Contents

Tourism Law
second edition

Tourism Law : Tutor's Manual

The accompanying *Tutor's Manual* supports and extends the book with materials, OHPs, exercises and notes

ISBN 1 85450 140 2

A4 looseleaf (with copying rights for student materials)

Tourism Law

2nd Edition

Jim Corke

ELM Publications

This second edition of **Tourism Law** is published October, 1993 by ELM Publications, Seaton House, Kings Ripton, Huntingdon PE17 2NJ (Tel. 04873-254 or 238 Fax 04873-359).

Printed by St Edmundsbury Press, Bury St Edmunds, Suffolk, England.
Bound by Woolnough Bookbinding, Express Works, Church Street, Irthlingborough, Northants, England.

ISBN 1 85450 028 7

British Library Cataloguing-in-Publication Data. A catalogue record for this publication is available from The British Library.

Principal Statutes Affecting Tourism Activities

x

xi

Table of Cases

xiii

xvi

xviii

Preface

This book has been written primarily for those studying Travel and Tourism on courses leading to the award of:

* BTEC Higher National Diplomas
* First Degrees

It is also intended to be of value to those seeking the professional qualifications awarded by the Institutes of:

* Travel and Tourism
* Leisure and Amenity Management

All who wish to gain an understanding of the nature of business operations need an awareness of the legal environment within which enterprises function. Any who act in ignorance of the law or who wilfully disobey its caveats do so at their peril. The company responsible is still counting the cost of the Zeebrugge disaster in March 1987. One of the victims has already accepted a settlement of £160,000. Many other claims have yet to be met. At the same time, the Belgian authorities are considering prosecution of those involved.

In the proceedings of the inquiry which followed the sinking, Mr Justice Sheen issued a timely warning that:

'All concerned in the management, from the members of the board of directors down to the junior superintendents, were guilty of fault, in that all must be regarded as sharing the responsibility of management.'

The disaster also illustrates the International dimensions of the law. While this text is based upon English law it also acknowledges Britain's membership of the European Community which by 1992 will have moved towards a closer association. As a party to international conventions, Britain recognises that law transcends even wider national boundaries, a matter long since realised by tourists.

Tourists are consumers of services within an environment extensively regulated by municipal and international laws. Consumer protection law has grown considerably of late in the United Kingdom,

Europe and in the world generally. The object of such law is to defend the untrained consumer against the businessman. Many consumer 'wants' have been artificially induced by clever psychological manipulation in advertising and salesmanship. Hidden persuaders aim to encourage the public to buy goods or services on terms and conditions suitable to the vendor. Such offers are often accompanied by credit sales agreements.

The role of the law makers is to promote legislative policy and to oversee its implementation via the appropriate agencies. For historic reasons associated with the development of the common law, enforcement has been left largely in the hands of local authorities in England.

Protection of the tourist has its roots in the common law. The Mercer's Case of 1368 is a very early example. It would have been well known to Chaucer's 'man of law' of whom the author said:

'He knew every judgement, case and crime Recorded, ever since King William's time.'

His pilgrims were drawn to the great cathedral. The tourists visiting Canterbury today are offered a range of attractions. They may watch a Marlowe play or examine the engine which drew the first regular passenger train in the world from Whitstable to Canterbury in 1830. They may go boating on the Stour or visit numerous monuments and archaeological sites both sacred and secular.

The essential ingredients of tourism might be said to be transportation, recreation and accommodation, provided by an industry which has developed to service them. Tourism is an essential part of the economy, accounting for 8% of the Gross National Product and providing much of the country's 'invisible earnings'. It is relied upon heavily to provide new jobs for workers made redundant by the impact of new technologies and the decline in the industrial base. Those who have benefited from the reorganised economy have additional 'wants' to be met by the leisure industry.

The service industries which cater for the tourist are in need of well educated recruits with management skills. It is hoped that this book will assist them in their chosen profession.

At the time of publication of the first edition of *Tourism Law* the Zeebrugge disaster focused attention on the need for improved safety management. Four years later the matter is still in high profile.

Zeebrugge did not so much close a chapter it opened a book. Passengers by air, rail and sea continue to be put at risk in avoidable situations. It is not possible to completely eliminate accidents but improved safety management could reduce their incidence and severity. In some ways the legislature has been swift to respond with new laws and in others remarkable dilatory. Apart from a few minor changes in the procedures to be completed before ships put to sea carrying passengers little of major consequence has yet taken place post Zeebrugge. We shall have to wait until 2004 before carriers are required to see that their vessels comply with revised structural regulations. In relation to inland water transportation little seems to have changed since the Marchioness incident on the Thames.

The question also needs to be asked, has the reaction by government been of the right order? After the fire at Kings Cross approximately 157 new regulatory provisions have been made with a view to minimising fires on London Underground. This has required the carriers to expend a disproportionate sum of money on this one hazard because the regulations introduced by the legislation are so prescriptive. This has had the effect of denying the carriers the ability in financial terms to carry out much needed upgrading of signalling, track and rolling stock. The result must be that while the risk from fire has been reduced there is now a much greater possibility of death and injury caused by defective equipment leading to a crash.

The same reaction to the rail crash at Clapham Junction and at Cannon Street has seen over emphasis on one aspect of safety risk with attendant neglect of others. People still continue to fall from the doors of trains which "mysteriously" open of their own accord whilst a rational explanation would seem to be that the type of door involved and indeed the whole carriage need to be replaced with modern rolling stock.

Economic considerations seem to be affecting safety elsewhere. Safety of Sports Grounds regulations have gradually been introduced but the full rigour of the original proposals has been somewhat watered down in relation to those operators who have complained of inability to afford much by way of change. At the same time a new set of safety hazards was revealed as a consequence of the Hillsborough disaster.

In relation to air carriage, relatively few changes have been made subsequent to the incidents at Manchester in 1985 and Kegworth in 1989 which left a total of 102 passengers dead. Reports of these accidents presented as a result of public inquiries show that deaths and serious injuries were preventable given better structural design of aircraft and evacuation procedures. The reports of the Air Accident Investigation Branch were accepted by the Civil Aviation Authority but little has been done by way of fire prevention or the introduction of smoke hoods. A major recommendation as to design of the passenger compartment has received even less positive support than in the case of boats and trains indicated above. There seems an overwhelming desire to treat the symptoms of malaise rather than to deal with the cause of the disease. This can only be explained in economic terms.

Safety has also preoccupied another area with an impact upon tourism. The Food Safety Act 1990 has introduced more rigorous regimes for the protection of the consumer as regards both unsafe and misdescribed food products. Food premises now have to be either licensed or registered and all food handlers must receive adequate training. Much stronger powers of enforcement have been put in place to accompany the new legislation. Good news for beer drinkers was issued by the DTI in December 1991. The Weights & Measures Act is to be amended so that customers will get a full liquid measure. Regrettably these provisions will not become effective until 1994!

The legislation on food safety was driven from Europe. Increasingly it seems that we must look to EC Directives to improve safety and other socio-economic problems in Britain. Whilst the record of compliance with EC Directives is relatively good in Britain in comparison to some of our partners the same cannot be said of the method nor content of many of the Regulations promulgated by UK Ministers. There seems to be creeping disease affecting Whitehall which takes the form of a minimalist approach to the introduction of EC law accompanied by obfuscation in wording which has led to the UK appearing more frequently than most of its partners before the European Court of Justice.

But it is to Europe that most eyes turn today in relation to measures affecting tourism, be this in respect of environmental, safety or consumer affairs. In 1989 consultations took place with the package travel industry and consumer groups on the proposed EC Directive on package travel, the aim of which was to harmonise the regulation Europe wide of all package travel and tours. The impetus for the Directive was to establish a common market in tourism by time the single internal market for the EC was in place. The Package Travel Directive 90/34 was duly enacted in Brussels with a deadline for compliance of 31 December 1992. Lengthy consultation processes with interested parties were instigated by the DTI throughout 1992. There was much wailing and gnashing of teeth by the travel industry and its representative bodies who seemed more concerned with protecting their own interests rather than those of the consumer. As late as October 1992 the DTI was still unable to state any date for the enactment of UK legislation to implement the Directive. The deadline was finally achieved at the 11th hour. The Regulations finally appeared as SI 1992/3288 - The Package Travel, Package Holidays and Package Tours Regulations 1992 on the 22nd of December and came into force with almost indecent haste for this variety of delegated legislation 23rd December 1992. It seems that the UK Government had heeded the warning that unless the EC Directive was made effective individuals could sue the Government for losses sustained as a consequence of its neglect.

In the event, the present edition of *Tourism Law* was held back so that a thorough review of the Regulations could take place with the consequent need to substantially change Chapter XI.

Again as a result of changes wrought in Europe, the issue of the Environment has come into high profile. Whereas this had been touched upon in passing in the first edition is has now become evident that because of environmental protection legislation gathering in size and content and affecting tourists as both victims of pollution and possibly themselves agents for pollution a separate Chapter should be devoted to the field in the new edition.

J A T Corke LLB MA
Bournemouth University at Poole in Dorset

CHAPTER I

The Nature Of Tourism Law

1. THE RULE OF LAW

In any community rules are necessary in order to regulate relations between the members. Those which derive from consensus become accepted norms and are the most effective. The making of rules requires both organisation and direction such that it becomes necessary for members to surrender autonomy to some form of government. By this means, power is devolved to individuals or groups whose ideas, right or wrong, become laws. These may best be described in terms of rules made by those having a monopoly of the use of force, compelling obedience.

Such a government was established in England by the Norman kings. Their authority derived from military conquest. A strong central executive was simply and effectively established by the grants of land to their supporters. The king *owned* all the land and those to

1

whom he *leased* it were his *tenants*. Power was firmly linked to land holding and property rights, a principle of English law which is still predominant today.

There was nothing in the country at the time which could be called a legal system. Citizens complaining that their neighbours had broken their obligations took their claims before local courts. Here the issues were tried in the light of the custom of the neighbourhood. The introduction of a national judicial system was a further step towards the centralisation of authority.

The government was effective despite bad roads and poor communications. Officials were sent out from the palace of Westminster into the country. They were to inquire on behalf of the Crown into local offences, faults in administration and slackness in the conduct of the king's affairs. Some of them were appointed repeatedly and became skilled in legal matters. Their involvement in the resolution of disputes, especially concerning land, saw their translation from civil servants to the first professional judges in English courts.

Justice on horseback

The difficulty in getting to Westminster to present a case before the royal courts resulted in *riding justices* going out with a *commission of assize* from the king to try both criminal and civil cases. They gained the confidence of local people and their law-making power grew with their popularity. Today judges still go out to hear cases in one of the six *circuits* into which England and Wales are divided. Although no longer on horseback, they still go on tour.

No one sat down and wrote out the legal system. There was no master plan. Its existence is due to generations of practical men doing their work in a way developed by their predecessors until there was reason to change. A *corpus* of law grew out of customs which commended themselves because experience taught that they worked. A judge faced with a question of law would ask himself how that question had been decided when last it had arisen. From this evolved the principle that a judge was bound to decide the issue in the same way that it had previously been resolved. This doctrine of *precedent* has come to characterise the *Common Law* which has grown from the custom of the people as it was understood and remembered by the touring judges.

The original local courts were gradually replaced by their royal

2

successors. In order for the system of *precedent* to work it was necessary to have a written record of the judges' decisions. Collections of cases were gathered into *Year Books*, so called because they were numbered by regnal year in the same manner as statutes. One such important decision was recorded at Canterbury in the 11th year of the reign of Edward III.

In *The Mercer's Case (1368)*[1] Justice Knivet was called upon to try a case in which a traveller had lodged at a *common inn*. During his absence from the inn goods which he had left in his room, together with some money, were stolen. He claimed that, according to the custom of the realm, the innkeeper was liable for the safekeeping of a guest's property left within the *hospitium* of an inn. The judge found for him. At the same time he decided that no criminal offence had been committed by the innkeeper such as would warrant his imprisonment. No previous decisions were cited only a claim of established custom. The judgment in this case itself created a *precedent* which has lasted until today.[2]

Public and private law

Justice Knivet's jurisdiction under his *commission of assize* extended to both public (criminal) and private matters. Today the two are considered separately, each in its own courts with their own rules.

Criminal law proscribes conduct which the state strongly disapproves. Treason against the state or theft from fellow citizens are both activities which cannot be ignored. The first is a threat to national security. The second could, if uncorrected, lead to public disorder. Wrongdoers are, therefore, punished as an act of public retribution.

Civil law has been the subject of similar reasoning. If left unresolved, disputes between individuals could also lead to violent confrontation. To prevent this, rules have been devised to determine the merits of arguments advanced by the contestants. The party with the stronger case will be entitled to the redress which he seeks from the other. The object here is not to punish the loser but to afford satisfaction to the winner.

Until the 19th century, the royal courts of justice were largely concerned with maintaining public order, defending the realm and preserving property rights. Actions on the case (torts) and contract obligations were being developed, but in a minor key.

Law merchant

The common law courts could find little time for the disputes which arose between merchants. For their part, those engaged in commerce viewed such courts as too hide bound by procedure and too long in their deliberations. Instead they had to resort to tribunals of their own choosing. These courts were scorned by common lawyers but provided an acceptable service to their customers. By the end of the 18th century, they had been absorbed into the mainstream of the courts of justice.

Their greatest contribution to the law has been the introduction of practical rules evolved from commercial expediency into the law of contract. In 1894, by resolution, the High Court reinvented such a court to deal with special issues 53 arising out of the dealings of importers, bankers, insurers and commercial agents. This court was officially recognised as the Commercial Court by the Administration of Justice Act 1970. It sits as a special court within the Queen's Bench Division of the High Court.

Arbitration, the reference of a dispute to an independent review body, was another ancient process devised by merchants. The most usual procedure is for a dispute to be adjudicated by a specialist experienced in the technical matter involved. Most commercial contracts include an *arbitration clause* within the terms of the Arbitration Act 1950. Arbitration is cheaper than a court action and may be particularly convenient where one of the parties is abroad. Subject to the supervision of the High Court, the award of an arbitrator is final and binding on the parties.

Law and society

The dominant concern of successive governments from the Middle Ages on wards has been with the maintenance of law and order. From 1285 *justices of the peace* were appointed from the ranks of *good and lawful men*. They were given wide powers that they might keep the *king's peace.* To this end also they were charged with the administration of local government. The whole of the local administration of the counties in England and Wales was in the hands of the Justices of the Peace until the County Councils were created by the Local Government Act 1888. Today their major role is sitting as justices at Petty Sessions:

4

'magistrates at Petty Sessions dispose of nearly 98% of all criminal cases, as well as exercising substantial civil jurisdiction which includes the disposal of matrimonial cases many times greater in number than those of the High Court. They handle almost the whole range of criminal and many of the civil matters which bring the average citizen into a court of law.'[3]

The Statute of Labourers, first passed in 1349, gave power to the keepers of the king's peace to stop agricultural workers leaving the land after the Black Death reduced the population of Britain from around 4 millions to 2½ millions in under two years. The Justices were unable to stem the tide which flowed from the country to the towns and began at the end of the 18th century. The rise of manufacturing industry and the growth of population saw urban centres unable to cope. Conditions in the towns deteriorated rapidly and disease became endemic. Executive action was necessary as a matter of priority.

The first in a series of Public Health statutes was passed in 1848, one year after the Town Improvement Clauses Act. That their provisions were soon put into effect may be judged from a case where a local board of health had made bylaws under the 1848 Act for the removal by the occupier of 'dust ashes, rubbish, filth, manure, dung and soil' *R v Wood (1855).*[4]

Other legislation provided for baths and washhouses, water-works, and street works. However, what is really remarkable is that the town authorities found time to provide other amenities instituted by statutes. Museums, libraries, art galleries, recreation grounds, town gardens, parks and ancient monuments were all legislated for by Parliament between 1845 and 1882.

While the Victorian poor were very poor, the majority of the nation grew increasingly prosperous. One result of the prosperity, allied to the promotion of healthier living by the authorities, was the growth of the holiday habit. Sea bathing had been popular since the end of the 18th century. With the coming of the railways and improvement in the roads stimulated by the bicycling lobby, it grew in popularity. Men and women bathed apart since it was the habit of men to scorn the use of costumes. Local byelaws were enforced at resorts such as Brighton, which did not initially ban such activities, compelling the proper use of bathing machines.

There was a growing practice for employers to grant Saturday half holidays and to give a week's annual holiday to many workers usually without pay! This, plus the impetus given by the Bank Holiday Act

1871, saw the increase in excursions by road and rail to popular resorts both on the coast and inland.

By the end of the 19th century, as a result of industrial growth, law was being used in a new way. Its purpose, whilst in some ways still restrictive of individual freedom especially in employment, was more and more directed towards social engineering. The result was that a healthier, better educated, population was responding to the forces of a laissez faire economy by becoming increasing consumers of services and goods.

Consumer protection

The origins of consumer protection may be traced to medieval statutes legislating against impure food.[5] The first law against adulterated food generally was part of the increasing social legislation of the 19th century.[6] It was not, however, such enactments which provided a remedy for the husband of a woman who died from drinking milk contaminated with typhoid, but the Sale of Goods Act 1893 - *Frost v Aylesbury Dairy Co (1905)*.[7]

This Act was passed in acknowledgement of the inequality in bargaining power that existed between sellers and buyers of goods. The concept dear to the common law of *freedom to contract* was illusory. When the maxim of *caveat emptor* (let the buyer beware) was added to this, it presented a formidable barrier to remedies sought against sellers of goods.

The method selected by Parliament was unusual for the time. Instead of proscribing malpractices, they used a device employed by the courts in commercial cases. In seeking to remedy defects in contracts, the courts *implied* terms into them on the grounds that (a) the parties would themselves have incorporated such terms had they stopped to consider the matter at the time the agreement was made, and (b) terms could be included so as to make commercial sense of the contract.[8]

The Act of 1893 implied, inter alia, statutory terms as to the 'merchantability' of goods and 'fitness' for the purpose of the same. It applied to commercial con tracts as well as to consumer purchases. Its provisions were to some degree thwarted by businessmen who made extensive use of *exclusion* clauses to deprive buyers of their rights. Despite the ingenuity of some judges, such clauses caught unfortunate travellers such as the illiterate Mrs Thompson who was seeking compensation for the negligence of an employee of a railway company -

6

Thompson v L.M.S. Railway (1930).[9] This area of consumer *dissatisfaction* was not resolved until the introduction of the Unfair Contract Terms Act 1977.

As in earlier times, Parliament called in aid the criminal law to proscribe practices of which it strongly disapproved, this time not so much for fear of the public taking the law into their own hands as the need to protect the public interest. The Weights and Measures Acts 1963-85, and the Trade Descriptions Acts 1968 and 1972, impose sanctions but they do not provide remedies to individual consumers.

Until recently, there were gaps in the protective legislation with regard to the provision of services and the supply of goods. The Supply of Goods and Services Act 1982 and the Consumer Protection Act 1987, Part III, have closed some of the remaining loopholes.

Where there are no contractual liabilities or where the statutes do not provide a remedy, the common law still has its part to play in this area. Where it is possible to prove fault in the tort of Negligence then, again with the ingenuity of the judiciary, redress may be available to such as those who consume snails with their ginger beer - *Donoghue v Stevenson (1932)*.[10] Or fault may be presumed because the defendant is in breach of a statutory duty - *Monk v Warbey (1935)*.[11]

The European dimension

The European Communities Act 1972 took Britain into membership of the 'Common Market' with effect from 1 January 1973. The result is, as stated by the Master of the Rolls:

'In any transaction which contains a European element we must look to the Treaty (of Rome) for (it) is part of our law. It is equal in force to any statute. It must be applied by our courts.'
Application des Gaz v Falks Veritas (1974) [12]

This has had some profound effects on English law. It has led to the enactment of anti-discriminatory legislation in the form of the Sex Discrimination Act 1975 and the Race Relations Act 1976. The strict product liability for defective goods, as embodied in the Consumer Protection Act Part I, had its origins in Europe. The Consumer Protection and Information Programmes launched by the Council of Ministers have, as two key themes, health and safety and the improvement of the legal position of the consumer. It is likely that

7

there will be effective initiatives in particular problems when the opening up of the internal European Market occurs after 1992.

The Director General of Fair Trading, Sir Gordon Borrie, predicts

'After the legislative surge in consumer protection measures of the 1960s and 1970s, the 1990s like the 1980s will be more a period of consolidation and relatively modest improvement.... Civil procedure generally, and not just the development of small claims and ombudsman procedures, will be more radically altered than the substantive law.... There is also of course a continuing need for adequate resources to be made available to local authorities to enforce the criminal law, to local authorities and others to provide advice facilities, and to my Office to enforce the regulatory controls under the Consumer Credit Act.'[13]

The phrase 'the rule of law' was coined by the jurist Professor A.V. Dicey[14] to indicate that no one, not even government, is above the law. He meant the law of England. That law has now been extended by British membership of the European Community and by our adherence to international conventions which have been incorporated into our law by Acts of Parliament. The tourist is perhaps in a better position than most to appreciate the breadth of law to which travellers and others are now exposed.

2. TOURISM - A DEFINITION

Most people would recognise an elephant but trying to describe the animal without the aid of illustrations is no easy task. Even with photographs it would still not be a simple matter to describe a tourist.

The United Nations Conference on International Travel and Tourism, held at Rome in 1963, described tourists as:

'any persons visiting a country other than that in which (they) have (their) usual place of residence, for any reason other than following an occupation, remunerated from within the country visited.'

The definition is defective in so far as it excludes domestic travel. The classification of 'visitor' adopted by the UN distinguishes between those who stay at least 24 hours at a location, and others. This latter group are identified as 'excursionists'.

The International Conference on Leisure, Recreation and Tourism sought a wider definition in 1981 and it did so by reference to activity rather than personality:

'Tourism may be defined in terms of particular activities selected by choice and undertaken outside the home environment. Tourism may or may not involve over night stay away from home.'

This definition has been criticised for being so wide as to include burglary or any of a hundred other activities.[15] It does, however, define tourists in terms of what they do rather than who they are.

Activities

In 1937, the League of Nations classified international tourists according to whether they travelled for pleasure, domestic reasons, health, to meetings, or on business. It also included those visiting a country on board a cruise vessel. The UN conference in 1963 added sport, religion and study to the list. Business and study (education) are usually excluded from many lists today. It is hard to see why unless it be on the grounds that the entire activity must be voluntary. Outside business hours, such travellers often enjoy recreational and leisure pursuits at their location for the time being with, for example, holiday makers. Many *students* combine study with pleasure as anyone who operates a *language school* in a seaside town in England would admit.

The use of 'meeting' opens another door. There exists a growing market for *conference* facilities, many of them provided in custom-built venues such as the Bournemouth International Centre. Others are catered to in some of the larger hotels. In addition to the usual catering services, a range of satellite operations provide amenities for delegates seeking to relax outside the environment of the meeting.

The range of amenities which are available to the seekers after rest and recreation is enormous. The fact that they may also be enjoyed by local residents as well as visitors does not make them any the less attractive to tourists.

An important characteristic of tourism is that it cannot be brought to the customer. The tourist must travel to the attraction. Nor, in many cases, can the product be stored. An unoccupied seat on a plane or a hotel bedroom, an unsold seat at the theatre or a garden festival, cannot be used later, they are *perishable* items which are not recoverable.

Travel

Any definition of tourism will include the element of travel. The distance travelled does not appear to be critical. It is distance combined with purpose that is the determining factor as to what constitutes activity for this calculation. A visit to a local supermarket by a resident of the locality would not qualify but by a visitor to a French supermarket, as part of an excursion on a cross-channel ferry, it should.

A fundamental difference between the tourist and other travellers is that, for the former, the planning and execution of the journey is part of the enjoyment whereas, for the latter, it is in the nature of necessity. Judging by the number of brochures for package holidays taken from the shelves of travel agents in comparison to the number of holidays actually booked, the perusal of such literature is a form of leisure activity in itself.

For the tourist, to travel is as important as to arrive at the destination. Some tourists appear to derive a perverse pleasure from swapping stories with fellow sufferers stranded at airports and other terminals world wide. The battle honours of Gatwick, Faro and Athens are paraded with pride.

Accommodation

For centuries, travellers have been consumers of hospitality services. Traditionally, monasteries were associated with *hospice* facilities. Often these were an adjunct to a tourist attraction provided for pilgrims. The Church in England was skilled in such activity before the arrival of the Normans. Great numbers of *tourists* travelled the 'Walsingham Way' to the shrine of the Virgin Mary set up in the reign of Edward the Confessor. A whole industry grew up around England's Nazareth.

By 1086, work had begun on a great abbey, together with an extensive complex of hostels to accommodate thousands of pilgrims, hundreds of merchants together with palmers and similar pedlars of religious souvenirs. Hard-headed Norman clerics made a takeover of the business after the Conquest aided by the government. *Plus ça change, plus c'est la même chose!*

The monasteries developed an infrastructure of glebe lands and bartons to feed the communities they serviced. Monastic breweries were much in evidence. The malthouse of Fountains Abbey could produce 60 barrels of strong ale every ten days. The brewhouse of the Benedictine Priory at Canterbury still stands, massively imposing. Some of these breweries were so successful that they survived the dissolution of the monasteries in the 16th century, albeit in secular hands.

The innkeeper carried on a *common calling* of England, together with other venerable tradesmen such as the 'common carrier' and the ferryman, and is still described in law while the carrier has almost disappeared and the ferryman, as such, is no more. The law recognised obligations arising from this 'common' status and still does so today. At common law, and now under the Hotel Proprietors Act 1956, an innkeeper may not refuse hospitality to a traveller without just cause. Turning away a man because of the colour of his skin was unlawful in England before the advent of the race relations legislation - *Constantine v Imperial Hotels Ltd (1944)*.[16]

The range of accommodation occupied by tourists is extensive. It ranges from 5-Star hotels to tents, holiday camps to boatels, guest houses, apartments and time share operations. Some, like the tortoise, carry their home on their backs in a multitude of caravans and motorised campers. Yacht charter, boat-hire and cruise liners attract their own devotees. The list is almost endless. The all-in travel/accommodation package is perhaps the one which the industry has itself done most to popularise.

3. THE INDUSTRY

The activities in which a tourist may engage depend upon the purpose for which he has chosen to travel to a particular destination. The industry which has been created to meet his *wants* has manufactured expectations which may not be fulfilled for him. It has adopted a psychological approach to selling the product. Marketing holidays has been likened to 'selling dreams'.[17] When the reality does not match the dream, the tourist is a disappointed consumer who may have legal grounds for complaining of misrepresentation or breach of contract.

Among the British Tourist Authority's estimated 20 million visitors to Britain arriving annually by 1992, there are bound to be some who are disappointed by the experience. It would be unusual if this were not so in an industry so large that it employs directly some 1.5 million people in Britain. They cater to the needs of the internal tourism industry of some 140 million trips taken annually, as well as to visitors from abroad.

The industry world-wide has created attractions as well as capitalising on natural and man-made phenomena already in existence. Disneyland is a greater draw than the Grand Canyon. When its counterpart is built near Paris, no doubt it will be a greater draw than the Tour Eiffel. The Cairngorms may not seriously rival the Alps, but Scotland has more castles, stately homes and parks to offer.

It has also been realised that attraction derives, in part at least, from the hospitality record of a particular location. The manner in which visitors are received, and the quality of service provided for them, can be a decisive factor for someone planning an annual vacation. This helps to explain the continuing attraction of established resorts like Blackpool faced with the competition from sun and sangria at the newer sites on the Spanish costas.

The industry is not without its critics on grounds other than over-*puffing* its wares. It is argued that while tourism makes no great claim on public funds, it does make heavy demands on public utility services. Water, sewerage and transport are some examples. What tends to be forgotten, perhaps, is that many of these services would be provided at a lower level were it not for the pressure exerted by the industry. Some services might disappear completely. At the present time the historic trans-Pennine railway from Carlisle to Settle is kept open by the joint lobbyists of conservation groups and local tourist agencies.

The impact of tourism

Any large influx of tourists is bound to have a measurable effect on the host community. Local newspapers carry letters from local residents annoyed by traffic congestion, noise and litter. Environmentalists are concerned for the ecology of certain sites. Despite warnings to tourists on the Greek island of Zante, their activities are still affecting the breeding grounds of rare turtles. It is doubted whether the two life forms can live side by side in harmony. Some degree of containment in respect of tourist activity is necessary in any area.

In Italy, the causeway to Venice has been closed several times because the city was physically incapable of absorbing any more visitors. Air pollution from vehicle exhausts has damaged monuments in Florence. In July 1987, a torrent of 7 million visitors arrived in the city seeking accommodation. Hotels of all categories could muster only

20,000 beds. Local residents, outnumbered 14:1 by tourists, complained that the marketing campaign launched for them by the Italian Tourist Board had been too successful.

No local or central government administration can ignore the tourist industry and the impact which it has upon people and places. Problems of temporary population increase are, however, predictable. That, after all, is at the heart of the industry's marketing strategy. With this in mind, it should not be beyond responsible national and local government departments to exercise planning controls to minimise pollution, congestion and degradation of both the natural and man-made environment. The legal infrastructure exists for such purposes.

4. THE LAW RELATING TO TOURISM

On first reflection there is no such creature as 'Tourism Law' in the sense that there is no developed body of law designed to regulate the activities of tourists and the industry which has grown to service their wants. Instead, there is an assortment of common law principles and statutory provisions designed primarily for other purposes.

Tourism law is, therefore, a hybrid and none the worse for being so. We may trace its ancestors with certainty and discover that they come from vigorous stock. Each adds greater strength to this new variety. The inter-breeding of Attraction-Travel-Hospitality has produced a genus which is more adaptable and hardy than many a pure-bred species.

The law which is examined in this book is that which relates to the activities of those who pursue leisure-time amusements away from their usual environment and of the industry which caters to their wants. No distinction is drawn between such amenities as may be provided for tourists alone, e.g. charter flights, and those which are shared with other users, e.g. taxis.

Tourists will, by definition, come into contact with certain phenomena more often than other people. Immigration controls, security checks, in-flight catering and tropical diseases are a few of the more unpleasant which come to mind.

Whilst relying upon the same public services as local residents, tourists may be more heavily dependent upon them for the enjoyment of their leisure-time activities. The local environmental health and trading standards officers carry out their tasks for the benefit of all yet their diligence will have a greater impact upon the enjoyment of a once-in-a-year holiday for a family than for locals. While a foreign family suffered at the hands of a restaurateur in Canterbury, the successful prosecution of him by the local officer may well have saved other visitors from future harm of this nature - *Meah v Roberts (1978)*.[18]

Public law

Much of the law which regulates tourism is in the public domain. The agencies controlling various aspects of recreation and leisure are creatures of statute.

British Rail is a statutory corporation which must provide transport services and facilities in accordance with the enabling legislation. Some of this is drawn widely to allow for commercial enterprise, whilst on safety and matters concerning the ownership and operation of premises and plant it has to meet standards higher than most of its commercial competitors.

The operators of both road and air services are required to obtain licences. The former from the Civil Aviation Authority and the latter from the Traffic Commissioners. The Civil Aviation Authority has wide powers to control air navigation and, like the Traffic Commissioners, operates a licensing function for the vehicles carrying the public. Whilst sea carriers are required to provide ships which measure up to the safety requirements of statutes, the operators, while governed in their activities by Merchant Shipping Acts going back to the 19th century, do not require an operator's licence as do other public carriers. In the wake of the Zeebrugge incident this defect must be remedied.

Local authorities, which are themselves statutory creations, are charged under various enactments with the supervision of an enormous range of services. Through a licensing system such activities as the operation of theatres, taxis, entertainment, riding establishments and cinemas are controlled. They are also given wide powers to assist the promotion of tourism in their local areas by providing amenities and advertising their attractions outside the vicinity.[19]

They act as enforcement agencies for trading standards, health and hygiene, bringing prosecutions or issuing enforcement notices. They share with the county councils the control over any planning matters concerned with land and buildings where permission is required for the carrying out of any development.[20] This includes change of use under the terms of the Town and Country Planning (Uses Classes) Order 1972.

Developments in National Parks or Areas of Outstanding Natural Beauty are subject to joint planning control which is in conjunction with the specialist planning boards for these designated locations. Strict controls are exercised in connection with planning permission affecting conservation areas and listed buildings. This last category is very wide, ranging from Elizabethan farm houses to an AA Box in the Lake District.

Magistrates are local justices but they are not part of the local government administration structure as once they were. Nevertheless, they still have considerable influence in the areas they serve, notably in the case of the granting of liquor licences. Licensing Panel membership is drawn from the magistrates' bench. The Panel hears applications for licences permitting the sale of alcohol to the public in hotels, clubs, public houses and restaurants. Appeals from decisions of the Panel go to the Crown Court.

Private law

The relationship between tourists and those who provide them with goods and services is almost invariably based upon contract. The booking of an hotel room, a train ticket, a seat at a theatre or a package holiday, is a matter of agreement between the parties. These are very often the subject of statutory provisions, particularly as regards formalities in respect of consumer credit. Where a contract is broken then the disappointed party may sue for the breach of an express term - *Jarvis v Swans Tours Ltd (1973)*;[21] or of an implied term - *Reed v Dean (1949)*.[22]

Where the complaint cannot be based on contract it may be possible, by the establishing of fault, to bring a claim in Negligence, as where a spectator is injured at a sporting event - *White v Blackmore (1972)*.[23] Where it is the condition of premises which causes the injuries sustained by a guest at an hotel, he may seek redress relying upon the Occupiers Liability Act 1957 - *Wheat v Lacon (1966)*.[24]

There are liabilities which may be incurred as a result of statutory provisions. A spectator injured by a circus elephant may be able to base a claim for compensation on the Animals Act 1971. A traveller refused a meal at an inn may bring an action within the provisions of the Hotel Proprietors Act 1956.

15

The Development of Tourism Act 1969, the only legal provision specifically related to the area, does not provide any remedies. It is principally concerned with the establishment of tourist boards and hotel development. A regulation made under section 18 of the Act does require the display of room tariffs[25] but, this apart, the statute has no direct application to the needs of the tourist.

The raison d'être of the Licensing Act 1988 through all its Parliamentary stages was the need to cater for tourists. It is another example of the law being painted on a broad canvas with some of the figures in the landscape being tourists.

NOTES:

1. (1368) YB Edward III 11 No 13.
2. See Kott v Gordon Hotels Ltd (1968) 2 Lloyds 228.
3. The Changing image of the Magistracy. Sir T. Skryme.
4. (1855) 5 E & B 49.
5. Assize of Bread & Ale 1266.
6. Adulteration of Food & Drink Act 1860. Sale of Food & Drugs Act 1875.
7. (1905) 1 KB 608.
8. See The Moorcock (1886) All ER 530.
9. (1930) 1 KB 41.
10. (1932) AC 52.
11. (1935) 1 KB 75.
12. (1974) Ch 381.
13. Consumer Protection Law for the 1990s. Sir G. Borrie JALT Vol 21 No 3 1987.
14. The Law of the Constitution A.V. Dicey (1885).
15. The Business of Tourism J.C. Holloway p 3.
16. (1944) KB 693.
17. Holloway Op cit p 5.
18. (1978) 1 All ER 97 (QBD).
19. Local Government Act 1972 ss 144 and 145.
20. Town and Country Planning Act 1971 s 23 (1).
21. (1973) QB 233.
22. (1949) 1 KB 188.
23. (1972) 2 QB 651.
24. (1966) AC 552.
25. Tourism (Sleeping Accommodation Price Display) Order 1977 SI 1877.

CHAPTER II

Tourism Law

1. CASE LAW

The law-making process in England is shared by Parliament and the judiciary. Today, statute law is pre-eminent as the source of new rules but the principles by which they are decided are judge-made. Decided cases are examples of the process in action.

The common law was established as the basis for development of a system by the end of the 13th century. In the absence of a body of law, the judges looked to custom and practice and developed these into rules and principles. Initially, the common law was the product of judicial reasoning. Cases were decided in the light of the facts presented before the courts. If problems had already arisen which had been resolved in a particular way then it was practical to reach the same decision in similar circumstances. Case law is, therefore, practical and based on experience. By making law in this way there is the opportunity for growth and development through the laying down of new principles or extending old ones to meet changed circumstances.

By the 18th century, one eminent commentator was able to write of *judge-made* law that it was the *common law* which was:

'the common sense of the community, the chief cornerstone of the laws of England which is custom........ from time to time declared in the decisions of the courts of justice ..... and explained in our reports.'[1]

Until the 19th century, case law was the main source of law, statutes were of relatively minor importance. Today the position is reversed and statutes have become dominant. There are many reasons why this should be so. Chief amongst them is the need to solve economic and social problems which cannot wait for case law to develop new rules.

The main concerns of the judges have been described as being:

'to preserve and protect the existing order. This does not mean that no judges are capable of moving with the times, of adjusting to changed circumstances. But their function in our society is to do so belatedly.'[2]

Although Parliament creates statutes establishing precise rights and duties, it does not apply them. This task is for the courts. In exercising their function judges create law by the meaning they give to statutes when they interpret them. The *creativity* of some judges has more than once caused government to complain. The response from the judges has always been that if their decisions are not what was intended by the statute in question then, since Parliament is the supreme law maker, it must pass another to make its wishes clear.

The judges are the enforcers of both civil and criminal law whether Parliamentary in origin or judge-made. Much judicial time is spent on interpreting legislation. This having been said it should be noted that 98% of all criminal matters begin and end in the Magistrate's Courts. The Justices are not concerned with interpretation but with application. Where they are in difficulties as to interpretation they may refer a matter of law by way of *case stated* to the Divisional Court of Queen's Bench.[3] A further appeal on a point of law may be made from the Divisional Court to the House of Lords. In this way, by interpretation and by applying principles, judges are creating law in action.

Criminal law

Much of the criminal law is now contained in statutory form but some offences are still tried by the rules of the common law, having been created by the common law courts, and definitions of them are to be found only in case law. Public Nuisance is one, refusal to receive as a guest and lodge a traveller by an innkeeper is another.[4]

Those offences which are most likely to affect a tourist will be the subject of statutory provisions. Misdescription of goods and false description of facilities and services in respect of accommodation are dealt with by the Trade Descriptions Act 1968. Misleading price indications in connection with these are now dealt with by the Consumer Protection Act 1987, Part III.

Disputes between individuals and the State are resolved by the trial of a criminal offence. The law recognises corporate bodies as *legal persons* so that a company may be prosecuted for an offence in the same way as an individual. Similarly, a company may be the party to an action before a civil court. Here the dispute is between private individuals for alleged breaches of obligations. In civil matters, unlike criminal cases, the parties may choose arbitration as the method of settling a dispute instead of trial before the courts.

It is in connection with the breach of some obligation that the traveller, spectator or hotel guest, is more likely to come into contact with the legal process. He may wish to seek redress for an alleged breach of contract or for an injury sustained as the result of the tortious action of the defendant.

Contract

The general principles upon which issues of contract are decided are essentially judge made. The rules have, however, been much altered by statutes.

The greatest period of growth in this branch of the law was in the second half of the 19th century, a time of increased prosperity for both the business entrepreneur and his customers.

In 1841, Thomas Cook arranged his first excursion in the domestic market and in 1866 launched his first venture in North America. Between these two events a courier for another tour operator brought a successful action for breach of contract against his employer who had booked him for the summer, then cancelled the appointment before his employment commenced. The court decided that the courier had a right of action for *anticipatory* breach: *Hochster v De La Tour (1853).*[5]

In the field of exclusion clauses, the courts were very active in discovering principles which would prevent the operation of conditions depriving customers of remedies for breach of contract. Many examples of such *creativity* were to be found in a series of *ticket* cases which continued until recent legislation provided a more comprehensive solution. But even where some exclusions may escape the statutory rules, those made by the judges wait on the sidelines. Where, for example, the conditions referred to by a ticket were obliterated by a rubber stamp and the paper was then folded before delivery to a steamship passenger, the company issuing the document were unable to avail themselves of exclusions which the court decided could not have been brought to the attention of the traveller at the time the contract was made: *Richardson v Rowntree (1894).*[6]

The courts have also examined contracts to discover whether or not they are enforceable agreements. They may lack one of the essential prerequisites such as a failure of consideration or, whilst not illegal, they may be discovered to be unlawful as against public policy. Where a coach owner hired a carriage to a prostitute it was held that he could not recover the moneys due either for the hire or for damage to the vehicle. It was said that he knew very well the purpose for which it had been hired: *Pearce v Brooks (1866).*[7]

In the laisser faire attitude adopted by the State towards business activity in the 19th century great play was made of the principle of freedom of contract. The parties were allowed to bargain freely as equals. It became apparent, however, that where one of the parties was in a much weaker bargaining position than the other there was no freedom. The stronger could impose his will on the weaker who must either take what was on offer or go without. In one area in particular the much vaunted freedom was illusory.

Standard form contracts

The purpose of a SFC is so that the person supplying goods or services may fix in advance all or any of the terms with the intention that they shall form the basis of many contracts between him and persons yet undefined as to their number or identity.

The origin of SFCs is to be found in the custom and practice of merchants. The standard terms used in their contracts had become settled over the years. They were in general use in such areas as carriage and insurance. It was possible to attribute fairness and reasonableness to such terms because the parties were usually fairly matched in bargaining power.

The more recent adaptation of SFCs to goods and services provided to consumers cannot be said to have been conducted on an equal basis. Inequalities have been apparent from the earliest ticket cases to the widespread use of such documents in connection with *package holidays*. SFCs are used as a means whereby an operator claims the right to unilaterally vary a contract, to impose compulsory arbitration clauses or to limit the time within which claims against the operator must be brought.

Concern over such standard clauses goes back to the 19th century. Until 1977 the battle against them was largely waged by the judges. They devised a variety of weapons for the purpose of rendering onerous restrictions inoperative. They created the doctrine of *fundamental breach* but increasingly those responsible for drafting such clauses in contracts found ways of including *judge proof* terms. The judges for their part felt that they had no general power to strike down these devices as unreasonable on the grounds of public policy alone. It was left to the Unfair Contract Terms Act 1977 to deal with them more effectively than the common law had found possible.

The UCTA bans certain types of exclusion clauses and permits reliance on others only if they satisfy a test of *reasonableness*. There have been few cases to help clarify what this test is and the dicta in the old case of *Moghul S.S. (1889)*[8] equating reasonableness with 'the good sense of the tribunal' still seems the most satisfactory descriptor today.

Recent cases have produced no definitive interpretations and only a mixture of guidelines which may be taken into account by the courts. It would appear that consumers e.g. tourists, are more likely to succeed when alleging that a clause in a contract is *unreasonable* than a business enterprise and that clauses which seek to limit liability rather than to exclude it are more likely to be upheld. It would also appear that time limits which are very restrictive, small print and unnecessarily complex and obtuse wording of clauses are likely to fail the test for *reasonableness*.

The 1977 Act did not regard *arbitration clauses* of themselves as being equivalent to exclusion clauses such that it appeared that even a very restrictive arbitration provision was not controlled by the UCTA. This apparent lacuna was sealed by the Consumer Agreements

Arbitration Act 1988 which provides that such a clause cannot be enforced unless the consumer has consented to it in writing and after the matter in contention has occurred.

The provisions of the UCTA do not prescribe penalties for the inclusion of exclusion clauses which are *unreasonable* in contracts and it has been the practice to include them with what appears to be the intention of intimidating customers. In conjunction with these statements it is customary to include a phrase similar to 'This guarantee does not exclude your statutory rights'. Were this advice to customers not included then the exclusion could be construed as misleading or a failure to inform customers of their statutory rights and would constitute a criminal offence.

Despite the Act some contracts still escape regulation. Those pertaining to insurance are a prime example. Others are to be found where the terms of international conventions govern SFCs. Thus the Athens Convention imposes limits on levels of compensation for losses sustained by passengers carried on ships. The convention is part of English law by virtue of its incorporation by the Carriage of Passengers and their Luggage by Sea Act 1974. Section 28(3) of the 1977 Act specifically allows limits set by the convention to be exempt from its general provisions.

It must be emphasised that the great majority of contracts are not challenged. They are brought to a conclusion by performance which is to the satisfaction of the parties. Others may be ended by agreement or be found to be frustrated. This concept is also the creation of the common law. It relates to a situation where the object for which the contract was designed cannot be fulfilled through no fault of either of the parties and the contract is at an end as a consequence. Two cases based on the illness of King Edward VIII and the postponement of his Coronation illustrate the point.

In the first, a room had been hired which was on the Coronation route. When the event was put off, the hirer declined to pay the agreed price. It was held that the owner of the room could not sue for the previously agreed rental: *Krell v Henry (1903)*[9]. In the other, a steamer had been hired from which it was intended that a party should watch the King review the fleet at Spithead as part of the celebrations. In this case the contract was held not to have been frustrated because the boat was capable of other uses not dependent on the Coronation: *Herne Bay Steamboat Co v Hutton (1903)*.[10]

Many other examples of common law principles applied to contracts can be discovered, these are but a few relating to circumstances in which tourists may find themselves. However the parties to a contract are not always personally concerned with the conclusion of the agreement. It may be brought about as the result of actions of an intermediary.

Agents

Such an arrangement will arise where one person (the agent) is authorised to make contracts with third parties on behalf of another (the principal). There are various types of agent and methods of appointment. Almost without exception the rules which regulate the position of an agent were created by the common law.

For most practical commercial purposes agency is created by appointment under the terms of a contract. The agent must exercise care and skill when performing his duties in accordance with the terms of his appointment. His duty is to his principal on whose behalf he is acting. Once the contract is made the agent drops out of the scene, his duty done. The obligations under the contract are a matter for the parties to it not for the agent. However, if the agent has represented to the third party, innocently or otherwise, that he has the authority of the principal to act but this is not the case, he becomes liable to that person for breach of *warranty of authority*. Package holidays are usually negotiated for by agents acting on behalf of tour operators who have appointed them for this purpose. The agent owes his duties to the operator. He is not the agent of the customer. An important change in the relationship between the travel agent and the customer has been introduced by the Package Travel, Package Holidays and Package Tours Regulations 1992 (See Chapter XI). Section 4 states:

(1) No organiser or retailer shall supply to a consumer any descriptive matter concerning a package or any other conditions applying to the contract which contains any misleading information.

(2) If an organiser or retailer is in breach of paragraph (1) he shall be liable to compensate the consumer for any loss which the consumer suffers in consequence.

This provision supplements the criminal sanctions of the Trade

23

Descriptions Act 1968 and the Consumer Protection Act 1987 by providing a civil remedy for information which is misleading but not supplied knowingly or recklessly which defences are allowed in the 1968 and 1987 statutes.

Compensation payable by the retailer (travel agent) could be for direct financial loss or consequential loss for disappointment suffered by the customer.

An agent may also be someone who acts in that capacity for his employer by virtue of his employment. Thus a receptionist at an hotel concludes an agreement for accommodation between the hotel company and the guest. In the case of a corporate body its actions must be conducted via its agents by the very nature of such a creation of the law. It is a legal person but only an artificial being.

Where agents act in this capacity as employees they may, if they have the authority or appear to have it, alter express terms which their employer has laid down for particular contracts so as, in one case, to deprive the employer of the benefits of an exclusion clause: *Curtis v Chemical Cleaning and Dyeing Co (1951).*[11]

Where a person is in possession of goods which are not claimed by the owner, such that the person in possession must act to protect the goods and he cannot contact the owner for instructions, he becomes an agent of necessity. Any expenses which he incurs in safeguarding the goods may be claimed by way of indemnity from the owner who is regarded as the principal vis a vis the agent of necessity: *Great Northern Railway v Swaffield (1874).*[12] In the golden age of the railway the situation which gave rise to agency of necessity was not uncommon. Most of these circumstances arose in connection with horses. From the number of cases it could be supposed that horses were being abandoned throughout the system in the 19th century!

Where the goods have been delivered into the custody of such an agent, as distinct from them merely coming into his possession, he is also in the position of bailee of those goods.

Bailment

This is a very ancient concept recognised by the common law and almost entirely governed by it. Today it is usually created by contract but this is not essential.[13]

It consists of a delivery of goods by one person into the custody of another for a limited purpose, on condition that when that purpose has

24

been achieved the goods shall be returned. There are various types of bailment.

Goods may be deposited for safe keeping e.g. at a cloakroom or left luggage office. The bailee cannot use the goods and must take reasonable care of them. Should he, through negligence, fail to redeliver them to the depositor or his agent no exclusion clause will protect him from liability: *Alexander v Railway Executive (1951)*.[14]

Where goods are hired, the bailor warrants the fitness of the goods e.g. a car, and the bailee must take reasonable care of them in accordance with the terms of the contract. He will not be liable for loss by theft or accidental fire occasioned without negligence.

An innkeeper who exercises his right of lien over goods against an unpaid bill for accommodation is a bailee of those goods and, similarly, if he takes the property of a guest into safe keeping at the request of that person.

A pawnbroker is also a bailee of goods pledged for security against an advance of money. The goods are redeemable on payment of the loan plus interest. This old profession is undergoing something of a revival as a means whereby money may be speedily borrowed without too much formality against property which would not be considered for security by banks. Pawnbrokers were regulated by the Pawnbrokers Act 1872 until recently when they came within the provisions of the Consumer Credit Act 1974.

The transactions which have been examined to this point have been mainly the subject of agreements creating obligations. Where these are breached they may give rise to an action for compensation or other remedy. Where no agreement can be discovered giving rise to an obligation it may be possible to bring an action under another head. For example, the hirer of a tricycle was injured when the saddle slipped. It was held that the drafting of an exclusion denying his claim was ineffective so as to refute a claim for negligence if this could be established: *White v John Warrick & Co Ltd (1953)*.[15]

Torts

The law of torts has its origins early in the development of the common law. It still relies upon the judges for its growth rather than on statute. Torts are acts or omissions causing injury for which the victim may recover unliquidated damages at common law and which are not exclusively crimes, breaches of contract, or a failure to discharge an equitable obligation.

It should be noted that a single incident may give rise to a prosecution for a crime and an action in contract and tort. Thus, where a taxi driven carelessly is involved in an accident causing injury to the passenger, he may sue for breach of contract, the driver having failed to perform the same with reasonable care and skill. He may also sue for the tort of negligence and the police may prosecute the driver for a statutory offence against the Road Traffic Acts. There is no bar to an action because a conviction has been obtained in the criminal courts and no bar to a prosecution because a claim has been upheld in the civil courts. The two branches of the law operate under separate rules and principles and, unlike Justice Knivet's day, in different courts.

Torts are notoriously difficult to classify. Some defy classification and are referred to as *innominate*. One such is the failure by an innkeeper, without lawful excuse, to accommodate a traveller.

The oldest of the torts is trespass upon which all such actions were once founded. It may be committed against the person, e.g. for exclusion from an hotel where the guest was staying and from which he was unlawfully excluded: *Warner v Riddifor (1858)*,[16] or against property.

Trespass to land is familiar to most people. This is mainly due to the posting of signs which warn that *trespassers will be prosecuted.* Such notices betray an imperfect knowledge of the law. The tort consists of an unlawful entry upon land or buildings in the possession of another. Only where that other has a statutory power of exclusion can such an entry constitute a criminal offence. The sign may be correct in relation to land in the possession of the Ministry of Defence or British Rail, for example, but not in the case of ordinary landowners. However, it is intended that legislation shall be introduced which makes it a criminal offence to camp on the land of another without that other's express permission. This provision is designed to restrict activities which have become associated with the 'New Age Travellers' and other groups of mobile communes. Equally it could affect individual 'fly' campers as well as groups of people acting in unison.

The tort may also be committed by someone who enters lawfully but who, having been asked to leave, refuses to go. In such circumstances, the occupier may use reasonable force to expel the intruder. He must himself take care lest he commits a trespass against the person of the unwanted visitor.

The action for trespass to goods has been subsumed within the provisions of the Torts (Interference with Goods) Act 1977. The Act creates a new form of tortious liability - wrongful interference with goods. If a traveller makes off with the luggage of a fellow passenger this would constitute an act of trespass. If a baggage handler were to misuse articles in transit this would also amount to *interference* of a tortious nature.

Torts which are concerned with the protection of land will not be of direct interest to a tourist although they will affect those who provide amenities for him. A hotelier, for example, whose business is affected by noise and dust from building works may seek a remedy within the tort of Nuisance: *Andreae v Selfridge & Co Ltd (1938).*[17] Nuisance may also be occasioned by the activities of prostitutes: *Thompson-Schwab v Costaki (1956).*[18] It may result from the smells emanating from a restaurant: *Adams v Ursell (1913).*[19] All of these have been held to be indirect *invasions* which unreasonably interfered with the peaceful enjoyment of land. Direct *invasion* of land may also constitute nuisance - *Leakey v National Trust (1980)*[20] when a burial mound subsided.

Where something is brought onto land which is not naturally found upon it and is kept there, and it escapes from the land causing damage as a natural consequence of such a break out, then an action may lie at the suit of an injured party. This tort is known by the name of the original case which established the common law rules which govern it: *Rylands v Fletcher (1868).*[21] The dangerous *escape* there was of water which had been stored up in a reservoir and caused flooding when it leaked onto adjacent property. In a later case the *escape* was of caravan dwellers who caused damage by polluting land nearby: *Att. Gen. v Corke (1933).*[22]

The providers of amenities, particularly those operating site attractions, will need to have regard to their neighbours lest their activities in producing noise, smells or dangerous escapes, lead to action being taken against them in the courts. Their negligent behaviour may be the basis of such proceedings; it may also amount to a separate tort.

Negligence as a tort consists of an 'omission to do something which a reasonable man would do, or doing something which a reasonable and prudent man would not do': *Blyth v Birmingham Waterworks Co (1856).*[23] More recently it was explained in terms of a 'duty of care' which is owed by one man to his 'neighbour': *Donoghue v Stevenson*

(1932).[24] It would seem that the objects of negligence are infinite. A negligent mis-statement by a travel agent, unaccompanied by a disclaimer, could be actionable at the suit of a party who suffers loss as a consequence of reliance upon the information: *Hedley Byrne & Co v Heller and Partners (1964).*[25] Failure to detect a mechanical fault in a vehicle which crashes injuring a passenger may result in an award of compensation: *Barkway v South Wales Transport Co (1950).*[26] A diner who is ill after consuming a meal bought by someone else may not have an action based on contract but may succeed in negligence: *Buckley v La Reserve (1959).*[27] A spectator injured by a firework at an organised display has recovered compensation for his injuries: *Whitby v C.J. Brock (1886).*[28]

It has also become established that liability for harm may be attributed to a defendant as a result of the actions of a third party. The commonest case in English law is the liability of an employer for the actions of his servant committed in the course of the latter's employment.

Vicarious liability

The reason for imposing such liability is one of policy. It provides a financially credible person against whom an order for compensation can be made and it concentrates the mind of management upon the need to achieve reasonable standards of safety within the organisation.

The common law did not provide for vicarious liability to attach to a master where a crime was involved. The courts have modified this stance in the case of certain statutory offences. Notable amongst these are abuses of licensing laws. The serving of alcohol to under-age drinkers is a prevalent offence. An employer who knows his staff are guilty of such acts, but does nothing effective to control them, is himself guilty. Similarly, where he delegates control of the business to staff: *Allen v Whitehead (1930).*[29]

It is in tort, however, that the principles are most often encountered. A most extreme case is to be found where the driver of a petrol tanker, whilst discharging fuel into an underground tank, lit a cigarette and threw away the match! An explosion occurred causing extensive damage for which his employer was held liable: *Century Insurance v Northern Ireland R.T.B.(1942).*[30]

An over zealous employee, seeking to guard his master's property, who assaults the person he mistakenly believes is stealing from his master will be unlikely to make the latter liable: *Warren v Henlys Ltd (1948)*.[31]

As with agency, the rules and principles of this liability have been written by the judges. There are some who would wish to see them, and others, contained within statutes.

The Law Commission

The Commission, established in 1965 was charged, inter alia, with:

'keeping under review all the law...... with a view to systematic development and reform, including in particular codification of the law ...... (and) simplification and modernisation of the law.'[32]

Should that day ever come, it is doubtful whether the obfuscation which so often afflicts legislation will diminish the need for judges to interpret statutes. It is more likely that their workload will increase. Law in action will still be viewed through cases and principles devised by the courts.

2. LEGISLATION

Parliament is now the supreme law-making body. It can make or repeal any previous statutes or common law. Once an Act has been passed, and the date set for its commencement has been arrived at, it must be applied by the courts. It consists of formalised rules which are to be observed in the future by all those to whom it is addressed either expressly or by implication. It is unusual for a statute to take effect retrospectively.

The majority of bills which become law are *government* inspired and promoted. They are, therefore, political decisions made by the party in power. Bills are introduced by private members,[33] some in the House of Lords, but these are in the minority.

Until the 19th century, legislation occupied a minority share of the law-making process. The social revolution which occurred in Britain after 1815 changed the situation irreversibly. The common law was unable to meet the demands made upon it by new towns and industries. It had never been designed to do so. Executive action was necessary and successive governments seized the initiative. A notable example is to be found in the case of the development of the railways. So massive was the growth in personal mobility which this called forth that, in the period 1830-1930, more than 200 Acts of Parliament were passed regulating their activities.

Even the *common callings* of England, which had existed for centuries, were regulated by statute. Common carriers were constrained in their trade by the Carriers Act 1830 and innkeepers by the Innkeepers Act 1878. Both of these are still in force while the Innkeepers Liability Act 1863 has been repealed by the Hotel Proprietors Act 1956. Some statutes lie dormant awaiting repeal. The Sunday Observance Act 1677 which prohibits people on pain of fine from assembling outside the confines of their own parishes on the sabbath for any sport or pastime is still extant.

Where a volume of law has become contained within a variety of statutes, subordinate legislation and judicial interpretation, it may become necessary to *consolidate* it under one head. A prime example is the Road Traffic Act 1972, while the original Sale of Goods Act was brought up to date by its namesake of 1979.

Pressure groups

Whether or not a Bill becomes law may be determined by the effectiveness of pressure brought to bear by interest groups upon ministers and individual Members of Parliament. Government policy may be determined:

'In semi-secret by a triad of ministers, civil servants and pressure group representatives, with Parliament hovering critically and vocally in the background, sometimes able to influence policy even in a radical way, at others being forced to accept a series of faits accomplis.'[34]

A whole network of organisations exist whose purpose is to communicate views of interest groups to the appropriate organs of government. In the great debate over licensed hours for England and Wales, proposals for liberalising existing controls on the sale and supply of liquor have been widely canvassed by the Brewers' Society and the British Hotels, Restaurant and Caterers' Association. For the opposition, Alcohol Concern has spearheaded the resistance.

If causes espoused appeal to the government of the day it may adopt them and appear to be responding to the pressure of *public opinion*. In many cases it is doing no more than responding to demands which it has itself instigated. There is no doubt that the lobby from the drinks industry was given the nod by the government prior to the 1987 General Election. A potential vote-winner was appreciated by the policy makers and included in the party manifesto. The benefits to the tourist industry which liberalisation of licensed hours would bring have been widely canvassed. The Licensing Act 1988 is now on the statute books.

Legislation is not the only, or even the main, activity in which government must engage. Consequently, it is just possible to find time for a maximum 60-70 enactments in any one year. There is also, very often, a pressing need to introduce legislation. In addition, there is much technical detail for which Parliament has neither the time nor the expertise to deal. Over the years Parliament has leant increasingly upon various agencies to introduce and implement administrative detail. It has been criticised for surrendering law-making to others who are chiefly ministers, local authorities and statutory corporations e.g. British Rail.

Delegated legislation

The greatest criticism of this form of law-making is that, unlike its parent statute, the statutory instrument which is the device used, is given too little scrutiny and is insufficiently challenged. In part this is true. However, whereas a court of law cannot question the validity of an Act of Parliament, it can challenge delegated legislation on the grounds that it is *ultra vires*. By this the courts mean that the minister or other initiator of the regulation has exceeded his authority. Only if the enabling statute has conferred the power may it be exercised by the designated person: *Laker Airways Ltd v Department of Trade (1977)*.[35]

Statutory instruments are also void if they conflict with EEC legislation. In addition, local authority byelaws may not only be declared 'ultra vires' but can be declared void by the court if they are found to be unreasonable: *Parker v Bournemouth Corporation (1902)*.[36]

The growth of delegated legislation has been rapid. From 1894 to 1913, the annual production of statutory instruments was an average of 1238 annually. Since 1964 that annual figure has risen to over 2,000.

Very many Acts concern the tourism industry and it would be a lengthy process to list them all. In connection with transportation the principal statutes have been the various Road Transport Acts 1930-1985; the Transport Acts 1947 and 1962 which have had the most

31

effect on the railways; Merchant Shipping Acts 1894-1984 and the Hovercraft Act 1968; Air Acts 1911-1986. The movement of travellers is controlled primarily by Public Health and Immigration Acts.

The provision of goods and services is regulated by a wide range of consumer protection legislation combined with industry-specific statutes. The Food Safety Act 1990, Licensing Acts 1964 and 1988 and the Hotel Proprietors Act 1956 are the principle examples of this latter group.

In the field of leisure and recreation the list expands to even greater proportions. Legislation regulates the operation of Cinemas, Theatres, Gambling, the Safety of Sports Grounds and the display of animals in Zoos.

More general laws have an impact over the whole range of tourism activities. The most significant of these are the statutes whose concern is focused on safety. The Health and Safety at Work Act 1974, and the Regulations made under it, is concerned not simply with working conditions as they may affect employees. Every employer owes a duty to conduct his undertaking in such a way as to ensure, so far as is *reasonably* practicable, that persons not in his employment, but who may be affected by it, are not exposed to risks to their health and safety.[37] Employees have a duty to take reasonable care for the health and safety not only of themselves but of other persons who may be affected by their acts or omissions at work.[38] The Act is concerned with enforcement through criminal sanctions; it is not a vehicle for claims for compensation.[39] New Health and Safety at Work Regulations came into force in Januay 1993 as a consequence of EC Directives made under the provisions of Article 118A of the Treaty of Rome. These Directives form part of the EC's programme for improved safety and are an essential ingredient in the progress of the Single European Market.

These new Regulations require a higher standard of care than those of the present HASAW Act 1974. Under EC law it is not sufficient that a *reasonable standard* is the level of safety to be achieved. If harm does occur as a consequence of a deriliction of an imposed obligation then *reasonableness* will be no defence.

A major priority in safety matters is the prevention of loss and damage caused by fires. The Fire Precautions Act 1971 was passed to improve fire safety standards. Section 1 empowers the Secretary of State to designate certain premises in respect of which a fire certificate is required. One of these is addressed to Hotels and Boarding Houses and another to places where people congregate - public houses, restaurants and discoteques etc.[40] This Act, and the Regulations associated with it, also provides criminal sanctions, not civil remedies.

Of major concern to those who cater to the wants of the tourist is the Occupiers Liability Act 1957. The duty owed by an occupier of premises, which had been contained in complex common law rules, was synthesised into this Act. It imposes a duty of care upon those who are in physical control of premises and those who reserve a right to such control when they lease property to others: *Stone v Taffe (1974)*.[41] The duty applies to all lawful visitors but not to trespassers. This latter group were governed by the common law until the Occupiers Liability Act 1984 was passed to simplify their position.

The duty concerns the safety of the premises and certain things done or omitted to be done on them. Because of the wording of the Act, it is probably better to consider its provisions as applying to the static condition of the premises, while 'things done or omitted' are still governed by the common law principles of negligence from which the Act derives. Thus a loose stair carpet which causes a guest to fall and injure himself in an hotel would be the subject of the Act's provisions, while the actions of a clumsy waiter spilling hot soup on a diner at the hotel would not.

The occupier's obligation is described in the statute as a *common duty of care* which is 'to take such care as in all the circumstances of the case is reasonable to see that the visitor will be reasonably safe in using the premises for the purpose for which he is invited or permitted by the occupier to be there.' The occupier can protect himself to a certain degree by warning visitors and displaying notices as to specific dangers.

The 1957 Act specifically states, in section 2 (3) (a), that 'an occupier must be prepared for children to be less careful than adults.' The standard of care owed to them has been established by a series of cases preceding the Act: *Glasgow Corporation v Taylor (1922)*;[42] *Phipps v Rochester Corporation (1955)*.[43]

It is also necessary to draw a distinction between those vehicles, ships and aircraft, which are regarded as *premises* by the Act and those which are 'exceptions', governed by the rules of the more onerous common law.[44] The effect of this is that, in the case of contracts for the 'hire of, or for the carriage for reward of, persons or goods in any vehicle, vessel, aircraft or other means of transport', the duty of care is not discharged unless 'all' reasonable care and skill have been taken to ensure the safety of such forms of transport.

The statute provides defences for occupiers against whom breaches of duty are alleged and, in addition, the Law Reform (Contributory Negligence) Act 1945 assists them in reducing damages by allowing the conduct of the plaintiff to be used in assessing levels of compensation.

Other statutory provisions may give rise to claims by those suffering loss or damage through the activities of others. In cases where a statute provides criminal penalties it may also be possible to assert that its provisions impose a statutory duty the breach of which gives rise to a civil claim for damages. Such liability is sometimes called *statutory negligence* but this is not an entirely accurate description. Each statute needs to be examined in order to determine whether or not it does allow a right of action to the complainant.

This is not the case with the Animals Act 1971 which consolidated the previous common law provisions and created a strict liability in respect of damage caused by animals, i.e. liability without need to prove fault on the part of the defendant. All those who operate tourist attractions featuring animals, and tourists accompanied by animals, are subject to the provisions of the Act.

In addition to domestic legislation, laws made outside the UK will affect the activities of tourists at home and abroad.

3. THE INTERNATIONAL DIMENSION

There are two branches of International Law. The first, Public International Law, is concerned with the regulation of dealings between states in the international community, e.g. rights of passage on the high seas and overflying of national territory by foreign aircraft. The second is that area of law which is sometimes referred to as the *conflict of laws* and includes the resolution of disputes between individuals which have a *foreign* element, e.g. where a contract has not been performed to the satisfaction of one or other of the parties. So, for example, a British passenger on a Polish cruise liner is injured by an Italian sub-contractor conducting a day trip around Naples. The question arises as to who is liable and which national law shall apply. In such a case, the contract may contain a clause to the effect that 'Any action covered by the Athens Convention may be brought in any Court specified in Article 17 thereof. Any other action, suit, or proceeding arising out of or connected with any contract between Chopin Lines and the Passenger shall only be brought in London. All proceedings including arbitration shall be governed by English Law both as to liability and the amount of damages whether or not they be covered by that Convention and wherever they may be brought, heard or disposed of.' Many contracts for carriage of an international nature contain such clauses.

The issue here is of a *private nature* but the Athens Convention was the subject of international agreement by governments. It became part of English law by virtue of its inclusion within the Merchant Shipping Act 1979, Schedule 3. The provisions did not come into force until an order in Council - a form of delegated legislation - gave them the force of law with effect from 1 January 1981.[45]

This process of incorporation is necessary for such laws to become a part of English law. As was stated forcibly by the Master of the Rolls:

'It is elementary that these courts take no notice of treaties as such. We take no notice of treaties until they are embodied in laws enacted by Parliament and then only to the extent that Parliament tells us.'

Blackburn v Att. Gen. (1971)[46] per Lord Denning M.R.

Originally, customary rules of international law were deemed automatically to be part of the common law but this view was denied, first, in *R V Keyn (the Franconia) 1876*[47] and by other authorities since. However, judges are not prepared to interpret Acts of Parliament in such a way that they conflict with international law. There is a presumption that Parliament, in making the law, did not intend to breach international law: *Corocraft Ltd v Pan American Airways (1969)*[48] Where a statute is clear and unambiguous, the judges will need to be especially *creative* if they are to rule that the Act is a breach of a 'customary' rule of international law.

The term *Treaty* covers a range of forms under which international rules are made, there being no established format. The term itself is usually reserved for the most formal agreements concluded by heads of state and are expressed in terms such as to bind contractually the 'High Contracting Parties': *Phillipson v Imperial Airways Ltd (1939).*[49]

Convention is the term used to denote formal instruments of a multinational character, e.g. the Warsaw Convention 1929 governing international carriage by air. The rules were agreed by the signatories at the time and provision was made, as in all such agreements, for other nations to *accede* to the terms later by ratification.

A *Protocol* indicates a lower grade of agreement. It is usually concerned with matters of interpretation of a particular convention. Thus the Hague Protocol 1955 was an extension of the provisions of the original Warsaw Convention to carrier's servants and agents. Further modifications have since been added by the Guatamala Protocol of 1971 and the Montreal Protocol of 1974. Not all parties to the Warsaw Convention have agreed to these and so are not bound by them, e.g. the USA.

Lower down the scale still come *Declarations*, usually resulting from *resolutions* by diplomatic conferences. These may become accretions to the original convention when ratified by a sufficient number of signatories. The Montreal Resolution 1975 is an example of this in relation to carriage by air.

The overall effect can be one of some confusion. Carriage by air is a particularly good example in that a number of *regimes* for air travel now operate depending on whether a country has signed the original or amended Warsaw Convention and whether it has ratified all, some, or none of the modifications; or has also signed the Guadalajara Convention 1961.

The original Warsaw rules were embodied in the Carriage by Air Act 1932. The later modifications were incorporated within the Carriage by Air Act 1961, whose terms were brought into operation by statutory instrument in 1967. Britain also included the Guadalajara Convention in the Carriage by Air (Supplementary Provisions) Act 1962. The other Protocols and Resolution have not yet attracted sufficient national signatures to become effective.

Other Conventions dealing with road, rail and sea travel have received similar attention. They have either been included in domestic legislation or are awaiting further action. One international agreement requires no further action to make it part of our domestic law, the Treaty of Rome.

The European Community

Britain joined the Community officially with effect from 1 January 1973. The Treaty was signed by the government on behalf of the Crown and the legislative act of passing the European Communities Act 1972 made the Treaty part of English law. In the words of section 2 (1) of the Act:

'All such rights, powers, liabilities, obligations and restrictions from time to time created or arising by or under the Treaties, and all such remedies and procedures from time to time provided for by or under the Treaties, as in accordance with the Treaties are without further enactment to be given legal effect or used in the UK shall be recognised and available in law, and be enforced, allowed and followed accordingly; and the expression 'enforceable Community right' and similar expressions shall be read as referring to one to which this subsection applies.'

These provisions mean that the UK is bound by existing and future treaty obligations and those which the Community makes with external states. These all form part of the municipal law of member nations without the need for further administrative action. Laws are also made by way of Regulations, Directives and Decisions published by the Council of Ministers or the Commission. They either take effect immediately or require the appropriate form of municipal legislation for their adoption.

Wherever Community law conflicts with domestic law there is a presumption for interpretation by the courts that the former shall prevail. UK statute law is to be read subject to Community law. This anticipates that Parliament will not pass legislation which is inconsistent with Community law. Where there is a question either as to the application of Community law or as to its interpretation, the matter is to be referred to the European Court of Justice: *McCarthys v Smith (1979).*[50]

The UK government has one of the best records in the EC for the implementation of Directives. It is unfortunate that this record does not extend to implementation in the manner or as to the content of UK legislation in this regard. Omissions and obfuscation in UK statutory implementation of Directives has caused the UK to be taken to task by the Commission and the ECJ on more occasions than almost any other national government. Government Ministers have indicated that they do not like 'red tape' from Brussels and that they will seek to reduce the 'burdens' on British business. This may very well land the UK before the ECJ on even more occasions in the future. Only by the skin of its teeth did the DTI manage to get the provisions of the EC Directive on Package Travel 90/314/EEC in place by the deadline of 31 December 1992 and it remains to be tested as to whether SI 1992/328 has satisfied the provisions of the EC Directive.

It should be noted that most of English municipal law is not affected by membership of the European Community. Community law is mainly concerned with restrictive trade practices (Competition law) and the free movement of labour, capital and services. English domestic law of contract, tort and crime is not directly affected by UK membership of the Community. It remains to be seen what closer union, post-1992, will mean in terms of integration and a move towards political unity.

NOTES

1. Commentaries on the Laws of England. Sir W. Blackstone. Vol I p 23.
2. The Politics of the Judiciary. J.A.G. Griffiths p.241.
3. See Bennett v Markham & Another (1982) 1 WLR 1231 (QBD).
4. R v Higgins (1948) 1 KB 165.
5. (1853) All ER 12.
6. (1984) AC 217.
7. (1866) LR 2 Exch. 213.
8: 23QBD 598CA
9. (1903) 2 KB 740.
10. (1903) 2 KB 683.
11. (1951) 1 KB 805.
12. (1874) LR 9 Exch. 132.
13. See Samuel v Westminster Wine Co (1959) C.L.Y. 173.
14. (1951) 2 KB 882.
15. (1953) 2 All ER 1021.
16. (1858) 3 CB (NS) 180.
17. (1938) Ch 1.
18. (1956) 1 W.L.R.335.
19. (1913) 1 Ch 269.
20. (1980) QB 485.
21. (1868) LR 3 HL 330.
22. (1933) Ch 89.
23. (1856) 11 Exch. 781.
24. (1932) AC 562.
25. (1964) AC 465.
26. (1950) AC 185.
27. (1959) C.L.Y. 1330.
28. (1886) 4 TLR 241.
29. (1930) 1 KB 211.
30. (1942) AC 509.
31. (1948) 2 All ER 935.
32. Law Commissions Act 1965 s 3(1).

33. Licensing (Restaurant Meals) Act 1987.
34. Governing Britain. A.H. Hanson & M. Walters p178.
35. (1977) QB 643.
36. (1902) 86 LT 449.
37. s.3.
38. s.7.
39. s.47.
40. SI 1972 No 238; SI 1976 No 2009.
41. (1974) 3 All ER 1016.
42. (1922) 1 AC 44.
43. (1955) 1 QB 450.
44. Occupiers Liability Act 1957 s.5.
45. SI 1980 No 1092.
46. (1971) 1 W.L.R. 1037.
47. (1876) 2 Exch. Div 63.
48. (1969) 1 QB 108.
49. (1939) AC 332.
50. (1979) 3 All ER 325.

CHAPTER III

Rights of Passage

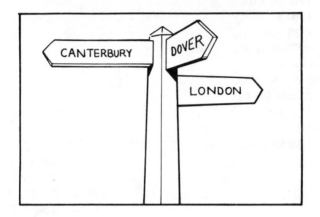

1. HIGHWAYS

People travel for a variety of reasons - business, duty, pleasure. They may go on foot or use personal transport, or they may travel as passengers in any number of types and descriptions of vehicle. What all travellers share is the control which exists to a greater or lesser degree over the routes they take to reach their destinations.

Air travellers are controlled by the rights of overflying national territory agreed by international conventions. Domestic flights with-in the UK have been controlled since the earliest days of flight in order to protect the public on the ground from dangers resulting from accidents and the possibility of mid-air collisions. Rail travellers are dependent upon the willingness of the carrier to transport them over the routes which he dictates. Only on the high seas is there a true freedom of choice as to the route selected.

In the UK, the Crown has long recognised the right of its subjects to navigate the waterways and coastal waters and to travel the public highways. These may range in scope and sophistication from footpaths and bridleways to motorways. A highway has been described as:

'A way over which there exists a public right of passage, that is to say a right for all Her Majesty's subjects at all seasons of the year freely at their will to pass and repass without let or hindrance.'

This dictum of Mr Justice Willis in *Ex parte Lewis (1888)*[1] encapsulates the attitude of the common law to the use of a highway once it is in existence. It does not describe the *way* nor the method of its creation.

Dedication

At common law the existence of a highway is established by presuming *dedication* of a way to the public and their acceptance of it.[2] The elements of *dedication* and *acceptance* are important in the creation of rights of passage. Those routeways which have been in existence and continually used since before the year 1189 are regarded in law as having been established by prescription. The choice of this year is purely arbitrary for the purpose of setting a 'time whereof the memory of man runneth not to the contrary'.

In all other cases, prescription is established by the fact of use by the public for a time whose length has never been precisely determined. It is usually taken as being of such an extent as to create the presumption of public *acceptance*. The common law doctrine is based upon the notion that the owner of the sub-soil over which the highway runs so conducted himself as to imply that he had granted public right of passage, that he had *dedicated* the land for this use.

A landowner who seeks to deny a *right of way* to the traveller will need to produce evidence that he and his predecessors in title did not so dedicate the route. As proof of this he may show that, from time to time, it has been barred to the public in such a manner as to signify that there is no *way* over his private property, e.g. by means of the regular and periodic use of a gate or other closure.

Since the great increase in road traffic which occurred in the 19th century, it has been increasingly common to find rights of passage established by statute. Most recently, the Highways Act 1980 treats twenty years of uninterrupted passage as sufficient to establish a right by prescription.[3]

The 1980 Act is a consolidating statute. It has collected together the provisions of earlier Highways Acts 1959-71, amendments to them and decisions of the courts. The *twenty year rule* is no more than a recognition of the presumption of dedication which in some instances has existed for much longer periods: *Eyre v New Forest Highways Board (1892).*[4]

The National Parks and Access to the Countryside Act 1949 makes special provision for the creation of long distance recreational routes. Recommendations as to their adoption are made by the Countryside Commission to the Secretary of State. The purpose of such advice is so that the public should be entitled to make 'extensive journeys on foot, horseback or bicycle (excluding motor vehicular transport) along the route which passes over land for the whole or the greater part not normally used for motor vehicles'.[5]

Closure of highways

The rule of the common law was 'once a highway always a highway'. Mere non-use did not extinguish rights of passage, but natural causes - coastal erosion or landslip - could. Occasionally, private roads leading to such highways might be closed by their owners thus effectively rendering them unusable, though not extinguishing their use.

Today, closures are effected under statutory provisions. The regulation of such closures is contained in the Highways Act 1980.[6] Routes may be closed, either temporarily or permanently, for a variety of reasons. The most frequent cause is temporary denial of access for repairs or improvements to the roads. The procedure for closure usually requires an order to be made by local Magistrates, who have long and historic duties over highways.

The 1980 Act makes it clear that its provisions do not prejudice powers contained in other statutes. Various powers over routes and access to land are contained in Military Lands and Defence Acts. Byelaws made under these enactments allow closures in the national interest and for reasons of public safety.

Right of way

Public rights over a highway are restricted to use for passage from one place to another. This includes such purposes as may be reasonably incidental to such purpose, e.g. mending a puncture. Activities not of this nature may render the traveller a trespasser both as to the highway and to adjacent land. The use of a roadway for the purpose of spying on horses engaged in training gallops by a racing tipster is a case in point: *Hickman v Maisey (1900)*.[7]

Obstruction of the highway is both a statutory offence[8] and the common law crime of Public Nuisance. It is, in effect, a denial of the right of passage which, if left unchecked, could lead to the public taking the law into their own hands and creating a breach of the peace.

Public Nuisance may take various forms and may be committed by both private individuals and public bodies: *Campbell v Paddington Corporation (1911)*[9]. In this case, the local authority obstructed a highway by erecting a grandstand for the purpose of viewing a procession. It should be noted that this common law offence can only be committed when the number of persons which it effects are sufficient to constitute a *class*, e.g. road users generally or local people particularly.

The Road Traffic Acts give powers to the police for stopping road users in order to check for a wide range of offences. These powers have become accepted as a part of everyday life even if, at times, under protest. What is less acceptable to some is the closure of roads by the police in connection with marches or rallies (particularly in Northern Ireland) and in order to deny use of the highway to such members of the public as 'flying pickets' during the miners' strike of 1985.

The powers which are used by the police on such occasions arise out of those which they, together with the military, have possessed historically for the preservation of public order. The Public Order Act 1986 is the first major statute in this field for fifty years. It abolishes the principal common law offences and replaces them with a wide range of statutory provisions amongst which are measures to control public use of highways. The full effect of such powers will need to be judged in the light of experience over the next few years. There can be no denying that they are a radical departure from previous practices governing public rights of access in the UK.

There are some 140,000 miles of rights of way criss-crossing England and Wales. Increasingly these have become obstacle courses. An unpublished report by the Countryside Commission in 1989 showed that 62% of paths were not signposted; once on a path there was a 63% chance of encountering gates or stiles which were closed or difficult to use; after getting over walls and fences there was a 7½% chance of finding that sections of the paths were obliterated by agriculture. This report from Travers Morgan for the Commission was the first attempt to analyse the extent to which routes are fully open to the public. As a consequence the Government has committed itself to making sure that the 108 miles of public footpaths and 27,000 miles of bridleways and 5,000 miles of unsurfaced roads are fully open by the year 2000. Farmers who plough up paths are liable to prosecution and grants have been made to ensure that existing routes remain open.

2. ACCESS TO LAND

For the traveller, the ability to gain access to his chosen destination is as important as his right to use the highway. Access to land in Britain is largely a matter connected with the *ownership* of land or rights over it.

Ownership

The concept of *ownership* of land is foreign to English law. It recognises *estates* or interests in land but not of absolute ownership. The reasons for this are historical. As a result of the Norman Conquest, all lands are held of the Crown. By the Law of Property Act 1925, the forms of legal landholding were reduced to those familiarly known as freehold and leasehold. The freeholder holds his lands indefinitely, the leasee for a term of years determined in advance. Both forms of holding may be transferred to others. Nevertheless, every occupant of land is, in theory at least, a tenant ultimately of the Crown. Land has always been regarded as a national asset and public control over it is a logical extension of State authority.

Modern statutes allow for land to be controlled by planning authorities and government ministries. Compulsory purchase of land is no more than the reassertion of Crown rights. It is often fiercely opposed by those effected and the law provides safeguards by means of enquiries and appeals against decisions. In the end, it is usually the power of the State which carries the day.

Crown lands

Land may be owned by the monarch in his or her personal capacity or by the Crown exercising control through a Department of State. By far the largest land-holder in this respect is the Ministry of Defence. For many years this organ of government and its predecessors has acquired land in the interest of defending the realm. Armies need accommodation and land upon which to practise the arts of war. Numerous statutes have been enacted to meet the needs of the three services.

A series of Defence Acts was passed during the period 1842-73. These were succeeded by the Military Lands Acts 1892-1903 and, later, by the Defence of the Realm (Acquisition of Land) Acts 1916-20. Chief amongst them is the Military Lands Act 1892 whose provisions largely regulate the position of such properties today.

Some of these enactments were meant to be temporary in nature with lands being acquired compulsorily from their owners upon a presumption of return to them at a future date. Some were returned, but others remain in military hands. Others were recovered, as in the case of Critchell Down, after years of struggle against bureaucracy. Many former inhabitants of villages in Dorset and Wiltshire have died waiting for the return of their homes.

Many of the Defence lands are in areas of great attraction for tourists but the public is denied access to them on an open basis. When they are opened, movement is restricted by notices warning of unexploded pyrotechnics.

Other lands are closed because they are occupied as military cantonments or for more sinister reasons. The island of Gruinard in the Hebrides was used for testing bacteriological warfare agents nearly fifty years ago. It is still contaminated by anthrax and is likely to remain so into the 21st century.

The occupation of areas of outstanding scenic beauty by the military is the subject of much continuing public complaint. In particular, the use of Dartmoor and of large tracts of the North Yorkshire Moors has attracted particular attention from conservationists and public interest groups.

Unauthorised visitors to Ministry of Defence property are not only trespassers but run the risk of prosecution for offences committed either against the legislative provisions themselves or byelaws made under their authority. In many cases, members of the public may have no prior knowledge that such powers exist. Ignorance of the law is no excuse against criminal charges.

Private property

In English law, there is no such concept as the Jus Spatiandi known on the continent of Europe. There is no right to *wander at will* which this concept embodies. The nearest English equivalent is the right to unimpeded passage over the public highway. Most land is subject to proprietorship which allows the occupant to deny access to those visitors he wishes to exclude.

Visitors to private property may enter premises as lawful visitors or as trespassers. From the earliest times, the law protected land-owners by allowing them to bring civil actions in trespass. The reasons for modern exclusions are developments of these ancient rights. 'Today actions in trespass to land are available to protect land from the interference of outsiders ... by those who trample on farmers' crops, or those who come to spy on the private homes of the rich and famous'.[10]

The act of trespass results from a voluntary intrusion by one person into the space under the control of another. It is a wrong against the possession of property by that other. In this sense *possession* means the legal right to exclude others from the land whether the possessor is present in person or not. In order for an act of trespass to occur it need not be accompanied by physical damage to the property. Entry without damage of some sort is, however, unlikely to attract more than nominal damages awarded by a court.

Those who exercise a *right of way* over the land of a private owner are not trespassers unless they act in such a way as to exceed the right of passage. In certain instances, statutes grant rights to visitors. The National Parks and Access to the Countryside Act 1949 allows rights of entry onto land for outdoor recreation. These are arrived at by agreement between local planning authorities and landlords or by compulsory access orders.[11] If such visitors abuse their rights by damaging the property then they too become trespassers.[12]

Despite many notices proclaiming trespass as a crime which will be prosecuted, uninvited visitors do not often face criminal sanctions. They will encounter such penalties where statutes so provide. The Railway Regulations Act 1840 allows for the prosecution of trespassers upon British Rail property.[13] Other examples are to be found in the case of summary offences connected with municipal parks.[14] Similarly, the National Trust possesses powers to make byelaws to protect Trust property by the threat of criminal prosecution.[15]

Protection of the right of possession extends to the air space above the land as well as the soil beneath. In acknowledgement of rights over air space, which may be possessed by a landowner, the Civil Aviation Act 1982 provides that:

'No action shall lie in respect of trespass....... by reason only of the flight of an air craft over any property at a height above the ground which...... is reasonable, or the ordinary incidents of such flight.'[16]

Nevertheless, the Act allows damages to be recovered for injury caused by taking off and landing or of things or persons falling from an aircraft! Commercial aircraft and recreational flights by individuals in 'planes or microlites are included in these provisions but not aircraft in Her Majesty's Service.

Access to land may thus be limited, excluded, or in some cases extended by operation of statute. It may also be allowed for in other ways.

Common lands

Historically, common land was that which was enjoyed by a number of people with established rights. Originally, these were in connection with grazing livestock but, with the passage of time, recreational use has also been established. Many a village green came into existence as a common amenity in this regard.

The Commons Registration Act 1965 includes recreational use to be registered along with other activities. Failure to register rights under the Act leads to their extinction. It further allows that, even in the absence of rights of common, recreational uses for land may be registered. In so doing, the Act recognises the antiquity of certain practices which, in the absence of evidence to the contrary, should be protected.

These rights rely for their protection on the needs of local people not of the public at large. This does not prevent the extension of such enjoyment of the land to the general public. The Law of Property Act 1925 granted the public rights of enjoyment and exercise on any land which is a London metropolitan common or *manorial waste*, or a common wholly or partly within an urban area.[17]

The intention of Parliament seems to have been to prevent in-fill within urban areas, particularly by property developers with an eye to prime sites. The need for the urban population to have access to open spaces seems to have been a major concern of legislators. In some cases, the land in question is subject to old manorial rights although the lord of the manor has long since disappeared with the advance of urbanisation. Where it is not possible to discover his identity, local authorities have statutory powers of management conferred upon them.[18]

Concern for the future of such land is a major feature of the work of Britain's oldest national conservation group, the Open Spaces Society. An attempt by the Society to get a private members' bill through Parliament to restrict the sale of manorial titles narrowly failed to gain approval in 1977.

The sale of England's biggest village green at Old Buckenham, near Diss in Norfolk, took place in 1987. The 50 acre site was auctioned in London and sold for £30,250 to a local farmer. The parish council had maintained the green for a number of years but their bid was defeated. The fate of the land is as yet unknown but the owners of ancient grazing rights dating from the 18th century are investigating their claims to ownership.[19]

Over 8,500 commons in England and Wales have been registered since the 1965 Act - an area of over 1.3 million acres - yet the public has no right to enter more than 20% of these areas. In 1958 a Royal Commission recommended that public access to common land should be recognised by law. In 1987 the government did promise legislation but to date this promise remains unfulfilled. In the meantime loopholes in the 1965 Act are being exploited and commons are being *deregistered* fenced off and built upon.

Open access to the shores

Except where open spaces are provided for by statute, there is no general right of access to open spaces. Such amenities often exist only because of specific rights of commons. The foreshores and beaches which surround Britain are governed by a similar collection of ancient privileges.

The sea bottom, from the low water mark out to a three mile limit, is Crown property. The Crown has traditionally allowed its subjects freedom to navigate such waters and to fish them. These privileges have been extended to tidal areas on the coast when the seas cover the foreshore and extend up rivers. When the tide is out, the public appear entitled to cross the foreshore for the purpose of reaching the sea for activities such as navigation or fishing: *Williams Ellis v Cobb (1934)*.[20] The issue of what constitutes the foreshore was examined in some detail in *Ingram v Percival (1968)*.[21] The Queen's Bench Divisional Court considered the question best resolved by local justices with knowledge as to *ebb or flow*, whether lateral or vertical in movement.

The foreshore technically comprises that strip of land which lies between high and low water marks and along river estuaries. Originally, all such land was held by the Crown. Much of it still is, but much more has been granted to private owners. Land bordering the sea may also become part of the foreshore because, with time, the sea has retreated. It becomes private property as well and, in both cases, unless a right of way over the property exists, those who venture onto it become trespassers.

The presumption exists that all the foreshore is Crown land unless a claimant can prove to the contrary. Even where the land is Crown property, as with private land at the sea's edge, there is no right to bathe from it: *Brinckman v Matley (1904)*.[22] Still less is there a right to keep and hire out deck-chairs to the public: *Ramsgate Corporation v Debling (1906)*.[23] As one writer puts it succinctly:

'There are no absolute rights to sit in a deck-chair, to play games, to paddle, to collect sea shells, driftwood...... or even to take a stroll on the beach. Bathing in the sea is normally on sufferance.'[24]

Land around ports is invariably in private ownership, whether this be by individuals or corporations. It is on such a basis that commercial development of amenities such as marinas has taken place.

Often the Crown has granted leases of the foreshore to local authorities whose parishes abut the shore. Such bodies make and enforce byelaws regulating the use of the shore and the conduct of those who may cause obstructions or annoyance on the beach or its approaches. Such regulations also extend to the noise of boats and their emissions together with the speed at which they are allowed to travel.

A newspaper report at a popular resort on the south coast highlights some of the problems facing enforcement agencies:

'Hot weather has brought with it more boats afloat than ever before ...... inexperienced people are rushing around in very high powered boats......

swimmers are most at risk....... so far (the police marine section) have stopped dozens of speedboats ... in areas where speedboats are prohibited. They have warned some and in certain cases taken action for prosecution.'[25]

The use of byelaws has brought unusual defendants before the courts: *Llandudno U.D.C v Woods (1899)*.[26] In this case, the Justices did not feel that an Anglican clergyman preaching a sermon on the beach should be prevented by an injunction even if, technically, he was a trespasser.

Where a local landowner has blocked the access to the beach deliberately, he has been held entitled so to do even where this moved other local residents to violent objections: *Behrens v Richards (1905)*.[27]

Local Justices may show a marked reluctance to support the actions of local landowners as being against the public interest but the fact remains that private property rights are paramount in English law. It has been left to Parliament to take action for access to certain parts of the natural heritage.

National Parks

The National Parks and Access to the Countryside Act 1949 makes special provision for the Countryside Commission to secure public access to open country where this is 'wholly or predominantly of mountain, moor, heath, down, cliff or foreshore (including any banks, barriers, dune, beach, flat or other land adjacent to the foreshore)'.[28]

These provisions are extended by the Countryside Act 1968 to rivers and canals and adjacent land allowing of rambling, boating or picnicking.[29] Access can be secured in several ways. Local planning authorities can acquire land, secure access agreements with landowners, or make compulsory access orders. The agreements reached or orders made under the 1949 Act create a *licence* for the public to enter and enjoy the land but they must not abuse their privileges.[30]

A good example of what the legislation was designed to achieve can be seen in the 'Borden' agreement reached between the Duke of Devonshire's private family trust and the West Yorkshire County Council in 1960. Thousands of visitors are now enjoying the Yorkshire moorlands without being treated as trespassers or running the gauntlet of the Duke's gamekeepers.

That there are not more successes is due, in part, to the dilatory way in which some local authorities have responded to the initiatives allowed in Part V of the 1949 Act. The statutory provisions themselves do not fulfil the full extent of the recommendations of the Hobhouse Committee which reported in 1947. This wanted automatic, universal access to land. As it is, the Act has not been able to prevent enclosure and loss of land to intensive uses.

The legislation also gives central government the power to intervene. Local authorities are required to produce maps of open country in their areas. These are subject to review by the Secretary of State as are local plans for securing access. In almost every case ministerial action has been conspicuous by its absence.

This leads to the conclusion that, apart from rights of the public over highways, there is little which can be said to exist by way of right in connection with access to land. This has prompted one noted activist to claim:

'At present the only circumstance in which full access will occur is in the event of a benevolent landowner volunteering to open up his prize domain. Given the characteristic attitudes of the landowning classes there are not many such benevolent people.'[31]

A continental view

English law recognises no right of access to land unless there is some clear indication to the contrary. In France the presumption is reversed. Unless a landowner puts up notices at prescribed intervals on his land telling his countrymen to keep out, a right of access is assumed. In Sweden, there is the right of *Allemansrattan* allowing few restrictions. In both France and Sweden, the approach to *ownership* of land is fundamentally different to the British experience. As regards foreign travel, the position is not so dissimilar.

3. THE INTERNATIONAL TRAVELLER

Every sovereign state has an absolute discretion to decide whether it will permit its subjects to travel abroad and whether it will admit aliens. Each state exercises its authority in order to control immigration and emigration. In this regard it is notable that:

'Few subjects arouse quite the same degree of passionate and partisan argument as the presence of aliens upon State territory. The condition of

51

their entry, if it be allowed at all, the treatment due to those admitted and the permitted circumstances of their expulsion are matters commonly consigned without further inquiry, to the realm of sovereign State powers.'[32]

International travel, by definition, involves the crossing of national frontiers. The nationality of the traveller will determine whether he possesses the ability to enter a country, to remain there, to leave or, perhaps, be expelled.

Under English common law, citizens were prohibited from quitting the realm without leave of the Crown. The reason for this is not hard to discover. The king had need of money and men to perform military service. Free exit from his dominions would have enabled his subjects to evade their responsibilities.

One of the rights wrested from the king by Magna Carta was for every free man to leave the realm at his pleasure in time of peace. By the 18th century, this had been extended to a right to leave at all times subject only to the power of the royal prerogative to detain a person by the issue of a writ.

Nationality

A state is free to determine the identity of its citizens. It may decide to create different classes of persons to whom it may accord rights, in accordance with their status, and impose corresponding obligations upon them. Between 1815 and 1905 no aliens were excluded or expelled from Britain. They were treated in similar fashion to nationals. In 1914, the British Nationality and Status of Aliens Act defined British citizenship. It reflected the intention of Parliament to create a common status for nationals of the British Empire. It was never uniformly applied and those countries of predominantly white settlement discriminated against members of the *eastern empire*. The British Nationality Act 1948 attempted a radical change. It recognised the right of independent Commonwealth nations to enact their own citizenship laws. The Act speaks in terms of the status of British subject but nowhere defines the meaning.

Between 1949-1962, the spirit of the Act was observed in respect of unconditional rights of entry to Britain for citizens of the United Kingdom and Colonies and also those from the independent Commonwealth countries. Aliens, on the other hand, were not permitted to land in the UK without immigration control at approved ports of entry. Wide discretionary powers were given to immigration officers to refuse admission to aliens whose presence they believed was undesirable. Also, at this time, concern was being registered over the increased immigration of citizens of the *new Commonwealth*.

A campaign against coloured immigration led to the Commonwealth Immigration Act 1962. For the first time, a distinction was drawn between citizens of the UK and Colonies and other nationals from the independent countries of the Commonwealth. Following the *Africanisation* of countries in East Africa, the Commonwealth Immigration Act 1968 set out to control the large numbers of Asians resident in these countries who sought entry to the UK. Unless they could demonstrate *substantial connections* with the UK, they were made subject to a *special quota voucher* system.

All the previous legislation was consolidated in the Immigration Act 1971 which is the major legislative control operating today. The Act employs a concept of *patriality* to describe the status of those who 'shall be free to come and go into and from the United Kingdom without let or hindrance except such as may be required..... to enable their right to be established'.[33] A *patrial* may be questioned or detained in order to establish his status. Non-patrials are subject to such controls as may be necessary to regulate the conditions of entry and stay.

The 1971 Act grouped millions of former British citizens in the same category as aliens. The Act lays down the guide lines but the regulations made under its authority control the movement of travellers coming to Britain for a variety of reasons - employment, education and tourism. The controls are effectively imposed by means of the use of administrative discretion, uncontrolled by judicial process or statutory bodies.

Further changes have been made by the British Nationality Act 1981. Three categories of citizen were created by the Act - British citizens, citizens of dependent territories and British overseas citizens. Only the first named group have a right of residence in the UK. The Act was largely a government response to fears of the consequences when Hong Kong returns to Chinese rule in the 1990s. The statute gives the Home Secretary additional discretionary powers intended to be freed from any judicial control. The controls over aliens are now subject to other considerations arising from Britain's membership of the European Community.

EEC membership

Articles 48 and 49 of the Treaty of Rome call for free movement of labour within the Community. All discrimination on national grounds within the Community is removed to create a category of *Community worker*. Rights of movement are to be subject only to considerations of public order, security and health. Later Directions have expanded the interpretation of the Treaty of Rome.

In 1974, a Dutch national was refused entry to the UK because of religious affiliations. She brought an action under Article 48 of the Treaty. The European Court of Justice ruled that individuals had rights as citizens of the Community which could be enforced by them in municipal courts. It also ruled that individual nations had the right to refuse admission on the grounds of *ordre publique*. This allows member states to use discretion as to what is considered as effecting national interests. On these grounds, the plaintiff was denied entry to the UK: *Van Duren v Home Office (1974)*.[34]

Directive 64/2220 effects those EEC nationals who wish to provide services, or participate in some non-salaried activity, on the territory of another member state, e.g. tourism, together with their families. Members agree to permit the entry of EEC nationals upon presentation of a valid passport or a national identity card. As a result, formal entry requirements amount to little more than a check on identity of EEC nationals moving between member states.

Human rights

The Universal Declaration of Human Rights was not drafted in the form of a Treaty and is, therefore, a statement of moral standards not of law. It has not created international law nor does it constitute domestic law in the countries of the signatories.

The European Convention for the Protection of Human Rights and Fundamental Freedoms was adopted by the Council of Europe in 1950. The Convention and its Protocols went further than the UN Declaration since they impose legal obligations upon the signatories and they are drafted so as to avoid the vagueness of many international agreements. The European Commission of Human Rights was established to report on allegations of violations at the request of member states or individuals, groups or non-governmental organisations, if the member state against whom the allegation has been made agrees. Cases are heard before a Court of Human Rights. A state can refuse to comply with a judgement and the Commission has no powers of enforcement save public opinion.

As regards freedom of movement required by the Convention, no state has adhered to unrestricted travel. With the exception of the clearly defined terms of the EEC Treaty, no international agreements have removed the power of any state to dictate the terms upon which it will accept visitors or potential residents. Some degree of flexibility is given by the European Convention on Establishment 1955. Its object is to facilitate movement for citizens of the signatories on both a prolonged or short term basis. It states that 'each contracting state shall facilitate the entry into its territory by nationals of other parties for the purpose of temporary visits and shall permit them to travel freely within its territory except when this would be contrary to *ordre publique*, national security, public health or morality'[35] The inclusion of *ordre publique* demonstrates a significant toleration for the discretionary powers reserved to themselves by national governments. The use of *facilitate* betrays a similar air of caution in the wording of the Convention. What at first appears as a charter of rights and duties seems, in reality, to be little more than a gentlemen's agreement.

Such measures as these may ease the passage of tourists and other visitors between the territories of the signatories of such agreements. In practice, however, municipal law will determine the manner in which visitors will be received. It will continue to regulate the conditions under which they are permitted to remain in countries, other than their own, together with the duration of the visit.

NOTES

1. (1888) 21 QBD 321.
2. Halsbury's Laws of England Vol 21 para 1.
3. s 31(1) and (2).
4. (1892) 36 JP 517.
5. Part IV.
6. ss. 116-122.
7. (1900) 1 QB 752.
8. Highways Act 1980 s. 137.
9. (1911) 1 KB 869.
10. Landscape, Land Use & the Law J. Harte p. 337.
11. s. 60.

12. Schedule 2.
13. s. 16.
14. Town Gardens Protection Act 1863 s. 5.
15. National Trust Act 1971 s. 24.
16. Civil Aviation Act 1971 s. 76(1).
17. s. 193.
18. Commons Registration Act 1965 ss. 8 & 9.
19. The Guardian 26 and 27 October 1987.
20. (1934) 1 KB per Lord Wright at p. 21.
21. (1968) 3 All ER 657.
22. (1904) 2 Ch 313.
23. (1906) 4 LGR 495.
24. The Countryside and the Law. C.Fox p. 177.
25. Bournemouth Evening Echo 10 July 1987.
26. (1899) 2 Ch 705.
27. (1905) 2 Ch 614.
28. Part V.
29. s. 16.
30. s. 16.
31. This Land is Our Land. Marian Shoard p. 396.
32. International Law & through Movement of Persons between States. G.S. Goodwin-Gill p. vi.
33. Immigration Act 1971 s. 1 (1).
34. (1974) 3 All ER 78.
35. Article 1.

CHAPTER IV

Movement Control

1. THE PASSPORTS REGIME

In the broadest sense, a passport is a document which allows a traveller to go about his business without let or hindrance, a token of safe conduct issued by one in authority addressed to whomsoever it might concern. 'Proclaim it through my host, that he which hath no stomach to this fight, let him depart; his passport shall be made.'[1] Today, it is recognised as an official document granted to a named person or persons, facilitating travel in foreign countries by authenticating the identity and citizenship of the bearer and granting access to diplomatic offices.

Originally, it was issued to someone engaged on the king's business. The last passport signed personally by the monarch was in 1778. After this date, they were signed by the Secretary of State and over the next hundred years the document took on its modern form. The Public

Records Office holds details of all of those issued since 1795.

A passport is recognised internationally for the purpose of movement across national frontiers. It is 'a document of identity which a State will generally require alien travellers to have in their possession. As a general rule, it is for the municipal law of the State which the traveller seeks to enter to determine the form of the passport or visa it requires'.[2]

Requirements for entry into the UK are contained in regulations made under the powers created by the Immigration Act 1971. Travellers, of whatever nationality, are required to produce a valid passport to the immigration officials on demand. The document, or other form of identity, must be such as is acceptable as proof of the bearer's identity and nationality.

Issue

There is no statutory authority for the issue of British passports. They are issued by the Passport Office under the power of the royal prerogative exercised by the Secretary of State. No citizen is obliged to hold a passport and, in theory at least, there is no limit on the number which may be held at any one time by a single individual. There is a long history of antipathy towards the holding of any form of identification document by British citizens. Only in time of war has the government insisted on identity cards being carried.

The present format of the British passport dates from 1921. The small book design was agreed with other countries at the League of Nations, where twenty-two signatories decided that passports should be issued in English and French. Whatever the form, there are frequent complaints over the 11 to 12 weeks which it takes to process an application.

Some members of the European Community have long wanted to abolish passports as a move towards the ideal of free travel which is contained in the Treaty of Rome. The major opponent to this has been Britain whose governments have been fearful of *illegal* immigration from the *new Commonwealth* by the back door.

A compromise was reached. National passports will continue in use for Community citizens but from 1989 they *are* of a common format. They are in a much smaller book size, machine-printed and readable, with a maroon cover. Other changes include the abolition of joint passports for husbands and wives.

Applications for British passports currently exceed 2 million annually issued from six Passport Offices. An alternative, which is widely accepted in Western Europe, is the British Visitors Passport. These can be used for holidays or unpaid business trips for up to three months' duration. They can be obtained over the counter at main post offices in mainland Britain and are valid for one year from the date of issue.

The concept of free movement across national boundaries is an ideal of various international conventions[3] but the municipal law of individual nations is the ultimate determinant of the need for documentation. This is well illustrated by the action of Yugoslavia in 1987. Industrial action by the UK passport issuing staff led to long delays for British holidaymakers. As a solution to the problem, the Yugoslav government agreed to admit bearers of British Visitors Passports, which under normal circumstances would be unacceptable in that country. The relaxation of the regulations was quite clearly done for economic reasons.

The refusal to issue a passport, or to deny admission of a traveller without one, is a clear barrier to free movement. The wording of the British document is in the form of a 'request' to foreign nations that they 'allow the bearer to pass freely without let or hindrance and to afford the bearer such assistance and protection as may be necessary'. The person making the request is 'Her Britannic Majesty's Principal Secretary of State for Foreign and Commonwealth Affairs'. The Minister is claiming no right to travel either expressly or by implication.

The issue of a British passport is entirely a matter for the Foreign Office. It can be refused to an applicant on a mere whim,[4] with no explanation for the denial. There is no process of administrative review of the decision; no appeal against it lies to any court of law; no payment of compensation for refusal is available to one who suffers loss as a result. It would appear that documents have been withheld on political grounds alone. Refusals have been made in the case of scientists wishing to attend conferences in the USSR[5].

From this, it would appear that the issue of a passport is a matter of foreign policy and, consequently, the subject of arbitrary executive control. The same view prevails in the United States where issue is governed by statutes and various regulations. Nevertheless, the American courts have deduced that the right to travel is enshrined in the Constitution and may only be restricted by due process of law.

Refusal of a passport to an American scientist on the grounds that he was a communist was held to be unlawful in the Supreme Court: *Kent v Dulles (1958).*[6]

Withdrawal

A British passport is so worded that it remains the property of the Crown. The consequence is that a demand for its return may be made at any time without explanation.

In response to criticism Government spokesmen have declared that in practice:

'Passports are withheld in four classes of case: (i) in the case of minors suspected of being taken illegally out of the jurisdiction; (ii) in the case of persons who have been repatriated to the United Kingdom at the public expense and have not repaid the expenditure incurred on their behalf; (iii) in the case of persons believed on good evidence to be fleeing the country to avoid prosecution for a criminal offence; (iv) in the case of persons whose activities *are so notoriously undesirable or dangerous that Parliament would be expected to support the action of the Foreign Secretary in refusing them a passport.*'[7]

However, it should be noted that if the effect of denial is to prevent an individual travelling freely within the European Community the Foreign Secretary could be in breach of the Treaty and the Convention on Establishment. He would have to answer such a charge by claiming that he acted on the grounds of *ordre publique*, public security, health or *morality*.

In the absence of published rules for refusal or withdrawal the only guidelines for the reasons are government statements of general policy[8]. Rarely have the courts been called upon to consider the effect of the possession or not of a passport: *R v Brailsford (1905).*[9]

It appears that some two and a half thousand passports are seized annually. Few are on political grounds. The majority are those of tourists who become stranded and are repatriated on government loans. It would be possible for Regulations made under the Immigration Act 1971 to classify reasons for passport denials but this has not been done, it would appear, for policy reasons.

Protection

The prime virtue of a passport has been held to be the protection which it affords the bearer: *Joyce v D.P.P. (1946)*[10] - 'possession of a passport by a British subject does not increase the Sovereign's duty of protection, though it will make his path easier. For him it serves as a voucher and means of identification ... (The) Crown in issuing a passport is assuming an onerous burden and the holder of the passport is acquiring substantial privileges ... (The) holder may demand from the State's representatives abroad and from officials of foreign governments that he be treated as a British subject'.

The better view might be that it is not the possession of the passport which calls forth the right to protection but the *status* of the individual as a citizen. In this respect the document is 'a voucher and means of identification'.

Stranded tourists may call upon the help of the local Consul on the basis of their nationality. They may be expelled or returned to the UK by officials of foreign governments. To this latter group, the passport is an indication that the country which issued the passport will re-admit its nationals and owes an obligation to foreign countries so to do. The bearer of the *voucher* may have nowhere else to go and the passport's value as a document of 'returnability' should not be underestimated. A traveller without valid documentation signals to potential hosts that, should the latter wish to expel an unwelcome guest, they may have no place to send him.

Immigration controls

The Immigration Act 1971[11] regulates the procedures for entry into the UK. Anyone entering or leaving the country is examined to establish *patriality*. The holder of a valid British citizen's passport need produce no further evidence of *patriality*. Failure to produce such evidence makes the person liable to a fine upon summary conviction. However, the immigration officer may not detain such a person, only report him with a view to prosecution. Any attempt at detention, it seems, would leave the official open to a charge of false imprisonment.

In practice, a traveller without documentation would find difficulty in entering the country for which he is bound and also upon his return to the UK. Realising the problems which it may cause them, carriers make it a condition of the contract for carriage that passengers shall be in possession of valid documentation. If the passenger is unacceptable to the country of destination, the carrier may be faced with the cost of returning their passenger whence he came. Regulations were introduced in 1987 by the Home Office to the effect that carriers of passengers seeking entry without the necessary papers will face heavy fines.

The only grounds upon which the holder of a valid British passport may be denied admission to the UK appears to be under the Prevention of Terrorism (Temporary Provisions) Act 1976. The object seems to be to restrict the movement of people from Northern Ireland to mainland Britain. The Act was originally designated *temporary* but has been repealed and re-enacted (1984).

A returning British national may not be refused entry on health grounds. Persons requiring hospitalisation may be placed in quarantine under the public health legislation.

Expulsion

The right of any nation to expel unwanted visitors is internationally recognised. Such expulsion must be made in good faith and in the case of EEC citizens and those covered by the European Convention it may only be upon those grounds specified in the international agreements. It is no easy matter to prove bad faith: *R v Governor of Brixton Prison ex parte Soblen (1963).*[12]

Visitors are usually deported because they have committed a breach of municipal law. Breaches which:

'In the opinion of Her Majesty's Government if the law... permits the expulsion..... of persons whose presence is dangerous to public order, an expulsion on such ground lawfully carried out according to the municipal law could not be taken exception to, on any ground of international law, by a power whose subjects had been so expelled': *Haiti Case (1894).*[13]

Provided the powers are not exercised arbitrarily, all States possess the right to deport aliens at their discretion on grounds appropriate for them.

In the UK the power of expulsion is exercised under the power of the royal prerogative. In addition powers of exclusion were provided by the Aliens Act 1905 and more recently, in the case of non patrials, by the Immigration Act 1971.[14] The grounds for such expulsion are:

1. Failure to comply with a condition of entry or to depart at the expiry of the time allowed for stay.

2. Where the Secretary of State deems it to be conducive to the public good - not defined.

3. Where a person having attained 17 years is convicted of an imprisonable offence and the court recommends deportation.

Under the terms of the Immigration Appeals Act 1969, appeals may be made to the courts but not if the Home Secretary certifies that deportation is for the public good or where a court has recommended deportation. Additional powers exist for the repatriation of illegal immigrants and the mentally ill.

Extradition

The UK has treaties with many countries for the return of people wanted in connection with offences committed abroad. The most notable recent case being that of people involved in the riots at the Heysul football stadium in 1986. At the request of the Belgian authorities those accused were extradited to stand trial.

The treaties do not apply to *political* crimes. This has caused some difficulty in the past. In order to meet the need to deal with security the Suppression of Terrorism Act was passed in 1978, the same year as the ratification by the UK of the European Convention on the Suppression of Terrorism.

Visas

The UK together with many other nations, USA and Russian Republics included, have as a pre-entry requirement a document of permission authorising admission of the bearer held in addition to a valid passport. Such *visas* are obtained by application to the embassies or consulates of the countries concerned. These are valid for a specified period of use. In the case of the UK, they will cover the visitors to whom they apply for a period of up to six months' stay. Not all countries require such formal documents. Treaties making them unnecessary have been concluded between the UK and 50 nations including all Western Europe and the USA. The latter country, in February 1988, announced that there is to be a gradual phasing out of the requirement for UK visitors to the USA to hold visas.[15]

Immigration officials require to be satisfied that visitors are entering the UK for a permitted purpose. Even with their bona fides established, it is still necessary for the officials to be sure that the visitor can support himself during his stay and will not be a burden to the social services. Above all, it is necessary to ascertain that the visitor has the resources to ensure that he can pay for carriage out of the UK when that time comes.

Criticism of the system has been levelled at the government on the grounds that it discriminates against non-white members of the Commonwealth. In reply, it was stated that the effect of the mandatory penalty applied to carriers, who did not ensure that passengers had the necessary documents for entry to Britain, had been an effective deterrent with greater checks on documentation by all concerned.[16] A warning was given by the Home Secretary that he would not hesitate to increase the statutory penalty under the Immigration (Carriers Liability) Act 1987 if he discovered that carriers were including the cost of the possible fine in the price of the tickets they issued.

Once in the country lawfully, visitors enjoy the same freedom of movement as UK citizens. It should be noted that hotels are obliged to record and keep records of guests for examination by authorised officials. The details which must be obtained are more extensive in regard to foreign visitors than for UK travellers.[17]

Alternative documents

In 1963 the United Nations Conference on International Travel and Tourism recommended that States should seek to abolish the need for passports by treaty agreements. Some already exist where nations have common land frontiers, e.g. the agreement between Belgium and Luxembourg in 1945. Once in the UK, there is freedom of movement to the mainland and off-shore islands and to Eire.

Freedom of movement is also fundamental to the ideal of the Treaty of Rome. But the passport regime remains unless a member state decides otherwise. Movement in the EEC is possible on 'simple production of a valid identity card or passport....... (issued) in accordance with (a state's) own legislation ...... showing in particular the nationality of the bearer'.[18] This is an over-simplification of a system which still allows EEC members to exercise various controls, subject to supervision by the courts.

Where British Visitors Passports are accepted, the UK has

reciprocated by accepting national identity cards in conjunction with visitors cards. In practice this means the citizens of Western European countries. EEC nationals are required to be in possession of identity cards with no further documentation deemed necessary.

Special arrangements also exist in relation to the recognition of group passports for such activities as organised educational visits. Seamen and aircrews are also treated according to rules allowing them special category status. All visitors are nonetheless required to comply with other controls.

2. CUSTOMS DUTIES

From the mid 19th century until 1932 Britain was essentially a free trade country. Duty was levied on liquor and tobacco together with some other specified items but there were no general duties on imports or exports. Under the Import Duties Act 1938, revenues were raised generally for the first time. This, and later legislation was consolidated into the Import Duties Act 1958.

The Act itself does not impose duties but gives power to the Treasury to direct which goods shall be taxed at what rates. All goods are classified under the Customs Tariff 159, whether or not duty is to be levied upon them. The EEC Treaty provides for a common customs union for the members but full harmonisation is still in the future.

Collection and enforcement

The Commissioners of Customs and Excise are appointed by the Crown and control over their activities delegated to the Treasury.[19] The officers who have very wide powers of investigation and enforcement are, however, appointed by the Commissioners. They have, inter alia, authority to board aircraft, ships and vehicles generally. They may detain and search them and confiscate items or impound cargoes. They may act as immigration officers[20] and also exercise powers in connection with the prevention of infection and the spread of disease which could be carried on aircraft and ships entering the country.[21] Their activities in relation to the movement of passengers have brought them into high profile and made them the centre of criticism in recent years.

65

Powers of search

A customs officer has powers of search in connection with premises, persons and places where he has reasonable grounds for believing that there are items chargeable to duty which has not been paid. This is extended to include items which are subject to prohibition or restriction. The test of reasonable belief is an objective one, i.e. did the officer act on such grounds as would have aroused suspicion in a reasonable person.

This is at the heart of the controversy over officers' duties. There appears to be growing evidence of purely random searches of passengers arriving from certain ports of departure. A number of incidents of strip-searching have been reported in the press giving rise to accusations of excessive zeal on the part of the officers concerned.[22]

The searches are being used to discover *prohibited articles* under powers provided under the Customs and Excise Management Act 1979, section 164. These powers allow a customs officer, or a person acting under his authority, to search a passenger or any article in such person's possession. It is the intimate body searches which have given rise to most complaints. Out of 43 million travellers in 1986 46,000 were searched, 816 intimately. Of these 224 were found to be in possession of *prohibited articles*, drugs concealed internally.

The customs officers have much greater freedom of action than police officers. The Police and Criminal Evidence Act 1984 allows for intimate body searches, specifically detailing such in section 55. The 1979 Act governing customs officers does not. The wording of section 164 uses the vague expression 'search him'. It does recognise that there is an inherent danger in this by providing specifically under section 164(3) that women and girls may only be searched by and in the presence of female officers.

An added danger is that, although a complaint may be addressed to a magistrate against a search, it has long been established that the justices have no power to rule on whether the suspicion of an officer was reasonable or unreasonable: *Anderson v Read (1902).*[23] They may only consider whether the proposed search is genuine or a mere pretence by the officer to justify his interference or annoyance of the complainant. This is because the legislation makes the officer, not the magistrate, the judge of what type of search there should be.

It is submitted that the 'reasonable grounds' of s.164 should be read as meaning that the grounds are only reasonable if the officer has a

66

genuine belief that smuggling is taking place. It is further submitted that had it been intended to permit intimate body searches Parliament would have included this power specifically as it did in the Police and Criminal Evidence Act 1984.

There is no right to carry out such a search without the consent of the accused. Any officer who does so should be guilty of an assault as should anyone, e.g. a doctor acting under his supervision. In view of some of the searches which have been carried out, the time when officers' actions may be challenged by the travelling public may not be far off.[24]

There are suspicions that customs officers were becoming over-zealous as a response to staffing cuts. In an attempt to improve their conviction rate the pursuit of suspected offenders was carried out to the limits of their powers. These allow them to prevent drug importation and other smuggled items by pursuit of couriers to business premises and to the profits of the organisers. This brought them into conflict with the police which at times amounted to outright antagonism between the rival law enforcement agencies. As a result, the customs officers have withdrawn to their own territory and have become more active on their home ground.[25]

Whatever the reasons, the hurriedly constructed Act of 1979 needs amendment or a directive from the Commissioners to enforce its vague provisions more sensibly. Antagonising both the travelling public and other enforcement agencies is not in the interests of anyone but the real offenders.

Arrest

Any person who has committed an offence against the customs and excise Acts, or who is reasonably suspected of having committed an offence, may be detained. The arrest may be made by any officer of customs and excise, or any constable, member of the armed forces, or coastguard at any time within three years of the offence having been committed. Prosecutions must also be commenced within three years of the alleged offence. Anyone who impedes an officer or prevents him from the execution of his duties may be prosecuted, as may persons who attempt such acts.[26]

In pursuing their duties of entry and search, customs officers do not need to apply to magistrates for search warrants. They have their own general warrants. These go back to the 16th century. They are issued to the Commissioners at the beginning of the reign of each monarch by the Queen's Remembrancer in the Crown Office of the Supreme Court. Their use has been much criticised but they do allow officers to act speedily, enhancing their chance of apprehending offenders, e.g. when pursuing drug smugglers. Their retention has been approved by a Committee on Enforcement Powers of the Revenue Departments no doubt with drug abuse much to the fore and the opening of the Channel Tunnel on the near horizon.[27] The coming ashore of the latter will create added problems not only for the customs and excise but other control agencies as well.

3. PUBLIC HEALTH

The first Public Health Act was passed in 1848. From a small beginning, the volume of legislation increased and killer diseases such as cholera were gradually brought under control by the end of the century. Cholera is still listed amongst 'notifiable diseases' in the Public Health (Control of Diseases) Act 1984 together with plague, relapsing fever, smallpox and typhus.

The introduction of diseases by visitors to the UK has been recognised for many years. Flying the yellow plague flag on ships may have had some effect in days gone by, but more sophisticated methods are necessary in an age of mass communication by air. Public health controls at ports of entry are the means whereby disease and its spread is contained today. Every traveller can expect to encounter health checks on departure and arrival.

Port health authorities

The Secretary of State has the power under the 1984 Act to establish port authorities by means of statutory instrument. Port health districts and authorities are found from the local authority whose area of responsibility includes within its boundaries a designated port which has customs controls. This link with local authorities goes back to the 19th century.

The Minister possesses wide powers to prevent the spread of diseases. He has authority to maintain and supplement the list of notifiable diseases and for making regulations in connection with such matters. He may take action to treat affected persons, prevent the spread of disease and any dangers to health from vessels and aircraft arriving at any place. The 1984 Act recognises international obligations by providing for control over departures from the UK such as may be 'necessary or expedient for the purpose of carrying out any treaty, convention, arrangement or engagement with any country'.

Powers of regulation extend to requiring signals to be flown marking infected craft; questioning passengers and crew of infected vessels or aircraft; detaining the same and persons on board.

Two sets of Regulations currently apply to ships and to aircraft containing detailed rules for the safeguarding of public health.[28] These and other Regulations contain provisions for dealing with any person who wilfully neglects or refuses to obey or carry out any provisions contained in the legislation which itself imposes penalties. The Regulations specify treatment of persons suffering from diseases and allows for such persons to be detained in hospitals specialising in the treatment of specific diseases.

Anyone seeking to avoid such quarantine regulations needs to be aware that the 1984 Act provides that anyone who exposes others to the risk of infection knowing that he is suffering from a *notifiable disease* faces penalty. The Act makes special mention of likely places where such infection might occur - streets, public places, places of entertainment or assembly, clubs, hotels, inns or shops. Penalties are also imposed for any such person who travels in any form of public transport.

The regulations extend to carriers by making them responsible for fumigation, decontamination and detoxification and the cost of the same. Knowing this, carriers should be ever vigilant for signs of illness amongst passengers in their charge.

Certificates of vaccination

Vaccination is a worldwide method of disease control. Individual countries have their own regimes for entry of visitors. Many demand valid certificates of vaccination as a pre-entry requirement to their territories. Often the granting of a visa will be conditional upon presentation of the necessary certificate of vaccination. The World Health Organisation monitors controls and designates countries as infected areas for the purpose of identifying the appropriate vaccinations. All travellers from such areas must be protected. Immigration authorities are vigilant in this respect. If the appropriate certificates are not held a tourist could find that a vaccination at the port of entry will be ordered followed by up to fourteen days in quarantine.

The certificate must be in the approved international form or it will not be accepted. It must be authenticated by an official health authority. Travel Agents may be able to give advice on the certificates required for a particular destination but many prefer to direct clients to the local offices of the Department of Health and Social Security.

Controls over passengers on matters of health extend not only to the person of the traveller but to his baggage and items which he may have in his possession, including animal products and plants.

4. PRESCRIBED ITEMS

The 'prescribed items' covered by the customs Acts are supplemented by other statutory controls on items which travellers may seek to export or import.

The Animal Health Act 1981 is a consolidating statute which extends to both live animals and animal products. The Minister of Agriculture Fisheries and Food (MAFF) is empowered to make regulations to prevent the spread of animal diseases. Wide powers of investigation are given to inspectors appointed by the Minister and local authorities. The enforcement of the legislation is delegated to police authorities.

To date controls have been effective in preventing deadly diseases such as anthrax and rabies spreading in Britain. The 1981 Act makes special mention of rabies. Regulations concerning the disease are constantly reviewed and updated.[29] Those who seek to evade the quarantine regulations by smuggling pets into the UK face heavy penalties.

Foodstuffs

Measures designed to prevent the spread of disease to animals in this country also extend to animal products both cooked and raw. A health certificate issued in the country of origin is required before the importation of fresh, chilled, frozen, smoked or cured meats is permitted.[30] Where food originates outside the EEC the Regulations extend to canned products. Enforcement is by port health authorities or local authority health departments.

Plants

Controls against diseases also extend to plants. Cultivated plants require a Phyto-Sanitary Certificate issued by a plant health officer in the country of origin which is required to be produced to customs officers on arrival in the UK. A wide variety of vegetables will also require the same certificate.

Wild flowers and plants require a licence issued by MAFF who will require to be told when such items are likely to be imported. These will be held for at least 21 days for inspection. Certain species may only be imported under licence from the Department of the Environment who are concerned to protect endangered species both at home and in conjunction with conservationist bodies in other countries.

Because of the many endangered species of animals and plants, both at home and abroad, legislation has been passed designating individuals and groups in need of protection. The Endangered Species (Import and Export) Act 1976 contains detailed and lengthy lists of species. These are added to from time to time with amendments derived in part from other UK legislation, e.g. The Wildlife and Countryside Act 1981.

The many controls on travellers and their baggage are a small price to pay for health and safety. Despite their range and complexity they do not seem insuperable barriers to the tourist and his enjoyment of the travel experience. Which does not mean that weak or oppressive legislation, or excessive use or abuse of authority, should go unchallenged.

NOTES:

1. Henry V Act IV Scene III.
2. Goodwin-Gill op cit Ch 3 n.32 p 25.
3. Universal Declaration of Human Rights 13(2).
   European Convention on Human Rights - Fourth Protocol Art.2(2).
4. Freedom the Individual and the Law. H.Street p 294.
5. Ibid pp 294-295.
6. (1958) 357 United States Reports 116.
7. 209 HL Deb 860 16 June 1958 and HC Deb 265 (Written answers) 15 Nov 1974.
8. Going Abroad - A report on passports - Justice paras 29, 46-47, 51-55.
9. (1905) 2 KB 730.
10. (1946) AC 347.
11. Schedule 2 para 3(1).

12. (1963) 2 QB 243.
13. (1894) 6 B.D.I.L. 124.
14. s. 3 (5) (a) and (b); s. 3 (6).
15. *The Guardian* 27 Feb 88.
16. *The Guardian* 12 Mar 87.
17. Immigration (Hotel records) Order SI 1972 1689.
18. Directive 68/2360.
19. Customs and Excise Management Act s. 6.
20. Immigration Act 1971 s.4(2).
21. Public Health Act 1936 s.143.
22. The Unfortunate Traveller. *The Guardian* 25 Apr 87.
23. (1902) 86 LT 713 DC.
24. *The Observer* 1 Nov 87.
25. Beyond the Bounds of the Duty Men. *The Listener* 29 Oct 87.
26. s.16.
27. Cmnd.9440.
28. Public Health (Ships) Regs 1979: Public Health (Aircraft) Regs. 1979.
29. Rabies (Importation of Dogs, Cats and other Mammals) Amdmt Order 1986.
30. Imported Food Regs. 1968.

CHAPTER V

Road Transport

1. THE ESSENTIALS OF TRANSPORTATION

The two basic components of transportation are the *way* and the *carrying unit*. The nature of the former will determine the choice of the latter. As an island, Britain was only accessible by boat until the advent of the airplane and later the hybrid land/water vehicle, the hovercraft. Inland, the choice lay originally between navigation of the inland waterways and travel by road. Later the choice was widened with the advent of the railroads.

Travellers may now choose between personal forms of transport, e.g. the bicycle, horse or car, or elect to be carried as passengers in vehicles provided by others. Choice will be dictated by preference, cost and availability. A particular route may be serviced by alternative

73

modes of transportation. A visitor from mainland Britain to the Channel Islands may travel by boat or plane. He/she may take combined carriage, e.g. a coach to an air terminal, a flight to the chosen destination, and from there a taxi to an hotel.

Roads

Until the 19th century the choice lay between roads and such natural waterways as connected centres of population. Chaucer's pilgrims would have followed a road which was little better than a track beaten out by men and animals. Often in winter the roads were impassable. In 1380 Parliament was unable to meet because too few members were able to reach Westminster.

The designation of *king's highway* seems inappropriate when the Crown did not bear the cost of building or maintenance of roads and bridges. This fell largely on the great landowners, who needed to visit their scattered estates, and the Church, which was both land-owner and manager of site attractions for the faithful. Men contributed to religious charities as acts of piety and the Church used some of this revenue on the roads. This reliance on benevolence was insufficient to meet the need, especially after the dissolution of the monasteries. In its place a system of *statute labour* was initiated. The Statute of Mending the Highways was passed in 1555, requiring that each parish provide men and materials to maintain the roads which ran through its boundaries. Men were sent to labour on the roads for a set number of days each year supervised by an elected *surveyor*. Justices of the Peace were charged with seeing that the work was done but many of the parish who could afford to pay, commuted service to cash leaving the poor and infirm to do the work. By the 18th century the days set aside for roadwork had become equated with holidays and little work was done by labourers relieved of toiling in the fields. Inefficient as it was, this system was not repealed until the Highways Act 1835.

Streets

In the towns, those whose property adjoined the roads were charged with their repair. Few landowners honoured this obligation until an Act of 1540 compelled them to pave the streets on pain of fine. The Justices of the Peace, who were often burgesses of the towns, were given powers of supervision but no money was forthcoming from the king's Treasury. The practice grew of paying money at a local *rate* for the work to be done on a commercial basis.

Turnpikes

The first Turnpike Act was passed in 1663 for repairing the road leading north of London through the counties of Hertford, Cambridge and Huntingdon.   In return for repairing the dilapidated roads the gentry in the counties concerned were allowed to erect gates and barriers and to levy tolls. The money raised was to be expended on the roads.   In 1706 the first Turnpike Trust was established.   These commercial ventures were viewed as a way in which enterprising men could raise money, repair the roads and make a profit at the end of the year. They were not popular with local people who did not see why they should pay for using 'their' roads. In some places riots occurred, tolls were burned and gate-keepers attacked.   Despite their shortcomings the turnpikes did provide a service which in places was excellent and in others deplorable. The more popular made money, many others returned debit balances year after year. With the coming of other forms of transportation in the 19th century the turnpikes declined rapidly but the last of them, on Anglesey, was not extinguished until 1895.

As the turnpikes declined the burden fell more onto the parishes. Attempts were made to group them together for greater efficiency but rivalry and self interest defeated all but a few efforts. The Highways Act 1862 created *highway districts* compelling combinations of parishes to levy a highway rate. Finally in 1888 the reform of local government saw the responsibility for main through roads placed upon the new County Councils.

Tourist lobby

While the main roads were gradually improved, other secondary routes, in the charge of urban and rural district councils with limited funds, remained narrow and treacherous.   Popular agitation for their improvement coincided with the rise in popularity of the bicycle in the 1880s. The Bicyclist Touring Club was founded in 1878 and was absorbed into the Cyclists Touring Club in 1883. For many the bicycle was a means of escaping from the towns into the countryside for recreation. They were joined by a new leisured motoring class and together these groups called for road works on all highways.

In 1910, a Road Board was set up funded with monies derived from motor car licenses and petrol taxes. Funds were made available to County Councils who began tarring the surfaces of the main roads. Apart from intervention in ad hoc road schemes such as the London to Holyhead road in 1810 this was the first planned policy for roads organised by central government.

Modern roads

There was a great increase in road traffic of all types in the 1920s. Buses and coaches began to compete with the railways on a network of cross country routes. The Road Board was replaced in 1919 by the Ministry of Transport. Roads were classified by size and importance and the County Council acted as agents for the Ministry in road building and improvement. Private motoring as well as road haulage increased rapidly.

The Special Roads Act 1949 authorised the construction of national trunk routes to be known as *motorways*. These were placed under the direct control of the Ministry of Transport and the first *motorway* was built in 1958. This was the eight mile bypass for Preston on what was later to become the M6. In 1959 the first 75 miles of the M1 were built leading north from London.

Unlike railways, road operators do not build or maintain their 'ways'. Monies are made available from public funds which derive in part from vehicle taxation, fuel tax and taxes on vehicles. Other funds are subscribed from local rates. Responsibility for the trunk roads lies with the Ministry of Transport which usually requires the County Councils to act as its agent for these routes in addition to their responsibility for other major roads. Unclassified roads are the responsibility of District Councils who also have charge over bridleways and footpaths. The powers and duties of these *highway authorities* are to be found in the Highways Act 1980.

The responsibility of these bodies is to take notice of changing patterns of highway use and to maintain the roads in a state which is safe and fit for ordinary traffic. The use of the term *ordinary* relates to the prevailing use of the route at any one time.

In the past highway authorities were liable only for the negligent discharge of their duties. Under the 1980 Act they can now be held responsible for inactivity as well[1]. Their defence to that charge is that they have taken such care as in all the circumstances was reasonably required to ensure that the highway was not dangerous to traffic. Inactivity may derive from lack of funds and in this respect tolls have been mentioned again in Parliament. The travelling public has become used to paying bridge and tunnel tolls. It is only a short step to introducing tolls on major roads to help pay for their upkeep, as in France.

2. VEHICLES

The earliest form of transportation in general use was the wagon. It was designed as a load carrier and in this sense the term is used today to describe goods vehicles of various types. Wagons also carried passengers and their personal effects. It is not possible to determine with any certainty what proportion of goods were carried in comparison to passengers but *stage wagons* were running regularly from London to Oxford in 1575. Records of 1690 show *coach* and *wagon* services connecting all parts of England[2]. The two terms were used so indiscriminately that it is not possible to describe the vehicles accurately nor the traffic which each carried.

Common carriers

The public nature of the service provided by the wagoner can be seen from the special status accorded to him in law. Where a carrier held himself out as willing to provide a service to any who would pay him, the law accorded him the title *common*. This distinguished such a man from other carriers who would only accept special commissions. The law placed upon him, as with other followers of 'common callings' like the innkeeper, obligations which, if he failed to discharge, would make him liable in tort and triable on indictment for a crime.

In respect of both goods and passengers he was obliged to carry for all for which he had space in the vehicle. He might refuse goods which were in an unfit or dangerous condition or passengers whose conduct or persons gave good cause for rejection. Once on board, the law regarded the carrier as an 'insurer' of goods in his charge. Should any items be lost he was held strictly liable to the owner for their value. Theft and pilferage were frequent perils for goods in transit and by making the carrier liable in this way the law sought to reduce the risk to the consigner. In recognition of this onerous burden, the carrier was allowed to exclude liability for certain categories of goods entrusted to him and to limit, although not exclude, his duty in respect of others. This facility was accorded statutory recognition in the Carriers Act 1830 which is still in force.

The liability of common and private carriers towards their passengers is identical. They must both observe a high standard of care for those they carry but they will not be held liable for injuries sustained in incidents beyond their control.

Another class of carrier is sometimes described, the public carrier, said to contain those who hold themselves out as willing to carry passengers in accordance with a publicly displayed timetable and conditions. The carrier reserves the right to pick and choose amongst his fares but in practice seldom exercises this power. In such circumstances it can be asserted that the offer of carriage is made to the whole world and is capable of acceptance by those who present themselves in a fit condition to be carried and are willing to pay the fare. It would be unreasonable for such operators to refuse to carry someone who meets the conditions. Failure to carry would constitute a breach of contract[3].

Passengers are also entitled to carry a reasonable amount of luggage with them. Sometimes a maximum may be stipulated and it is an implied term of the carriage that it should not prove a hazard to other travellers. In such a case it seems likely that, in so far as this luggage is concerned, a public carrier as described above is also a common carrier as regards passengers' luggage. The Carriers Act 1830 speaks of the 'stage coach proprietor' which tends to support the view. This was a point made in: *Clarke v West Ham Corporation (1909)*[4]. The point is also made in the earlier case of: *Lovett v Hobbs (1680)*[5] where the carrier was of the class which would be classified today as a taxi.

This case described the carrier as the driver of a 'hackney carriage' a phrase repeated in the Town Police Clauses Act 1847. This and later statutes make the taxicab driver one who is very like a common carrier. A cabby plying for hire or reward must, unless he has reasonable excuse, drive to any place, including private property, within the district for which his vehicle is licensed or any lesser distance fixed under a byelaw, to which he is directed by the hirer. A refusal to do so constitutes an offence punishable by fine[6]. Subject to certain exclusions he must also carry the luggage of his fares. Similar provisions apply under the London Cab Order 1934. The driver cannot normally be compelled to accept a hire for carriage of more than 6 miles or one hour's duration[7]. In the case of travellers wishing to go to London Heathrow Airport, a distance of 20 miles is substituted for that which may usually be compelled[8]. In such circumstances the driver may bargain for the fare and is not limited by the fixed tariff: *Goodman v Serle (1947)*[9].

In determining the status of a carrier the type of vehicle used is irrelevant. Vehicle design has come a long way since the early wagons. Nevertheless, one form of road vehicle which was contemporary with wagons in the carriage of passengers and their luggage is still used today, albeit vastly changed.

Coaches

The use of the description *coach* first appeared in England in the 16th century. In 1657 a thrice weekly service by coach from London to Chester was advertised. It was the popularity of such vehicles amongst the leisured classes which gave an impetus to tourism. The pamphleteer J Cressel wrote in 1681:

> 'These stage-coaches make gentlemen come to London upon every small occasion, which otherwise they would not do but upon urgent necessity, nay, the conveniency of the passage makes their wives often come up, who rather than come such long journeys on horseback would stay at home. Here when they come to town, they must presently be in the mode, get fine clothes, go to the plays and treats and by these means get such a habit of idleness, and love to pleasure.'[10]

By the middle of the 18th century the coach in general use was a rigid roofed, closed vehicle holding 4-6 passengers with the body suspended above the carriage with steel springs. To maximise the space, *half-fares* were allowed to ride on the roof amongst the luggage. Because of the frequency of accidents, legislation was introduced in 1788 to limit the numbers of such outside travellers. Fines were imposed, often collected by the custodians of the turnpikes.

The spread of the turnpikes and the introduction of *mail coaches* heralded the heyday of the coach. The mail coach operators were obliged to carry the Royal Mails but in return were allowed to keep the fares as compensation for being required to carry the mail at reduced rates. The mail coaches were fast, carried armed guards and travelled overnight. They introduced an increasing number of people to travel, stimulated road improvements and an increase in the number of inns. It was their misfortune that their success in promoting travel led to a rapid switch of passengers to the railways after 1830.

They had established a nationwide network of fast, reliable and regular transport. They could not compete with the railways to whom they lost not only their passengers but their trained travel staff. Contrary to some reports, coaching did not die out. A decline of coaches on the through routes was predictable but where they adapted to localised travel by carrying passengers from outlying areas to railway stations they survived remarkably well.

They also discovered a niche for themselves in the new Victorian holiday trade. Horse drawn coaches provided excursions to the seaside in the 1850s and railway trippers were encouraged to enjoy *charabanc* rides in the West Country on combined rail and road excursions as late as 1908.[11]

After the introduction of railways, the history of road transport is largely that of short haul and town services. The horse-drawn omnibus became a common feature of public transport. Tramcars were introduced in Birkenhead in 1860 and then in recent years declined and all but disappeared except on the Isle of Man - which retains some horse drawn carriages - and Blackpool where they are not only a tourist attraction but a popular means of local transportation. More recently, however, the experience of continental countries has shown that tramcars are both economic and environmentally friendly as well as efficient. UK enthusiasts have always known this. Now there is something of a rennaissance for trams. Greater Manchester has introduced a regular service and other northern cities are examining the possibilities. Such developments have met with less favour in the south where only the futuristic proposals for Southampton attracted much support but were opposed on grounds which had more to do with start up cost than efficiency and public need.

A close relative of the tramcar, the trollybus, enjoyed a brief heyday between 1911 and 1960. So far this form of transport has survived only in transport museums but the merits of the trollybus are being re-examined to see if after all they too may have a part to play in modern urban transportation in the UK's congested towns and cities.

3. MODERN TIMES

The introduction of the motor vehicle and the bicycle opened up a new era for road transport. Motor buses in the towns were, from the start, used by locals and visitors alike. They provide valuable interconnecting links for travel termini, especially in London. Some intrepid tourists have journeyed the length and breadth of the land on interconnecting local services.[12]

The first municipal buses entered service on the streets of Eastbourne in 1903. This in turn led to extended distance services and the motor-coach, derived from its horse drawn predecessor soon appeared. In 1905 they were taking excursionists to Brighton in the south and to Blackpool in the north.[13] In 1925 the first long-distance scheduled coach services began, connecting London and Bristol. The Greyhound company followed in the tracks of the early mail coaches which had begun the same run across England in 1784.

A whole network of coach services grew rapidly in the 1920s. London Victoria Coach Station opened as did many others in towns up and down the country. Road traffic generally profited from the struggle of the railways to meet ever-rising operating costs. Anyone who wanted could run a bus or coach service. Controls were operated by local authorities but these were inadequate to deal with *pirate* carriers who in many cases ran dangerous vehicles and made their drivers work excessive hours. Safety and maintenance of vehicles was minimal and primitive, accidents frequent. In 1929 the Royal Commission on Transport met to examine the whole question of what to do about public road transport.

Regulation

The Report of the Commission led to the Road Traffic Act 1930. These new laws were a milestone in the history of public road transport and remained little altered in their application to public service provision of transport until 1980.[14] The Act sought to restrict operations rather than to encourage competition which had led to such poor standards of safety.

The Act had safety as its primary objective. The method chosen was licensing of both routes and vehicles and their crews. Buses were treated as short haul vehicles and coaches as through carriers although the distinction drawn was purely arbitrary.

The licensing of Public Service Vehicles (PSV) tackled the safety of the buses and coaches. Vehicles were required to pass rigorous tests and obtain a certificate of road-worthiness. Owner operators required a PSV licence for each vehicle they put into service. All drivers had to pass a proficiency test and conductors were also tested as to their duties.

The Road Service Licence (RSL) was used to regulate the activities of those who wished to carry passengers at separate fares whether locally or long distance. Those who carried under a single contract, e.g. party bookings, were exempted from the RSL provisions but not the PSV regulations. Many operators sought to evade the RSL requirement by claiming to carry, by single contract, all on board a vehicle but were largely unsuccessful: *Victoria Motors (Scarborough) Ltd v Wurzel (1951)*.[15]

RSLs were granted for routes agreed by Traffic Commissioners (TC) for a particular area. The system was criticised from the beginning because the TCs tended to base their judgements on the three principles of priority, protection and public interest. The last of these seemed to many to come a poor third after the interests of existing carriers and the protection of alternative operators, e.g. the railways.

When granting RSLs the TCs had wide powers to attach conditions to the licence. They were concerned mainly with such matters as fixing fares, stopping places and the publication of timetables and tariffs. The result was that the large carriers profited at the expense of the small man. In the towns, municipal transport undertakings established monopolies. The private carriers concentrated on inter-city routes and the less profitable country services.

The two regulatory licensing systems continued largely unchanged until 1960 when the Road Traffic Act consolidated the legislation which had developed since 1930. The system of licensing was set out in Part III of the Act. It divided vehicles into two groups, 'Stage Carriers' (short distance, low fares) and 'Express Carriers' (long distance, minimum fare 5p!). Both of these groups required RSLs. A third group 'Contract Carriers' required no RSLs. This was made up of those adapted for carrying less than eight passengers and used for conveying them to a 'special occasion', e.g. a race meeting; *private parties* not organised by the carrier nor by the organiser for reward and having only minor fare differentials; 'shared taxis' where not more than 4 passengers were carried whose custom had not been solicited by the cabby; carriage of overseas *tourists* when such travellers had been resident outside the UK when the booking was made on their behalf. The four limited exceptions were set out in Schedule 12 of the 1960 Act.

Nationalisation

The Transport Act 1947 set out to provide an integrated transport system for the UK. With the exception of carriage by air, all public transport was transferred to the British Transport Commission (BTC). The duties of the Commission were performed by various *Executives*, e.g. the Road Passenger Executive (RPE). It was originally combined with road haulage of goods but the two soon became separated. Until 1962 the RPE published plans for services but carriage remained in the hands of the operators. The Transport Act 1962 abolished the BTC replacing it with 4 *Boards* and the Transport Holding Company (THC) all under the direct control of the Minister of Transport.

The THC was an entirely new, nationalised undertaking in the form of a *holding company* more usually associated with private commercial undertakings. Those bodies whose securities were transferred to it are listed in Schedule 4 of the Act. They included, inter alia, a large number of road passenger undertakings, shipping, travel and tourism operations. Under the Transport Act 1968 the THC lost its long distance operation to a newly formed National Bus Company (NBC) and the Scottish Transport Group (STG).

The principal function of the NBC was to carry passengers by road. It could, if it chose, carry goods in addition to luggage, operate travel agencies and carry by ship or hovercraft. Both the NBC and the STG were required to *cooperate* with municipal carriers as well as British Rail. They faced a rising tide of private car ownership and the need to service country routes where British Rail had discontinued passenger services to stem the rise of its escalating costs. The THC limped on with nothing more than a few travel agencies for a little while longer. In 1971 the THC and its subsidiaries, including Thomas Cook, were sold off.

Deregulation

The Transport Act 1980 set out to change the licensing system for public passenger carrying vehicles. It was felt to be time to redraw the boundaries originally set by the 1930 Act.

PSV licences were redefined and classified according to size of vehicle. Henceforward PSV criteria were only to be applied to vehicles adapted to carry 8 or more people as passengers, bringing regulation in line with EEC levels. Shared taxis, hire cars, vehicles carrying private parties and tourists below this size were excluded from the need to have a PSV licence.

Modern standards of safety were substituted for older regulations as prerequisites for the granting of a vehicle licence. In addition, an operator no longer needs to be licensed for each vehicle he puts on the road. A single operator's licence is now issued to a suitable applicant. They may be either *standard* or *restricted*.[16]

An applicant for a *standard* licence must demonstrate to the TCs that s/he is of good repute, of good financial standing and professionally competent.[17] A licence may be *restricted* with reference to both the number and descriptions of vehicle which may be operated by the holder.

With both types of licence the TCs may stipulate certain restrictions which are to operate, e.g. where the vehicles of the operator may pick up and set down passengers. If the operator ceases to fulfil any of the qualifying criteria, his licence may be revoked.

Express services were redefined with reference to distances travelled (above a 30 mile radius) with no conditions as to minimum fares. The intention was clearly to benefit 'excursions and tours'[18] as much as inter-city links.

'Stage carriers' were defined as meaning providers of local services. RSLs were abolished in the case of 'express carriers', being retained only for local transport by stages. In the case of these services, the grant of RSLs for excursions, tours and special events was made easier to obtain.

The Public Passenger Vehicles Act 1981 consolidated the provisions of the Road Traffic Act 1960, as amended, and the Transport Act 1980. This paved the way for more deregulation.

The provisions of the Transport Act 1985 are mainly concerned with the deregulation of bus services, the 1980 Act having dealt with what were ostensibly coach services. The 1985 Act finally abolished the RSL system still in force for omnibuses, with the exception of the London Passenger Transport Area. Instead a system of registration for services was instituted under a reconstituted regime of TCs.

The classification of *stage, express and contract* has been repealed. In its place a distinction is drawn between local services and others for which operators PSV licences are required. The definition *local* describes a service 'using one or more public service vehicles, for the carriage of passengers by road at separate fares other than one (where the passenger) is set down .... fifteen miles or more..... from the place where he was taken up'.[19] Exceptions in favour of local excursions organised privately are made available and certain vehicles are allowed to operate under a *permit* system.[20]

'Excursions or tours' are defined in terms of 'a service for the carriage of passengers by road at separate fares on which passengers travel together on a journey, with or without breaks, from one or more places to one or more other places and back'.[21]

The General Provisions relating to the granting of PSV operators licences contained in Part II of the 1981 Act remain in force save for section 28 which is repealed. Some minor modifications were made regarding the attachment of conditions to licences and to disqualifications. Part III of the Act contains provisions for the *denationalisation* of the NBC.

The so called *market forces* much trumpeted in the 1980s did not result in increased competition to the benefit of the consumer. After a brief flurry of small enterprises and examples of bus racing along the routeways not witnessed since Victorian days, the small carriers were squeezed out and the large private monopolies have come to predominate. Once these had settled down in the new found world post de-regulation the system has operated much as before with private having replaced public enterprise. The profits earned have given rise to some carriers actively proposing to enter the market and become rail carriers. Echoes from the past seem to recall that it was rail carriers who dealth a death blow to the waterways - as they did to the stage coach. Perhaps the wheel is turning full circle and the road carriers are about to gain their revenge on the railways!

The last bastion of public bus service, London Buses, seems about to fall victim to privatisation. Despite the crying need for an integrated passenger service for the Capital City it seems that dogma once again rules the day and profit comes before people.

In addition to the deregulation of bus and coach services, the Acts of 1980 and 1985 liberate other services in the private sector. The 1985 Act introduces new regulations allowing for the use of 'licensed taxis' and 'licensed hire cars'. The former have long been regulated by a system of licences going back to the 17th century[22.] Taxis have been in use for local travel as well as interconnection with road, rail and air terminals for a number of years. Taxis, or hackney cabs, are still defined in terms of section 37 of the Town Police Clauses Act 1847 and section 6 of the Metropolitan Public Carriage Act 1869.

4. HACKNEY CARRIAGES

The term *hackney* is derived from an old French word meaning an ambling horse. It was used as early as the 17th century to denote a form of light coach used mainly in towns. These were so popular and numerous that the Thames watermen complained loudly that their trade was being taken away. In the early years of the century the first *stand* for carriages plying for hire was set up in the Strand by a Captain Bailey. The cabmen, as they became known, were a motley collection and travellers complained of being pestered by insolent drivers touting for hire. For a time cabs were banned from the streets of London then returned under licence.

On and off the cabs competed with other forms of personal conveyance in towns. Sedan chairs enjoyed a certain vogue as did the Bath chair designed by James Heath in 1750 and lasting until the last licensed chairman retired in 1947. No form of town transport was a serious competitor for the hackney cab despite the reputation of their drivers as surly, dishonest and bullying towards their fares. Their carriages were often run down and second-hand, drawn by inferior horses. Often they doubled as hearses, ambulances and police vans. Not infrequently they were found to be dirty and verminous.

The system of licences was profitable both to the Hackney Coach Office which issued them and also to the drivers since it restricted competition. A licence was a valuable commodity. When in 1832 it was proposed to close the office, the drivers rebelled. Fares were charged on estimates of mileage and any passenger who dared haggle over a price was subjected to abuse or worse. There were calls for some form of meter to be introduced to stop these abuses[23] but the *taximeters* were not adopted until 1899. Not until the advent of the motor cab was the device widely in use. The London cabbies held out longest against them until forced into submission by the licensing authority.

The licensing powers for the Metropolitan Police Districts and the City of London are held by the Home Secretary for whom they are exercised by an Assistant Commissioner of the Metropolitan Police (ACMP). Both vehicles and drivers must hold a licence. The vehicle must pass a safety test and the driver must be a fit and proper person. Penalties for the use of unlicensed cabs and for those not displaying the correct distinguishing marks are levied by the ACMP. Licences may be revoked by the ACMP but they are valuable possessions and cannot be taken away lightly or in an unjust manner: *R v Metropolitan Police Commissioner ex parte Phillips (1987).*[24]

Within the jurisdiction of the ACMP no private car may carry a sign using the words *taxi* or *cab* or *for hire* without penalty.[25] Regulations are in force for numbers of persons to be carried as passengers in a cab, stands, fares assessed by time and distance. Various offences still exist under Victorian statutes - magistrates can fine drivers for wanton or furious driving or causing hurt or damage to persons or property by carelessness or wilful misbehaviour, or of drunkenness, insulting language or gestures.[26] Waiting for fares at unauthorised stands is likewise an offence: *Eldridge v British Airport Authority (1970).*[27]

Outside London controls are effected under the Town Police Clauses Acts and byelaws passed under local government enactments. Licensing authorities are the District Councils. No vehicle may ply for hire without a licence. A vehicle which is unlicensed breaches the law if it is displayed for hire on the highway or private property: *Bateson v Oddy (1874).*[28] Where licenses have been issued for vehicles they must display the appropriate plates.

District Councils may appoint such *stands* for taxis as they deem fit. Notices will stipulate times of use and the numbers of vehicles allowed to wait in *ranks*. During such designated hours, other vehicles may not use the facility.

Private hire vehicles

Under the Local Government (Miscellaneous Provisions) Act 1976, drivers of private vehicles wishing to hire out their vehicles for reward must apply for a licence. If such vehicles seat fewer than 9 passengers they may be licensed as Private Hire Vehicles (PHV), not being taxi cabs. More capacity than this requires a PSV licence. Registers of PHVs are kept open to public inspection by the authorities. To obtain a licence the applicant must show that the vehicle is suitable, safe, comfortable and insured. The driver must be a fit and proper person and the vehicle must carry an authorised licence plate or disc.

PHVs, like taxis, must be available for such mechanical inspections as are required by the licensing authority to a maximum of three times in any one year. Any authorised officer, or any police constable, may stop and inspect a vehicle at any time to examine a taximeter wherever one may be affixed to a taxi. Where a vehicle is not a taxi, e.g. PHV or other private vehicle, it may carry no sign suggesting that it is a cab.

PSV - taxicab

By definition, a taxi did not engage in the carriage of passengers at separate fares and so did not come within the classification of PSV within the Road Traffic Acts. Unless adapted to carry more than 8 passengers, no taxi needs a PSV and never required an RSL.

However, a taxi could fall foul of the PSV regulations if passengers were charged separate fares. If it were to do so it would be classified as a stage or other carrier. Taxis have always enjoyed some exemptions as indicated earlier in connection with RSL exempted uses of contract vehicles.

The 1985 Act sought to simplify the arrangement to accommodate changing usages of hired vehicles. It provides that licensing authorities may introduce *schemes* in their areas whereby PHVs and taxis may be hired out at separate fares without becoming subject to PSV operators' licensing.[29] Any such *scheme* must designate *authorised places* from where vehicles may be hired. Provisions may be made as to fares, stops and other matters. It effectively allows a 'microbus' operation for the benefit of the public. As an alternative, the holder of a taxi licence can apply to the TCs for a restricted PSV operator's licence for one or more of his taxis without needing to meet the particular requirements of the 1981 Act. The new provisions do not allow the taxi operator to organise tours or excursions.[30] The *special licence* holder is seen essentially as someone who is providing a localised bus service and is not in competition with coach tour operators. In the event that the local authorities may be tempted to use the new provisions as a way of restricting taxi licences, the 1985 Act states that hackney licenses are only to be refused where there is no significant unmet need for their services.[31]

The intention of the legislation, introduced from 1980, has been to increase competition and restrict local authority discretionary powers in the licensing of passenger vehicles of all descriptions. As a clear indication of the latter move, a local authority is obliged to introduce a special *scheme* if more then 10% of its taxi licensees so request[32] Whilst the authorities may make provision for stopping places for buses, coaches and taxis, the Act does not suggest how the additional need for parking spaces is to be met.

Parking

The pressure for parking space of all kinds has intensified. This much has been appreciated by the Department of Transport whose interest, however, seems to be limited to the opportunity to charge parking fees. The Ministry has made no suggestions as to where the additional spaces may be found.

'Tourists are important people ..... Many tourists are only in London for a short time. The coach provides comfort and convenience. It is an increasingly popular way to see the sights of London. For many tourists it is the best way to get around .... but popularity has brought problems. Tourist coaches contribute to congestion ..... Parking facilities are in short supply particularly near popular tourist attractions.'[33]

The Ministry goes on to point out the dangers of street parking such that coaches will have to pay for off-street facilities. It does not explain that the increased cost will undoubtedly be passed on to the consumer by the coach operator. The matter will again be passed on to hard pressed local authorities who will have to find the spaces by unpopular compulsory purchases if necessary.

Safety

Department of Transport figures show that per mile of travel, a passenger in a bus, coach or train is ten times less likely to meet with a fatal accident in transit than he would if travelling by car. At the same time, road travellers are 3 times more likely to be injured in a bus or coach than they are in a train.

There is little evidence to show why coaches have accidents. Most seem to result from the actions of other road users. Some are caused by driver error, others by excessive speed. To reduce malpractices, the Bus and Coach Council drew up a voluntary code of conduct for its members which includes the fitting of tachographs to all coaches. These records are inspected by the operators to show whether or not drivers are exceeding EEC regulations. Under these, drivers may not drive more than 8 hours per day, no more than 48 hours in a week and 92 hours per fortnight. Every driver must take a break from the wheel every 4 hours. All UK drivers are required to hold a PSV licence renewable every 5 years.

For a number of years the UN has sought international safety standards for coaches without success. Although crashes are comparatively few in number, the injuries sustained seem disproportionately high. There has been a demand by consumer bodies for greater strengthening of roofs to minimise roll-over crushing. Little has been done to achieve this by the industry to date.

Except for London taxis, no records exist of accident statistics. There were some 3,000 accidents to London taxis recorded in 1985: 1432 passengers were slightly injured, 159 seriously hurt and 10 killed. There are no regulations for hours worked by cab drivers nor any compulsory breaks from driving. There is nothing to stop a cabby working around the clock then falling asleep over the wheel.

The new regime introduced by the 1985 Act will mean more people using taxis and PHVs on pre-set routes at standardised fares. It would seem necessary to introduce greater regulation of drivers through the licensing system. More spot checks on the condition of vehicles will be necessary together with examinations of insurance documents. The legislation may in consequence produce more controls not less.

NOTES:

1. Highways Act 1980 s.58.
2. Angliae Metropolis. T. Delaune.
3. After Carlill v Carbolic Smokeball Company (1893) 1 QB 256 (CA).
4. (1909) 2 KB 858.
5. (1680) 2 Shaw KB 127.
6. Town Police Clauses Act 1847 s.53.
7. SR & O 1934 No 1346 para 34.
8. London Cab Act 1968; London Cab Order SI 1047/272 para 3.
9. (1947) 1 KB 808.
10. British Museum Document 816 mi2 (162).
11. The History of Passenger Transport in Britain J. Joyce p 164.
12. Ibid p 157.
13. Ibid p 165.
14. Hansard Vol 974 col.1120.
15. (1951) 2 KB 520.
16. Transport Act 1980 s.20.
17. Ibid s.21.
18. Ibid s.44 (now in Public Passenger Vehicles Act 1981 s.82).
19. Transport Act 1985 s.2(1) and (2).

20. Ibid s.2(4) and s.19.
21. Ibid s.137.
22. Act 14 Car.II c2.
23. Roads and Vehicles. A. Bird p 144-45.
24. (1987) *The Guardian* 10 Nov 1987.
25. London Cab Act 1968 s.4 and London Cab Act 1973 s.1.
26. London Hackney Carriages Act 1843 s.28.
27. (1970) 2 All ER 92 DC.
28. (1874) 38 JP 598 DC.
29. Transport Act 1985 s.10.
30. Ibid s.12.
31. Ibid s.16.
32. Ibid s.10(4).
33. Tourist Coaches in London HMSO Dd 8933846. 1986.

CHAPTER VI

Carriage By Road

1. RULES OF THE ROAD

The earliest regulations affecting the carriage of passengers by road are to be found in the rules imposing obligations on *common carriers*. Today the rules governing the relationship between carrier and passenger are still largely those created by the courts. The great majority of travellers are carried in accordance with standard form contracts. The harsher effects of the terms which they contain have been ameliorated by the courts over the years and more recently by statutory intervention against unfair exclusion clauses.

Statutory intervention has also resulted in terms being implied into contracts which protect the rights of the traveller as a consumer of services. The Supply of Goods and Services Act, for example, requires that the provider of services should use reasonable care and skill in his performance of the contract.

Legislation is also the means whereby the terms of international conventions are incorporated into English law. The Geneva Convention on the Contract for the International Carriage of Passengers by Road (CVR) will be incorporated by the Carriage of Passengers by Road Act 1974 on a day to be appointed in the manner prescribed by section 1(1) of that Act. Once the Convention has been ratified by the British Government it will become part of English law.

Carriers owe a common law duty of care towards the passengers they transport by road. Failure to live up to the standard required may lead to an action in tort founded either on Negligence or, where appropriate, for breach of duty imposed by statute. In addition, the premises used by carriers are subject to the provisions of the Occupiers Liability Acts 1957 and 1984 and the Health and Safety at Work Act 1974. Vehicles too come under the description of 'premises' governed by the common law which imposes higher standards of care than statute.

2. THE CONTRACT OF CARRIAGE

Since the earliest days, carriers have been required to display a high regard for the safety of their passengers. They were never regarded as *insurers* of their safety and so no strict liability was imposed upon the carrier as was the case with goods. In every contract for carriage, it is an implied term of the agreement that the passenger will be carried with reasonable safety having regard to all the circumstances[1]. A driver who chooses to drive too close to the kerb will be responsible for injuries to passengers which are the foreseeable consequence of his accepting a risk of dangers which he knew or ought to have known: *Hale v Hants and Dorset Motor Services Ltd (1947)*[2]. However, if the dangers were something quite out of the ordinary which could not be anticipated, liability may not be incurred by the driver: *Hase v L.G.C. (1907)*[3].

A passenger usually enters a contract by purchasing a ticket. The mutual obligations of the parties arise from the conditions under which the ticket was issued. Carriers have long been able to contract-out of implied terms by including express conditions in the agreement contradicting any implied obligations. No implied term can of itself override express conditions. The usual means of effecting this in carriage was for the ticket issued to a traveller to refer the recipient to the carrier's standard terms upon which he was prepared to convey passengers and their belongings. These usually contained conditions which gave the carrier generous protection against claims brought by a passenger based not only in contract but also in tort.

Although not willing to accept all tickets as evidence of the terms of the contract, it has long been held by the courts that a ticket issued to a passenger is more than a mere receipt for monies paid and that, by reference in the document to conditions contained elsewhere, these form the basis of the agreement. Most tickets are issued prior to a journey commencing. It is not clear what precisely is the position where they are received by the passenger after the journey has begun, as where they are presented by a conductor to a bus passenger after the latter has entered the vehicle and often when it is in motion. No exemption clauses referred to on the ticket can be valid if they are not brought to the attention of the party to whom they are addressed until after the contract has been concluded.

It has long been the case that a contract of carriage commences when the passenger boards a bus and is concluded when he alights from it: *Wilkie v L.P.T.B. (1947)*[4]. Now that many buses are one man operated the position may be the same or the contract may not be formed until the fare is offered and accepted upon entry.

The effect of exemption clauses has been further reduced by statutory provisions. Where such imposed terms seek to disclaim liability for death or injury resulting from the carrier's negligence, they will be ineffective. The Transport Act 1962 prohibited the Boards set up under the Act from sheltering behind such terms. Similarly, the Road Traffic Act 1960 makes void any terms in a contract which seek to exclude or restrict the liability of any person for the death of, or personal injury to, any passenger while being carried in, entering or alighting from a vehicle, or which in any way seeks to deny enforceability of such liability.[5]

The Unfair Contract Terms Act 1977 applies to all forms of contract. In addition to preventing exclusions relating to personal injury, the statute provides that liability may be excluded or limited for loss of property, e.g. luggage, or for financial loss, provided that he who seeks the benefit of the exclusion can prove that such exemption is *reasonable*[6]. The provisions of the Act apply to all who seek to use such devices in the course of business.

The 1977 Act also prevents the imposition of terms restricting the right of an injured party to bring a claim by setting a time limit during which such claims must be brought. A written term which binds the complainant to submit a claim to arbitration is at present lawful and enforceable[7]. Consumer Arbitration Agreements Act prevents unfair arbitration clauses.

At common law the carrier owes a duty to passengers to take them to the agreed destination within a reasonable time and at a reasonable speed. He may seek to exclude liability for delay caused by failure to complete the journey within the time specified on the timetable. Coaches may also be withdrawn from service, or re-routed. Departures may be delayed or postponed. A properly drawn exclusion clause can protect a carrier from the consequences since the common law only implies a duty to perform the contract without delay and this may be negated by an express term. However, where the carrier has agreed terms by special contract, he may not hide behind an exclusion clause so as to enable him to render performance of the contract which is fundamentally different from that which was agreed, or to render no performance at all[8].

If damage is occasioned to the luggage of the passenger, a term in the contract or a notice displayed will not exclude the carrier's liability unless it satisfies the test of reasonableness set out in section 11 and Schedule 2 of the 1977 Act. In addition, it must be noted that exclusion clauses operate contractually and cannot be used to protect a person unmentioned by the contract, e.g. an employee or agent of the carrier. Such persons may, however, be protected by a *Himalaya clause* which is often used as a term in a standard form contract.

Safe carriage

At common law, the carrier's obligation is to carry his charges safely and, should harm befall them, it is necessary to show that he is at fault. 'A carrier's obligation to his passengers whether it be expressed in contract or in tort, is to provide a carriage that is free from defects as the exercise of all reasonable care can make it': *Barkway v South Wales Transport Co Ltd (1950)*[9].

In order to succeed in an action against a carrier, it is necessary to show that he, his employees or agents, were negligent: *Mottram v South Lancashire Transport Co (1950).*[10] Where the injury complained of is the result of an act or omission of the defendant it will be for him to disprove fault. The court will apply the maxim 'res ipsa loquitur' (the thing speaks for itself) which may be countered by a reasonable explanation by the defendant. The reason for this rule, which is usually applied in transport accident cases, is that the ordinary passenger has no way of knowing exactly what caused the accident. It may be human error on the part of the driver, or a mechanical defect in the vehicle. It may be the result of something outside the control of the carrier, e.g. the conduct of another road user. In the absence of a reasonable explanation by the carrier, the court will assume that the accident was caused by the want of care on his part: *Prescott v Lancashire United Transport Ltd (1953).*[11]

Generally speaking, a carrier will not be liable for harm which results from a latent defect in the vehicle which could not be reasonably detected. He must keep abreast of technical improvements and modern safety standards but this does not mean that he must modify his vehicles each time a new and improved device comes onto the market. It will be sufficient if he uses known and practical precautions such as a *reasonable* carrier would be expected to do. The Court of Appeal in *O'Connor v B.T.C. (1958)* held that it was not:

> 'universal law that every......omnibus or taxi cab ...undertaking which trades for reward must have the latest standard of design.....Economically and practically it would be impossible and would involve carriers, who on one day were apparently fulfilling their obligations, becoming, by some improvement, automatically in breach of duty to their customers on the next, or at least within such time as the improvement could have been known and adopted.'[12]

The standard by which the carrier's conduct will be judged is assessed as that of the reasonable man (or carrier) who finds himself in the same position as that in which the defendant found himself. This is much subject to the creativity of judges, one of whom was once said to have credited the reasonable man with the agility of an acrobat and the foresight of a Hebrew prophet!

The Occupiers Liability Act 1957 imposes a *common duty of care* upon an occupier to all lawful visitors to his premises. This is described by section 2(2) of the Act as a 'duty to take such care as in all circumstances of the case is reasonable to see the visitor will be reasonably safe in using the premises for the purpose for which he is invited or permitted to be there'. This will be the standard which needs to be observed at, say, a coach or bus station but the standard of care is higher in the case of vehicles. Implied terms in contracts of carriage are exceptions under section 5 of the Act and are not governed by it but by the more onerous rules of the common law. The result of this is that the carrier's duty of care is not discharged unless 'all' reasonable care and skill have been used to see that the vehicle is safe. The effect of this is that the carrier will be vicariously liable for the actions of independent contractors contrary to the general rule of the common law.

Consequently, a passenger may hold a ticket issued by one carrier but is in fact carried in a sub-contractor's vehicle which, if it prove defective and an accident to the passenger results, makes the issuing carrier liable. This is because there is an implied term in the contract that the passenger will be carried with due care throughout his journey by whomsoever is the *actual* carrier. Such a situation could be covered by an express exemption clause in the contract coupled with a 'Himalayan' clause but this would have to satisfy the statutory requirements mentioned earlier.

Breach of statutory duty

A particular statute may impose liability on a defendant. If this duty is broken he may be liable for the injury which he causes to another which is occasioned by the breach. Some statutes while imposing duties do not give civil remedies. The Health and Safety at Work Act creates duties but, in section 47, specifically denies the use of breaches of its provisions to someone seeking compensation.

The plaintiff must show in all cases that the injury which is the subject of his claim is one which the statute cited was intended to prevent. Road Safety provisions are the subject of Road Traffic Acts 1960-72, as are regulations made by subordinate legislation authorised by the statutes. The breach of a duty imposed by the enactments does not, however, make the carrier liable to his passengers per se. A breach will, nevertheless, be prima facie evidence of negligence on the part of the carrier. If an accident occurs as the result of, say, exceeding the speed limit, the court will apply the *res ipsa loquitur* maxim.

There are some exceptional cases where the breach will be sufficient to sustain an action for damages when injury results. The Road Traffic Act 1960 requires that all motor vehicles shall be driven by insured persons. Owners of vehicles who allow uninsured persons to drive will be held strictly liable to all who suffer loss as a result of the negligence of such drivers: *Monk v Warbey (1935)*.[13]

In respect of all lawful travellers, fare paying or gratuitously carried, the standard of care will be the same in all cases where breach of a duty of care is alleged. In the case of persons on board without the express or implied permission of the carrier e.g. those who have not yet been discovered to be evading payment of the fare, the carrier's only duty is to avoid causing them harm through intentional or reckless acts.

3. PAYMENT OF FARES

A passenger has an obligation to pay for the services which he receives under the contract of carriage. He is not entitled, for example, to use a day return ticket other than in accordance with the conditions under which it was issued. If he wishes a different service than that for which he has paid, he must agree this with the carrier, his servants or agents. At common law a passenger has no right to break a journey at an intermediate stop and rejoin the vehicle later. Express terms in a contract may allow him to do so. If he travels to a point beyond the one for which his ticket is valid he must pay the full fare for the extra distance. He may be required to pay the total fare for the journey or only the difference between his original destination and the new one thus:

Bournemouth to Heathrow	£7 return
Bournemouth to Victoria	£9 return
Heathrow to Victoria	£1 return

A traveller with a ticket to Heathrow who carries on to Victoria may be required to pay either £1 or £2 depending on the terms under which the ticket was issued: *Covington v Wright (1963)*.[14] Such a traveller is allowed credit for that part of the journey for which he has already paid.

Tickets remain the property of the person who issued them and must be produced at any time during the journey or delivered up to the carrier, his servant or agent. A ticket may not be transferred to a person other than one to whom it was issued without the authority of the issuer. This does not mean that a traveller may not employ an agent, say his wife, to purchase a ticket on his behalf.

Offences

Fare dodging seems to have become a national pastime and as a consequence special provisions have been made to protect carriers from fraudsters. The Road Traffic Acts 1930 and 1960 make express provision.[15] If a passenger is suspected, on reasonable grounds, of contravening any of the PSV Regulations he must, upon request, give his name and address to a driver or conductor. If he has actually infringed any Regulation he may be removed from the vehicle by such persons or by a police officer at their request. Unlike railway regulations there appears to be no power to arrest such a person.

Every passenger must have a valid ticket for his journey. If, for whatever reason he has not been called upon to pay his fare and he leaves the vehicle without tendering payment with the intention to avoid so doing, he is guilty of an offence: *L.P.T.B. v Sumner (1935).*[16]

A passenger who refuses to leave the vehicle upon completion of the journey in respect of which a fare has been paid, after being requested so to do by the conductor,[17] commits an offence. Attempting to use an expired, altered or defaced ticket is an offence as is the use of a *non-transferable* ticket by someone other than the person to whom it was issued.

Conduct of passengers

The PSV Regulations also cover misconduct by passengers. They are designed to prevent travellers endangering themselves or others, or annoying fellow passengers by such activities as spitting. Persons whose dress or clothing is in such condition as to present a hazard to the vehicle or those on board may not be permitted to enter or if aboard, remain. In most vehicles there is a prohibition against smoking in part of the vehicle, which must be observed.

Other prohibitions are against obscene language; the use of radios or musical instruments; singing. Passengers must not enter parts of the vehicle to which they are denied access nor enter or leave the same other than by the authorised doors. People who offend against any of these Regulations or those exhibiting riotous, disorderly or indecent behaviour may be removed from the vehicle. Again, there is no power of arrest conferred by the Regulations.

Taxis

In normal circumstances a cab driver cannot be compelled to accept a hiring of more than one hour's duration or outside the area for which he is licensed. Every cab must be fitted with an authorised taximeter. This must be set in motion by the driver as soon as the cab is hired. It may only be stopped once the hiring is at an end. Subject to a minimum charge, the fare may include a hire charge and a further sum calculated from a scale based upon speed, distance and time. Further charges may be authorised for other allowable additions e.g. night hirings, public holidays and carriage of excess luggage. No addition is allowed for the cab having been ordered by radio: *Bassam v Green (1981)*.[18]

When a hiring is accepted for a journey greater than that which the driver is compelled to accept, he may bargain a special fare rate with the hirer: *Goodman v Serle (1947)*.[19] In areas outside London this must not be a sum greater than would have been recorded on the meter for a journey within the licensing area. Any agreement to pay more than the authorised fare outside London is invalid: *House v Reynolds (1977)*.[20] Any excess overpaid may be recovered in the local Magistrates' Court. There is no objection to a fare being agreed which is below the authorised rate. Taxi drivers may not seek to charge higher fares by purporting to ply for private contract hire except where such hire is allowed by local regulations. Passengers who refuse to pay a fare may be sued for a civil debt. Those who run off without payment will be liable to be charged with *bilking* (qv).

4. LUGGAGE

Passengers seem always to have been allowed to carry with them a certain amount of luggage without extra charge. A proportion of the fare was notionally allotted for the transportation of items sufficient for the personal needs of the traveller. Under the Road Traffic Act 1960, the TCs could impose conditions as to quantity and charges for excess baggage when granting RSLs. Since the abolition of the licensing system and the break up of the NBC the amount of personal luggage to be carried and any charges in connection with it will be regulated in the contract of carriage.

The carriage of luggage is only an ancillary to the main purpose of the contract and the carrier reserves the right to set limits as appropriate. He will be entitled to refuse items which he considers hazardous, for if he were to load them and they harmed other passengers or their property he could be liable to them for breach of contract or in negligence: *Hanson v London Transport Executive (1952)*.[21] Any excess over the permitted amount will be charged for and the carrier may exercise a lien over luggage for any sum due which has not been paid.

Descriptions of luggage

Passengers' luggage is that which they require for their personal use or convenience with reference to their immediate needs or the ultimate purpose of the journey. Unlike the British Railways Board, the road transport industry is not a unitary undertaking and has no precise definitions of what constitutes luggage which may accompany a traveller.

It would seem that the term is reserved for hand luggage and should not include *tools of the trade* of the passenger. By definition it is apparent that items should consist of articles packed in a case or bag of some kind. Articles carried on the passenger's person are not luggage, but what of a coat carried but not worn, or an umbrella; is a folding bicycle in a bag luggage but an ordinary cycle not? These are points which the carrier should resolve at the time the contract is made. If the carrier allows items to be transported with their owner which are not normally deemed to be luggage he will be stopped from denying liability for them later. The same may be said of excess baggage which is carried but not charged for.

In the case of animals it is probable that small ones kept in a carrying case may be regarded as luggage. In the absence of a hazard or nuisance being caused to other travellers on the vehicle there seems to be no reason why they should not be carried as luggage in the absence of express contractual provisions.

Liability for loss

A common carrier is an *insurer* of luggage and must bear losses subject only to the excepted perils unless he has limited his liability by special contract. In the case of private carriers, the question of liability will depend upon proof of fault on the carrier's part: *Houghland v R.R.Law (Luxury Coaches) Ltd (1962)*.[22] It will also be necessary to show that the loss or damage to luggage occurred during transit. At common law this is determined as beginning when the items are received into the care of the carrier or his employees acting within their real or ostensible authority. Such luggage will have been delivered for carriage a short time before the commencement of the journey. Often it is loaded by the passenger himself on the directions of a driver or attendant.

Transit ends when the carrier unloads the goods onto the pavement or road at the end of the journey. Where the passenger transfers from one coach to another it is seen as his responsibility to also reload the luggage unless the contract allows otherwise. During any such time as the luggage is not covered by the contract of carriage the carrier may still be liable if he or his servants are shown to be at fault in its management. If a servant of the carrier takes the goods into his custody and they are lost or damaged by his wilful or negligent act or omission his employer will be vicariously liable. He may seek to protect himself by an exclusion clause in the contract, subject to all the qualifications as to the effects of such provisions considered earlier.

Taxis

Very often travellers using taxis are accompanied by luggage. Because of this, London taxis have developed a unique feature. Since the introduction of motor cabs there has been no seat beside the driver to allow for the carriage of a sizeable quantity of luggage. It was an obvious attraction to the passenger who could see that the driver had the property under his personal scrutiny for the duration of the journey. He had a greater control over it than if it were carried elsewhere. It also made it more difficult for the driver to deny liability in the case of its loss or damage.

Unless a taxi is specially adapted, no luggage may be carried upon its roof. A vehicle which is improperly loaded by the driver will be prima facie evidence of negligence should damage or loss occur. At the end of the hiring, or as soon as practicable thereafter, the driver is required to search the vehicle. Any property which cannot be handed to its owner immediately must be handed in at a police station within 24 hours unless previously claimed by the owner.

It would appear that under the provisions of the Town Police Clauses Act 1847-1889, the proprietor of a cab operation is liable to third parties for torts committed by a driver which are within the apparent scope of the latter's duties. This will be so even where the driver is not an employee of the proprietor. This is a departure from the usual rules of vicarious liability but the limit of compensation to be paid by such proprietors has remained at £5 for many years. Since drivers are required to be insured against liability to passengers the luckless passenger would be better advised to sue the driver if needs be.

Left luggage

At most major terminals there is usually a facility for luggage to be deposited. When this occurs, it is covered by a different regime from that of carriage. The contract is now one of *warehousing*. He who undertakes responsibility in this manner does so as a *bailee for reward*. Any loss or damage occasioned to such goods whilst in his possession will be assumed to have been the result of his negligence unless he can prove to the contrary. The contract may be governed by such terms as are agreed between the parties at the time of deposit and very often these have included exclusion clauses which may be effective in protecting the bailee.

Upon depositing the goods, the bailor is handed a ticket as a token of their receipt and the means by which they may later be recovered. The ticket will in variably inform him that it is witness to the standard form contract governing the bailment. These terms often endow the bailee with generous exemptions. To deny their operation the depositor may seek to show that he was unaware that the ticket was a contractual document: *Chapleton v Barry U.D.C. (1940)*.[23]   It is also usual with left luggage offices for there to be displayed a notice of the terms of deposit in clear view of the depositors.

A bailee may, by the use of well drawn exclusion clauses and sufficient notice to the bailor, absolve himself from much liability. But where there is a failure to redeliver the goods upon presentation of the ticket, the bailee will be unable to plead the exemptions. To allow him to do so would be to allow him to deny the very purpose for which the contract had been made: *Woolmer v Delmer Price Ltd (1955)*.[24] Such exemption clauses would not be regarded as reasonable within the terms of the Unfair Contract Terms Act 1977. An exclusion for damage to goods which have been bailed may satisfy the requirements of the statute depending on the circumstances of a particular case.

In the absence of effective exemption clauses the duties of a warehouseman are:

1. To protect the goods against loss or destruction - Torts Interference with Goods Act 1977 section 2(2).

2. To exercise reasonable care and skill in the discharge of his duties - Supply of Goods and Services Act 1982 section 13.

3. To deliver the goods to the rightful owner. Delivery to the wrong person constitutes the common law tort of conversion.

4. To redeliver the goods without unreasonable delay. An implied term in the contract.

At many terminals today, lockers are provided for the use of travellers wishing to deposit luggage. In such circumstances, the provider of this facility does not act as a warehouseman. He merely gives the depositor a licence to use this amenity. Only where the licensor can be shown to have caused loss or damage by wilful wrongdoing on his part, or that of his servants or agents, will he be liable. A faulty lock on the compartment used by the traveller may result in liability of the depositor if it can be shown that he could not have discovered this for himself. Alternatively, the licensor may show that he has done all that a reasonable man could do to ensure that his equipment was secure.

5. INTERNATIONAL CARRIAGE

On 1 March 1973 the Convention Relative au Contrat de Transport International des Voyageur et des baggage par Route (CVR) was published in Geneva. The UK Government indicated a clear intention to include the provisions in English law but this has not yet been done. The English text of the CVR is included as a schedule to the Carriage of Passengers by Road Act 1974. Section 14 of the Act provides that the CVR terms will come into effect when sufficient states have ratified the Convention and a commencement order is made.

A Protocol to the Convention was also agreed in 1979. Provision has been made in the Carriage by Air and Road Act 1979 for it to be implemented at a date yet to be announced.

The CVR applies to every contract for the international carriage of passengers and their luggage by road for reward. The journey must cross the territories of more than one of the states who are parties to the Convention. It will apply to contracts for combined carriage where one of the segments of the journey is by road. This will be so where the land segment is not *international* e.g. by road to Dover and sea to Calais, and extends to damage sustained where the vehicle is being carried by some other form of transport e.g. ship. This is conditional upon the passenger being inside the vehicle or entering or alighting from it at the time of the injury.

Documentation

Passengers must be issued with documentation by the carrier which contains a *Geneva Statement*. Absence, irregularity or loss of the ticket will not invalidate the cover but the ticket must be printed with the name and address of the carrier. The ticket is transferable at any time before the commencement of the journey.

The carrier is required to issue, at the request of the passenger, a luggage registration voucher giving the number and nature of items consigned to him. It must bear a *Geneva Statement*. By the issue of the voucher, the carrier is deemed to have accepted luggage which was, prima facie, in good order when it was received by him.

Redelivery takes place when the carrier hands over the items listed on the voucher presented to him by the bearer. If the person presenting himself cannot produce the same, the carrier may require him to provide proof of identity and if he is not satisfied with this, adequate security against delivery of the goods.

Personal injury

The carrier may be liable to compensate a passenger for death, wounding or any other bodily or mental injury, sustained whilst the passenger was on board the vehicle or entering or alighting from it. He will be liable for injuries resulting from the mental or physical failing of the driver; any defect or malfunctioning of the vehicle; or from any wrongful act or neglect of any person from whom the carrier hired the vehicle. He will not be liable in circumstances where no due diligence on his part could have prevented the occurrence. The national law of the country where the case is to be heard shall determine which persons are entitled to compensation and the extent of such injuries which are the subject of a claim.

Loss or damage to luggage

The carrier is liable for loss (or partial loss) and damage to luggage during the whole period of transit. If the luggage is not collected upon arrival at its destination the carrier must deposit it in a safe and convenient place. Luggage not redelivered within 14 days of the voucher holder claiming it is deemed to have been lost.

Luggage under the CVR includes personal effects worn by the

passenger. The carrier will be responsible for all luggage, the loss of which is attributable to an accident. Where items are stolen or disappear in the aftermath of an accident he will only be liable for such as were actually in his custody. The carrier will be relieved of liability if loss or damage results from the *inherent vice* of the goods or in circumstances which he could not have avoided had he used all due diligence. (In respect of loss or damage to luggage.) He will be responsible for loss or damage to luggage occasioned by the defects of the vehicle and the acts and omissions of third parties to the same extent as in the case of personal injury to passengers.

Financial limits

The CVR sets upper limits for compensation payable by a carrier in the event of death or personal injury expressed in terms of *gold francs*. The parties may contract for higher limits if they wish. Any nation which is a party to the Convention may set higher limits or no limit and in the 1974 Act Britain has done so where a carrier has his principal place of business in the UK.

Similar liability limits are set for luggage with reference to each piece and a total in respect of each passenger. The same rules apply to items worn by passengers. Again the amounts are expressed in *gold francs*.

The Protocol of 1979 replaces the *gold franc* with a unit of account expressed in terms of 'Special Drawing Rights' (SDR) as defined by the International Monetary Fund. The 1979 Act allows for an equivalent amount in sterling which is the value of SDR on a given date.

If loss or damage results from the wilful misconduct or gross negligence of the carrier or a person for whom he is responsible, the carrier cannot rely on the limits of compensation set by the CVR.

Exemptions from liability

In addition to those exceptions indicated earlier, the carrier may be relieved of liability in whole or in part if loss or damage was occasioned by the wrongful actions of the passenger. This includes actions which would not be expected of someone conducting himself in a reasonable manner. The carrier will not be held liable for the loss or damage caused by a nuclear incident if the law of a contracting state which governs liability fixes such liability upon the operator of the nuclear installation.

Claims

Claims in respect of luggage under the CVR rules must be commenced within one year of the vehicle having arrived at the destination of the passenger, or the date when it should have arrived had the journey been completed. If the passenger takes delivery of the luggage without complaint at such time, this is prima facie evidence that the items were redelivered in good order. Any complaint must be made to the carrier within 7 days of actual receipt of the luggage by the passenger. It may be made orally or in writing unless the loss or damage has been checked and agreed by the carrier and the passenger at the time of redelivery.

In respect of claims for death or personal injury, these must be made within three years of the date on which persons entitled to claim became aware of such entitlement or ought to have had knowledge of it. In any event, such period may not exceed 5 years from the date of the accident. Any statement in the contract of carriage which seeks to exclude the provisions of the CVR is null and void.

Choice of forum

A claimant may bring proceedings in any court of a contracting state such as is agreed between him and the carrier. Alternatively, he may bring such action in the court of the state where the loss or damage occurred; or the place of departure or destination of the vehicle; or where the carrier had his principal place of business or was habitually resident or had a place of business from which the contract of carriage was made.

Any proceedings to enforce liability imposed on the carrier by the CVR are governed by the Convention. In this way it is intended that international travellers by road shall be protected in like manner to those who journey by air, rail or sea. Despite pressure in the United Nations, safety standards for long-haul vehicles have not been significantly increased while, at the same time, accidents have been rising in number and severity.

NOTES

1. Supply of Goods and Services Act 1982 s. 13.
2. (1947) 2 All ER 628 (CA).
3. (1907) 23 TLR 616.
4. (1947) 1 All ER 213.
5. s. 151.
6. Unfair Contract Terms Act 1977 s. 2(1).
7. Ibid s. 31(2).
8. Ibid s. 3(2) (a) and (b).
9. (1950) 1 All ER 403.
10. (1950) 1 All ER 392.
11. (1953) 1 WLR 232.
12. (1958) 1 WLR 346.
13. (1935) 1 KB 75.
14. (1963) 2 QB 469.
15. Road Traffic Act 1930 s. 84 and Road Traffic Act 1960 s. 147.
16. (1935) WN 96.
17. The title 'conductor' now also includes stewards or attendants.
18. (1981) RTR 362.
19. (1947) 1 KB 808.
20. (1977) 1 All ER 689.
21. (1952) CLY 2451.
22. (1962) 1 QB 694.
23. (1940) 1 KB 532.
24. (1955) 1 QB 291.

Chapter VII

The Age Of The Train

1. EARLY RAILROADS

The poor state of roads in the 18th century led to the use of horse drawn wagons running on wooden rails, later replaced with iron to carry heavier loads. An early attempt at carrying passengers was tried by the Oystermouth Railway in South Wales in 1807, lasting until 1827. Also in South Wales, experiments with a steam *tram wagon* were carried out by Richard Trevithick at Pen-y-darran in 1804. The same engineer constructed a small circular track near Oxford Circus and ran railway rides as a leisure attraction in 1808. These ventures were not a commercial success, but they demonstrated that steam power, allied to a rail-road, was an idea worth developing.

In 1825, the Stockton to Darlington Railway was inaugurated using George Stevenson's engine, the *Locomotion*. Amongst a motley collection of wagons was one hastily improvised *passenger coach*. It resembled a shed on wheels and bore the name *Experiment*. The railway itself was designed for goods traffic, allowing horse drawn coaches to be used for passenger travel over a short stretch, but it was not a serious rival to the local stage coach service.

The world's firsts

On the 4th May 1830, the Whitstable to Canterbury Railway was opened. It marked the beginning of regular steam hauled passenger services which spread rapidly during the next hundred years. This railway soon witnessed an early attempt at an integrated passenger service. In 1836 a steamer-rail-coach link between London and Dover was established. Passengers could embark at London Bridge on the coastal steamer, *William IV*, bound for Whitstable via Gravesend. The railway took them on to Canterbury from where a coach followed the good turnpike to Dover and the cross Channel packet. The line also catered for excursionists in 1832 and issued the first season tickets and family railcards in 1834.

The link between travel and the hotel trade was not lost on the Directors of the railway. They issued 'untransferable complimentary tickets' to Innkeepers in East Kent, the most favoured being given framed engravings of the opening of the railway as a sales promotion. The railway was a pioneer of tourism as well as transportation.

Unfortunately, the historic railroad was closed in 1952 having, in the years between then and its inauguration, become part of a rapid growth in private rail companies and, finally, of a nationalised British Rail. Its fate was followed by the closure of the Oystermouth line in 1960. The *Invicta* engine which hauled the first train in 1830 now stands in a new museum in Canterbury, adding to the city's tourist attractions.

2. THE GOLDEN AGE OF STEAM

The success of the early trains as mass transporters of people and freight enabled the railway companies to meet the heavy capital costs of building and maintaining the *permanent way* and providing stations and rail terminals. They also had the benefit of controlling their own roads with regulations governing services and dictating conditions for the carriage of passengers. All undertakings had to be established by an Act of Parliament because of the need to both acquire land and develop the system. By 1914, there were 27 main line railway companies and nearly one hundred smaller undertakings. The industry remained in private ownership until 1947.

Railways offered reduced costs and increased capacity. They could carry goods and passengers more cheaply than the road carriers whose trade went rapidly into decline after 1840. Canal companies were bought up by the railways and competition for heavy freight was eliminated.

At first, Parliament adopted a laisser-faire attitude to the new industry, not wishing to stifle growth. For some time the only restrictions upon the companies were the limits set for maximum rates in the enabling legislation. Despite attempts to encourage the companies to lease the use of their lines to other carriers to prevent monopolies, it was soon realised that lines could not be run economically on such a basis. The rail-road could not be treated in the same way as the highways which allowed access to all who would pay the tolls.

Statutory provisions

The Railways Clauses Consolidation Act 1845 preserved the principle of allowing commercial enterprises to lease time to run their own carriages on the railways, but this never materialised. For many years the railways were *common carriers* and, except on restricted grounds, could not refuse to carry passengers or their luggage. The Transport Act 1962 abolished common carriage, substituting conditions of carriage. The value of the railways as public utilities was realised and, beginning with the Railway and Canal Traffic Act 1854, they were obliged to for ward and deliver 'traffic' which included passengers and goods. They were required to provide reasonable *facilities* - enlarging stations, promoting through traffic and maintaining the services. This statutory duty was abolished by the Transport Act 1962,[1] enabling the British Railways Board to close lines on economic grounds. A mechanism and system of public enquiries was established under the Act,[2] but in practice objectors to closures have little hope of success in preventing them. In any event, the Minister possesses the power of closure without consultation.

By 1850, the railways carried some 67 million passengers annually. The numbers rose spectacularly - 150 million in 1860; 1,300 million in 1910. Railway stations became the hub around which towns grew.

111

Buses, coaches and taxis fed them with travellers which they carried on ever-expanding routes. Because of its unique position, the railway system became the testing ground for statutes which sought to develop public utilities and which, through both common law and statutory interpretation by the courts, was to develop rules which both contemporary forms of transport and later introductions were to follow. Many of the rules relating to road and air travel borrow heavily from the mass of experience accumulated by 150 years of railway operations.

Amalgamations

In the years leading up to the Great War, the railways enjoyed a period of unprecedented prosperity. Many major works were undertaken with rival companies outdoing one another in erecting magnificent buildings to attract custom. The trend towards amalgamation continued and was accepted by government as inevitable. During the War the railways were subjected to direction by the state for the first time in order to coordinate the war effort. By the end of hostilities there were calls for *nationalisation* to be continued and extended. Instead a compromise was reached between the champions of state control and the free market forces. The Railways Act 1921 ushered in a new policy for the railways. Compulsory amalgamations became the order of the day with more than one hundred companies swallowed up by the four super-carriers which emerged. In each of the regions which they served, the London and North Eastern, the London Midland and Scottish, the Great Western and the Southern Railways enjoyed monopoly powers.

To safeguard the interests of the public, control over rates and charges was taken out of their hands. In future, tariffs were determined by the Railway Rates Tribunal, an independent body. The provisions of the Victorian statutes which compelled the railway companies to treat all their customers equally were retained in their entirety. However, with their rates *capped* and the cost of maintaining services rising, the railways began to lose out to the road transport companies who were not burdened with restrictive legislation and had no *permanent way* to maintain.

Decline

In an effort to assist the railways, the government allowed them to run road transport undertakings[3]. In addition, local rates were lowered so that overheads on railway property were reduced, and the passenger duty which had been levied for many years was abolished. Despite these measures, the industry still declined in competition with the roads. Some companies looked round for new ventures. The Great Western inaugurated a Cardiff to Plymouth air service in 1934 and shortly after, all four super-carriers joined with Imperial Airways to run an extended inland air network. The companies were agitating for radical reforms when the Second World War broke out in 1939. Once more the companies came under direct state control.

A Railways Executive Committee was set up and a Controller Of Railways appointed in 1941. There was no time or money for repairs and development. It was a case of make do and mend. At the end of the war, the railways were all but exhausted. A massive injection of capital was necessary to restore the whole system and to bring it up to modern standards. It was, therefore, decided that the railways should stay under public control and be brought under one statutory corporation.

3. NATIONALISATION

The Transport Act 1947 was designed to promote an efficient, economical and integrated system of public transport within Britain for both goods and passengers carried by land and the inland waterways. To run the enterprise, the British Transport Commission was established and endowed with very wide powers. Its task was to maintain a freedom of choice for the travelling public but it directed this by discontinuing some services and discriminating in its system of charges between others. The BTC acquired interests in a wide range of amenities catering to passengers' needs - hotels, cafeterias and other ancillary activities. It was not in tended that the BTC should make a profit, but it was required to meet its running costs.

In 1948 the entire railway network was placed under the control of the Railway Executive. A few *private* lines survived e.g. the Romney, Hythe and Dymchurch Railway established by private Act of Parliament in 1925. Again the Victorian legislation requiring that reasonable facilities be provided and anti-preferential treatment of customers, were maintained in unaltered form. This hampered the development of the system, but some help was given in the form of a new tariff of charges being introduced, replacing those established in 1921 and 1933[4]. This did not solve the difficulties created by such schemes and, in recognition of this, all such regulation of charges was swept away in 1962[5].

In 1955, a strike for better pay and conditions highlighted the problems of the BTC which told the Court of Enquiry, set up to examine the dispute, that it could not meet its statutory obligation to provide services and pay higher wages. The Court refused to accept this as an excuse. In 1960 BTC losses exceeded £100 million and a White Paper entitled 'Reorganisation of the Nationalised Transport Undertakings' placed the blame squarely on the BTC. The Transport Act 1962 abolished the Commission and replaced it with five new bodies, one of which was the British Railways Board (BRB). The 19th century legislation which had restricted the activities of the railways was repealed. Henceforth, the BRB was to enjoy complete autonomy in deciding what services and facilities to offer and the charges for both goods and passenger carriage. The Board, together with its Regional Boards, was given the same commercial freedom as private enterprises with one notable exception. It was not permitted to use exclusion clauses in its standard conditions of carriage which denied or limited liability for the death or personal injury to passengers. Nor could it restrict in any way the time or manner in which such claims might be made against it[6].

The first Chairman of the BRB was Dr (later Lord) Beeching who instituted an investigation of the Board's finances. Despite existing debts accrued by the BTC having been written off by the government, the railways were still operating at a loss. Wholesale closures of *unprofitable* lines together with their stations ensued; yet the system still continued to make losses. A White Paper on 'Railway Policy', published in 1967, recognised that the break-even target for the system was socially and economically unacceptable. Commercial viability might be desirable but it came second to the nation's need for a sound rail network.

The Transport Act 1968 made a determined effort to set up an integrated transport system. Part II established Passenger Transport Authorities (PTA) and a Passenger Transport Executive (PTE) for areas outside London. A PTE is required to consult with all carriers in its area to establish an integrated system of multi-mode transportation. The Transport Acts of 1980 and 1985 have much altered the roles of PTAs and PTEs with the result that there is little coordination between road carriers and British Rail.

Part IV of the 1968 Act was principally concerned with the

problems of the BRB. Regional Boards were abolished and the services of the BRB were divided between socially necessary but loss-making services, which were to be aided with Treasury support from public funds[7], and the remainder which were expected to be run on a commercial basis. With a change of government in 1970, the BRB was again in difficulties because of a call for restraint in price increases coupled with a duty to provide services accepted as loss making.

Into Europe

When Britain joined the EEC in 1973, it became necessary to alter the provisions of the 1968 Act. EEC regulations prohibit subsidies to transport undertakings with few exceptions. The Railways Act 1974 amended the law but allowed the Minister to make such proposals for payments as are allowed by the Community rules.

Article 77 of the Treaty of Rome allowed subsidies to be paid to meet public service obligations. This was seen by the European Commission as capable of too wide an interpretation, so Regulation 1191/269 called for the ending of payments in respect of public service obligations, inserting in their place permission to provide aid in order to maintain *adequate* transport services. This has been interpreted very widely by the UK.

The 1974 Act allows support for British Rail on grounds which are not strictly within the terms of the EEC Regulation. BRBs problem under the 1968 Act has been in separating out which parts of the system should be supported as providing *adequate* levels of service and which have to be commercially viable. The Government still supports those parts of the network which it thinks necessary, with no apparent indecision as to whether this conflicts with EEC rules. The Transport (Finance) Act 1982 repealed the 1974 Act and raised the limits by way of payments in aid to the BRB.

The level of grant support dropped by 25% between 1983-86. A further 25% reduction has been budgeted for 1986-89. In 1988, the Inter City Service enters its last year of qualifying for Public Service Obligation funding. At present the main target for support is the commuter sector. It is doubtful if the BRB could maintain service at the present level, despite 1988 fare increases, without financial support. Substantial *windfall* revenues are forecast when the Channel Tunnel opens. Many observers believe this will be the signal to return the railway network to private ownership, for which the need to comply with EEC rules, however reluctantly, can be used as a *persuasive* reason.

Throughout the 1980s there was much talk of *privatisation* but opponents from all political parties raised objections on a variety of grounds. It is difficult to see how the system could operate both efficiently and safely. Efficiency, it seems, would be achieved by selling off regional networks to private carriers and/or selling the right to carry goods and passengers in owner operated rolling stock. So called *unprofitable* lines such as the south coast route Southampton to Brighton would be closed. The result would be that only profitable lines would remain - profitable that is to the operator who would in effect run a monopoly with little by way of regulation if the other national enterprises which have been sold off are any measure of what we may expect. The whole process smacks of government bereft of ideas selling off public assets for private gain. The much heralded Channel link to London has been the subject of much controversy and anxiety for the people of Kent. Now it seems everything is to be sacrificed to cost cutting. The line at present seems destined to terminate at St Pancras which is itself a Victorian masterpiece in terms of its architecture but when built was the ruination of the company which paid for it to fulfil Scott's dream. Even this route will not be in operation until the year 2000 while on the other side of the Channel the French fast track operation will be ready by the end of 1993.

Powers of the BRB

The general duty of the Board is to provide 'railway services in Great Britain and, in connection with the provision of railway services, to provide such other services and facilities as appear to the Board to be expedient, and to have due regard as respects all those railway and other services and facilities to efficiency, economy and safety of operation'[8].

To these ends, BRB has carried goods and passengers by road when occasion demanded, provided shipping services (Sealink ferries) and, under the Railway Companies (Air Transport) Act 1929, engaged in carriage by air. The Board also possesses powers to provide and manage hotels, food and drink, and places of refreshment wheresoever it deems expedient. Many of the hotels have been sold and catering facilities and the 'Travellers Fare' operations are being franchised or sold off at present.

4. SAFETY OF PASSENGERS

Government concern for the safety of railway operations appeared at a very early point in their history. The Railway Regulation Acts 1840-1844 required the Board of Trade to be satisfied that, before granting powers to a railway company, such undertaking could be operated without danger to the public. The Board had also to give its approval to any byelaws which were to govern the conduct of the enterprise. In 1919, the powers of the Board were transferred to the Minister of Transport. The Ministry is concerned with all transport matters, which requires specialist areas to be placed in the charge of Under Secretaries of State. The Railway Directorate is charged with duties in connection with rail matters. In this it is supported by an Inspectorate which oversees railway operations. Inspectors must approve any new works which are proposed in connection with passenger traffic; investigate accidents and hold inquiries; advise the Minister; consult with the responsible officers of BRB.

Accident

Major railway accidents and fatalities are unusual occurrences in Britain. When they do take place, detailed public inquiries are instituted by the Secretary of State for Transport under powers derived from the Regulation of Railways Act 1871, sections 3 and 4, and extended by section 125 of the Transport Act, 1968.

A comprehensive list of such accidents, which must be reported, is prescribed under the legislation[9]. The list includes all accidents to passenger trains and those on lines which are used to carry passengers. It is possible to bring criminal charges of manslaughter, but few have been brought and no persons convicted. Incidents which would give rise to charges of *involuntary manslaughter* are those involving neglect of duty, gross negligence, or recklessness. The degree of negligence, or other fault, required to maintain a charge is considerable. It would have to be shown that there was such a disregard for human life and the safety of others that it required action by the state in the public interest: *R v Benge (1865)*.[10]

Manslaughter by recklessness is perhaps best seen as an extension of gross negligence, but the line between the two is hard to define with certainty. It may be seen as the sort of activity where a driver of a train saw signal lights but carried on because they were only

117

preliminary in nature and he had never been stopped before. This is the most likely explanation of the finding arising out of the accident at Lewisham in 1957 when 90 passengers died.[11] Other less serious offences are interfering with the permanent way or with signalling equipment, throwing anything at a train with intent to injure or endanger the safety of persons on board.[12]

Major accidents have continued to occur on the rail system - Clapham, Cannon Street, Kings Cross to name but three. The cause would seem to lie primarily with failures in maintainance, use of rolling stock long past its useful life, signals defects and a general reluctance to provide financial support for an enterprise long starved of cash. All it seems is to be resolved by privatisation.

Safety on the system has been continually and justifiably under attack. There is a lamentable record of passengers - or as BR now likes to refer to them, *customers* - falling from high speed trains. In the five years 1986-1991 more than 100 people fell to their deaths from Inter-City trains. At first BR claimed that most of these fatalities were caused by *passenger behaviour* - drunkeness, suicide or foolhardiness. Later after commissioning a private inquiry BR admitted that the consultants employed 'were unable to establish causal links between these incidents and any of the possible reasons for doors opening during running'. The answer it seems 'a mystery'!

If as seems likely the accidents were the result of faulty systems and lax supervision, how much safer will the *customers* be in a cost cutting privatised operation?

Compensation

A fare-paying passenger who is injured in an accident may bring an action founded in contract or tort: *Kelly v Metropolitan Railway (1895)*.[13] A person who is carried on a *free pass*, or who is otherwise a lawful but non fare-paying traveller, may only sue in negligence since no contract exists between him and the carrier. Those representing the estate of a deceased person may sue in contract or tort as the case may be.

Standards of care

The obligation of the carrier is to provide a means of transportation which is as free from defect as all reasonable care can make it. This common law duty is objective and would make the carrier responsible for the faults of an independent contractor however reputable he might be in, say, carrying out repairs to a coach. Only a fault which was undetectable would absolve the carrier from responsibility: *Redhead v Midland Railway (1869)*.[14] In some cases, it is difficult to see how the court arrived at its decision objectively: *O'Connor v BTC (1958)*.[15] A guard's van of a type usually coupled at the end of the train was instead placed in the middle and no liability was attributed to the railway for the death of a child who fell from it. The court seems to have applied the *subjective* test appropriate to the Occupiers Liability Act 1957, when it was the common law test that should have been adopted.

On this point, Kahn Freund writes of the 1957 Act that it: 'determines the standard of liability towards persons who lawfully enter railway stations, coach terminals and such buildings, but it has nothing whatsoever to do with obligations towards fare paying passengers'.[16] It is surely right that the standard of care is much higher in respect of a passenger being carried in a train than one who is simply on railway premises. Even in the case of such persons it has been said that they are there 'exactly on the same terms as a person who has got a ticket to travel': *Stowell v Railway Executive (1949)*.[17] In this case a person who slipped on grease from fish boxes at Paddington station was able to recover damages. The court is here suggesting raising the standard to that of a passenger in the course of carriage whereas in *'O'Connor'* the converse is asserted.

Proof of fault

Some degree of fault must be capable of being attributed to the carrier if he is to be held liable. He cannot be held responsible for the wrongful actions of a passenger which cause harm to other travellers: *Hanson v LTE (1952)*.[18] This principle appears to hold good even where the railway know that violence to a passenger may occur: *Pounder v N.E. Railway Company (1892)*.[19] This may well not be the case where British Rail know that passengers on a football special are likely to cause problems and they fail to police the train adequately. Older cases do suggest that railways are not bound to guard against wilful disorder on the part of passengers. Today, with British Rail holding a monopoly of rail travel and with the British Transport Police established by statute,[20] it is submitted that the BRB have a duty to protect the travelling public especially when they have provided trains for groups of people engaging in a particular activity so as to make a profit from such enterprise.

Duration of transit

It is not clear when the contract of carriage is concluded so as to make the carrier liable to perform the carriage with reasonable care and skill, as required by the Supply of Goods and Services Act 1982. In 1965, it was said: 'It is a very common thing for a person who arrives late at a station to enter a train without taking a ticket, because he has no time to do so, but with the intention of paying during, or at the end of, the journey. Such a person is undoubtedly a passenger, and probably a fare-paying passenger from the moment he enters the train'.[21] The problem has been compounded by the practice of British Rail operating *open stations*, encouraging passengers to enter trains without checks at the platform. It is probable that the duty of care for a passenger's safety begins once he enters the station with the intention of boarding a train and lasts until such time as he clears the station at his destination. It is hard to see why it should be limited to the time during which he is actually on board a train. In any event, the traveller will be pro-tected against the negligence of the carrier, his servants or agents, during the whole of the time that he is on railway property. Such liability operates separately from obligations derived from contract.

In the case of international carriage by rail (q.v.), the railway is liable where damage is caused by an *accident* (not defined in the Convention) arising out of the operation of the railway and occurring while the passenger is in, entering, or alighting from the train.[22] The Convention specifically reserves for municipal law the determination of the railway's liability to pay damages for injuries other than those described in its terms.[23]

Special damages

Passengers entering or alighting from trains are at risk and carriers are expected to display a high order of responsibility for their safety. Platforms present particular hazards for travellers. They must be neither too high nor too low for their purpose: *Manning v L. & N.W. Railway (1907)*.[24] They must not be slippery: *Osborne v L. & N.W. Railway (1888)*.[25] Overcrowding may lead to dangers: *Hogan v S.E. Railway (1873)*,[26] as may platforms which are unlit: *Martin v G.N.*

120

Railway (1855).[27]

Dangers occur where the platform is not long enough to accommodate a train, or the carriages stop short of the platform or overshoot. Sometimes, because of the curvature of the train, there is a gap between the carriages and the platform. In all such cases the adequacy of the warnings given to passengers will be tested. The railway may, in such cases, raise the defence of contributory negligence against the traveller who is injured after not heeding a warning: *Rose v N.E. Railway (1876).*[28]

There is a general duty upon the carrier to ensure that doors are properly shut before the train departs: *Brookes v L.P.T.B. (1947).*[29] If the door flies open while the train is in motion, in the absence of evidence to the contrary, it will be assumed that this is due to the fault of the carrier: *Inglis v L.M.S. Railway (1941).*[30] Before doors are closed by railway staff, warnings should be given to those who may be mounting or alighting from the train: *Bird v Railway Executive (1949).*[31]

Res ipsa loquitur

The traveller may find it impossible to discover the precise cause of his injury, which may have resulted from the failure of some mechanical device on the train or connected with signalling equipment. In such cases, the rule of evidence employed by the courts is to require the defendant to demonstrate that he was not responsible. It is presumed that, by the nature of the accident, it arose from a defect which is the railway's responsibility. 'When an accident happens on the railway, as the railway system and the trains thereon are entirely under the control of the railway company, it is for them to explain, if they can, how the accident happened without fault on their part': *Easson v L.N.E. Railway (1944).*[32]

In the case of carriage doors, passengers have a right to expect that they will be properly fastened and that, if they are not, it is the fault of the railway: *Gee v Metropolitan Railway (1875).*[33] In the light of modern technology, the railway may seek to show that the door is foolproof but, unless they can show how it opened, this defence may avail them nothing. Where a statute requires specific devices to be in operation, e.g. automatic brakes, failure of such items may give the basis for a claim even if liability for breach of statutory duty cannot be used.

The duty of a carrier will not readily be discharged by the courts. During a journey, a passenger is at the mercy of the carrier. He can do nothing to ensure his own safety in a vehicle which is driven by another and over whose progress he has no control. The duty of reasonable care for the safety of passengers and of their luggage will, therefore, arise primarily out of the contract of carriage and the implied terms as to the safety of the traveller which are contained within it.

5. THE CONTRACT OF CARRIAGE

As with other forms of transportation, the contract for carriage by rail will most often be evidenced by the issue of the appropriate form of ticket. The ticket will, by reference, notify the traveller of the conditions under which the carrier will undertake to convey him to his chosen destination. For many years, the railway ticket has been acknowledged by the courts to represent to the traveller the express terms of carriage set out in regulations, byelaws and conditions drawn up by the carrier. Even where a passenger was illiterate, the terms of the contract were deemed to bind her so as to exclude the carrier's liability for injury: *Thompson v L.M.S. Railway (1930)*.[34] Had Mrs Thompson been travelling today, the terms of the contract under which she was denied compensation would have fallen foul of the Transport Act 1962 and the Unfair Contract Terms Act 1977.

Fares

Passengers have a duty to pay the appropriate fare. Tickets are usually issued at stations but they may be purchased on board the train. Where a passenger has no ticket nor the means of paying, provided he has no intention of evading payment, he may still travel lawfully. He may give his name and address to the ticket collector, indicating that he will pay within a reasonable time.

A passenger is not entitled to any services other than those purchased by the ticket on which he is travelling. If he obtains additional services, he must pay for them. Travel is to the destination indicated on the ticket and via the route shown. A ticket is not transferable to another, but it may be purchased on behalf of a traveller by an agent acting on his behalf.

A source of irritation to many travellers is that they are forced to stand while first class accommodation is available. Even if all second class places are taken, such a traveller may not occupy first class seats or standing room without paying the first class fare, or the difference between that and the price which he has paid for his ticket.

Carriers' obligations

Since 1962, the railways have not been common carriers of either goods or passengers. A traveller has no right to be carried other than under the conditions of a special contract which restricts the expectations he may have of the services which will be provided for him. Reference to the British Rail Conditions of Carriage show that a traveller has no right to be carried on any particular train or in accordance with the published timetable. Trains may be suspended or discontinued at any time without prior notice. Any delay or detention occasioning loss or damage is not actionable. No accommodation on board is guaranteed in a particular train or compartment of the class shown on the ticket.

In some circumstances the unlucky traveller may be able to claim a refund of all or part of the fare he has paid. Such a traveller who has to change trains to reach his destination may discover that the connecting train has departed leaving him stranded. The BRB Conditions tell him that 'Reasonable consideration will be given to application for refund in accordance with Condition ...'! So far, the Unfair Contract Terms Act has not been invoked to challenge the reasonableness of such denials of liability. Protection is afforded by the inability of the Board to deny liability for death or personal injury caused by negligence. A passenger who travels in a class other than that for which he holds a valid ticket does not lose protection by virtue of that action alone: *Vosper v G.W.R. (1928).*[35]

A person who travels on a train intending to avoid the fare, or part of it, has a bare licence to be on the train. Once such licence is revoked, i.e. he is asked to leave, he remains on the train as a trespasser. The railway owes him no higher duty of care than that which is owed to trespassers generally under the Occupiers Liability Act 1984.

Luggage

It is a long established practice to allow passengers to travel accompanied by a reasonable amount of personal luggage. There was no precise definition as to what comprised such luggage but it was generally accepted that it should conform in both shape and size to the popular conception of baggage.

Today, British Rail Conditions of Carriage are more specific as to both weight and description. Excess baggage must be paid for and some items have particular conditions attached to their carriage, e.g. motor cycles, animals and perambulators.

The Board only accepts liability for goods in transit. This is the time between them being taken on board the train and when they are unloaded onto the platform at the agreed destination and the passenger has had a reasonable opportunity to claim them. The conditions deny liability should the route be subject to deviation. However, a claim may be made for delay if the passenger can show that this was the result of the neglect or default of the carrier. In such cases, limits are set as to the amounts of compensation which will be paid. It is of interest to note that, although the railway is no longer a common carrier, the exclusions of liability allowed by the Carriers Act 1830 are used as the basis for exemptions under BRB Conditions.

Luggage is defined as meaning 'articles which passengers may keep with them on the train without inconvenience to other passengers or which can be readily accommodated in the guard's or luggage van'. The ownership of the goods accompanying the traveller are no longer of relevance as was formerly the case: *Meux v Great Eastern Railway (1895)*.[36] At common law, animals were not considered to be luggage but the Board's Conditions allow for small animals to be carried in boxes for no extra charge, while whippets and greyhounds must be kept chained and muzzled in the guard's van!

No mention is made of the time at which such goods may be accepted for transit. At common law, before the 1962 Act was passed, it was recognised that passengers usually presented items for carriage in the guard's van some short time before the train departed. Provided the interval between loading and departure was not excessive, the railway would accept liability for loss or damage upon proof of its negligence towards the goods: *Steers v Midland Railway (1920)*.[37] It is presumed that this is still the case in the absence of conditions to the contrary.

Prior to 1962, the railways assumed responsibility for such loss as was occasioned by the negligence or wilful misconduct of their staff. Luggage handed to a porter prior to departure came within this protection: *G.W.R. v Bunch (1888)*.[38] Such was not the case where a porter took delivery of luggage at the point of arrival: *Hodgkinson v*

124

L.N.W.R. (1884).[39] The matter of porterage is now covered by the Board's Conditions. The Board accepts liability in such circumstances and upon such conditions as would apply to such luggage in transit.

Left luggage

There was nothing in the common law which obliged a carrier to act as a warehouseman and to store baggage. However, railways long provided such facilities by special contract. There was no duty to do so but items would be kept, provided they were not deemed objectionable or dangerous.

The relevant terms under which left luggage will be accepted are contained in Part IV of the current Conditions published by the BRB. Items may be stored in the left-luggage office, or elsewhere, at the Board's discretion. Once bailed to the railway, the bailor may not have access to goods but may withdraw them in whole, or in part, upon production of a valid receipt and upon payment of the charges due.

If no receipt can be produced, the goods may be handed over to an applicant who can prove that he has lost his ticket and is entitled to claim the items lodged with the Board. Such a person will be required to sign an indemnity in favour of the Board. The Board has a lien upon the goods deposited against payment of the charges due. Whilst in their custody, the Board claim the right to open or destroy goods without liability, or even to dispose of them as they will. All such claims could be challenged under the statutory provisions as to reasonableness. The limit of liability is also set and may be challenged in view of the fact that a traveller may have no alternative place in which to deposit his possessions. To set an arbitrary limit on loss, attributable to the negligence of the Board, appears to be unreasonable.

The Board no longer seeks to contract out of liability for misdelivery of goods which have been bailed into its custody. Where such is attributable to the negligence of its servants, the Board accepts liability. The Conditions suggest that it is for the owner to prove negligence but under the law of bailment, inability to redeliver the goods by a bailee is prima facie evidence of negligence: *Alexander v Railway Executive (1951).*[40]

6. BYELAWS

Contractual terms by themselves have never proved sufficient to cover all the activities which are involved in the running of a railway. Parliament recognised this and granted powers to the railways to make byelaws to meet the need. Most recently, the 1962 Act empowers the BRB to make byelaws for the regulation of the use or working of the railway, the regulation of travel upon it, and the maintenance of good order. Specific powers are made available to the Board to deal with such matters as the evasion of fares, smoking and other nuisances, the prevention of interference with, or obstruction of, the permanent way. Such byelaws as were in existence before 1962 are preserved in accordance with section 67 of the 1962 Act. Once such byelaws have been made and confirmed in the prescribed manner, they become law and apply to all concerned. It was no longer necessary to display them on special notice boards, instead copies were kept available at booking offices for consultation by those who wished to see them. This has now been repealed and it is sufficient to keep a copy at BRB Head quarters.

At one time, the byelaws contained no provisions as to arrest for their breach. Now any person who fails to give his name and address to a constable who, having reasonable cause to believe that a byelaw has been broken, requests it, may be arrested. The same applies to any person who refuses to leave any railway premises or vehicle when called upon to do so.

The byelaws create a wide range of offences. These include wilfully damaging railway property; interfering with vehicles, lifts or automatic doors; spitting; entering a train in a state of intoxication; throwing articles out of train windows; smoking in prohibited places; using obscene or offensive language; behaving in a riotous, disorderly or indecent manner; molesting passengers; trespass on railway premises; entering or leaving a train when it is in motion.

A special offence of misusing a communication cord was established by statute as early as 1868. Today, it is covered by the British Railways Act 1977, section 13. The prosecution must establish intent to misuse, which the defendant may counter by pleading just cause. The test is whether a reasonable man, hearing the explanation by the accused, would accept that such a person's action, viewed subjectively, is a good defence.

Offences against railway byelaws are prosecuted before the criminal courts. Penalties are fixed under the terms of the byelaws which may duplicate other legislation. So, for example, the Regulation of Railways Act 1889 imposes penalties for avoidance of fares, as do the byelaws. Some byelaws make regulations but provide no sanctions for their breach, e.g. entering carriages as passengers are trying to leave.

7. INTERNATIONAL TRAVEL

International agreements on rail travel across national boundaries have long been in existence. Britain did not become a party to such agreements until after the Second World War. The two Berne Conventions were signed on behalf of the UK in 1952. That which covers the carriage of passengers is entitled the Convention Internationale Concernant le Transport des Voyageurs et des Baggages par Chemin de Fer (CIV). The original CIV was replaced by another in 1961. None of these agreements was incorporated into English law. Instead, BRB were given the option of including their terms within Standard Conditions on a voluntary basis, which was accepted.

The 1961 Convention was revised in 1970, but, once again, it was not included in municipal legislation in the UK. In 1970 also, an *Additional CIV* was passed and included in the Carriage by Railway Act 1972. The odd result was that the BRB observed the CIV by voluntary incorporation into standard form contracts of carriage and the Additional CIV as required by statute.

The provisions of the Conventions only apply where passengers are carried on international carriage documents and where travel is exclusively over lines listed by the agreements. Such lines are listed and updated by the Convention Central Office in Berne.

In 1980, a fundamental revision of the Conventions was undertaken. The result was that a single Convention, covering freight as well as passengers and their luggage, was agreed. The new agreement is the Convention Relative aux Transports Internationeaux Ferroviaires (COTIF). The Convention both revises and amalgamates the previous Conventions. The UK ratified COTIF in its entirety. Its introduction was anticipated by the International Conventions Act 1983. Provision was made in section 11(3) for COTIF to become part of English law by Order in Council once the minimum number of nations specified in the Convention, 15, had ratified the agreement. The Order was made 1 May 1985. The Carriage by Railways Act 1972 was repealed. The Uniform Rules (CIV) under Appendix A to COTIF now provide a unified set of rules for the carriage of passengers and registered luggage under international travel documents over the territories of at least two states who have ratified the Convention, provided that carriage is exclusively over lines listed in accordance with the provisions of COTIF.

The rules govern liability of the railways for damage resulting from death, personal injury, or other bodily or mental harm, sustained by a passenger as a result of an accident in the course of international carriage by rail. Hand luggage is also covered but not loss occasioned by delay, whose regulation is left to municipal laws.

Obligations of the carrier

There is a general obligation to carry passengers who present themselves to the carrier, subject to his right to refuse to carry any considered unfit, e.g. an intoxicated person. Such passengers must be in possession of valid through tickets for the journey.

Exemptions

A railway is relieved of liability, or such liability may be reduced in part, where the accident was the result of actions unconnected with the operation of the railway and the carrier could not have avoided or prevented the consequences; or the accident resulted from the fault of the passenger concerned or from his abnormal behaviour; or the accident was caused by a third party and the consequences could not have been avoided by the railway despite the exercise of all due care.

The CIV specifically prohibits any of its rules being excluded by special contracts. Attempts to set lower limits of compensation are also overruled as are efforts to reverse the burden of disproving liability by the carrier.

Actions for compensation for death or injury can only be brought against the railway on whose system the accident occurred. Where an action would lie in this respect, claims may also be made for loss sustained by damage to, or partial loss of, any article which the passenger had with him on his person or as hand luggage. All claims must be in writing.

Compensation

The amount of damages to be awarded are to be fixed in accordance with municipal law. The limits are set in terms of Special Drawing Rights (SDR). The limit for passengers is 70,000 units per person and

700 units per person for luggage. These may be converted into national currencies. The limits are removed where the damage results from the wilful misconduct or gross negligence of the carrier. These categories of wrong doing, as with the term *accident* used in COTIF, are not defined.

Proof of claim is by production of a valid ticket or other evidence. Actions are time-barred in the case of injury to passengers 3 years from the date of the accident. Where claims are made by dependants of deceased persons, such claims must be brought within 3 years of death, or 5 years from the date of the accident, whichever is the earlier.

A claimant in person loses his right of action if he does not present a claim within 3 months of becoming aware of his right to claim, subject to certain exceptions, as where he can show fault of the carrier, delay could not have been avoided by the claimant, or if the carrier learns of the occurrence by other means.

Luggage

The CIV definition is much wider than that used by the BRB. Anything is accepted as *registered luggage* which is contained in trunks, baskets, suitcases, travelling bags and similar receptacles. Unless, that is, it is a prohibited item in the state of the carrier concerned. The railway may examine items for their suitability and may, where appropriate, charge an excess.

The carrier undertakes to deliver the luggage to a person in possession of a valid voucher at the destination to which it has been registered. Under CIV the carrier may be liable for total or partial loss caused by delay. Missing articles are presumed lost if undelivered within 14 days of a request for their delivery. The passenger must establish the value of the items lost and produce a valid luggage registration voucher or other proof of claim.

Contract of carriage

Carriage by rail in the UK is principally governed by the terms of the contract between the *carrier* and the *customer*. This contract is governed by a SFC the terms of which are presently contained in Passengers' Conditions of Carriage issued by BR (BR 25833/2 June 1988) which state in paragraph 74 'these Conditions shall be governed in all respects by English law and any individual bringing an action on these Conditions submits to the exclusive jurisdiction of English courts'. This in turn means that the SFC is subject to statutory provisions designed for consumer protection. That having been said, it remains the case that the Conditions are designed first and foremost for the benefit of the carrier.

Much has been publicised lately in terms of the so called Citizens Charter which has begat little Charters one of which is BRs Passenger Charter. One is tempted to recite lines from Lear - 'a tale told by an idiot, full of sound and fury, signifying nothing.' At best such Charters are an 'opiate for the masses' at worst a sham. They have no force in law, not even enjoying the status of Codes of Practice which at least have evidential standing before the courts. The best hope for the travelling public is that in due course EC law may make the railway system a better and safer form of travel. In the matter of health and safety where EC law is introduced by *qualified majority voting* it is not open to maverick national governments to veto legislation on the grounds, inter alia, that national economic interests must not be harmed.

NOTES

1. Transport Act 1962 s. 43(6).
2. Ibid s. 43 (4)(a).
3. Railways (Road Transport) Act 1928.
4. British Transport Commission (Passenger Charges) Scheme 1952.
5. Transport Act 1962 s. 43(1)(a)
6. Ibid s. 43(7).
7. Transport Act 1968 s. 39.
8. Transport Act 1962 s. 3(1).
9. Railways (Notice of Accidents) Order 1965 SI N 2119.
10. (1865) F & F 504. See also R v Pittwood (1902) 19 TLR 37.
11. *Times* 24 April 1958.
12. Offences Against the Person Act 1861 ss.32-34. Malicious Damage Act 1861 ss.35-36.
13. (1895) 1 QB 944.
14. (1869) LR 4 QB 379.
15. (1958) 1 WLR 346.
16. The Law of Carriage by Inland Transport 4th Edn p. 503.
17. (1949) 2 KB 519.
18. (1952) CLY 2451.

19. (1892) 1 QB 385.
20. British Transport Commission Act 1949 s. 53. Transport Act 1962 s.31(2)(e).
21. Kahn-Freund op cit n16 p. 499.
22. Uniform Rules (CIV) Art 26(1) Appx A to COTIF.
23. Ibid Art 29.
24. (1907) 23 TLR 222.
25. (1888) 21 QBD 220.
26. (1873) 28 LT 271.
27. (1855) 16 CB 179.
28. (1876) 2 ExD 248.
29. (1947) 1 All ER 506.
30. (1941) SC 551.
31. (1949) WN 196.
32. (1944) KB 421.
33. (1875) LR 8 QB 161.
34. (1930) 1 KB 41.
35. (1928) 1 KB 349.
36. (1895) 2 QB 387.
37. (1920) 36 TLR 703.
38. (1888) App Cas 13.
39. (1884) 14 QBD 228.
40. (1951) 2 KB 882.

CHAPTER VIII

Contracts of Passage

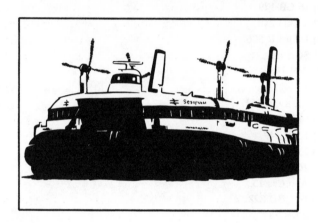

1. WATER TRANSPORT

The potential of waterways as means of communication were realised very early in the history of mankind. For many years, passenger transport was confined to bridging the narrow seas and following river courses. The first contract of passage was, in all probability, in the nature of a ferry service. The activity was recognised in England as one of the *common callings*, the profession of ferryman being of a class which included the innkeeper and the carrier. Later, when bridges had been built and tunnels dug, the trade declined. Modern examples can still be found, usually in the form of *chain* or *floating* bridges such as that which connects Sandbanks with Studland in Dorset.

Since Britain is an island nation, off-shore ferries are needed to connect outlying islands and to join the UK to mainland Europe. The Channel Tunnel will undoubtedly capture a good proportion of the cross-Channel trade, but the sea link will still be maintained, especially with northern Europe and the Iberian peninsular.

By comparison to the early roads, rivers and coastal waters were smooth highways. The value of the inland waterways can be seen from many early petitions to the Crown against the blocking of rivers and the competing claims of millers, fishermen, merchants and carriers. Magna Carta, in 1215, decreed that public waters were the King's Highway open to all his subjects. This was not a new concept, merely a declaration of established principle. It did not stop barriers being built, and statutes appeared ordering them to be removed on pain of fines. There were continuous battles for rights of passage on the Severn and the town of Gloucester was challenged over its imposition of tolls on the river.

A human barrier was created by the watermen who charged high rates for carriage of both goods and passengers. Matters were so bad on the Thames and Medway that legislation was needed to stop the worst excesses. The real barrier was the natural silting which occurred on the rivers. Towns co-operated in clearing the obstructions and sponsored Bills in Parliament for the opening up of new, previously unnavigable, rivers to commercial transport.

The industrial expansion of the late 18th century created a demand for better communication for freight carriers than could be provided by the existing road system. Between 1750 and 1830 some 4,000 miles of canals were constructed in the UK. The Bridgwater canal in Lancashire was built in 1759 to transport coal and heralded a new age in transportation which saw Birmingham rise to prominence as the centre of a great network of *navigation* canals.

Canals were built and primarily used for the movement of freight, but passengers were also carried. By 1792, the Bridgwater canal was earning £1,500 per annum in revenue from this source. Once the railways opened, the canals were doomed to decline. The railway companies bought out the canal owners and thus stifled competition from water carriers. The canals never recovered their lost carrying trade but many are today enjoying a new lease of life as valuable amenities for leisure and recreation.

The railways were, however, unable to buy up the sea. This has remained a highway open to all, subject only to the rights of territorial waters and the rules of navigation secured by international agreements. The main restrictions on its use are the charges for use of specialised terminals and docks. Some costs can be reduced, in the case of the carriage of passengers, by using new forms of transport which require less port facilities than other modes. A prime example being that of the Hovercraft (q.v.).

Steamships

In the same way that steam engines transformed carriage by land, steam-powered ships changed the waterborne trade. They were used first on the inland waterways and on coastal navigation but later, their use revolutionised transmarine services across the world. The earliest patent for a steamship was registered in 1736 but progress was slow and not until 1802 was the use of a steam-driven boat demonstrated successfully in the UK. In that year, the *Charlotte Dundas* displayed her prowess on the Forth-Clyde canal. Early British interests in steamships were centred on the Clyde. The first *steamer* to run a regular service left Glasgow, bound for Greenock, in 1812 with twenty passengers aboard. In 1814, a Clyde ship left for London via the east coast. In 1815, a regular summer service was inaugurated on the Thames between London and Gravesend, the first of many other ventures on the river.

In 1816, a steamer was sold to a French company and became the first such ship to cross the Channel. In 1819, a steam assisted vessel left Georgia and crossed the Atlantic in thirty days. This marked the beginning of a new era for sea travel.

At first, steamships confined themselves to coastal waters and acting as ferries. As they became more sophisticated and safer, they ventured further. Their early development owed much to the tourist trade. Many excursions on the Clyde and the Thames pioneered the way ahead. Such trips were very popular. There was much public demand and some water-ways became crowded with boats. Accidents were not infrequent and the dangers from these new vessels was the subject of a Parliamentary inquiry in 1831.[1]

This revealed that vessels were often not built strongly enough; that they carried too many passengers; their speed raised questions of safety on the waterways. To curb the abuses by carriers, vessels were required by law to be licensed, speed restrictions were imposed for the use of inland waters, and limits were placed on the numbers of passengers who could be carried. Such measures have continued to the present day in respect of vessels used to carry passengers in territorial waters.

The conditions of the roads drove many travellers to use the coastal steamers where it was practicable to journey from one part of the UK to another. In 1880, Arthur Conan Doyle chose to remove his household from Plymouth to Southsea by steamer rather than trust himself to the roads. Where a sea route paralleled a coach road, many passengers chose the sea, especially during the summer months. An added advantage was that there were no tolls to pay, no turnpikes.

The advent of the railways did not have the profound effect on the carriage by water that it had upon the roads. People used the steamers mainly for pleasure and to engage in the new occupation of the Victorian middle classes, tourism. Popular attractions, like the Isle of Wight and the Isle of Man, thrived on the steamer-borne tourist trade. Paddle steamers were crossing to the Isle of Wight until 1950. In addition, the railways served as feeders to the ferries, particularly those crossing the Channel, and to the new transmarine port facilities built to cater for the growing Atlantic routes.

Transmarine travel

The first ship to cross the Atlantic, propelled only by steam, made the voyage in 1838. The inadequacies of paddle propulsion were overcome by the use of screw propellers. In 1843 the SS *Great Britain*, built by Brunel, became the first ship with an iron hull and screw system to be put into service. Today she stands as a tourist attraction in Bristol dock.

The way was now open for commercial expansion, fuelled by the need to communicate with distant parts of the world. The British company Cunard, founded in 1840, took a leading role in the development of transmarine carriage. A regular 14-day service to North America, combining passenger, cargo and mail transport was established, which lasted until the introduction of air travel in the 20th century.

The diesel turbine replaced the steam engine in many ships and extended their range. Until 1956, the number of transatlantic sea crossings was increasing but gradually declined thereafter as turbo-jet aircraft were introduced and the cost of air travel was lowered. No regular passenger shipping lines cater for travellers on the route to North America today. The main terminal at Southampton has been demolished and replaced by a yachting marina. The great *floating hotels* have turned their attention to other forms of income generation.

Cruise liners

In the 1960s, the shipping companies found themselves faced with ever-increasing operating costs and a falling demand for their services. The industry returned to its Victorian roots for a solution. Cruising became the means by which the decline could be at least partially halted. In the 19th century, the Peninsular and Orient Steam Navigation Company (P&O) had become aware of the attraction to tourists of its routes to the East, via the Mediterranean and the Suez Canal.

During the 1920s and 1930s, cruising became popular with the leisured classes. In the 1960s, the task for the shipping lines was to open up the market to a wider audience. In 1963, Cunard took the *Queen Elizabeth* off the North Atlantic run for a 5 day cruise off the Bahamas. This venture proved so successful that her sister ship, the *Queen Mary*, joined her in 1964 and both became used increasingly as floating leisure centres. The experience gained with these two ships led to a new design for the *Queen Elizabeth 2*. She was built not to compete as a carrier in competition with the airlines but as a leisure and tourist attraction.

Towards the end of their lives, many other former liners were employed on cruising but few were suited to the new role, lacking the refinement and amenities with which to attract tourists. There were some exceptions, P&O's *Canberra* for one, but the needs of this new industry have called for ships to be built as leisure cruise vessels, not adaptations from older designs.

The cruise market has a high appeal with regular sailings provided by P&O and Cunard, together with a number of East European and Scandinavian lines. A development instituted by the tour operators, Clarksons, has shown what can be achieved by combined travel modes. Before the company went out of business in 1974, it had launched the idea of combining flights to the Mediterranean linked to cruises on low price, locally-based, ships in the area. For a while, Thomson Holidays took over the idea but did not develop it. It has, however, become a feature of some of the longer-established companies, allowing passengers to fly out to, or back from, cruise ships, thus maximising their available sea time with shorter on-board packages for the tourist.

Ferry services

Thirty years ago, it was not possible to drive a car on board a sea ferry. Today they are commonplace and have proved a marked success story for the shipping companies, particularly on the short European sea routes. Until the 1950s, ferries were operated as miniature passenger liners, many being owned by railway companies. One unique form was the 'Night Train' from London to Paris. This featured the transportation of railway sleeping cars across the Channel as a joint venture between Southern Railway and SNCF French Railways.

The earliest carriage of cars and their passengers was undertaken in 1928 by Townsend, operating from Dover to Calais, but the vehicles were loaded as freight by cranes. In 1953, a Car Ferry Terminal was opened at Dover following a rapid expansion there of the Eastern Docks. In 1965, Townsend introduced the first British 'roll-on, roll-off' ship, the *Free Enterprise II*. At the time serious doubts were registered as to the seaworthiness of such a design. These doubts have come to the fore again following the Zeebrugge disaster and other sinkings. It is likely that legislation will be needed to compel safety standards in an industry which appears to be dragging its feet over ship design.

Many other operators have joined in the competition for the ferry market. Townsend's, having taken control of Thoresen Car Ferries in 1968, were themselves later to become part of P&O. British Rail responded to competitors by offering its *Sealink* services. In addition, they introduced a cross-Channel hovercraft service to compete with the Swedish carriers, Hoverlloyd.

The first hovercraft crossing of the Channel had been made only 9 years earlier in 1959. A remarkable leap forward for this type of craft resulted from very small beginnings by its designer, Christopher Cockerell, on the Isle of Wight.

In 1984, Sealink was *privatised* and sold to Bermuda-based British Ferries Ltd. Many more operators have entered the field in the last 15 years to capitalise on the increase in car ownership and the demand for car space on ships during the tourist season. Since Britain's entry to the EEC, and the relaxation of travel control, many more travellers have been taking short break excursions by car ferry to the continent. By 1980, over 200 ferry services were operating around the coasts of Europe. Many new designs have appeared including *Jumbo* car ferries and larger hydrofoils operating mainly in the Baltic. Some shipping experts believe that the largest of the latter group will be capable of carrying 3,000 passengers on three decks, and travelling at 108 knots, by the end of the century. These developments will call for a re-appraisal of the safety standards in ship design and operation, and for new rules in municipal and international legislation.

2. COMMON LAW

'The contract of carriage of passengers by sea is an ordinary contract for the conveyance of persons. Much of the law governing the contract of passage is the common law that applies to all contracts.'[2] This comment, by a leading authority on Shipping Law, is doubtless true when passage is compared to the specialised world of carriage of goods by sea. This has evolved over many years to meet the particular requirements of those dealing in international cargoes. At the same time, it is also true that the law which governs the vessels which carry goods to a large degree, regulates passenger ships. The cargoes may differ, but the rules which are concerned with the condition of vessels, safety at sea, and the conduct of the master and crew are almost the same.

There are probably no common carriers of passengers by sea today, passengers being carried instead by special contracts whose terms are governed by statute and international agreements. Nevertheless, the standards set by the common law require a high level of safety to be demonstrated by the carrier towards his passengers. He has a duty to see that they are carried in vessels, the safety of which has been assured by the taking of all reasonable care. He will only escape liability if he can show that any loss or injury sustained by those in his charge was the result of causes beyond his control, or that of third parties to whom he lawfully entrusted the maintenance and operation of his vessels. The passenger in a ship is entitled to the same high duty of care under the contract of passage as he is when he is being conveyed in a coach, a plane or a train. More so, perhaps, since *perils of the sea* have long been recognised as requiring special rules particularly in marine insurance.

A shipowner is not obliged to carry passengers, but if he holds himself out to the public as ready to carry those who present themselves in accordance with published conditions, then he owes such persons a duty not to refuse to carry them without good reason. A traveller who makes for a port to take ship for a passage home suffers a severe disadvantage if the carrier refuses to carry him because of some capricious whim or seeks to hold the traveller to ransom for a higher price. If the traveller has already booked passage, the carrier must convey him in accordance with the terms of the contract or be in breach.

To hold such persons to be *public carriers* does not deny them the opportunity to write in standard clauses which will absolve them of liability for delays or cancellations caused by the state of the tide, strikes or other *forces majeur*. 'It is beyond all doubt that the first and most general obligation on the part of public carriers of passengers, whether by land or water, is to carry persons who apply for passage'.[3] The existence of such a *third class* of carrier is not accepted by all authorities[4] but there is no reason why such a class of carrier should not exist in law.

Terms

A shipowner provides a service under the contract of passage which must be carried out with reasonable care and skill. The standard of care in contracts is the same as that in tort. 'It is well established law that it is sufficient if (the supplier) exercises the ordinary skill of an ordinary competent man exercising that particular art': *Bolam v Friern Hospital Management Committee (1957).*[5]

Over the years, the common law has established various rules which are applied to carriage of passengers by sea. These reflect the nature of the contract as being not only for the transportation of the traveller but also for matters arising from the fact that, apart from short journeys, the shipowner must also arrange for food and accommodation for those on board.

There is a requirement that adequate accommodation is provided for the passenger: *Adderley v Cookson (1809)*[6] and that there is regard for the comfort of those on board, at least to the extent of seeing to it that a passenger can get into and out of a berth provided for him: *Andrews v Little (1887)*[7].

Passengers on sea voyages are likely to be accompanied by a greater amount of luggage than is perhaps the case with other forms of carriage. This bespeaks the need to provide reasonable facilities for the stowage of such baggage. Storing it in a vacant toilet where it is damaged does not appear to meet the terms of the contract: *Uppertown v Union Castle Mail SS Co (1902).*[8]

The owner or master of the ship must make reasonable provision for feeding passengers although 'it is not because a man does not get so good a dinner as he might have had, that he is, therefore, to have a right of action against the captain who does not provide all that he ought': *Young v Fewson (1838)*[9]. Unlike passengers in coaches or trains, those on board ship in the middle of the ocean are reliant on the shipowner for the necessities of life. They cannot alight from the ship and seek out other accommodation or an alternative menu. Where the vessel is detained they must needs look to the shipowner or his agents to provide for them. It appears, from older cases that, if a ship is unavoidably detained, there is no action available for diminution, or even deterioration, of provisions or water: *Corbyn v Leader (1833)*.[10] In the changed conditions of modern food storage technology, it is difficult to imagine such a circumstance occurring today. A ship which breaks down at sea should always have enough contingency supplies on board and can summon assistance by radio to be delivered by an air drop if necessary.

In the absence of a valid exemption clause, it would appear that a carrier will be liable to a passenger for injuries sustained for failing to put up weather boards in rough weather: *Austin v B.T.C. (1956)*.[11] Such liability will also attach to a carrier who does not take adequate precautions against injuries caused by the playing of games such as deck quoits: *Glynn v Royal Mail (1955)*.[12]

In the absence of a contractual term, there is no obligation for a ship to carry a doctor. In practice, many of the larger cruise liners do so. At common law there is an implied term that sufficient medicines shall be carried on board to meet the reasonably anticipated needs of passengers.

Deviation and delay

In the case of ferries, it is common practice to exclude liability for failure to adhere to a published timetable and to allow the withdrawal or cancellation of a service which has been advertised. Similarly, other carriers may seek to avoid the consequences of deviation from a route or delay in its completion. If the exemption seeks to deliver a service which is fundamentally different to that for which the passenger has contracted, the term may be struck down as unreasonable.

Where the shipowner has not successfully avoided liability the carrier may be required to pay compensation to a person who has been inconvenienced for reasons which may be reasonably attributed to the breach of contract: *Crane v Tyne Shipping Co Ltd (1897)*.[13] Where a failure to depart on time amounts to a misrepresentation, an exclusion clause may not serve to deny liability: *The Emily (1850)*.[14]

At common law, a carrier is obliged to prosecute a voyage with reasonable despatch such as is allowed by the circumstances of the voyage: *The Melbourne (1853)*.[15] It has long been the practice to modify a contract to allow for contingencies which may affect a voyage.

The first issue is to determine what is the *proper route*. Usually the contract simply stipulates the ports of departure and destination. The route to be followed is that which is set out in the contract and failing this, that which is usual: *Evans v Cunard SS Co (1902)*.[16] In a cruise contract, the ports of call will be set out in the form of an itinerary. In such circumstances it is usual to find a statement to the effect that:

'Tramplines are unable to guarantee that the ship will call at every advertised port or follow every part of the advertised route. Tramplines reserve to themselves and/or the Master the absolute right to decide whether to omit any such port, whether to call at additional ports and whether to deviate from the advertised route. Provided such decision is reasonably taken Tramplines shall be under no obligation or liability to the Passenger.'

Deviation from the route is also allowable for such matters as have long been the concern of mariners - the saving of life at sea, avoidance of imminent dangers, to effect repairs to the ship at a port of refuge, even if, in this last case, this was a breach of the warranty of seaworthiness.

Seaworthiness

In every contract for carriage by sea, there is an implied term that the shipowner will provide a ship as fit and seaworthy as care and skill can render it. To be seaworthy, a vessel 'must have that degree of fitness which an ordinary, careful and prudent owner would require his vessel to have at the commencement of her voyage, having regard to all the probable circumstances of it': *McFadden v Blue Star Line (1905)*.[17]

The ship must be in a good state of repair, sufficiently fuelled and ballasted and manned by an efficient crew. Seaworthiness covers more than simply whether a vessel is watertight. The degree of seaworthiness required will be decided in the light of the type of voyage and the cargo carried. A high standard will be required where the 'cargo' consists of passengers.

The ship must be in a fit condition at the start of the voyage and, if repairs are necessary during the journey, they must be carried out by the shipowner where it is reasonable for him so to do. Failure to discharge this duty will amount to negligence on his part.

In the ordinary course of events, it is for the plaintiff to prove *unseaworthiness*. As with other forms of carriage this could work against him. Here, again, the law will apply the maxim *res ipsa loquitur*, it being for the defendant to disprove his liability.

The shipowner is only liable for defects which a careful and reasonable examination would reveal and will not be held liable for *latent* defects. Where he has taken delivery of a new vessel he may be able to rely on the fact that he has dealt with a reputable builder. But in addition, a prudent, reasonable purchaser would be expected to have carried out the precaution of having a marine survey of the ship. This has not always proved sufficient. Where a *loss* is involved, the use of a reputable builder and marine surveyor, both using state of the art technology may not be enough to save the shipowner from liability: *Amoco Cadiz (1984).*[18]

This level of responsibility was imposed by an American court. In England, the level demanded in respect of new ships may not be so burdensome upon a shipowner: *Angliss & Co v P&O (1927).*[19] However, liability will attach to him for the negligence of even the most carefully selected ship repairer: *Riverstone Meat Co v Lancashire Shipping Co Ltd (1961).*[20]

Negligence

A shipowner, even a common carrier, is not, nor ever has been an *insurer* of passengers' safety. In the absence of a special contract, the carrier's liability will depend upon fault. In most contracts, carriers will include terms to the effect that they will not accept liability for the death, injury or sickness of any passenger, or in respect of the loss or damage to luggage or goods belonging to, or travelling with, any such person unless the same is due to the negligence of the carrier, the Master, crew, servants or agents of such carrier.

Because accidents at sea can so often result in much more serious consequences than those on land, it is not surprising that shipowners should seek wherever possible to limit their liability. Even where they do this successfully for themselves, it may not be sufficient to protect others acting on behalf of the owner unless they are specifically, and unequivocally, named in the contract: *Adler v Dickson and Another (1955)*.[21] Since this case, all such contracts of carriage have included a *Himalaya* clause, the name deriving from that of the ship on board which Mrs Adler suffered her injury. Such a clause had been used much earlier to protect the Master from liability for negligent navigation resulting in a collision and the loss overboard and drowning of a passenger: *Haigh v Royal Mail Steamship Co (1883)*.[22] In both cases such exclusions would today fail to escape the Unfair Contract Terms Act, insofar as the negligence caused death or personal injury to the plaintiff.

Exclusions using the *Himalaya* clause can operate to protect third parties if the exclusion is reasonable. The use of a clause denying liability for loss sustained by *any cause whatsoever* would not pass the test today: *Budd v P&O (1969)*.[23]

Even where the exclusion is reasonable, it must still be brought to the attention of the party against whom it is being asserted before the contract is concluded: *The Dragon (1979)*.[24] This applies equally where the exclusion is contained in standard conditions of carriage to which a passenger is referred in a ticket: *Williamson v North of Scotland and Orkney & Shetland Steam Navigation Co (1916)*.[25] Terms and conditions not brought to the attention of the passenger prior to or at the time of making the contract cannot be part of the contract: *Hollingworth v Southern Ferries Ltd (1977)*.[26]

If a passenger suffers loss or injury due to the negligence of another ship, e.g. in a collision, then that shipowner will be vicariously liable for the actions of his servants. If both the carrier and the other vessel are to blame, then they are jointly and severely liable.

Passage money

If there is no provision in the contract as to time of payment for passage money, then it falls to be paid at the accustomed time, e.g. subject to the usage of the port. If the money is paid in advance, and the ship is lost before the commencement of the voyage, the money must be refunded: *Greeves v West India & Pacific SS Co Ltd (1869)*.[27]

Where payment for passage is due at the commencement of a voyage and it is not made conditional upon the successful completion of the same, then even if the money is to be paid at the place of destination it is due, notwithstanding that the vessel and all on board are lost during the voyage: *Moffat v East India Co (1808).*[28]

Where passage monies remain unpaid, the Master has a lien on the passenger's luggage against payment: *Wolf v Summers (1811).*[29]

3. STATUTORY PROVISIONS

A series of statutes, the Merchant Shipping Acts 1894-1984, regulate shipping operations. They comprehensively cover many aspects of carriage by sea.

A ship's Master had absolute control over passengers at common law, he could confine them on board or cause them to be removed. Such powers are now re-inforced by statute.[30] In particular, the Merchant Shipping Act 1894 allows the Master of a *passenger steamer* to arrest persons guilty of offences. These include being drunk and disorderly, molesting fellow passengers, evading the payment of passage money, interfering with the operation of the ship, or impeding or molesting crew members. Such persons are liable upon summary conviction to fines.[31]

The term *passenger steamer* includes every ship, British or foreign, propelled by any form of mechanical power and carrying passengers to, from, or between any places in the UK. It does not include ferries worked by chains or similar methods. 'Passenger' includes anyone on board except the Master, crew or owner and the latter's family and servants.

Safety

The Master of any passenger ship must render passenger returns to any person designated by the Secretary of State. Overloading of ships can cause serious safety hazards. The Zeebrugge ferry disaster drew severe criticism from the Court of Inquiry for failure to keep proper records of those on board. In November 1987, a Sealink ferry turned back to Boulogne after members of the seamen's union reported the ship as carrying more than 200 passengers over its capacity.[32] The dangers were vividly demonstrated when the ferry *Dona Paz* sank in the Philippines in December 1987 with the loss of approximately 1,400 lives. The precise number will never be known. It may even have exceeded that of the *Titanic* which sank in 1912 with the loss of 1,500 lives.

A passenger vessel carrying more than 12 passengers must be

surveyed at least once a year. Only such ships as are exempted by the Secretary of State may proceed to sea on any voyage or excursion without a certificate of survey.[33] Where a certificate is issued, it is valid for a year and must be displayed on board. Under the regulations, ships which are either constructed to carry passengers or which habitually or substantially operate for such purpose must be examined: *Duncan v Graham (1951)*.[34]

Any vessel attempting to operate without a certificate can be detained by a customs officer and the Master fined. It is an offence for the owner or Master to carry more passengers than the certificate allows on penalty of a standard fine and an additional fine for every person carried in excess of the number prescribed. The falsification of a certificate renders the offender liable to an unlimited fine and/or imprisonment not exceeding 2 years.

In addition to a passenger certificate, those vessels registered in the UK require to have a general or qualified safety certificate. Ships registered elsewhere qualifying as *convention ships* must have an equivalent document.[35] A condition of all such certificates, wherever issued, will be that *convention ships* must not carry passengers on more than one deck below the waterline.

In the time which has elapsed since Zeebrugge it appears evident that the safety of passengers and crew is not the first priority in the design of ferries. Almost six years after the disaster which cost so many lives the recommendations in safety for roll-on roll-off ferries have gone largely unheeded. Still today perhaps as many as 9 out of 10 do not fulfil the criteria. Admittedly, the cost of compliance is significant but companies do not seem to regard refitting of their ships as urgent - as urgent as that faced from competition with the Channel Tunnel for example. No voyage can ever be completely safe but in weighing the cost of human lives against the chance of profit the latter seems to carry more weight in the industry.

Examination of such vessels still reveals inadequate safety procedures, old fashioned equipment and confusing signs. This despite the report by Lloyds Register for the Department of Transport commissioned after Zeebrugge which revealed that in terms of passenger deaths for each unit of distance or time travelled, ferries were one of the most dangerous forms of public transport. It appears that not until the year 2004 will the requirements as to the naval architectural design of ferries be enforced by law in the UK.

The tardiness of national governments generaly is reprehensible at home and abroad as is the reluctance of the International Maritime Organisation to be pro-active in the matter. There are some signs that the UK government as a Port State Authority may not wait for the co-operation of fellow IMO members but may unilaterally demand that ships wishing to use British ports meet UK standards. Yet such standards as have so far been implements on British ferries have only scratched the surface for what is required.

4. INTERNATIONAL CARRIAGE

As with other forms of transport, the carriage of passengers by sea is the subject of international agreements. The Athens Convention was signed in 1974 and, under section 16 of the Merchant Shipping Act 1979, that Convention was to become part of English law on a day to be appointed. The Convention, reproduced in Schedule 3 to the Act, became applicable to all contracts made after 1 January 1981.[36]

In the UK, the Convention applies to both international voyages and those made entirely within territorial waters with no intermediate port of call outside the UK. The Convention had limited application until sufficient states ratified its terms. This was effected on 28 April 1987. Henceforward, the terms apply where a voyage involves calls at ports of at least two convention states.

The Convention allows limits to be placed on the levels of compensation for death, personal injury, or damage to luggage. The Unfair Contract Terms Act makes provision for such limits not to be a contravention of its provisions.[37] However, there is no application of the Convention to breaches of other contract terms. Actions may be maintained for disappointment, inconvenience, or distress where the conditions in which a passenger is carried do not meet accepted standards. Terms which seek to render a service substantially different from those contracted for will still be caught by the 1977 Act. A plaintiff in any action must show that the matter in issue occurred during the period of carriage.

Duration of carriage

The period covered by the contract of carriage is between embarkation and disembarkation. It does not include anything which occurs at a terminal building or on the quay side. It will include transfer from the ship by tender where this is included in the contract. Luggage is

146

covered as soon as the carrier takes it into his charge. Often it is transferred to the carrier some time before embarkation.

Luggage does not include animals or items shipped under a bill of lading. Liability for loss includes loss or damage to items resulting from failure to redeliver them within a reasonable time of the ship's arrival. Delay caused by industrial disputes is exempted from this rule.

The rules of the Convention relate to international carriage. This is defined as where points of departure and destination are in two different states, and round trips (cruises) to and from the same port, provided there is at least one port of call in another state.

Limitation

Limits of liability under the Convention are expressed in terms of Special Drawing Rights (SDR). Where loss of life or personal injury are concerned an additional Convention on the Limitation of Liability for Maritime Claims 1976 introduced a simplified regime for claims. This London Convention came into force in December 1986.

The Convention will apply only where the passenger is notified that he is being carried under its terms, e.g. on the carriage documents. It must also tell him that in most cases liability is limited and that claims for damage must be notified in writing to the carrier. Where loss or damage is caused, inter alia, by wreck, collision, defect in the ship, and is in the nature of personal injury or loss or damage to luggage in the custody of the passenger, the fault or neglect of the carrier, his servants or agents is presumed. It is for the carrier to discharge the burden of proof. Where the loss is of money or valuables, the carrier will not be held liable unless such items were delivered into the carrier's keeping.

A carrier may agree to higher levels of compensation than those set by the Convention but he may not set lower limits or contract out of liability. He will lose the limits set if it is proved that the damage resulted from an act or omission of the carrier done with intent to cause such injury, or recklessly and with knowledge that such damage would probably result.

Deliberate actions will be rare and *recklessness* difficult to prove. It involves a state of mind which accepts the risk knowing that injury of the type which results is probable. Such a situation could be envisaged where the Master of a ship proceeds at full speed in fog with her radar equipment switched on but not continuously monitored: *The Lady Gwendoline (1965).*[38]

The Zeebrugge disaster

On the 6 March 1987, the cross Channel ferry, *Herald of Free Enterprise* sank shortly after leaving the Belgian port. She was overloaded, had her bow doors open, rapidly took on water, and capsized with the loss of some 190 lives.

The owners, P&O Ferries, relied on the limits of the Athens Convention. Under the provisions of the Athens rules, the shipowner could limit liability only if he showed he was not at fault. The London Convention requires that the shipowner, or those acting on his behalf, must be shown by the plaintiffs to have acted recklessly and with knowledge that the damage caused would probably result. It also sets global limits for compensation as a 'fund' rather than individual claim limits.

The formal inquiry into the incident was conducted by a Commissioner of Wrecks and two Master Mariners sitting as assessors. They found that the loss of the ship was caused by serious negligence on the part of the Master. His Master's Certificate was suspended for one year and his later appeal against this suspension was rejected by the High Court. The Court severely criticised his conduct as below acceptable standards.[39] Negligence does not amount to recklessness for the purpose of setting aside the limits of the Convention.

5. HOVERCRAFT

A hovercraft is a vehicle designed to be supported, when in motion, wholly or partly by air expelled from the vehicle to form a cushion of which the boundaries include the ground, water, or other surface beneath the vehicle.[40] The Athens Convention excludes them from the classification of *ship*. One authority refers to them as 'monsters, partaking of the features of ships, aircraft and land vehicles'.[41]

The provisions as to carriage of passengers and baggage by hovercraft is governed by the same regime as for carriage by air.[42] All such vehicles used in the UK, with few exceptions, must be registered and carry an assigned mark. They may not be operated without the issue of an appropriate safety certificate issued by the Civil Aviation Authority. The vehicles may be inspected by the Civil Aviation Authority at any reasonable time. Certificates, which are renewable annually, may be suspended or varied at any time. They are issued as passenger, cargo or special by classification.

Operation

No vehicle may be operated for reward in the UK without a permit in connection with any trade or business. Each craft must have a designated captain for any journey and carry a full complement of trained crew. The captain must ensure that the vehicle is properly loaded and secured prior to departure and that it is in a fit condition. He must also ensure that, having regard to available information as to the route and the weather, the journey can be made safely. Each craft in use must carry first aid equipment of good quality sufficient in quantity for those carried.

The captain must keep operational records and log all accidents and casualties. The operator must keep a record of safety drills. Any authorised person must be allowed access to the records at reasonable times. The Secretary of State may suspend any certificate, licence, approval, permission or other document as a result of inspection reports made on the craft or their documentation, pending the results of any inquiry which may be ordered.[43] Contravention of the regulations by captain or operator can lead to a fine or imprisonment.

Carriage

The carrier is liable for death or personal injury of a passenger during passage, including entering and leaving the craft. He is also liable for luggage lost or damaged in transit.[44] Defences to claims by passengers are confined to contributory negligence on the part of the plaintiff and that the carrier took all reasonable measures to avoid the damage, or that it was impossible to take such measures.

The carrier may limit his liability for injury to passengers and for hand luggage. He is further entitled to limit his liability for baggage taken into his charge,[45] but will lose his defences, and the limits set for compensation, if he, his servants or agents are shown to have been guilty of acts or omissions with intent to cause damage, or recklessly and with knowledge that damage of the nature sustained would probably have resulted. Employees and agents are entitled to the same defences and limits as the carrier. Vehicles carried on board a hovercraft are not treated as baggage for the purposes of limiting liability, they are subject to a separate limitation.

6. COMBINED TRANSPORT

Where there is a combination of travel modes, e.g. rail/sea, road/sea, by public transport, the rail or road element is covered by the appropriate carriage rules, e.g. COTIF. The CIV rules in Annex A to COTIF are very similar in the case of hovercraft.

During the carriage by sea, the Athens rules prevail, except where the injury to a passenger occurs when the person is in, alighting from, or entering, a public vehicle which has been taken on board ship.

The combined transport rules only apply where there is a single contract of carriage covering all legs of a journey. When a traveller takes a coach, or buys an ordinary rail ticket and arranges a separate contract for the sea leg, then the Athens Convention will apply only to that part of the journey.

NOTES:

1. British Doc.1831 (335) VIII/1.
2. Shipping Law. Chorley & Giles p.327.
3. The Law of Carriers. J. Angell.
4. Law of Carriage by Inland Transport. O. Kahn-Freund p. 452 n.11.
5. (1957) 2 All ER 118 at 121.
6. (1809) 2 Camp 15.
7. (1887) 3 TLR 544 CA.
8. (1902) 19 TLR 123.
9. (1838) 8 C & P 55.
10. (1833) 6 C & P 26.
11. (1956) 2 L1 106.
12. (1955) 2 L1 21.
13. (1897) 13 TLR 172.
14. (1850) 7 LT 201.
15. (1853) 7 LT 183.
16. (1902) 18 TLR 374.
17. (1905) 1 KB 697 at 706.
18. (1984) 2 L1 304.
19. (1927) 2 KB 456.
20. (1961) 1 A11 ER 495.
21. (1955) 1 QB 158.
22. (1883) 52 LJKB 640.
23. (1969) 2 L1 70.

24. (1979) 1 L1 257.
25. (1916) SC 554.
26. (1977) L1 70.
27. (1869) 3 Mar LC 255.
28. (1808) East 468.
29. (1811) 2 Camp 631.
30. Merchant Shipping Act 1970 s 79.
31. Merchant Shipping Act 1894 s 287.
32. The *Guardian* 2 November 1987.
33. Merchant Shipping Act 1894 s 271: Merchant Shipping Act 1964 s 17(1).
34. (1951) 1 KB 68.
35. Merchant Shipping (Safety Convention) Act 1949.
36. The Carriage of Passengers and their Luggage by Sea (Interim Provisions) Order 1980 SI 1092.
37. s 28.
38. (1965) P 294.
39. The *Guardian* 21 December 1987.
40. Hovercraft Act 1968 s 4(1).
41. Shipping Law. Chorley & Giles p. 337.
42. Hovercraft (Civil Liability) Order 1979 SI 305.
43. Hovercraft (General) Order 1972 SI 674.
44. Hovercraft (Civil Liability) Order 1986 SI 1305.
45. Ibid Art 22.

CHAPTER IX

Travel By Air

1. THE PIONEERS

Carriers by air have no track to maintain, no roads to repair. The air, like the sea, is a free way. At the same time, the operating costs of aircraft are high. Airports require a great deal of space in which to operate with good access to transport feeder systems which bring their customers to them. The outstanding characteristic of air travel is speed and this has made it the best medium for long haul routes. While cargo is carried, the airlines are unique amongst carriers in that they were developed primarily to transport people.

The development of air travel has been remarkably swift since the first powered flight took place in 1903. In 1976, *Concord* entered full passenger service with flights at supersonic speeds. This European venture serves to emphasise the part played by its national carriers in the development of air transportation.

The first scheduled passenger service was flown by the company which is now Lufthansa. Internal flights in Germany began in 1919, the experience of military flying both there and in England was valuable to the pioneer carriers.

In England the first *commercial* flights were three seater tourist trips over Blackpool in 1919. In three months these 'joy rides' carried over 10,000 paying passengers. They flew daily without incident, prompting regular 'commuter' routes from Manchester to Southport and Blackpool. In July 1919 the first flight from London to Paris was made. Air Transport and Travel Limited (AT&T) used a converted light bomber to carry one passenger from a field close to what is now Heathrow International Airport. In 1920, the Dutch carriers KLM began flights from Amsterdam to London. Three quarters of the passengers on these early flights were tourists.

In 1920, AT&T encountered financial difficulties and closed. The high overheads and lack of revenue from tourist flights alone saw other companies encounter similar difficulties. Governments in European countries realised the merit in assisting their carriers to survive but not until 1921 was the pressure sufficient in England to produce some small measure of government assistance. Instead, smaller airlines amalgamated with the result that by 1924 one *National Carrier* had emerged, Imperial Air Transport. In return for a £1 million start up grant, and a promise of a further £1 million payable over the next 10 years, the company undertook to fly only British-made aircraft on regular flights. As Imperial Airways, the company survived until 1940 when its operations were taken over by the British Overseas Airways Corporation (BOAC).

The new carriers

The government-subsidised Imperial Airways dominated the overseas routes. Internal communication was developed largely on the initiative of the rail carriers. In 1934, the four main railway companies joined up with Imperial to produce a considerable net-work of domestic flights. At the same time, a consortium of operators grouped together to operate as *British Airways* with a subsidy from the government on certain European routes. By this time, the government had become very interested in air travel and the Maybury Report of 1937 recommended a scheme of licensing for economic public services. In 1938, the Cadman Report was critical of operators generally. The result was legislation which effectively *nationalised* most of Imperial's business together with that of the umbrella organisation, British Airways, creating a public corporation - BOAC[1]. The process of public ownership was completed with the setting up of British European Airways in 1946[2]. These two corporations dominated the market with smaller private carriers having a very small share.

Despite public ownership of the major carriers there was no coherent government policy for air transport. Eventually, an inquiry was launched in 1969 which produced the 'Edwards Report'. It made recommendations for civil aviation based on economic fares; a mixed economy of public/private carriers; the merger of BOAC/BEA; the foundation of a major 'second force' airline; a better system for licensing private enterprises; a unified system of air traffic control then being shared between the Air Transport Licensing Board (ATLB), the Board of Trade, and the Air Registration Board. These major proposals were given statutory effect by the Civil Aviation Act 1971. Out of the merger of BOAC/BEA came British Airways (BA). The second force carrier was created in the private sector from an amalgamation of British United Airways and British Caledonian (BCal). Air Traffic regulation was made the responsibility of the newly created Civil Aviation Authority (CAA).[3]

2. PUBLIC CONTROL

The CAA was established as a body corporate. Its constitution and functions are regulated by statutory provisions[4]. It is not regarded as a servant or agent of the Crown but all of its members are appointed by the Secretary of State. It belongs to that amorphous grouping of organisations known by the acronym *quango*. These bodies are characterised 'by specialisation of function, varying degrees of autonomy, and whole or partial exemption from the normal processes of accountability to Parliament, through Ministers'[5]. In law the CAA is classified as a 'tribunal' and as such comes under the supervisory regulation of the Council of Tribunals[6].

The CAA has very extensive supervisory powers granted under statutory authority:[7]

1. The licensing of air transport and of the provision of accommodation in aircraft.

2. Air navigation control.

3. Operation of airfields.

4. Registration of aircraft.

5. Airworthiness of aircraft and safety of air navigation.

6. Air Traffic control.

7. Certification of air operators.

8. Licensing of aircrews and airfields.

9. Prosecution of offenders.

It is required to exercise its functions in such a way as will ensure that British airlines provide air transport services which satisfy all substantial categories of public demand at the lowest cost, consistent with a high standard of safety and an economic return to efficient operators on the sums invested in providing those services[8].

Under the 1971 Act, which established the Authority, it was required to ensure that at least one British carrier not controlled by the British Airways Board (BAB) had the opportunity to participate in providing air services. This caveat was replaced, in the 1982 Act, by a vague generalisation requiring only that the reasonable interests of users of air transport services should be furthered.

The independence of the CAA may be judged in the light of the powers which the Secretary of State has to give it written *guidance* in the performance of its duties[9]. Under the 1971 Act, such power could not be exercised unless it had been approved by resolution of each of the Houses of Parliament. This safeguard was repealed in 1982. The CAA must now act in accordance with any direction given to it by the Secretary of State.

Air transport licensing

As early as 1911, statutory powers were created to control the overflying of aircraft so as to protect the public from danger.[10] Further measures for air safety were taken and consolidated into the Air Navigation Act 1920. A licensing system for inland flights was introduced in 1938 only to be revoked the following year. It was left to the public monopoly carriers to regulate their own flights and the Air Transport Advisory Council had ad hoc powers with regard to private flights.

Independent carriers were allowed to provide scheduled flights by the Civil Aviation (Licensing) Act 1960. It was stated, by the then Minister, that it was the intention of the Government 'to establish an independent authority to whom all airline operators can apply on an equal footing for licences to run regular air services'.[11] The ATLB was established by the 1960 Act.

The ATLB controlled all flights 'for reward or in connection with any trade or business'. No aircraft could be flown without an Air Operator's Certificate (AOC) and an Air Service Licence (ASL). The regulations applied to all UK registered aircraft operating anywhere in the world. Foreign aircraft required permission of the Minister before they might embark or discharge passengers or cargo in the UK.

The AOC ensured that operators were competent in the provision of public transport but it did not authorise the holder to go into the business of providing air transport. For this he would need an ASL. With few minor exceptions, an ASL was a prerequisite for all scheduled and charter services, provided by aircraft registered in the UK, and for certain foreign aircraft. This effectively stripped BOAC and BEA of their monopoly over scheduled services. A carrier needed an ASL for the particular service he wished to provide. An ASL was not needed for Charter flights, e.g. where passengers were carried in an aircraft whose capacity was at the exclusive disposal of one person and provided that none of the passengers paid a separate fare. The ATLB enjoyed almost complete discretion in the granting of ASLs. Appeals against its decisions lay to the Minister of Aviation. The criteria for the granting of an ASL were the fitness of the applicant; satisfactory insurance for liability; need and demand for the service proposed.

Demand was to be considered in the light of existing licensed services and tariffs; the possibility of duplication; the likelihood that there would be a 'material diversion of traffic' from existing or proposed services.

Aircraft which operated without either AOL or ASL, or were in breach of the terms under which they were granted, faced prosecution. In 1971, the powers of the ATLB were assumed by the CAA.

The CAA used the powers which it inherited from the ATLB to give route preference to the public corporation which dominated air transport, BA. The 'second force' carrier, BCal, was never allowed to compete successfully because the government introduced zoning in the allocation of routes. BCal were relegated to a complementary rather than a competitive role. The North American routes were allocated almost exclusively to BA and BCal had to make do with Latin America. In 1979, BCal and a few of the smaller carriers were allowed to compete in the more lucrative market across the North Atlantic and a price war began.

British Airways Board

BAB was set up in 1971 to operate the new public corporation. It was given wide powers to provide air services of all descriptions, including air charters, and was deemed to be independent, but strings attached it to the government as they did the CAA. In 1979, the incoming Government was pledged to a policy of *deregulation* of transport. As part of this policy, the property, rights, liabilities and obligations of the BAB were, under the provisions of the Civil Aviation Act 1980, vested in British Airways plc. Shares were sold to the public with a preferential holding retained by the Crown. A public monopoly was, at a stroke, replaced by a private one. BCal and the smaller companies immediately began to experience difficulties in competition. BA had held on to its large charter division, British Airtours, and many of the charter airlines, most of whom were associated with the major tour operators, recognised the dangers to them. In 1987 the predatory nature of BA was fully revealed in the take over bid for BCal. No longer shackled as a public corporation, the monopoly carrier could seek to further eliminate competition.

After much public opposition to the proposed *merger*, the matter was referred to the Monopolies and Mergers Commission. The Commission felt unable to block the proposal but a rival bid was entered almost immediately by Scandinavian Airlines System (SAS). Both they and BA gave as their reasons for takeover the need to compete in Europe with their rivals and to beat off the threat from the US megacarriers.

This new offer was referred to the *independent* forum of the CAA for it to decide whether or not the SAS bid would constitute foreign control of a British airline.[12] In the light of a modified bid by SAS, the CAA agreed that this feared foreign domination would not materialise. Since there was no right of appeal from this decision, BA used the device of requesting that all BCal's ASLs be revoked. The CAA was obliged to consider such a request under the 1971 and 1980 Acts. The effect was to depress BCal's advance bookings and to cause SAS to consider that it might be buying in to an airline with nowhere to fly.

This gave BA a chance to make an *improved* offer for BCal shares, accompanied by heavy hints that if the CAA did not revoke BCal's RSLs, the Minister would do so when BA exercised the right of appeal from a CAA decision to the Secretary of State. The writing was already on the wall for BCal after the CAA proposals for route redistribution had not been approved by the Minister. The result is that BA will dominate the world's two busiest international airports, Heathrow and Gatwick. The Air Transport Users Committee, and other consumer groups, await the outcome of the expanding monopoly of BA. The charter carriers are already concerned with the threat of the Ministry of Transport to *evict* their flights from Gatwick to make way for additional scheduled routes. The few remaining small scheduled operators fear that BA will use its powers of membership on airport committees to squeeze them out of the two main airports too, by manipulation of the allocation of runway space. They also see this as but a short step to eliminating them from the larger provincial airports, combined with unfair pressure on fares and buy-out tactics, and are concerned that BA wants to eliminate all but a few marginal services and control domestic routes and those to Europe. It seems that a government-supported takeover of BCal could be repeated in the case of, say, British Midland or Air Europe. The history of UK air services seems to be one of monopoly, whether public or private.

The recent unsavoury activities of British Airways in attempting to undermine the business of competitor Virgin Atlantic has seen a call for the DTI to examine BA's commercial practices. The episode does little to reassure *consumers* that legalised private monopolies work in the public interest.

3. NON-SCHEDULED SERVICES

The Air Corporations Act 1949 defined a scheduled flight as 'one of a series of journeys which are undertaken between the same two places and which together amount to a systematic service operated in such manner that the benefits thereof are available to members of the public from time to time seeking to take advantage of it'.[13]

Until 1960, the statutory carriers, BOAC and BEA, had a monopoly of such business and it now appears to be a de facto private monopoly for BA.

Pre-1960, certain operations in the nature of *tours*[14] were exempted from the need to hold RSLs. Some operators sought to use this to evade the provisions of the 1949 Act: *Ackroyd's Air Travel v D.P.P. (1950)*,[15] and faced fines or imprisonment as principals or accessories. A popular method was the formation of *clubs* for whom planes were chartered on a regular basis: *D.P.P. v Milbanke Tours Ltd (1960)*.[16] The passing of the 1960 Act rendered such practices obsolete.

In place of the previous restrictions, the 1960 Act requires an aircraft above a certain weight, registered in the UK, to hold an AOC if public transport is to be undertaken. In addition, both schedules and charter carriers require ASLs.

The proliferation of *clubs* and *affinity groups* in the 1960s attracted the tour operators who were constructing packages for their customers. The charter market appealed to them more than the high cost block booking of seats on scheduled flights. Charterers were also able to operate *on demand* and unlike scheduled flights, carriers could *consolidate* their flight by switching passengers to other planes in order to fill space more economically. Such *consolidation* often includes switching airports as well as planes and has been the subject of complaint from package tourists.

The idea of charters stems from the well tried practice of *charter parties* in the sea-carrying trade. Ships were originally chartered to a carrier by voyage, later these became *time* charters which were cheaper. A ship could be chartered with or without a crew.

Tour operators also realised the utility of such arrangements as it was a short step from this for them to operate their own aircraft and lease spare capacity to others seeking flights to the same destinations. In this way, tour operators could guarantee seats to their own customers and sell off surpluses at a profit. The trade was the saviour of many small carriers who are now more concerned than ever by the activities of BA.

With the rise of charters operated by tour operators, there was the increased risk of the dangers to tourists of collapse in the case of companies which over reached their resources. Since 1972, the CAA has required any tour operator who intends to run tours abroad, whether by charter or scheduled flights, to hold an Air Travel Organiser's Licence (ATOL).[17] The Authority considers the fitness of the applicant - although lack of experience is no bar - and his financial standing. It will require such a person to have some form of bonding in order to protect customers from the failure of the operator to meet his obligations. Such a licence is renewable annually and may be restricted in various details.

An airline is not required to hold an ATOL, nor is a travel agent who is only selling on behalf of an airline or a tour operator who himself possesses one. An operator who does not sell tickets to the public, but only to others in the trade, also requires an ATOL: *Jet Travel Ltd v Slade Travel Agency Ltd (1983).*[18]

If the CAA refuses an applicant, he may appeal to the County Court. If he is successful, the CAA must grant the licence. For offences in connection with licences, a person is liable to fine, or imprisonment where the case is heard on indictment before the Crown Court.

Arising out of the collapse of tour companies and the need for bonding, it was decided to provide other safeguards should bonding not prove effective. In 1975, the Air Travel Reserve Fund was set up[19] with an initial government grant and thereafter maintained by a compulsory levy from all ATOL holders. When the Fund reached £14 million the levy was discontinued. The Fund was wound up in February 1986 and the Agency controlling it was dissolved in the following June.

Air taxis

A modified form of the charter is the service known in the US as the *Air taxi*. The aircraft used are either helicopters or short take off and landing (STOL) air craft. The potential of the latter has been seen recently in the commencement of services from the new London City Airport. Scheduled flights may also operate using such aircraft in a manner which may make them 'Common carriers'. There are no decided cases on the point but *Air taxis* in the US are considered to be such and there is dicta in English law to suggest the possibility: *Ludditt v Ginger Coote Air (1947).*[20] The issue will turn upon whether or not the carrier has, by contract, reserved the right to refuse carriage: *Aslan v Imperial Airways (1933).*[21]

The principal use for such services would seem to be to meet the needs of business. They could also be used for inter-connecting services between long haul carriers, or for *excursions*, although the cost would be likely to deter most 'day trippers'.

The London City Airport was the first new airport to open for several years and was closed for a short period after a series of near misses due to inadequate air traffic control. Following reassurance as to safety, the CAA allowed operations to start again. The problem of providing sufficient airport facilities in recent years has caused most of the difficulties for operators seeking to expand services.

4. AIRPORTS

An airport is any area of land or water designed, equipped, set apart, or commonly used for affording facilities for the landing or departure of aircraft.[22] It includes any provision for helicopters and VTOLs, including the roofs of buildings. It has taken some years for the older term *aerodrome* to disappear from the language of the legislation.

Powers to establish civil airports are conferred upon the Secretary of State and certain local authorities approved by the Minister and the CAA. Any person may establish an airfield, subject to planning permission, but restrictions and prohibitions effectively prevent most proposals. No aircraft may take off or land at any places in the UK not approved as CAA aerodromes or licensed by the Authority.[23] All aircraft entering or leaving the UK may only do so via 'customs airports'.[24] In addition, a proportion of these must be designated as *sanitary airports*. International Health Regulations require these to be provided in relation to the volume of air traffic. They must be staffed with trained personnel and equipped to meet the needs of aircraft diverted to them.[25]

British Airports Authority

The BAA was established as a statutory corporation in 1965. The government airports of Heathrow, Gatwick, Stanstead and Prestwick were transferred to the Authority. It was charged with doing anything to facilitate the discharge of its duties as set out in the Airports Authority Act 1965. Subject to Ministerial approval the BAA was also empowered to manage any other UK aerodromes.

As part of the *privatisation* programme of the Government, the Airports Act 1986, Part I, provides for the BAA to be dissolved and for a new commercial company to take over its assets. Under Part II, the larger municipal airports are required to be sold off to private enterprise.

Under Part III of the 1986 Act, the Secretary of State for Transport has extensive powers in connection with the distribution of traffic to airports, within set limits, through the agency of the CAA. In Part IV, the larger airports, i.e. those with a turnover in excess of £1 million, are required upon privatisation to seek CAA approval for the levying of airport charges and are obliged to adhere to any conditions attached to such approvals.

In respect of certain airports, an upper limit of charges has been set with reviews at five-yearly intervals. Those so far affected are Heathrow, Gatwick, Stansted and Manchester International Airports.[26] To safeguard against unfair discrimination in charges, or predatory pricing, references of complaints may be made to the Monopolies and Mergers Commission.

The Minister of Aviation described the Act in glowing terms as 'providing the framework for our major airports to be released into the commercial world in which they belong. It provides a new stimulus to efficiency and innovation from which both the airports and their customers will benefit. The new legislation will have pro-found effects on the way our airports are structured and managed.' His further assurance that 'the new regulatory regime for airports will protect the airport users against any possibility of unfair trading practices or monopoly abuses' has a somewhat hollow ring to it after the BA saga of 1987/88.

5. PRICING

The airline industry has two entirely different methods for fixing air fares. The first is by way of free competition between carriers operating scheduled or charter flights. The second, which is found predominantly on UK-European services, is the 'system number two' where fares are fixed in collusion between two airlines, usually state-owned. The routes have been allocated by the national governments concerned and the fares have to be identical, with the proceeds being shared out by the airlines on a percentage basis. Fares are kept at a high level for reasons of government policy rather than the economics of the industry. The controls do not apply to charter flights. With planning and the use of reduced off-peak fares it is possible to keep costs down but at the expense of flexibility in travel arrangements.

The cartel system which is being operated is against Article 85 of the Treaty of Rome. This makes such price-fixing agreements between companies which share markets illegal. Despite this, no attempts have been made to take the European Commission to court or to pursue the issues raised in domestic courts. The result is that scheduled flights are, in the main, used by businessmen.

In 1984, the British and Dutch governments signed an agreement allowing BA to reduce fares without prior consultation with the Dutch carrier KLM. Instead, BA signed an undertaking with the carrier to keep identically high prices and to share the profits. They agreed a new low fare for London to Amsterdam but allocated so few seats, and made conditions of booking so restrictive, that few travellers could benefit. BCal did introduce cheap flexible fares on the route, as they did after a similar agreement between the British and Belgian Governments in 1985, while BA did not.

It appears that the carriers still intend to adhere to the cosy cartels they have created for their benefit. With BA now effectively controlling Heathrow and Gatwick, the outlook for the traveller is not good. EEC members declare intentions to secure a better regime for air travel but governments seem to back away from confrontation with the megacarriers which they have created or allowed to develop.

Regulation

The regulation of national and international routes derives primarily from the need to ensure safety standards. The issues of national economics and, in some cases the need to provide essential public utilities, are also of paramount importance at governmental level. Financial subsidies are also evident, paid to maintain essential but loss-making activities.

Control is effected by agreement at national government level and the licensing of carriers on scheduled routes. Such international agreements are usually reached on a bilateral basis. In 1946, Britain and the US concluded the *Bermuda Agreement*, later renegotiated in 1977 and ratified in 1980. The intention was to guarantee that a high percentage of trade between the two countries would be undertaken by their respective national carriers.

Such agreements for carriage on internal domestic flights - known as *cabotage* - are not necessary. A country will usually reserve such routes for its own carriers. The term, *cabotage* is another example of a borrowing from carriage by sea rules. Its definition extends to flights between the mainland of a nation and its overseas territories, e.g. in the case of the UK, the Falkland Islands or Gibraltar.

In 1978, the US passed legislation making price-fixing on international flights to and from its territories unlawful. Such cartel arrangements are in violation of US anti-trust laws. This is a parallel to Article 85 of the Treaty of Rome which is more honoured in the breach than in the observance in the EEC. In 1980, several major US carriers withdrew from the International Air Transport Association (IATA) tariff-fixing conference.

IATA

This is essentially a trade body for international air carriers who seek to fix scheduled air fares by means of *traffic conferences*. Tariffs, which are agreed between the participants, are subject to ratification by national governments. In the order of 80% of international air carriers subscribe to the negotiations of IATA. Its critics point to it as a 'club' responsible for high prices and the stifling of competition.

For various reasons, carriers are often left with more seats than they can sell at the officially fixed price so they sell them off at much reduced rates. Discounting in this way breaches IATA rules and may be technically illegal in municipal law but it is not illegal for customers to buy reduced price tickets.

Discounting

Only IATA approved travel agencies are allowed to sell the tickets of the Association members. This has resulted in a growth in the phenomenon of *bucket shops*. The attitude of the British Government to such enterprises has been equivocal since it believes that, in general, air ticket prices are too high. Another problem for those who might be required to prosecute such enterprises is that only those airlines who are required to register fares with the CAA can be in breach of English law. These are, in the main, British and US carriers covered by the Bermuda Agreement.

By 1981, BA was selling discounted tickets via IATA agents, thus risking prosecution. Large agencies such as Pickfords also entered the market. No prosecutions have been attempted in the face of various difficulties and many IATA agents now sell tickets in competition with the *bucket shops*. Once in possession of a ticket, the customer can enforce contractual rights against the issuing carrier. Ironically, the discounted tickets carry the name of the issuing agent and his IATA letters.

Charters

Another growth industry has been the practice of selling seats only on packaged charter flights. Technically such sales are illegal. By definition, all charter passengers must pay the same price to one organiser who arranges the flight for all concerned. The CAA does allow a limited proportion of such sales but these are regularly flouted. Few complaints are made in the UK but occur more often in Spain and Greece. To eliminate the difficulty this may cause in those countries, tour operators have been moving towards scheduled flights provided by some charter airline licensees.

Here again BA has, by the retention of British Airtours within its empire, caused concern to the small carriers. Because BA also operates scheduled flights it can readily switch from one market to another, effectively cutting out the opposition. It can lease aircraft from its long haul fleet to its subsidiary at cost price.

The major tour operators offer inclusive tours with only minimal accommodation facilities to avoid problems at destination areas. These *minimum-rated* packages are sold at prices as low as possible. Should a tourist be refused admission to his chosen destination by the local authorities, the operator may find himself facing an action for breach of contract. A suitably-drawn exclusion clause, brought to the attention of the tourist when the contract is negotiated, may serve to protect the operator.

Surcharges

Most tour operators list terms in their brochures which they describe as 'fair'. Included amongst these are clauses allowing for surcharges. These arise mainly out of the practice of the operator fixing his prices well in advance of the season for which the advertising is promoted. Costs are worked out at the exchange rates which prevail at the time of publication. The two principal ingredients of the package are the accommodation and the flight. The Association of British Travel Agents' (ABTA) Code of Conduct for Tour Operators states that the latter should only add surcharges for reasons beyond their control.[27] These relate to fuel charges. In respect of other factors, such as the variation in exchange rates for foreign currency, no additions should be made within 30 days of the commencement of the holiday.[28]

Where a client is surcharged, the operator is required to provide the client with a written notice of the main cost heads and, if so requested, a reasonable written explanation for the additional charges.[29] Investigations of such surcharges imposed by different operators for the same, or almost identical, holidays reveal wide variations. There have been no reported cases where, due to lower fuel costs, a refund has been paid to a tourist. As a market attraction, some operators have begun to offer *no surcharge* guarantees.

The effect of terms in the booking contract will continue to be determined by the interpretation capable of being put upon them. If they are ambiguous they will be construed 'contra preferentum'. Those which are misleading may fall foul of the Misrepresentation Act 1967 or the Consumer Protection Act 1987.

6. CARRIAGE OF PASSENGERS

IATA defines a passenger as 'any person, except members of the crew, carried in an aircraft with the consent of the carrier'. It does not include stowaways until they are discovered by the carrier and he allows them to remain on board. It would be difficult to imagine what else he might do at 40,000 feet!

There is nothing to prevent a carrier from refusing to accept a passenger. Even though a valid contract has been concluded, he may reject a passenger because of the latter's conduct, physical condition or the discomfort likely to be caused to other passengers; the objection of other passengers; if the person is a danger to himself or the aircraft; it is against the law of one or more countries over which flights are made; the aircraft is overloaded; or the passenger fails to observe conditions imposed by the carrier.

Overbooking

To refuse to carry a person because the plane is overbooked and there are no seats available, entitles the passenger who is turned away to a refund of his fare. The only proper reason for such refusal is safety. If a carrier deliberately over books as a commercial practice, he may face a penalty for a trade descriptions offence. A booking of a seat on a plane is a promise for a future event. If the promise was capable of being fulfilled at the time it was made it is not an offence. If the promisor knew it to be false at the time he made the statement then it will be an offence. Similarly, if a passenger is guaranteed a seat it will render the carrier liable: *BAB v Taylor (1976).*[30]

The carrier may seek to exclude liability by a term in the contract but it is unlikely that this would be regarded as reasonable even if overbooking is common to the industry. Most carriers operate a Denied Boarding Compensation Scheme on a scale £10-£100 together with a reimbursement of reasonable expenses. Since this is as much as most travellers could expect to get as a court award they would be advised to accept unless there are circumstances which call for a higher level of compensation. The validity of such a clause has not been tested in the courts.

In the US Supreme Court, the concealment of an overbooking from intending passengers has been held to be fraudulent misrepresentation: *Nader v Alleghenny Airlines Inc (1976).*[31] There is no reason why this should not be so in English law.

The conditions for the carriage of passengers by air are very largely governed by international conventions. Where the flight is internal, modified convention rules will be applied. These are designated 'Non International Carriage' (NIC) flights which cover both purely domestic journeys and those which are between countries where one or both are not signatories of a relevant convention.

International flights

It was realised, early in the history of carriage of passengers by air, that disputes might arise which had international implications. To deal with anticipated difficulties, the Warsaw Convention was signed by 23 countries in 1929. It made carriers strictly liable for damage caused to passengers and baggage, with some exceptions, in return for an agreed limit on levels of compensation settled in advance. The limits of the Warsaw Convention (WC) have long been criticised for having been set too low. Most often such complaint has been made by the US. The reason for the levels set were so that they should not discourage nations from acceding to the WC. It was felt better to get some agreed sum than no money at all. At the same time, when the WC was drawn up the industry was in its infancy and could not afford to pay out large amounts by way of compensation. High levels would have called for unacceptably high premiums for insurance of risk.

Amendments

The WC was first amended by the Hague Protocol (HP) signed in 1955. Not all those who had signed the original WC agreed to the HP. It raised the levels of compensation but not high enough for some states, notably the US. The US was so dissatisfied with the levels that it renounced the WC in 1965. To avert the difficulties which this would cause, the world's major airlines met at Montreal in 1966 and agreed that all of them would accept *special contract terms* imposed by the US for international carriage which included a point of destination or departure on US territory, or where such point was a stopping place en route for another destination. The WC had allowed for such agreements to be made since they gave no less than the limits of the convention. Many nations have increased the limits. Any airline seeking an ATL in the UK must accept a higher level with an upper limit of 100,000 SDRs - the same level as for NIC. Not all UK carriers need an ATL, e.g. air taxis, but most have accepted the NIC levels fearing higher compensation might be awarded in the courts.

As with other international conventions, the WC did not have direct application to English law. It was incorporated by the Carriage by Air Act 1932. The HP was introduced by the Carriage by Air Act 1961 which took effect in 1967, repealing the 1932 legislation.

Another difficulty arose when the *actual* carrier was not the person with whom the contract had been made, e.g. where such person had subcontracted the carriage to another. This problem was overcome by agreement reached in the Guadalajara Convention (GC) signed in 1961, given effect in English law by the Carriage by Air (Supplementary Provisions) Act 1962.

Further agreements were reached at Guatemala in 1971 and Montreal in 1975 which have not yet attracted sufficient signatures to become internationally accepted. Provision has been made to adopt them in the Carriage by Air and Road Act 1979 but it seems doubtful that they will ever come into effect because the US strongly opposes them.

The consequence of this is that there are now three regimes covering carriage by air, the key to which operates in a given situation is the wording of the ticket for the flight. The terms governing the carriage will be:

WC Party	WC Party	= WC Terms
WC Party	WC or HP Party	= WC Terms
HP Party	HP Party	= HP Terms
Domestic in UK		= NIC Terms
Non contracting Party (NPC)	WC/HP/NCP	= Non Convention Terms

International flights

While the limits set under the Conventions have almost universal application, in certain countries, notably the US, there are no agreed limits in respect of domestic flights. It is a matter of some importance, therefore, to determine what is meant by an *international flight. Holmes v Bangladesh Biman Corp (1988)*[32]

The Conventions regard it as being where, according to the contract, the place of departure and the place of destination, whether or not there be a break in the carriage, are situated within the territories of two parties to the Convention; or within the territory of a single party if there is an *agreed* stopping place within the territory of another state, even if that state is not a party to the Convention. The carriage will not lose its international character because the flight occurs entirely within one country, or is performed by different carriers: *Grein v Imperial Airways Ltd (1937).*[33]

A deviation from the contracted carriage does not operate so as to disentitle the carrier from relying on the terms of the Convention: *Rotterdamsche Bank NV v BOAC (1953).*[34] It is the contract which determines the regime, not the route.

The overall effects of the operation of Convention terms are:

1. Where death, wounding or bodily injury are suffered by a passenger, the carrier is strictly liable without need to prove fault.

2. The burden of proof in respect of the defences available falls on the carrier.

3. If the carrier cannot disprove liability, the financial limits are pre-set.

4. In certain circumstances, the defences and the financial limits will be denied to the carrier.

In each case, the terms applied will be determined by whichever Convention is indicated on the ticket.

Under the WC the ticketing is of crucial importance. Absence of any form of ticket deprives the carrier of the defences under the Convention and of the limits of compensation payable. Failure to include a *Warsaw statement* on the ticket had the same effect. Subject to these provisions, providing something resembling a ticket was issued, the carrier was protected: *Preston v Hunting Air Transport (1956)*.[35]

It will be sufficient that the ticket was issued to an agent acting for the passenger: *Ross v PanAM (1949)*.[36] But if the ticket is not issued until the passenger is on board the aircraft the terms will not apply: *Mertens v Flying Tiger (1965)*.[37] These are both US cases which have persuasive effect only in English courts. The US courts do not like limitations of the Conventions and seek to interpret the terms strictly. They have even struck out their application on the grounds that the print size used on a ticket was too small to be legible. This is not likely to be followed in the UK.

The HP makes amendments in respect of the ticket. If none is issued or is lacking a *Hague notice*, then the carrier loses the limits set for compensation by the HP but not the defences available to him under its terms. It appears that so long as some sort of ticket is issued to the passenger then the carrier is protected.

The Conventions apply only to *carriage by air*. There is no definition as to the meaning of this phrase in any of them. It clearly refers to the time when passengers are physically on board an aircraft. By analogy to cases in land and sea carriage, it will include entering or disembarkation but there are no English cases on this point. It depends on the location of the passenger in relation to the 'risk of air travel' at the time of the incident forming the basis of a claim against the carrier. The US case of *Day v TWA (1975)*[38] is likely to be of strong persuasive precedent in the English courts. Here passengers had passed through a security check when there was a terrorist attack at Athens airport. It was held that the carrier having displayed a degree of control over the movements of the passengers concerned, *carriage by air* had commenced.

Defences

The defences available to a carrier under the Conventions are:

170

1. That he, his servants or agents have taken 'all necessary measures to avoid the damage or that it was impossible for him to take such measures'. (Article 20.)

English courts have rarely had to consider this defence. It probably requires that a carrier must take such measures as a reasonable carrier would deem necessary in the circumstances (see *'Grein'*). In some cases, as where the aircraft is a total loss, it may be impossible for the carrier to discharge the burden of proof. Today, the evidence of the in-flight recorder, the 'black box', may aid him in showing that the event causing the loss could not have been foreseen or prevented. The HP extends this WC defence to servants and agents of the carrier.

The scope of 'accident' referred to in Article 17 has never been precisely defined. Decisions in the US show that they are willing to include a wide range of incidents. These have included 'hijacking' and terrorist attacks: *Evangelis v Transworld Airlines (1976).*[39]

2. Contributory negligence on the part of the passenger. (Article 21.) This is not so much a defence as a plea in mitigation of damages by the carrier.

This issue was raised in the case of: *Chisholm v BEA (1963)*[40] where a passenger was injured after disobeying an instruction from the pilot.

3. Actions which are not commenced by the passenger or his representatives within two years of the actual or designated time of arrival of the aircraft at its destination are 'time barred': *Adatia v Air Canada (1992)*[41].

Loss of limits

As already stated, failure to issue any kind of document resembling a ticket will deprive the carrier of the protections afforded under the Conventions. He will also lose them if he has been guilty of *wilful misconduct*. There is no precise definition of this phrase as used in the WC. It would appear to be something more serious than gross or even culpable negligence.

The best definition is probably that of Mr Justice Barry in: *Horobin v BOAC (1952).*[42] He applied what has become commonly referred to as the *traffic lights test*. Where a car driver is in a hurry, or does not keep a proper look out, and fails to see traffic lights change from amber to red, if an accident occurs he is guilty of negligence. If, on the other hand, he sees them change to red but thinks he can beat the traffic coming across his path, he has taken a deliberate decision to do what he knows is wrong. He may lack the intention to cause the accident but it is due to his *wilful misconduct*. Such a man, said Barry, appreciates 'that he is acting wrongfully and yet persists in so acting regardless of the consequences or with reckless indifference as to what the results may be'.

The issue also turns on whether it is an *objective* test which is employed or a *subjective* one. An *objective* test sets the action of the pilot against that which is expected of pilots generally. In England, the *subjective* test seems to be favoured. Here, instead of measuring the action complained of against an accepted 'norm', the plaintiff has to show that the pilot foresaw the risk and decided to accept it. The major decision to this effect saw a judge at first instance apply an *objective* test, only for the Court of Appeal to overturn his decision by substituting a *subjective* one. *Goldman v Thai Airlines (1983).*[43]

The case was decided under the terms of the HP. Article 25 had substituted for *wilful misconduct* under the WC, the provision that for the carrier to lose his right to the limits of compensation it would have to be shown that the pilot acted either *with intent to cause damage* or *recklessly and with knowledge that damage would probably result*.

Recklessly here can be equated to *wilful misconduct* as under the WC. Lord Justice Everleigh said, had the definition in Article 25 stopped here, then the case for the plaintiff would have been proven. However, the use of the conjunction *and* together with the words which followed it, required that it was necessary to demonstrate that the pilot knew that damage would probably, not possibly, result from his deliberate actions or, in this case, omissions.

The judge went on to conclude that the pilot should not have attributed to him knowledge which another, i.e. model pilot, might have possessed or which even he himself should have possessed. Clearly the *subjective* test is being applied here. Article 25 has to be read as one piece and all the elements must be present. Thus, for the carrier to have lost the ceiling of compensation under the Convention, it was necessary to show that the damage sustained by Mr Goldman was caused by the pilot's omission; that the pilot knew that damage would probably result but disregarded this; that the kind of injury sustained was that which the pilot knew would probably occur.

The Court of Appeal unanimously agreed that these three elements had not been present. The result seems to be that it is highly unlikely that a plaintiff will ever be able to satisfy the requirements of Article 25 as it is presently worded.

The upper limit of awards for death or personal injury under the HP is 250,000 gold francs (£12,290), which is double that under the WC. There is nothing to prevent higher limits being set by *special contract*. Many countries have done so. In the UK the limit is set in terms of SDRs. The limit now is 100,000 SDRs (£80,000).

Luggage

In issues involving loss, damage or delay affecting passengers' luggage, two categories of property are defined:

1. Hand baggage: 'objects of which the passenger takes charge himself'.[44]

2. Other baggage in the hold of the aircraft in which the passenger is travelling or in some other aircraft: 'such articles, effects and other personal property of a passenger as are necessary or appropriate for wear, use, comfort or convenience in connection with his trip'.[45]

In order for the carrier to benefit from the limits of the Convention the baggage must have been *registered* by him. The English courts have interpreted this as meaning that some form of documentation must have been completed: *Collins v BAB (1982).*[46]

In respect of hand luggage, the Convention requires no documentation. Where it is carried elsewhere, a baggage check must be delivered to the passenger. It is usual to incorporate this with the flight ticket. Whatever the method used, it must comply with the same rules as those for the documentation of passengers. If the carrier does not issue a valid ticket/ check as required, he cannot rely on the limits set under the Convention: *Westminster Bank v Imperial Airways Ltd (1936).*[47] The document issued is proof that the carrier has weighed the baggage and that he agrees to carry it on the route indicated on the check.

The IATA Conditions allow the carrier the right to inspect and reject baggage. This is noted as being in accordance with similar provisions in English domestic legislation (Carriers Act 1830). The carrier can request a search to be made of the baggage before it is accepted as he may in respect of the person of the passenger. Such searches are usually, in the first instance, mechanical and designed to guard against terrorist activities.

Acceptance of the baggage by the carrier is prima facie evidence that they were delivered to him in good condition in accordance with the contract. This may be qualified by a written statement as to the condition of the items delivered by the carrier to the passenger. The contract will show that the baggage will be redelivered to the person presenting the relevant document to the carrier at the destination agreed by the parties. This protects the carrier from charges of misdelivery.

Under Article 18(1) the carrier is strictly liable for the articles provided the destruction, loss or damage occurred during *carriage by air*. This covers any time when the items were in the custody of the carrier at any place: *Guardian Assurance v Sabena (1976)*.[48]

The defences available to the carrier are the same as those listed in connection with passengers. It should be noted that failure to carry out security checks will probably negate the defence of due diligence/ unavoidability should loss be attributable to something which could have been discovered by adequate search.

The additional defence of *negligent pilotage* available under the WC is effective no longer under the HP.

A claimant must notify the carrier of any damage within 7 days of the delivery to him of his luggage. The complaint must be in writing. Where items are missing from the luggage this will be treated as damage: *Fothergill v Monarch Airlines (1981)*.[49]

In the case of loss, this may be claimed in respect of individual packages/cases or of the whole quantity. Each item should be weighed and recorded in the baggage check or the courts will calculate the loss mathematically: *Bland v BAB (1981)*.[50]

A time limit for written claims in the case of loss is 14 days from the time when the luggage should have been delivered to the person in possession of the travel documents relating to the luggage.

Neither the WC or HP define what is meant by *delay*. It probably means abnormal delay in redelivering the luggage to the person entitled to receive it at the agreed destination. If the carriage is not completed within a reasonable time, the complainant has 21 days from the time of delivery to him in which to notify the carrier (the same time as delay affecting passengers). Where the luggage has not been taken into the carrier's charge, so as to qualify under *carriage by air*, the passenger may bring an action for breach of contract at common law.

Financial limits

The limit of liability under the HP is 250 gold francs per kilogram weight (£12.29).[51] The limit may be extended by *special contract* when the baggage is handed to the carrier who will usually demand an extra payment for this. If a carrier refuses to agree to such *added value* he may lose his limit of liability: *Klicker v Northwest Airlines Inc (1977)*.[52]

For hand baggage, the limit is 5,000 gold francs (£248.50) per passenger. There appears to be no reason why a *special contract* should not be agreed for this category as with other luggage delivered into the custody of the carrier. The carrier could, in both cases, prove that the passenger had *overestimated* the valuation put upon the items.

It is not likely that deliberate actions designed to harm passengers will be taken either by the carrier, his servant or agents. This may not be the case where baggage is concerned. Servants or agents may in the course of their lawful duties act unlawfully, e.g. steal items from luggage. In such cases the carrier will lose the limits of liability under the Convention: *Rustenberg v Pan Am (1977)*.[53] It would be necessary to show that the items were stolen by those acting for the carrier. This may, in practice, be extremely difficult to do.

The Warsaw System is in disarray and requires emergency treatment to recussitate it. It has been referred to by leading authority as the 'Warsaw Shambles'[54]. It has also been subject to criticism by senior members of the judiciary: *SS Pharmaceutical Co Ltd v Quantas Airways Ltd*.[55].

Non-international carriage

From June 1967, the provisions of the HP and the GC were applied with modifications to NIC.[56] These are that failure to issue a ticket or baggage check will not result in the loss of the carrier's protection. The limit of liability was set at 100,000 SDRs. The result is that NIC is governed almost entirely by statute with little scope for common law intervention.

The NIC rules govern not only those flights which are entirely 'internal' but those where either or both of the carriers is not party to any convention.

Airspace

Every state has exclusive sovereignty over the airspace above its territory. This was the basis of the Convention on Civil Aviation signed by 38 nations at Chicago in 1944. Subsequently, many more states have ratified the agreement. The Chicago Convention applies to overflying rights by civil aircraft. It does not cover scheduled international air services which are the subject of separate bilateral agreements. Examples of these are to be found in the International Air Services Transit Agreements 1944, the so called *two* and *five* freedoms.

Disputes between nations on such agreements are referred to the Council of the International Civil Aviation Organisation (IACO) with an appeal lying to an agreed forum or the International Court of Justice.

7. SAFETY

In the years 1971 to 1976, an average of 1,300 passengers were killed annually in air accidents. Even so, in terms of deaths per thousand miles travelled, air transport was safer than travelling by car. Controls on aircraft, their crews and matters which may affect the safety of carriage by air, exist to minimise the dangers.

Airworthiness

Failures in the airframes, engines or control systems can result in disastrous accidents. In 1985, the probable loss of a part of the fuselage of a Boeing 747 led to the deaths of 520 passengers and crew over Japan.

Subject to a few exceptions, an aircraft not in possession of a certificate of air worthiness may not fly. In the UK, such certificates are issued by the CAA. The authority requires to be satisfied as to the design and construction of engines, air frame and equipment for any aircraft in relation to the purpose for which the air craft is to be used. The certificate will state the period for renewal and be subject to variation, review or cancellation.

In addition, records must be kept of the maintenance carried out in respect of every aircraft for which a certificate is in force.

Air crews

About three-quarters of all fatalities are caused by human error, far more than result from mechanical failures in the aircraft. Tired crews are more likely to make errors. For this reason, statutory provisions regulate the hours which aircrews may fly during specified periods.[57]

It is the duty of the operator of aircraft to see that crews do not exceed prescribed limits. No precise hours are defined but they must be judged within 28 day cycles and adequate rest periods must be taken. Maximum flying duty periods are set and no more than 100 hours may be flown in total during any 28 day period. The limits may only be exceeded in exceptional circumstances. These may be authorised by the operator only if he is sure that by allowing excess hours to be flown neither the aircraft nor those on board will be at risk. Where hours are exceeded, on allowable grounds, a report must be submitted to the CAA. The most usual reason for exceeding the limits is the unavoidable delay in completing a particular flight which could not have been foreseen in advance.

The operator must keep a log of hours flown by aircrew members and each member must keep a personal record. Failure to do so can result in an operator losing his AOC and individuals losing their licences. A condition of pilotage in the UK is that all aircraft above a certain weight must carry two pilots in flight, both to be at the controls during take off and landing.

Standards of safety are high in the UK, but the International Federation of Airline Pilots Associations (IFALPA) would like higher international standards to be set by IACO. This UN agency was created under the Chicago Convention to agree and monitor safety standards. It has been accorded recognition in many states in order that it may carry out its duties.

In 1960, a European organisation for safety of air navigation was established, *Eurocontrol*. It was given recognition in the UK by the Civil Aviation (Eurocontrol) Act 1962. Certain of its provisions are now contained in the Civil Aviation Act 1982 which, together with the Civil Aviation (Eurocontrol) Act 1983, governs the present regime.

Air crimes

If an act or omission which takes place on board an aircraft would be a crime if it were committed on the territory of the state to which the carrier belongs, then it is also a crime in the air wherever the aircraft may be at the relevant time. This is the position established by the Tokyo Convention of 1963. Originally its provisions were contained in the Tokyo Convention Act 1967 but many of the regulations are now consolidated in the Civil Aviation Act 1982.

The legislation allows the commander to take steps to secure the safety of the aircraft by restraining, disembarking, or handing over to a competent authority, those passengers who have committed offences or who he reasonably suspects may have committed *air offences* or are about to do so. Such offences must be in relation to the flight, e.g. during such time as passengers are within an aircraft whose doors are sealed. In addition, any passenger or member of the crew may restrain a person believed to be a danger to safety, provided this is done on reasonable grounds. The commander of an aircraft must hand over offenders to the appropriate authorities, in whichever country he happens to be, at the earliest opportunity. In the UK the appropriate authorities are immigration or police officers.

Hijacking

Anyone on board an aircraft in flight who unlawfully, or by the use of force or by threats of any kind, seizes an aircraft or exercises control over it, commits the offence of hijacking. This offence has its origins in acts of piracy at sea which predate the present law. The nationality of the hijacker, the state of registration of the aircraft, or the place where the incident took place, do not affect the commission of the offence.

A Convention for the Suppression of Unlawful Seizure of Aircraft was signed at the Hague in 1970. It was given effect in the UK by the Hijacking Act 1971. A further Convention for the Suppression of Unlawful Acts against the Safety of Civil Aviation was signed at Montreal in 1971. This is included within the provisions of the Protection of Aircraft Act 1973. Both statutes have now been consolidated in the Aviation Security Act 1982.

Prosecutions for the offence of hijacking may only be brought in the UK with the consent of the Attorney General. A person convicted of the offence upon indictment is liable to imprisonment for life.[58]

The 1983 Act contains a variety of measures to protect a wide range of aviation matters outside the safety of aircraft in flight and of this book.

NOTES:

1. British Overseas Airways Act 1939.
2. Civil Aviation Act 1946.
3. Civil Aviation Act 1971.
4. Civil Aviation Act 1982 s. 2 Sch.2.
5. Governing Britain. A. Hanson and M. Walters. p. 187.
6. Tribunals and Inquiries Act 1971.
7. Civil Aviation Act 1982 ss. 3,20 and 85.
8. Ibid ss. 4 and 105.
9. Ibid s. 12(2) Sch.3.
10. Aerial Navigation Act 1911.
11. Vol 618 HC Deb 1225 2 March 1960.
12. Op cit n.8.
13. Civil Aviation Act 1982 s. 44(3) (Replacing 1949 Act).
14. Ibid ss. 4 and 5.
15. (1950) 1 A11 ER 933.
16. (1960) 2 A11 ER 467.
17. Civil Aviation (ATOL) Regs SI 1972/223.
18. *Times* 16 July 1983.
19. Civil Aviation (ATOL Reserve Fund) Regs SI 1975/1196 and 1977/1331.
20. (1947) AC 233 per Wright LJ.
21. (1933) 45 L1 316.
22. Airport Act 1986 s. 12.
23. Air Navigation Order SI 1972/129.
24. Civil Aviation Order SI 1972/231.
25. Public Health (Aircraft) Regs SI 1970/1880.
26. Economic Regulation of Airports (Designation) Order SI 1986/1502.
27. ABTA Code Para 4.15.
28. Ibid Para 4.14.
29. Ibid Para 4.17.
30. (1976) 1 WLR 13.
31. (1976) 426 US 490.
32. (1988) 1 FTLR 534 C.A.
33. (1937) 1 KB 50. See also Phillipson v Imperial Airways Ltd (1939) AC 332.
34. (1953) 1 A11 ER 675.
35. (1956) 1 QB 252.
36. (1949) 299 NY 88.
37. (1965) 341 F 2d 851.

38. (1975) 528 F 2d 31. Contra. Re Tel Aviv (1975) 405 F 154. See also McLean V McLean (1977) SASR 305 and McDonald v Air Canada (1971) 11 Avi Cas 17
39. (1976) 550 F 2d 152.
40. (1963) 1 L1 626.
41. The *Times* 4 June CA
42. (1952) 2 A11 ER 1016.
43. (1983) *Times* 7 May 1983.
44. Civil Aviation Act 1961 Sch.1 Art 22(3).
45. IATA Passenger Conditions Art 1.
46. (1982) QB 734.
47. (1936) 2 A11 ER 890.
48. (1976) 11 ETL 918.
49. (1981) AC 251. See Carriage by Road and Air Act 1979 s. 2.
50. (1981) 1 L1 289.
51. Op cit n 48.
52. (1977) 563 F 2d 1310.
53. (1977) L1 36.
54. Shawcross & Beaumont - Air Law Part VII
55. (1991) L1288
56. Carriage by Air Act (App. Prov.) SI 1967/480 Art 4 Sch.1.
57. Air Navigation Order SI 1972/129.
58. Aviation Security Act 1982 s. 6(1) and (3).

CHAPTER X

The Traveller's Rest

1. ACCOMMODATION SERVICES

All travellers who stay away from home overnight require accommodation, provided by friends, relations, or a variety of businesses which offer hospitality for reward. The stay may be brief or for a season and involve board and lodging or self-catering. Those who prefer to be more independent and provide their own *accommodation* in the form of tents, trailer caravans or *motorhomes* will require only essential *utilities* at the specialist camp sites which cater for their wants. Some travellers are provided for on board their chosen form of transport. Passengers on cruise ships or rented boats have no need to look further for their accommodation; sleeping cars are available for long distance rail travellers; some coaches are equipped with berths; air travellers on long haul flights have the use of reclining seats and aids to sleeping.

The form of accommodation which most usually comes to mind is, however, that associated with the hotel industry. The word itself is used to cover establishments which provide lodging and ancillary services for reward to the public generally. *Hotel* is commonly used to describe a more or less commodious establishment with up to date appointments, though this may not necessarily be the case, and is capable of being applied to holiday camps or villages where *guests* are catered for in individual chalets or caravans. However, it is more usual to find it reserved for the traditional form of amenity comprised of various buildings. It is in the traditional sense that it is used here, although the law which applies to *hotels* may in certain respects apply equally to holiday camps, self-catering apartments, caravan sites or *health farms*. For example, legislation which seeks to promote health and safety is universal in its application: fire is no respecter of persons or premises, insanitary conditions call for remedial action wherever they may be situated, and consumer protection should be available to all who buy goods or services whatever the circumstances.

The range of titles used in connection with the provision of accommodation for reward can lead to confusion and would benefit from standardisation. *Hotel* itself can include an *inn* which has a particular meaning in English law. *Inn* may be used as part of the title for a public house which offers no accommodation or only that which is described as 'bed and breakfast', which has the effect in law of a denial that the premises are an *inn*.

The designations 'private hotel', 'guest house', 'boarding house', 'guestel', seek in some way to indicate that the proprietor is denying that he is an *innkeeper*. He may not succeed, since the law looks to a man's deeds, not to his words, in determining whether or not to apply to his activities the peculiar obligations and rights which attach to the ancient *common calling* of innkeeper.

What all these commercial activities have in common is that the dealings between guests and 'hoteliers' will be subject to the law of contract. In most cases, statutory interventions apart, the parties may choose their partners; in most respects the *innkeeper* has no such freedom to contract.

2. THE CONTRACT OF BOOKING

Booking is used to denote that a contract has been entered into as between the customer and the provider of the service in some event or activity in which the parties have a mutuality of interest. The term can be used in respect of theatre tickets, seats on an aircraft or train, a restaurant table etc. It may form part of a package of mixed services. If either party to the contract defaults on his obligation then there is a breach of the contract. Thus, where a hotel accepts a booking for a wedding reception then cancels this at 48 hours notice prior to the wedding it can be ordered by the court to pay both general and special damages: *Hotson & Hotson v Payne (T/A Anglia Motel) (1988)*.[1]

The element of booking which is at the heart of the contract made by the customer is in the case of a hotel most usually for sleeping accommodation and ancillary services. The booking may be made in advance by letter, telephone or fax or arranged via an agent. It may also be made by a casual caller at the hotel who inquires as to the availability of rooms and on being informed of availability of the same seeks to reserve one or more for his use. In such a situation the issue of overbooking so far as that guest is concerned does not arise. Rooms are either available for him to occupy or they are not.

Where accommodation is booked in advance, and if requested confirmed in writing, the *hotelier* is in breach of contract if, upon arrival, the guest is not provided with the facility which he has booked. He will be entitled to compensation for expenses which he has incurred in travelling to the hotel and additional damages in respect of the cost of finding alternative accommodation and for such distress or disappointment as has been caused to himself or to the members of his party. The *hotelier* may also find that he has committed an offence against section 14 of the Trade Descriptions Act 1968. He will incur no liability if he provides a room which fits the description supplied to the guest but not one demanded by the guest upon arrival. Unless that is, the booking has been made for a particular room, e.g. the bridal suite, or a south-facing aspect with a balcony etc.

A hotelier may pick and choose amongst the applicants for his services unless, that is, he discriminates on the basis of race or sex. The Sex Discrimination Act 1975[2] and the Race Relations Act 1976[3] both make unlawful such discrimination in the provision of goods, facilities or services to the public or a section of the public. The innkeeper is even more restricted in his choice of guests.

Duty to receive

At common law, the innkeeper was under a duty to receive all travellers seeking food and/or shelter. Provided that they were in a fit state to be received, and willing to pay a reasonable sum, he was obliged to accommodate them. If he failed to do so then he committed an offence for which he might be tried on indictment: *R v Ivens (1835)*[4]. He would also face a civil action by the rejected person: *Constantine v Imperial Hotels Ltd (1944)*[5]. The facts of this case would also lead to an action under the Race Relations Act, if brought today.

The duty of innkeepers to receive guests is still governed by the common law as to the committing of an offence. In civil claims, the position is now regulated by the Hotel Proprietors Act 1956. The Act defines an innkeeper as one who holds his establishment out as offering sleeping accommodation to any traveller who presents himself without having to book in advance.[6]

It should be noted that the civil action is not based upon a breach of contract since none exists. It is an action founded in tort for failing to contract, one of the class known as *innominate* torts.

If the hotelier does anything to deny the status of an inn as regards his premises then this may be effective in relieving him of the liabilities attached to the calling. If he does not accept casual bookings but only those arranged in advance, he may be successful, e.g. a holiday camp would not qualify as an inn for this reason. He may indicate that he reserves the right to pick and choose amongst his clients, e.g. by using the word *private* before *hotel*, or the description *guest house*. A sign which says 'no coaches' or 'coaches by appointment only' may deny that the premises constitute an inn or may simply indicate that they are unable to accommodate large parties.

An innkeeper is also obliged to provide food and drink to travellers at all times. Late arrival is no excuse for not serving a traveller (see *Ivens*) or admitting him for the purpose of occupying a room. However, the traveller has no right to demand a particular room: *Fell v Knight (1841)*,[7] nor may he demand to sleep elsewhere than in a room, e.g. in a lounge, if the inn is fully booked: *Browne v Brandt (1902)*.[8]

An innkeeper is only required to receive *travellers*: *Sealey v Tandy (1902)*[9]. However, it appears that anyone away from home and in the course of a journey, no matter how short, must be regarded as a traveller at common law: *Williams v Linnitt (1951)*[10]. He is only obliged to receive such as appear able and willing to pay a reasonable sum for the services and facilities provided. In order to ascertain the financial status of the traveller, the innkeeper may request payment in advance: *Mulliner v Florence (1878)*.[11] An innkeeper who charges excessive prices is guilty of an indictable offence: *Luton v Bigg (1691).*[12]

The innkeeper's duty is towards travellers who need accommodation upon the road. He is not in business, *qua* innkeeper, to provide long-term boarding facilities. Guests, however reputable and willing to pay their bills, may outstay their welcome and be required to leave: *Lamond v Richard (1897).*[13]

At common law, the refusal of a traveller to supply his name and address is not of itself grounds for turning him away (see *Ivens*) but since the Immigration (Hotel Records) Order 1972[14] makes it an offence for a hotelier not to keep such information, refusal would seem, today, to be adequate grounds. Strangely, it does not appear to be an offence to give a false name, nor is the hotelier required to seek proof of identity from the person who presents himself.

Both at common law and under the terms of the Hotel Proprietors Act 1956, the innkeeper may turn away a traveller who is not in a 'fit state to be received', e.g. if he or she is drunk or behaves improperly: *Thompson v McKenzie (1908);*[15] is improperly dressed: *R v Sprague (1899),*[16] although if this case were heard today it would give rise to a decision based on sex discrimination on the lines of the decision in: *Gill and Another v EL Vino Co Ltd (1983);*[17] is annoying other customers by pestering them: *Rothfield v North British Rly. Co (1920);*[18] is dirty or verminous, or is accompanied by a dog of such description: *R v Rymer (1877).*[19]

It is debatable whether a person who is ill should be turned away. This has been held to be unreasonable at common law: *R v Luellin (1701),*[20] yet a person who is suffering from a notifiable disease commits an offence if he knowingly exposes others to risk, as does any person allowing him to endanger others.[21]

It is not necessary for an inn to hold a liquor licence in order that it be classified as such, a temperance hotel may in every respect qualify for the status: *Cunningham v Philip (1896).*[22] An inn, or any licensed premises, where prostitutes are allowed to congregate risks the danger of a fine and loss of a licence.[23] Any hotelier who allows his premises to be used by prostitutes runs the risk of prosecution for brothel-keeping or keeping a disorderly house. This latter offence may be committed by someone who allows his premises to be used by anyone for 'immoral purposes', the involvement of prostitutes is not essential, enthusiastic amateurs will suffice: *Winter v Woolfe (1931).*[24] From this, it follows that an innkeeper who believes that his potential guests are resorting to his premises for immoral purposes is justified in turning them away.

In general, a hotelier may decline to receive a guest's luggage, for whatever reason, but it is not so easy for an innkeeper to do so. He is required to take in a guest together with any luggage, even if such property does not belong to the traveller: *Robins v Gray (1895).*[25] He may only refuse goods which are dangerous or a potential source of annoyance to other guests.

An innkeeper was, and it would appear still is, obliged to receive a traveller's horse. In the same way he must receive a traveller's motor car, but he is not required to provide garaging or any special provision for it: *Winkworth v Raven (1931).*[26]

Terms and conditions

It is said that an innkeeper does not sell by contract but delivers goods to his guests as they require.[27] This may be so, but there appears to be nothing to prevent such a person making a contract with a traveller in respect of matters which fall outside his duty to receive guests and to have the duty of an *insurer* of the goods of a traveller which are brought within the *hospitium* of the inn (q.v.).

The express terms agreed orally, or in writing, between inn-keepers, and any other providers of accommodation for reward, and their customers will relate to the type and number of rooms required, the tariff of charges and the duration of the stay. Other matters may be included as necessary and usually refer to methods for settling accounts, deposits, cancellations, times for vacating rooms, meal times, security for items deposited with the hotel etc. Terms will vary with the amenities provided. They may be very extensive in the case of a five-star hotel and very basic in a guest house.

Where a booking has been made in response to a brochure or other form of advertising, the statements made must be accurate while allowing for the hotelier to engage in *puffing* his services. They must not be false to a material degree so as to misrepresent the facilities advertised. It is usual for advertising to carry statements to the effect that the management reserve the right to change prices without prior notification to potential customers and that rooms are subject to availability. These statements protect the hotelier in the unlikely event that the sending of a brochure to a potential guest is construed as an offer and not simply an invitation to treat.

If guests do not arrive to take up their reservations, the hotelier is able to look to the contract as the basis for compensation. If a small deposit has been paid he may be able to keep it all to offset his administration expenses. Where the sum involved is substantial, he may still be able to keep all of it if he has been unable to re-let the accommodation. He may not sit back and rely on being paid for the rooms without some attempt to mitigate his losses. A Hotel Industry Voluntary Code of Booking Practice exists, but it offers little more than the implied terms in the contract would provide together with the statutory regulations for consumer protection.

No claim can be made against a defaulting guest until after the date on which the reservation would have terminated. Only then is it possible to calculate the loss sustained by the hotel. As a rough guide to the amount which might be claimed, it is usual to look to about two thirds of the room price. This allows for deductions made for facilities not used, e.g. heat, light, linen, cleaning etc. If a long notice of cancellation has been given, allowing for ample time to re-let, it is doubtful if the hotel would recover much by way of damages even if a loss has been sustained. It is also doubtful whether the hotelier would wish to spend the time or trouble in pursuing the matter.

If, on arrival, a guest finds that the standards or facilities of the hotel have been misrepresented to him he may wish to repudiate the contract. The Development of Tourism Act 1969[28] provides for the grading of hotels in Britain but to date this has not taken place. There has been opposition to it by the industry and the British Tourist Authority have made no effort to impose a system upon hoteliers. With the notable exception of the Channel Islands, such grading as exists has been on a voluntary basis by motoring associations and local tourist authorities. Nevertheless, if some form of grading in use at a hotel suggests that it is of a certain quality, indicated by *stars* or *crowns* or any other device, then the customer is entitled to expect the hotel will live up to its boasts. If it does not, he may seek to repudiate the contract and the matter may well be taken up by the local trading standards officer.

One measure which has been introduced under the provisions of the 1969 Act is the Tourism (Sleeping Accommodation Price Display) Order 1977.[29] This requires current prices to be displayed prominently at the entrance to all hotels and guest houses having four or more letting bedrooms, or accommodation for eight or more persons. The display must show the cost of single and double rooms (maximum and minimum range will be sufficient), whether VAT is included in the price, and charges for service and any meals similarly included. Where rooms are let in advance, and a tariff sent to customers who may only book in this manner, i.e. there are no *chance* or casual lettings, or where rooms are normally let for 21 days or more, the requirement is waived. In all other cases, failure to display the tariff is punishable by a fine upon summary conviction.

Notices

Hotels display a variety of notices in addition to those required by law. These may seek to exempt the hotel from liability in respect of various obligations. Such notices, if they are to have any force by incorporation into the contract, must be prominently displayed at the place where the contract is made. It is not possible to alter a contract unilaterally or add conditions after the agreement has been reached in the hope that to do so will achieve the desired result for the hotelier. A notice on the back of a bedroom door will not be sufficient to absolve the proprietor from liability for the loss of items left in a bedroom caused by the negligence of the management: *Olley v Marlborough Court Ltd (1949)*.[30] Even had the notice been correctly displayed at the reception area in this case, it is doubted whether the exclusion would have satisfied the reasonableness test of the Unfair Contract Terms Act 1977 in view of the level of negligence shown by the hotel.

A notice denying liability for guests' property in a hotel would be completely in effective in denying the liability of an innkeeper towards his guests in residence. He is allowed, by the terms of the Hotel Proprietors Act 1956, to display a notice which limits the extent of his liability as an innkeeper. It is important to note that this does not deny liability nor does it protect him if the loss is attributable to his negligence or that of his staff.

Implied terms

In every contract for services, the requirement of section 13 of the Supply of Goods and Services Act 1982 that a business supplier will carry out the service with reasonable care and skill is implied. Allied to this is the term that the guest will be reasonably safe in his use of the facilities of the hotel during his stay.

The guest also has responsibilities under the contract. It is implied that he will not abuse the use of the premises, facilities, or services provided for him under the agreement. There are many ways in which damage to hotel property may be caused by guests. Accidents are not unusual but, unless wilful damage or negligence can be proved, it is unlikely that a hotelier will recover the cost from a guest.

The guest is also required to conduct himself in the manner required of a reasonable person frequenting public premises. Drunken or unseemly conduct which causes offence to other guests could be reasons for the management requesting a guest to leave (see *Rymer* and *Lamond*). If a guest refuses to leave, he becomes a trespasser and reasonable force may be used to expel him. The police have no authority to intervene unless it is likely that a breach of the peace will occur.

3. SAFETY OF GUESTS

It is a hotelier's duty to take reasonable care of his guests so that they are not harmed through the negligence of himself, his servants, or those acting under his authority. In this respect, the innkeeper is no different from any other category of hotelier. He is not, nor ever has been, an *insurer* of the safety of his customer. There is a warranty by the hotelier that, for the purpose of personal use by the guest, the premises are as safe as reasonable care and skill can make them.

Until 1957, guests relied on breach of this implied term, or the tort of Negligence, to maintain a claim against a proprietor. Because of the difficulty, in some cases, in determining who exactly was responsible for the condition of premises which caused the harm complained of, the Occupiers Liability Act was passed to protect both the persons and property of lawful visitors. Early cases were brought in Negligence. Now, the duty under the statute would be called in aid.

It establishes a 'common duty of care' which is owed by an occupier to visitors, a duty to take such care, as in all the circumstances of the case is reasonable, to see visitors will be reasonably safe in using the premises for the purpose for which they are invited or permitted to be there. The duty is not strict. The plaintiff must prove failure to observe the common duty of care and this standard may vary with the circumstances of the case.

The duty of a hotelier does not extend to every part of the building at every hour of the day and night. It is limited to those places where guests may be reasonably supposed to go in the belief that they have a right so to do. The liability of the hotelier may be reduced by any contributory negligence displayed by the guest which was, in whole or in part, responsible for his misfortune.

A plaintiff who fell and was injured in an unlit passageway, which he might reasonably be expected to use, recovered damages, no contributory negligence on his part having been shown: *Campbell v Shelbourne Hotel Ltd (1939).*[31] A guest who had not been shown the layout of the hotel was injured in responding to a fire alarm and was able to recover damages: *MacLenan v Segar (1917).*[32]

In the case of: *Walker v The Midland Railway Co (1886)*[33] a guest who chose to seek out a toilet, other than one which was clearly marked for his use, fell down a lift shaft and was killed. No negligence was attributed to the hotel. A guest who slipped on a driveway leading to a hotel, and injured her ankle, was unable to recover damages since the hotel was adjudged to have taken reasonable care: *Bell v Travco Hotels (1953).*[34]

In a somewhat unusual case, the plaintiff who alleged that he had been bitten by insects while using the defendant's Turkish Baths, was held able to recover compensation: *Silverman v Imperial Hotels Ltd (1927).*[35] On other occasions guests have been injured by falling chandeliers: *Collis v Selden (1868);*[36] ceilings collapsing: *Sandys v Florence (1878);*[37] chimneys giving way: *Duckes v Strong (1902).*[38]

In 1985 an accountant attending a luncheon party at the Ritz Hotel leant against a balustrade which he later claimed to have been unsafe by reason of its height having been reduced by several inches by reason of alterations to the flooring adjacent to it. He fell some 26 feet onto an iron staircase and thence onto a concrete floor. The judge at first instance held that what had occurred was not *reasonably foreseeable* and that the hotel was not in breach of the *common duty of care* required by the Occupiers Liability Act 1957. The duty which was owed by the Ritz to all visitors was said to be only one of *reasonable care* in the circumstances and this did not make the hotel an *insurer* against harm befalling visitors. The victim appealed and by a majority of 2-1 the Court of Appeal found for the applicant. In doing so it placed emphasis on the fact that evidence had been adduced at the trial that the balustrade was below the level recommended by British Safety Standards and that the judge from whose decision the victim was appealing had not given sufficient weight to this evidence: *Ward v Ritz Hotel (1992).*[39]

Where the visitor has exceeded the licence under which he was

190

allowed to visit the premises, he does not become an unlawful visitor so as to lose legal protection, unless the revocation of his licence is made clearly known to him by the occupier or his servant: *Stone v Taffe (1974).*[40]

Under the 1957 Act, an 'occupier' is someone who has control of the premises. Such control may be exercised by more than one person so that two or more persons may be liable for harm which befalls a visitor: *Wheat v E. Lacon & Co Ltd (1966).*[41]

Children

In determining the standard of care owed to visitors, the 1957 Act section 2(3) requires that 'an occupier must be prepared for children to be less careful than adults'. Where there is that which may be classified as an 'allurement' to children, the occupier should have a particular care: *Taylor v Glasgow Corporation (1922).*[42]

Notices

In some circumstances, a notice may help an occupier to establish the reasonableness of the precautions which he has taken. Section 2(4) of the 1957 Act states that: 'Where damage is caused to a visitor by a danger of which he has been warned by the occupier, the warning is not to be treated without more as absolving the occupier from liability, unless in all the circumstances it was enough to enable the visitor to be reasonably safe'.

The Unfair Contract Terms Act 1977, section 2(1), reminds those who post notices that: 'A person cannot by any reference to any contract term or to any notice given to persons generally or to particular persons exclude or restrict his liability for death, or personal injury resulting from negligence'. Negligence, as defined in section 1(1) of the Act, includes breach of the common duty of care imposed by the Occupiers Liability Act 1957. The defendant in *Bennet v Pontin's Holiday Camps (1973)*[43] would not succeed today.

Where an unusaul danger exists the occupier must not only warn the visitor as to the danger but he should also errect a barrier appropriate to the hazard to be guarded against which together with the notice displayed should be capable of dererring persons coming across it: *Rae v Mars (1989).*[44]

Fire Safety

The Fire Precautions Act 1971 was passed to improve safety measures in premises where members of the public gather. Under its provisions, the Secretary of State can designate premises in respect of which a fire certificate is required. To date, two designations have been made affecting hotels and public houses and restaurants.

The certificate allows premises to be used for a specified purpose, subject to the provision of means of escape in case of fire and reasonable provision of fire fighting equipment. Other requirements will stipulate the holding of fire training and practices and the means by which warnings of fire are to be given. The numbers of people allowed to be present on the premises at any one time may also be stipulated. Under section 7 of the Act, anyone who fails to comply with the provisions of the Orders or the statute will be prosecuted.

A copy of the fire certificate must be kept on the premises for inspection by authorised officers. Fire authorities have a discretion as to whether to order the closure of premises until defects are remedied, but they cannot be held liable necessarily for failure to do so: *Hallet v Nicholson (1979)*.[45] Failure to hold a certificate, or to meet the required standards, will not give rise to an action based on breach of statutory duty, but may be used as evidence of negligence on the part of a hotelier. Very small operations, which provide sleeping accommodation for not more than six persons (whether guests or staff), or no sleeping accommodation above the first floor or below the ground floor, do not require a fire certificate.

Safe work conditions

The Health and Safety at Work Act 1974 seeks to extend responsibility for safety beyond those immediately concerned in the work process. The Act applies to people not places. Section 3 imposes a duty upon employers to conduct their undertakings in such a way 'as to ensure, so far as is reasonably practicable, that persons not in (their) employment who may be affected thereby are not exposed to risks to their health or safety'. Section 4 is wide enough in application to cover a guest injured by operating a vending machine.

Section 47(1) states specifically that:

"nothing in this part shall be constrtued -

(a) as conferring a right of action in any civil proceedings in respect of any failure to comply with any duty imposed by ss. 2-7 or any contravention of s.8;

(b) as affecting the extent (if any) to which breach of duty imposed by any existing statutory provisions is actionable:"

However, s47(2) provides that a breach of duty imposed by regulations made by the Secretary of State under powers conferred upon him by the Health and Safety at Work Act 1974 shall, so far as such a breach causes damage, be actionable except in so far as the regulations provide otherwise. The common law remains the cornerstone of claims for personal injury and s 47(2) does not prejudice any right an individual may have at common law.

4. GUESTS' PROPERTY

The requirement that the provider of services should exercise reasonable care and skill, in carrying out his obligations under the contract, extends to the safety of guests' property. Where items are lost or damaged, a claim may be brought against the hotelier if lack of care, or negligence, can be established. In the case of the innkeeper, his liability is *strict*. He is regarded as an insurer of guests' property which has been brought within the *hospitium* of the inn, or which he has caused to be left outside: *Watson v People's Refreshment Association Ltd (1952)*.[46]

The liability of an innkeeper for loss or damage to the property of guests is an ancient one which can be traced back to the 14th century. Today it is contained in section 1 of the Hotel Proprietors Act 1956. The Act states specifically that the common law, as it existed before the statute was passed, shall still have effect save where it is altered by the legislation.

Innkeeper's liability

The Act requires that the innkeeper make good the loss or damage only if, at the time of the occurrence, the traveller had engaged sleeping accommodation at the inn. Vehicles, or any property left therein, or any horse or other live animal or its harness or any other equipment, are expressly excluded from the operation of the innkeeper's strict duty.

The innkeeper is able to limit the amount of his liability if he displays the notice reproduced in the Schedule to the Act. The financial limits were set in 1956, have not been altered since then and, however inappropriate today, would appear to apply still. It is a matter of doubt as to whether such limits will hold good in the light of the Unfair Contract Terms Act 1977. However, since the innkeeper's liability is not based upon contract, the 1977 Act would seem inapplicable. If it were held otherwise, section 2 speaks only in terms of attempts to restrict liability for negligence. The innkeeper's liability is strict and not fault-based.

The limits will be lost under the terms of section 2(3) of the 1956 Act where the property was stolen, lost, or damaged through the default, neglect, or wilful act of the innkeeper or his servant. The limits will also be lost where the property of the guest was deposited for safe keeping with the innkeeper in a sealed package, or where the innkeeper refused to accept items for safekeeping.

At common law, the innkeeper could escape liability if he was able to show that the loss or damage was caused by:

1. **Act of God**. This refers to some cause which could not have been foreseen, and, if foreseen, could not have been guarded against, e.g. flooding due to a cloudburst.

2. **An Act of the Queen's Enemies**. This relates to war damage. Whether it can be extended to terrorist attacks is doubtful. It was applied to activities of the IRA in Ireland in the 1920s, in the case of the common carrier, and may, by analogy, be applied to the innkeeper, but there is no direct authority on this point.

3. **Negligence on the part of the plaintiff**. There are a number of cases illustrating this point. A guest who left a large amount of valuable jewellery in her room was held to be negligent thus barring her claim: *Wright v the Embassy Hotel (1934)*.[47] The mere fact of failing to deposit articles of value with the management is not necessarily evidence of negligence: *Carpenter v Haymarket Hotel (1931)*.[48]

Failure to lock a bedroom door is not of itself evidence of a guest's negligence especially where it is the practice of the hotel to require guests to leave their doors unlocked so that cleaning staff may gain access: *Shacklock v Ethorpe Ltd (1939)*.[49] A guest who asks for a key, but is told that no-one will steal her things, is not negligent if she responds to such comments by leaving valuable items in her room and they are stolen: *Brewster v Drennan (1945).*[50]

Where the loss of the plaintiff's property was occasioned by the negligence of the defendant, the statutory limits of compensation did not apply: *Bonham Carter v Hyde Park Hotel Ltd (1948).*[51] Similarly, where the wilful act of the defendant's employee was responsible for the loss: *Kott & Kott v Gordon Hotels Ltd (1968).*[52]

The burden of proving that the innkeeper was at fault lies with the guest: *Whitehouse v Pickett (1908).*[53] If the guest is unable to prove that the innkeeper was at fault for the loss, and the latter is unable to show that the guest was to blame, it appears that the statutory limits will be applied: *Medawar v Grand Hotel Company (1891).*[54]

Bailment

Where the hotelier assumes control over the property of a guest, a relationship of bailor and bailee exists. It may come about by an employee of the hotelier taking the keys to a guest's car and parking it. Bailment ends when the keys are returned to the guest.

It may arise when the guest hands property to the management for safe keeping. Should harm befall the property while it is in the hotelier's possession, he will need to show that he took all reasonable care of it if he is to escape liability. Failure to have an attendant on duty at a cloakroom may make the hotelier liable for the theft of property left there if negligence of the plaintiff cannot be proved: *Samuel v Westminster Wine Co (1959).*[55] If an employee takes charge of a customer's coat and hangs it up for him, an act of bailment has occurred: *Ultzen v Nicols (1894).*[56]

Where a plaintiff has only a bare licence to leave items on the defendant's property no bailment exists: *Tinsley v Dudley (1951).*[57]

An innkeeper and other hoteliers share the same degree of liability for breach of terms in bailment. Unlike the innkeeper, the other categories of hotelier do not assume the mantle of insurers of guests' property. Liability will only attach to them if it can be shown that they were negligent, or that loss was occasioned by some wilful act on the part of the management or staff: *Scarborough v Cosgrove (1905).*[58]

The duties imposed upon an innkeeper arise out of the nature of his calling. In acknowledgement of the burdens of office, the common law and legislation allow to him the privilege of exercising a lien upon goods against payment of the bill for accommodation (q.v.).

NOTES

1. [1988] CLY 1047: also Jones & Jones v Villa Ramos [Algarve] 1988 CLY 1061
2. s. 29(1).
3. s. 20(1).
4. (1835) 7 C & P 213 see also R v Higgins (1948) 1 KB 165.
5. (1944) KB 693.
6. s. 1(3).
7. (1841) 8 M & W 269.
8. (1902) 1 KB 696.
9. (1902) 1 KB 296.
10. (1951) 1 A11 ER 278. Following Orchard v Bush (1898) 2 QBD 284.
11. (1878) 3 QBD 484 at 488.
12. (1691) Skin 291.
13. (1897) 1 QB 541.
14. SI 1972/1689 art 4.
15. (1908) 1 KB 905 at 907.
16. (1899) 63 JP 233.
17. (1983) 2 WLR 155 (CA).
18. (1920) SC 805.
19. (1877) 2 QBD 136 CCR.
20. (1701) 12 Mod Rep 445.
21. Public Health Act 1936 s. 148 (a) (b).
22. (1896) 12 TLR 532.
23. Licencing Act 1964 s. 175.
24. (1931) 1 KB 549 CCA.
25. (1895) 2 QBD 501.
26. (1931) 1 KB 652.
27. Halsbury V 1 24 para 1241 n.6.
28. s. 17 (3).
29. SI 1977/1877.
30. (1949) 1 KB 532.
31. (1939) 2 A11 ER 351.
32. (1917) 2 KB 325.
33. (1886) 55 LT.
34. (1953) 1 QB 473 CA.
35. (1927) 43 TLR 260.

36. (1868) LR 3 CP 495.
37. (1878) 47 LJQB 598.
38. (1902) CA unreported.
39. [1992] *The Independent* 21 May
40. (1974) 3 All ER 1016 (CA).
41. (1966) 1 All ER 582.
42. (1922) 1 AC 44.
43. (1973) *Guardian* 12 December 1973.
44. [1989] *The Times* 15 February
45. (1979) SC 1.
46. (1952) 1 KB 318.
47. (1934) 79 SJ 12.
48. (1931) 1 KB 364.
49. (1939) 3 All ER 372 (HL).
50. (1945) 2 All ER 705.
51. (1948) WN 89.
52. (1968) 2 L1 228.
53. (1908) AC 357 (HL).
54. (1891) 2 QB 11.
55. (1959) CLY 173.
56. (1894) 1 QBD 92.
57. (1951) 1 All ER 252.
58. (1905) 2 KB 805.

CHAPTER XI

The Holiday Trade

1. HOLIDAYS FOR ALL

The second half of the 19th century saw the growth of private travel and the increase in leisure pursuits. The rise in the number of people with sufficient disposable income to permit a choice of spending coincided with the coming of the railroads . As living standards rose so did expectations. Where the railways advanced, the frontiers of living and recreational space expanded.

Not all members of society benefited equally. The living standards of the new middle class rose significantly and leisure activity came more easily to this group than it did to the working man. Nevertheless, mid Victorian prosperity brought substantial benefits to a large part of the population. The better-off families could afford a week or so at the seaside and workmen could enjoy a railway excursion or a day trip on a steamer. An added impetus came with the passing of the Bank Holiday

Act in 1871. Then holidays with pay were negotiated by trade unions in the 20th century, tourism began to expand at a steady rate.

It was the railways, more than any other factor, which introduced people to the experience of life outside their own communities. At first, the railway companies failed to realise the potential of the tourist trade in their pricing. Instead they concentrated on the business traveller. It fell to entrepreneurs like Thomas Cook to recognise the possibilities for organised travel. After his first venture in 1841 had shown the way, he was soon chartering trains for organised excursions. By 1855 he had widened his horizons, and those of his customers, with an inclusive *package* to the Great Exhibition in Paris.

His success led the railways to reassess their markets. They began to take a keener interest in the cross-Channel ferries which they soon came to dominate. They became prime movers in the building of new hotels needed to replace old coaching inns linked to abandoned coaching routes. Speculative building boomed, unfettered by planning controls until 1909.[1]

An interest in healthy outdoor pursuits grew, first with the cycling clubs at home and mountaineering expeditions abroad. New market leaders appeared on the scene, with Henry Lunn introducing ski holidays to Switzerland in the 1880s. Organised travel became the order of the day. A huge range of guide books came on to the market. Some were of the standard of Baedeker, but others were trivial and far from accurate. Photography became a growing interest of private and commercial enthusiasts. Allied to travel guides, this gave an impetus to advertising in tourism.

The Great War was a temporary setback to the growing leisure industry. It also served as the proving ground for the aeroplane. Just as the motor coaches ate into the railway's business from 1920 onwards, the 'plane was to do the same to long-haul trade, once the monopoly of the shipping lines.

Many people organised their own holidays, booking trains or coaches, hotels or boarding houses, and planning their own amusements. The first radical change in this pattern of domestic holidays appeared in the 1930s. Early experiments were made by the Cooperative Movement. The commercial development of low prices all-inclusive holidays began with the construction of the first *holiday camp*, by the promoter Billy Butlin, at Skegness in 1936. This milestone was acknowledged on the 30th April 1987 by granting Grade II listed building status to the last remaining campers' chalet at the original site[2]. The success of this initiative resulted in a spate of imitators in the years immediately before and after the Second World War.

Like its predecessor, this war gave an impetus to air travel. The post-war surplus of aircraft led to an increase in travel on long-haul routes and a new breed of entrepreneurs emerged to capitalise on the opportunities. The advent of commercial jets in the 1950s set the scene for the modern *inclusive tour* or *package* holiday business. Private operators developed highly profitable charter services, having been denied access to scheduled flights by the state monopolies. The travel industry in its modern form grew out of the alliance between this new breed of air carrier and tour operators.

In 1950, Horizon Holidays offered a package holiday by air to Corsica. It demonstrated that the cost of travel could be significantly reduced by filling chartered aircraft. Accommodation costs could be reduced by taking up low cost units on and around the Mediterranean. By the 1960s, what began as a trickle became a flood with tourists from Britain joined by others from northern European countries.

2. PACKAGE TRAVEL, HOLIDAYS AND TOURS

On the 13 June 1990 the Council of Ministers of the European Communities formally adopted Council Directive 90/14/EEC (the Directive)[3]. Art.10 of the Directive states that it is addressed to Member States (MS) and Art.9 requires that MS shall bring into force the measures necessary to comply with the Directive before 31 December 1992 and provide the Commission with the texts of the main provisions of national law (NL) which they have adopted in the field governed by the Directive. The UK used the method common in our NL, the Statutory Instrument, in this case S.I.1992/3288. This S.I. was introduced by the Secretary of State for Trade and Industry and was passed by Parliament after some debate and had as its commencement date 23rd December 1992. Britain joined France and Holland as the only members to date to have implemented the Directive in their NL. The Commission in April 1993 has announced that it is to commence proceedings against the other 9 EC MS for non compliance.

In 1984 the Commission had declared a resolution on tourism which was immediately welcomed by the Council of Ministers[4]. This was subsequently translated into a draft directive in 1988[5] and in amended form this became the 1990 Directive.

When considering the contents and implementation of a directive within NL it must always be borne in mind that the *preamble* to the Articles is as much a part of the provisions of the directive as are the Articles themselves. Unlike the long title of a UK statute which does not form part of the legislation. This is of great significance since the European Court of Justice frequently repeats that the spirit of the EC legislation is as important as its substance, a position which derives its impetus from Articles 2 and 3 especially of the Treaty of Rome.

The Package Travel, Package Holidays and Package Tours Regulations (the Regulations) were introduced when the Secretary of State, as a Minister designated for the purposes of section 2(2) of the European Communities Act 1972, exercised his powers in relation to measures relating to consumer protection. This places the Regulations fairly and squarely in the EC context and the Department of Trade and Industry (DTI) as the department of state in the UK charged with implementation of the Directive.

During 1992 lengthy consultations with interested parties took place before the final Regulations appeared in the form on an S.I. Despite the somewhat frenzied responses which appeared at times during the protracted consultation period the final version differs only in minor points from the original consultation papers.

In February 1992 a spokesman for the DTI stated:

'We have copied the directive - that is exactly what we have done except for some rare exceptions. Because we have to implement the directive we have deliberately kept as close to the wording of the directive as possible.'[6]

The language used displays a certain lack of enthusiasm in the implementation of the Directive. Sticking to the words of the Articles themselves seems to the DTI to resolve any problems. It does not. When it comes to Art.7 particularly, which deals with the need to provide sufficient evidence of security for the refund of money paid over and for the repatriation of the consumer in the event of insolvency, the DTI may well find that a failure to implement the spirit of the Directive means that those measures it has chosen to implement by way of regulations 16-21 of the Regulations are not sufficient to discharge the requirements of the Directive.

The Directive

In its *preamble* the Directive voices the concerns of the Council of Ministers in regard to the tourism and the travel package. It states, inter alia:

'One of the main objectives of the Community is to complete the internal market of which the tourist sector is an essential part;

national laws of Member States concerning package travel, package holidays and package tours .... show many disparities .... which gives rise to obstacles to the freedom to provide services in respect of packages and distortions of competition amongst operators established in different Member States;

Tourism plays an increasingly important role in the economies of Member States; the package system is a fundamental part of tourism; the travel industry in Member States would be stimulated to greater growth and productivity of at least a minimum of common rules were adopted in order to give it a Community dimension; .... this would not only produce benefits for the Community citizens buying packages .... but it would attract tourists from outside the Community seeking advantages of guaranteed standards in packages;

disparities in the rules protecting consumers in different Member States are a disincentive to consumers in one Member State from buying packages in another Member state.'

The *preamble* then proceeds to set out what it perceives to be the priorities which the Directive itself seeks to achieve on behalf of the consumer whose interests are to be paramount. These may be summarised as:

1 Safeguarding the position of the purchaser of packages who of necessity is involved in the expenditure of substantial amounts of money in advance of the supply of services in a State other than that in which he is a resident;

2 Protecting consumers irrespective of whether or not they are direct contracting parties, transferees or members of a group on whose behalf another has contracted for package services;

3 Avoidance of false and misleading information being provided by organisers and/or retailers of packages;

4 The promotion of full, comprehensive written contract terms which are also comprehensible to the consumer;

5 Avoidance of surcharges except in certain conditions;

6 Rights of providers and consumers to withdraw from the contract before the due date of departure;

7 Obligations of the organiser of the package as regards a failure to properly perform contractual obligations either for his own part or by any other supplier of services forming part of the package, unless such failure is not attributable to any fault of the organiser or supplier.

8 Supporting the liability limitations set by international conventions - Warsaw, Berne, Athens, Paris (qv) and allowing by contract the limitation as to liability for damage other than personal injury provided always that such limits are *reasonable*;

9 Requiring arrangements for providing consumers with information and the handling of complaints;

10 Benefiting consumers and the industry by placing an obligation upon organisers and/or retailers to provide sufficient evidence of security in the event of insolvency.

There is a sense in which those who are required to implement the Directive in NL of MS should regard these exhortations as 'commandments' which while not absolute duties upon organisers and/or retailers should be seen as duties of strict liability with only the defences allowed within the legislation.

The preamble concludes by stating:

'Member States should be at liberty to adopt, or retain, more stringent provisions relating to package travel for the purpose of protecting the consumer'.

203

The DTI have admitted that, with some minor additions, the UK Regulations do not seek to promote a more stringent regime than is to be found in the Articles of the Directive. In some MS, notably Holland which claimed 70% at least of these provisions already existed in its consumer protection laws, the opportunity has been taken in specific instances to beef up the floor of consumer rights established in the Articles of the Directive.

The prime areas of concern set out in the Articles as being suitable for protection may be seen as the protection of the consumer from false and/or misleading information whether such is contained in brochures or otherwise (Art 3); the provision of full contractual information, specifically as regards those matters set out in Annex to the Directive, as a minimum and in writing (Art 4); making the organiser and/or retailer liable for cancellations prior to departure and failures by himself and/or other parties to provide the consumer with suitable alternatives or compensation (Art 4); the liability which is *personal* to be organiser and/or retailer party to the contract in respect of failure to properly perform the obligations arising from the contract, irrespective of who is actually responsible for the breach, except where such failures are attributable to the consumer, unforeseeable or unavoidable circumstances or force majeure (Art 5); the need to provide security for refunds of monies paid by the consumer and for repatriation when these arise due to insolvency (Art 7).

The key to the liability of the organiser and/or retailer in these respects is to be found in the meaning of the words 'package, organiser, retailer consumer and contract' as set out in Art 2.

Article 2

For the purposes of this Directive:

1. 'package' means the pre-arranged combination of not fewer than two of the following when cold or offered for sale at an inclusive price and when the service covers a period of more than twenty-four hours or includes overnight accommodation:

    (a) transport;
    (b) accommodation;
    (c) other tourist services not ancillary to transport or accommodation and accounting for a significant proportion of the package.

The separate billing of various components of the same package shall not absolve the organizer or retailer from the obligations under this Directive;

2. 'organizer' means the person who, other than occasionally, organizes packages and sells or offers them for sale, whether directly or through a retailer;

3. 'retailer' means the person who sells or offers for sale the package put together by the organizer;

4. 'consumer' means the person who takes or agrees to take the package ('the principal contractor'), or any person on whose behalf the principal contractor agrees to purchase the package ('the other beneficiaries') or any person to whom the principal contractor or any of the other beneficiaries transfers the package ('the transferee');

5. 'contract' means the agreement linking the consumer to the organizer and/or the retailer.

The Directive makes the key point that it is for MS to translate the requirements of the Directive into NL (Art 9). It is not for the Council of Ministers or the Commission to dictate how this is to be done, only to ensure that it has been done in accordance with both the letter and the spirit of EC law. It becomes all the more regrettable then if NL does not fulfil the expectations of EC legislation and the issues have to be argued at length and at no little expenditure of money before national courts and/or the European Court of Justice (ECJ).

In the UK it is a fundamental legal principle that the primary authority is the best. In this respect it is held to mean the primacy of legislation as enacted by Parliament. In the EC context where conflict or uncertainty exist then EC law is paramount. Whatever the Regulations say with regard to packages, the Directive will take precedence. When NL has failed to implement EC law then it is open to an individual who has suffered loss to bring an action against a national government for redress and compensation: *Francovich v Italian Republic (1990)* and *Bonifaci v Italian Republic (1990)*[7].

3. THE REGULATIONS

The method by which the DTI has sought to implement the Directive is to embody in a S.I. regulations which are a mixture of administrative procedures, public (criminal) law and statutory terms which are to be automatically incorporated in contracts to regulate the conduct of individuals and set standards for enforceable obligations inter se.

The Regulations to some extent complement existing UK law but where there is a conflict between the *status quo ante* and the Regulations the latter will prevail as being, initially at least, the determinant of EC law - the Directive.

In UK terms, the criticisms of the legal controls on package transactions has centred largely on the conflict between voluntary and mandatory regulation. On the one hand there exists the licensing system operated by the Civil Aviation Authority (CAA) via the issuing or withholding of Air Tour Organisers Licences (ATOL) conditional upon the holding by tour operators of a valid financial bond which is a guarantee of financial resources being available to meet calls by passengers should an operator fail. The fund derives from a bond arranged with a bank or insurance company which is supervised by the Tour Operators' Study Group (TOSG) which operates within the overall umbrella of the Association of British Travel Agents (ABTA) which also has in membership travel agents who are the customers of the tour operators which has lead in the past to questions of conflict of interest within ABTA.

ABTA bonds its travel agent members such that in the event of collapse it can meet demands of both customers and tour operators. Behind the ATOL system there stands the Air Travel Trust fund, at one time financed by a compulsory levy on operators to provide a reserve of monies to meet emergency needs of the victims of company collapses. The levy was stopped by the UK government in 1986. Its fund continued but has been so severely drained in recent years that it declined from some £26 millions in 1990 to some £3.5 millions at the time of writing. The government is presently considering ways in which the Fund may be replenished.

An ATOL licence is needed where any part of the package contains a non scheduled air carriage component. The provisions administered by the CAA are statutory, the Authority itself having assumed powers created for it by the Civil Aviation Act 1982. Thus there is for packages with an air component a statutory licensing system and a back up reserve fund also the creature of statute - the Air Travel Reserve Fund Act 1975.

On the other hand, for non air carriage components in packages there is no such statutory regulation, instead there is a voluntary system operated principally by ABTA whereby in order to be ABTA members providers of surface packages are required to undertake bonding. In return for this, members came under the STABILISER arrangement operated by ABTA which dictates that for those in membership with ABTA an exclusive dealing agreement operates whereby members selling through agents may not sell through non ABTA agents. Similarly ABTA travel agents are not allowed to sell any foreign package holidays not organised by an ABTA members. The arrangement does not impact upon domestic holidays nor those in Eire. There is also the provision that ABTA members can sell the foreign package holidays of surface carriers of the Bonded Coach Holidays element of the Bus and Coach Council (BCC) and the Passenger shipping Association (PSA). These together with the 18 main tour operators offering air travel combine to create a monopoly system for ABTA.

In 1982 the STABILISER arrangement was referred to the Restrictive Trade Practices Court originally set up by statute in 1976. The Court found that the system supported ABTA's intention to provide financial protection for the public and was not against the public interest. It did find elements in SFC terms imposed by ABTA which were restrictive and ruled them unlawful. With STABILISER thus modified the system has operated to the present time.

Now there are signs of the breaking of ranks consequent upon the adoption of the new Regulations. In the light of these it is not difficult to see that a further reference to the Court could result in STABILISER being adjudged against the public interest. Recently, British Airways Holidays broke ranks and engaged in trading with non ABTA agents. ABTA determined to sue but realised that in view of the new Regulations its previous contractual arrangements were non-enforceable if not illegal. It has, therefore, been seen as dead. But it has not yet been buried.

Under the DTI Regulations, provisions exist in order to ensure the letter of Art 7 of the Directive, if not necessarily its spirit. But the danger has always been apparent that there were rogue elements in the travel trade who would pretend membership of ABTA to gain in the travel trade who would pretend membership of ABTA to gain the caché of its authorising stamp of approval on their transactions but who were not members and who were unbonded. In addition, there exist, quite legitimately, tour operators who until now operated outside ABTA, some of whom were bonded and some not. It has been the collapse of such as 'Land Travel' in 1992 which has lead to calls from ABTA and others for a full licensing system for tour operators, on the lines of ATOL, for surface packagers.

Such a proposal for a licensing and back up fund was present in the draft directive on packages issued in 1988 but is absent from the 1990 Directive. ABTA and others set up a clamour for a full licensing system but this was turned down by the DTI on, it would appear, economic grounds. The CAA declined to operate an extended system and when the DTI examined the number of potential operators who could be involved it discovered some 20,000 as opposed to the 160 ATOL businesses. This persuaded it to opt for a financial security system in the Regulations which appears to have produced the worst of the possible choices. The tri-partite system which now exists in response to the Directive's provisions is that sufficient security must be demonstrated by requiring either that:

"organisers may be bonded to an approved body for a certain percentage of the organiser's turnover. Of the approved body has a reserve fund the draft regulations permit bonding to a lower percentage of turnover or

"organisers may arrange insurance against insolvency to the benefit of the consumer or

"organisers may place pre-payments on trust for the consumer until the service against which the pre-payment has been made have been performed: there are special arrangements for organisers not acting by way of business - the *escrow* system.

Organisers and or retailers must also show evidence of security for repatriation in cases of overseas travel.

Calls made upon the ABTA bonded scheme which existed within its contractual membership rules and incorporating a Code of Conduct more rigorous than proposed by the DTI resulted in resources being stretched to the limits in the last few years as operators and agents' businesses collapsed in an adverse economic climate not aided by political difficulties in the Middle East and elsewhere. Strong representations were made to the DTI during the consultation period in 1992 prior to the Regulations becoming law. The result has been a partial victory for a properly bonded scheme for surface travel packages on the lines of ATOL and the ATTF.

In its representations the industry bodies began seriously to question whether or not the DTI understood the nature of the businesses it was seeking to control, albeit reluctantly it seemed. The DTI finally agreed to the setting up of the Travel Protection Association (TPA) whose constituent members will be ABTA, TOSG, BVV the PSA, all previously under the ABTA umbrella, together with Association of Independent Tour Operators. Its arrival was welcomed by CAA, somewhat prematurely since it will not be able to operate effectively until late 1993 and then funding for its back up fund will not be in place until late 1994. The DTI are aware of the dangers of another unbonded company, such as 'Land Travel', collapsing leaving some 2,500 people on holiday with 50,000 forward bookings with the Bath based company unprotected. None of these received recompense and the company's debts exceeded £2 million. It is one thing to pass legislation requiring adequate security provision, such as the Regulations now in force, and quite another matter to police it adequately especially when the system set up by the DTI is confusing for the public at large and almost impossible for the authorities charged with responsibility to enforce it. In order to finance the ATP fund the DTI is to allow a levy of £1 per head of consumer which in 12-18 months should produce an estimated fund of some £5 million. In the meantime it appears that STABILISER will soldier on until the new fund allows it to wither on the vine.

The whole system is overly complex and possibly, in time, the DTI will come to realise the wisdom of having a unitary system for the package industry involving licensing and reserve funding. The mixture of voluntary and compulsory, as in the past, has revealed the dangers of such a system.

The industry has called for *bonding* as the best safeguard of financial security but the DTI has allowed *insurance* and *escrow* provisions to be used as alternatives under the Regulations. Danger signs are already apparent as small operators find that they cannot afford the insurance route and run, in some cases, for shelter under the bonded wing of the bigger operators which in the sense of true competition has little to commend it. As insurance premiums continue to rise some operators seek the escrow method of depositing monies in trust to ensure pre-payments security. This impacts severely on the cash flow for businesses who rely heavily on monies paid up front by consumers of package services to buy in the very services the tourist wants. *Regulation 19* deals with this method of security with rules as to its operation but it is a notoriously difficult system to police effectively. Some firms of solicitors and accountants are already offering services as trustees but this in itself is no guarantee of the safety of monies in their or others hands so far as the consumers are concerned.

Bonding is provided for under the terms of *Regulation 17*. This requires that the other party to the contract, not being the consumer, has to ensure that a bond is entered into by an *authorised institution* under which the institution binds itself to pay to an *approved body*, of which that other party is a member, a sum calculated in accordance with the provisions of Reg.17(3), for which a minimum amount is set by 17(4). An *approved body* for this purpose is one for the time being approved by the Secretary of State. Applications were invited post commencement of the Regulations w.e.f. 1 January 1993. It was realised that such bodies would most likely come from the ranks of the industry organisations. So it has proved to be. ABTA, TOSG, AITO, PSA and BCC have all been approved together with a new organisation - The Association of Bonded Travel Organisations. More will doubtless appear.

By *authorised institutions* the regulation means a person authorised under the law of a MS to carry on business of bonding in the manner required by Reg.17. In practice this means banks and insurance businesses throughout the EC.

The requirements of the Regulations as a whole are to be enforced by the weights and measures authorities in the UK. This of course means by the Trading Standards Officers (TSOs). During the consultation period their professional body, the Institute of Trading Standards Officers (ITSO), protested that the system envisaged by the Regulations was unenforceable. Some areas akin to existing duties in connection with Consumer Protection legislation were bad enough in their eyes, but the requirements as to the security for financial provisions dismayed them. They were advised by the DTI that in this aspect of their duties spot checks were not necessary and that they should only investigate where they has suspicions of unlawful trading. This, responded the ITSO, would require enormous resources, including time and the professional assistance of actuaries and accountants otherwise the provisions for security in the Regulations would be no more than cosmetic.

The rejoinder of the DTI was to effect that TSOs were not required into the adequacy of whichever of the three possible forms for ensuring security was used, only to see that something in the nature of at least one of them was in place! After all, the DTI argued, no consumer could expect to be completely secure! As regards all the issues requiring to be policed under the Regulations the department did not expect to see a flood of prosecutions. None of these suggestions has allayed the fears of the TSOs, some of whose members are now engaged in mutual information exercises with ABTA and other bodies to solve the riddles posed by the DTI regime as presently constituted under the Regulations.

The consumer might fare better under the terms of existing consumer protection legislation as regards individual financial safeguards. Under the terms of the Consumer Credit Act 1974 s.75 where goods or services of more than £100 are bought using a credit card then the consumer can look to the card company to recompense him for unsatisfactory services bought by this method. Some card companies even offer free or low cost insurance which would enable a stranded tourist to get home in the event of a company collapse. A tourist would then be best advised to buy a package with his card, preferably direct from a tour operator with no intermediaries.

Existing consumer protection laws

Prior to the advent of the Regulations no specific legislation was aimed at package travel. Consumer protection was provided by a hotch-potch of voluntary measures, as previously outlined, and general statutory provisions together with the common law.

An operator who knowingly or recklessly misdescribes services in promotional material or brochures connected to bookings faces criminal prosecution under the Trade Descriptions Act 1968 s.14. Where convictions are obtained by TSOs Courts could require the guilty party to pay compensation to the victim under the Powers of the Criminal Courts Act 1973 s.35. The levels of compensation so awarded have always been relatively small compared to what might be obtained by a civil action.

In order to maintain such a civil claim the plaintiff could call in aid the Supply of Goods and Service Act 1982 s.13 which requires the provider of services to exercise reasonably care and skill. Any exclusion clauses in contracts would only avail the would be beneficiary of them provided that they did not fall foul of the Unfair Contract Terms Act 1977 s.3, satisfying a statutory test of *reasonableness*. Pre-contractual statements are also covered by the Misrepresentation Act 1967. All these legislative provisions require the victim to sue for common law rights in tort and/or contract. Where negligent mis-statements have caused loss to the plaintiff and a special relationship exists between him and the defendant then an action in Negligence could provide the answer

It would be better for the consumer if he did not have to sue at all to get compensation but rely instead on the provisions of the criminal law with accompanying sanctions to protect him from harm in the first place by preventing the climate for injury or damage. Failing that, an adequate system of compensation based on a bonded liability in some for would be preferable. The mixed regime of the Regulations appears designed to marry the two areas of consumer protection into one for package consumers.

Regulation 4 provides a right to a consumer to be compensated for *misleading information* supplied in relation to a package.

Regulation 6 declares that any particulars supplied in a brochure whether or not they are those which the Regulations expressly require to be given shall be *implied warranties* for the purposes of any contract to which they relate.

Regulation 9 states that the contract shall be in written form and is specific as to certain matters of content - vide *Schedule 2* to the Regulations. This provision helps to maintain an action rather than giving rise to one initially.

Regulations 10 to 13 allow for the consumer to transfer his booking to approved persons such as to give rise to rights to be vested in others; prevent surcharging, except in certain situations; disallow significant unilateral variations of contract terms before departure without agreement by the consumer; allow withdrawal by the consumer and, within limits, cancellation by the organiser without penalty in certain circumstances.

Significantly, Reg.13(4) specifically disallows overbooking as a reason entitling the organiser to cancel by reason of *unusual or unforeseeable* circumstances beyond his control which could not have been avoided even had *all due care* been exercised on his part.

Regulation 14 deals with the situation where a significant proportion of the services due to be provided under the contract is not provided or the organiser becomes aware that he will not be able to procure the same, allowing the consumer to agree to a suitable substitution with appropriate recompense for price differentiation, as applicable. Compensation may also be appropriate as well. If the organiser cannot meet his obligations as contracted for, or the consumer declines to accept alternatives, the organiser has an obligation to arrange equivalent transportation to that contracted for back to the consumers point of original departure or to another agreed destination and, where appropriate, offer compensation in addition.

This is a valuable new right which is enforceable by disappointed tourists. Second only in importance, it is submitted, to that which follows it.

Regulation 15. The organiser of the package is liable to the consumer for the proper performance of contractual obligations whether or not he is the designated performer of such obligations or they are to be performed by another. Thus, the disappointed guest in a hotel in Spain can look to the *organiser* who cannot then deny responsibility by passing on to the hotelier. The aggrieved *consumer* retains a right of action against the hotelier but does not have to look to the latter in place of the *organiser*.

The *organiser* is also liable to the consumer for any damage caused to him by improper or non-performance, unless this is the result of actions of a third party over whom the *organiser*, or the actual supplier of the service, had no control and which are unconnected with the services contracted for. Such interventions must be either *unforeseeable or unavoidable*. If the *consumer* himself is the author of the misfortune then he will not have a cause of action. Only in specified conditions will the *organiser* be allowed to exclude liability for non proper performance of the contract terms.

Pre-existing case law had already gone some way to deal with some of the situations which arise in connection with improper or non-performance by the organiser. Some of these are examined in Chapter XII. Other examples can be found in *Didgeson v Airtours (1992)*[8] where it was held not to be the duty of a tour operator to advise clients of the danger of diving into shallow pools where common sense dictated that the plaintiff should have looked first for himself; *Kemp v Intasun Holidays (1987)*[9] - a sudden and unforeseen asthma attack brought on by conditions in a dusty hotel could not be attributed to the tour operator who had no special knowledge of the circumstances of the client's health. The Court of Appeal held that damage was too remote, which would still be the case on the facts today and further would, it is submitted, be defended by the provisions of Reg.15(2)(c). In *Duthie v Thomson Holidays (1988)*[10] failure to provide accommodation as contracted for made the operator liable.

Example of cases which could be differently decided today under the Regulations are to be found in *Gibbons v Intasun Holidays (1987)*[11] loss of a suitcase by a sub-contractor - operator found not liable; *Toubi v Intasun Holidays (1987)*[12] overbooking by hotelier - operator held to have done his best - it was all the fault of the hotelier!

Cases which could still be decided either way under common law or the Regulations: *Jones v Villa Ramos (Algarve) (1988)*[13] dispute over the use of facilities at apartment complex; *Wilson v Pegasus Holidays (1988)*[14] misrepresentation as to standards and facilities.

Prosecutions

The Regulations also provide for prosecutions by the TSOs with a requirement of notification to the Director General of Fair Trading who has a duty of overview *(Schedule 3)*.

Criminal offences are committed under the terms of certain sections where prosecution is the only course since *Regulation 27* provides that they do not give rise to civil proceedings at the suit of an individual.

Regulation 5 relating to offences in relation to brochures. In particular, adequate information concerning issues set out in *Schedule 1*. This provision catches organisers and retailers but, as regards the retailer, he must know or have reasonable cause to believe that an offence is contained in materials supplied to him which he makes available to a possible consumer.

Regulation 7 failure to provide certain information with reference to passports, visas, health and other specified matters.

Regulation 8 failure to supply information in good time concerning matters specified in paragraph (2) of the regulation.

Regulation 16 failure to secure the financial interests of the consumer for the refund of monies paid over and for repatriation in the event of insolvency.

Regulation 22 false statements made in connection with the deposit of trust monies in escrow contrary to the provisions of *Regs. 20* and *21*.

Regulation 5 is in some instances already covered in Trade Description Act provisions. The others are new offences.

In relation to these offences, *Regulation 24* provides the *due diligence defence* which has echoes in other existing Consumer statutes. The defence consists of the defendant showing that he took all reasonable steps and exercised all due diligence to avoid committing the offence as charged. Its provisions, as regards the plea of *act or default of another* and *reliance on information given by another* seem to have been lifted straight from pre-existing legislation i.e. Food Act 1984 and the Trade Descriptions Act 1968.

Interpretation

The DTI showed a marked disinclination to offer any guidelines of substance during the consultation process preceding the introduction of the Regulations in their final form, admitting that much would probably be needed to be tested in the courts. Eventually some 18 pages of Guidance Notes appeared at the end of December 1992. The DTI authors are at pains to point out that they offer some interpretation of certain provisions in the Directive BUT are not intended to

'replace the Regulations or the Directive and ultimately only the European Court of Justice can decide the effect of the Directive'

and, one is tempted to add "whether or not the UK government has done all that it ought to have done and not left undone those things which it should have done" in keeping with the spirit as well as the letter of the Directive.

The main points of interpretation in the notes which will probably not be so contentious now as they were when the consultation period was underway are the meanings of:

Organiser - this must in all probability catch some travel agents at some time who put together a package using their professional expertise to meet the demands of a client; but possibly not when the client himself directs the agent to book certain specific individual items. Even so, if he accepts payment on his own behalf he is probably acting as an organiser. Where he accepts payments on behalf of an organiser he is unlikely to be himself acting as such.

Occasionally -	it is suggested that no travel agent who now and then organises packages on his own behalf is likely to be able to avail himself of the provision as to 'occasional' i.e. exempt provider. It is submitted that anyone in business, as distinct from the pure amateur, who puts together a package is likely to be an organiser and caught by the full impact of the Regulations, bonding et al.
Other tourist - *services*	are those which from a significant part of the deal and, therefore, contribute to the requirements necessary for the package to come into existence if their absence or presence is a determinant factor in causing the deal to be struck between buyer and seller.
Significant -	Aroused much interest, and still does, particularly in relation to educational or business type activities. This is most likely to be a prime area for litigation before the courts - as difficult to quantify as the concept of *reasonableness* derived from the common law.

Regulation 3 makes the point that subject to *Regulation 16(3)* the regulations apply to packages sold or offered for sale in the UK regardless of the place of establishment of the operator. They do not apply to packages sold in other countries by operators established in the UK. Some see this as a loophole which the DTI, after receiving trade submissions, refused to close. There are fears in the industry that if other countries interpret the Directive in a more relaxed way than the UK, tour operators will choose to have their base in the MS offering the most amenable climate for their activities.

The closing shot for the DTI was delivered by the Consumer Affairs Minister who stated confidently:

'This is a significant step forward in consumer protection. After extensive discussion and consultation with industry and consumers, I am confident we have struck the right balance in the way we propose to implement this important Directive. These Regulations aim to provide protection for package travellers without making the cost of holidays prohibitive by imposing unfair burdens on the smaller operators'.[15]

The Consumers' Association sees the position somewhat differently. In its journal, *Which*, it stated:

Government claims that the new regulations implementing the Directive on Package Travel are a major benefit to consumers have a hollow ring after a Minister was forced to admit that it cannot deter rogue operators which are determined to trade without protecting customers money .... Six weeks after the regulations became law the Minister stated that it is impossible to .... regulate against people acting corruptly, or lying to trading standards officers and to overseers of their business. The government is therefore admitting that the regulations fail to achieve their objective - to ensure that consumers are guaranteed protection if a tour operator goes bust'.

From the start it has been Article 7 which has been seen as the main difficulty and it was the major reason for the protracted consultation period in 1992. It was doubtless the main reason why upon enquiry of the DTI at the close of September 1992 I was given the answer to my question as to when we might expect to see the definitive Regulations on the shelves - "We haven't a clue"!

In some circumstances it will be necessary still for consumers to rely on existing common law for redress in matters where the Regulations do not operate. Where they are definitive they will need to be applied, subject always to the caveat that it may be necessary for a Court to decide - even if that Court is the ECJ and it takes years to bring a case before it.

4. TRAVEL AGENTS

Notwithstanding the provisions in the Regulations that a travel agent may render himself to be an *organiser* and therefore be required to make financial provisions as to financial security for consumers monies and for repatriation as necessary, this does not stop him from being regarded in law as an agent. In which case he is bound by the common law when he so acts. Where he acts or is deemed to act as a principal, under the Regulations he will also be deemed to be in cases where packages are involved, an *organiser*.

The common law position

An agent does not make a contract on his own behalf. He acts for a principal. Once the latter has been united with his customer, the agent withdraws from the scene. The law recognises many forms of agent who may come into existence in several ways. In the case of a travel agent, it would be unusual for him to be appointed other than by express agreement with the principal. This will usually be contained in a written format and is universal for ABTA members.

In practice, the agent will act for a number of principals whose packages he promotes. In return for the services he offers, he will be paid commission agreed with individual operators. An agent will not usually adopt a positive selling role, but act more in an advisory capacity to a customer who comes to him with an idea of the type of holiday package he wants. Brochures are made available to the client who may select those which appeal and seek further information or advice from the agent. The customer chooses a preferred option and the agent confirms whether or not it is available. If it is, the agent books the holiday, collects fees on behalf of the operator and, at the appropriate time, forwards the ticket to the customer. These are standard practices but will vary in detail with different agents and operators.

The primary duty of the agent is to his principal. But he also owes duties of professional competence to the client he introduces. Such obligations are not contained in the contract which the agent is instrumental in promoting. That contract is private to the parties who are joined together by it: *Montgomerie v UK Steamship Association (1891)*.[16] If issues arise from the terms of the contract, they fall to be resolved between the operator and the individual tourist since the agent is not a party to the agreement.

An agent is required to adhere to the terms of his agreement with his principal. This will require him to follow such lawful instructions as the principal may choose to give him in connection with his duties. These may be contained in the document creating the agency, or arise from established customs and trade practices. The agent's actions only bind the principal if the former possesses actual authority for them, or the principal allows a third party to believe that this is the case.

The main practical difficulty for the third party, in this case the customer, is that he cannot be expected to know the terms of the agreement between principal and agent. In this respect, the law takes the view that the third party is entitled to rely on appearances. If an agent appears to possess the authority which he professes then the third party need look no further. It may be that the agent is exceeding his authority, but in the ordinary course of events that is not a matter which need concern the third party: *Watteau v Fenwick (1893)*.[17]

On the other hand, if it is known to the third party that the agent does not have the authority to act in the way which he claims, then the principal will not be bound by the terms negotiated: *Kinahan and Co v Parry (1910)*.[18] Where the third party has good cause to doubt the agent's powers, he must seek to satisfy himself of the true position. He may not simply rely on outward appearances or professed authority in such circumstances. Where authority is lacking, the principal may elect to be bound by an agreement purported to be made on his behalf. He may *ratify* such a transaction which has the effect of legitimising the actions of the agent as though at the time of the negotiations with the third party he had real authority: *Bolton Partners v Lambers (1889)*.[19]

Anyone who professes to act as an agent, in effect promises to those concerned that he has authority for his actions. If he has no authority, or he exceeds his powers such that the principal will not ratify any agreement made in his name, a third party may sue an agent for *breach of warranty of authority*. Such a warranty attaches to the agent and makes him personally liable even where he may have acted innocently and in the genuine belief that he had the authority claimed: *Young v Toynbee (1910)*.[20] It will be necessary for the third party to show that he has been misled. If it should prove that he knew of the defective agency, he will not succeed in an action against either the principal or the purported agent.

The agent as principal

An agent who does not disclose that he is acting for a principal, runs the risk that the third party will proceed against him for the acts or omissions of the hidden principal. Where the agent gives the impression that he is acting on his own behalf, the third party may maintain an action against the agent or the principal when he discovers his existence and identity. He must choose one or the other, but, if the agreement is well worded, he may choose to proceed against the alternative defendant even after litigation has commenced: *Clarkson Booker v Andjel (1964)*.[21]

There have been a number of US decisions where the third party has been able to hold the agent directly liable: *Bucholz v Sirotkin Travel (1974)*[22]. This case turned on the fact that the customer had asked the agent to construct a package for him. He did not buy an existing package. The agent chose to take one off the shelf and use that. When it proved unsatisfactory, the customer was allowed to hold the agent liable since he had not asked that he be put into contact with the operator whose package it was. Under the Regulations it is most probable that an agent acting in such a manner would be regarded as an *organiser* even though he supplied complete, as it were, an existing package created by another.

Under US law, where an agent acts for an 'undisclosed' principal, but the third party knows of his existence if not his identity, he may still sue the agent: *Seigal v Council of Long Island Educators Inc (1973)*.[23] In English law, the third party may only proceed against the agent if it can be shown that the identity of the 'undisclosed' principal is such that, had it been known to the third party, he would not have made the contract: *Said v Butt (1920)*.[24] In the case of a package, the Regulations would once again determine the liability.

Where either the existence or the identity of the principal is unknown to the third party, the principal is entitled to intervene and sue upon the contract unless to do so would work an injustice: *Humble v Hunter (1845)*.[25] In such circumstances, the third party may use any defence or counter-claim he might have used against the agent before he became aware of the existence of the principal.

In the UK, it is standard practice for a holiday brochure to incorporate the terms and conditions of the contract of booking. These will remind the customer that the travel agent is acting on behalf of a named tour operator and that the customer's contract is with the latter. Such standard form contracts will usually be required to conform to the Tour Operators Code Of Conduct drawn up by ABTA for its members.

Agent for the customer

There is no reason why the agent should not act for the customer or be held to do so. The matter has never been directly tested in the courts. In 1974, with the failure of Court Line and its subsidiary Clarksons Holidays, it seemed likely that there would be cases brought by customers seeking to recover monies in the hands of travel agents holding such sums for Clarksons. If the agents could be held to be acting for the customers, and not for the operator, the monies were not available to the liquidators of the company but should be returned to the customers. This could still prove a valuable protection for consumers where the Regulations operate BUT the bonding of other obligations for establishing security is non existent or inadequate to meet the calls upon it - or where a trustee of an escrow is fraudulent.

Those who supported this contention argued that a travel agent was the equivalent of an insurance broker. Such persons are held by insurance practice to be the agents of the insured parties not of the insurers: *Anglo-African Merchants Ltd v Bayley (1970)*.[26] They, like travel agents, sell the products of more than one company. They advise on the merits of various insurance packages as travel agents do in respect of holidays.

The issue is far from clear since the Government stepped in before the matter could be brought before the courts. Money was repaid to the customers concerned from the newly-created Air Travel Reserve Fund which had been pump-primed with Government cash.

Because of the written contracts appointing agents on behalf of operators, required by ABTA, it seems likely that a customer would have difficulty in asserting the agent was acting for him not the operator. The Consumers' Association has long wished to make the high street travel agent liable to the customer instead of an operator in some distant office. It is interesting to note that a freight for warder acts for the shipper not the carrier and people who are packaged might feel entitled to ask why they should fare worse than goods!

Conflict of interest

Since travel agents sell on behalf of various operators at the same time, and also advise customers, there seems to be an element in such transactions which works contrary to the legal concept of an agent's duty to his principal. Usually, an agent may not accept employment from a second principal unless he makes a full disclosure to the first in time, and receives his consent to double employment: *Fulwood v Hurley (1928)*[28]. It must be assumed that custom and practice in the travel trade implies such consent on agency agreements.

Or it may be that the role of the travel agent is simply that of one who books on behalf of an operator, in the same way as theatre and other such tickets are sold on an ad hoc basis. This is a *bare agency* in law and is, in reality, hardly an agency at all in the accepted sense of the term. But if instead of simply displaying brochures and taking bookings, the travel agent has sought to offer services in the nature of 'travel consultancy' then a conflict of interest would appear to exist. This could be denied by reverting to the view which holds that the agent acts not on behalf of the customer, but only as the appointed representative of he who pays his commission. There is no contract with the customer since he gives no consideration to the travel agent for the services provided to him.

An agent who supplies false and misleading information is liable, under the Regulations for a criminal offence *Regulation 5* - where the agent gives the customer a false interpretation s to what the provisions in a brochure mean. Additionally, under *Regulation 4* the consumer may maintain a civil action - based upon the manner in which the Regulation is establishing a special relationship as in *Hedley Byrne v Heller (1963)*[28] and the line of cases stemming from it as to liability for negligent mis-statement.

It is just possible that the customer has a collateral contract with the travel agent: *Shanklin Pier Ltd v Detel Products Ltd (1951).*[29] The consideration given by the customer is that of entering into the main contract with the tour operator. Such a position would not arise if a travel agent confined himself to simply acting as a booking agent, and did no more than pass on information supplied to him by the operator, and made it clear that this was all he was doing. But if the travel agent wishes to be regarded as more than an intermediary for transferring tickets, then he should accept the responsibility which goes with professional status.

Whether or not the travel agent is liable in contract to the consumer is still a matter of conjecture. What is certain is that the ABTA Code of Conduct (1985) requires that 'Travel Agents shall make every effort to ensure that their clients are not sold tours, holidays or travel arrangements incompatible with their individual requirements'.[30] This stops some way short of the requirement of section 13 of the Supply of Goods and Services Act 1982, but raises the issue of the standard of *reasonableness* to be expected of an expert or professional adviser on interpreting section 13.

Liability in tort

Where a *special relationship* exists between the parties, he who causes financial loss by the making of a negligent mis-statement to the other will be liable to him: *Hedley Byrne & Co v Heller & Partners Ltd (1963).*[31] The House of Lords was unanimous in this decision that 'If someone possessed of a special skill under takes, quite irrespective of contract, to apply that skill for the assistance of another person who relies on such skill, a duty of care will arise'.

If the customer does not seek the advice of the agent, but relies on the brochure provided by the tour operator, he has no claim against the agent, unless, that is, the brochure contains a mis-statement amounting to a misrepresentation known to the agent. This is clearly where the provisions on misleading information supplied by a retailer contained in the Regulations derive their substance. The ABTA Code also requires that agents 'shall ensure that their counter staff carefully study all tour, holiday and travel programmes and brochures'.[32] In which case, an agent will be liable for mis-statements he could have detected - a position re-enforced in the Regulations as a defence.

A travel agent may protect himself by a disclaimer notice. This would need to be communicated to the client before he acts on the statement and must indicate that the agent is not taking care. It seems unlikely that any agent would seek to protect himself in this way. He would in effect be saying 'I don't know that what I am saying is correct and you should not rely on anything I say'! He would be better to say that he too is relying on the information received from the operator whom he will contact for further clarification.

If the agent is subsequently told by the operator that information in the latter's literature is incorrect, the agent has a duty to disclose this to the client. He could seek to rely on this being done by the operator direct but there is a general duty to disclose by one, if not both of them: *With v O'Flanagan (1936)*.[33] The agent must, under the Regulations inform the consumer of changes notified to him by the organiser.

Whilst a travel agent cannot be expected to warn customers of all possible problems associated with a particular holiday, he should warn of those he knows, even if he has not been expressly notified by the operator: *Freemantle v Thomas Cook (1984)*.[34] As indeed of those matters specified in the Regulations - even if the DTI seems to believe that all that is necessary is to make periodic enquiries of foreign embassies in order to satisfy the letter of the Regulations!

Booking arrangements

An agent who incorrectly fills out details when booking the client's holiday, or who fails to notify him of altered travelling arrangements, may also find that he is caught by the Regulations which will establish on behalf of the consumer the standard of care required to make the agent liable in negligence. Where the client proceeds against the operator, the latter may seek to resist the claim by raising the error of the agent as his defence. Alternatively, he could join the agent as co-defendant.

In trying to mitigate their neglect, the defendants could seek to show contributory negligence on the part of the plaintiff. This might arise where the client had not checked the accuracy of the details on the travel documents sent to him prior to the departure date - but the Regulations seem to preclude this.

The agent or the operator could counter a claim brought against them by alleging that the loss sustained was the result of matters over which neither had any control as in *Kemp*. If the operator was found liable, he might seek indemnity from the agent if it could be shown that he was in breach of the terms of his agency agreement.

The liability of travel agents, *qua* agents, arises independently of the Regulations. The services which the agent sells may not be in the form or of the nature which will constitute a package within the format decreed by the Directive/Regulations. At least two of the ingredients prescribed must be present in order to bring the provisions into operation.

Thus, the agent may book a hotel only which included a local car service to and from the local airport/ferry or rail station. The tourist has himself arranged the air/ferry/rail part of his activity. The car hire will not count as a *service* for the package requirement but only operate in the nature of a *facility*. Nor does it count as transport in the sense meant by the Regulations.

Similarly, the agent may book a ferry crossing which includes a cabin; a flight which has a relining seat for passenger comfort. Neither of these facilities would count as accommodation, only as a *facility*. Nevertheless, as regards these examples the agent still has legal obligations arising out of the service he has provided to the customer/consumer even though they do not, as constituted, add up to a package so as to bring the Regulations into play.

Where the package elements are lacking the common law and/or statutory provisions may make the agent liable so as to enable the disappointed party to seek redress from the agent if this is appropriate in the circumstances.

5. PROFESSIONAL STANDARDS

There is at present no legal requirement for travel agents to be licensed to operate in that capacity neither for the purpose of the Regulations nor for any other trading activity. The industry generally regards the Regulations at least to be defective in this respect.

ABTA was founded in 1955 as a voluntary body and has included in membership both tour operators and travel agents. The relationship between the two groups has not always been harmonious yet it did allow for a degree of regulation to the advantage of the consumer. It also allowed ABTA to insist on bonding of members both for the purposes of protecting the consumer and the tour operator/travel agent financial relationship under the STABILISER provisions. As indicated earlier this is now in a state of terminal decline due to the introduction of the Regulations.

Still for those in membership, with the new regime in place the provisions of the ABTA Codes of Conduct provide a degree of control over the activities of the members who enter into a contractual agreement with ABTA to observe the standards set. These in some cases are more rigorous than the Regulations. Indeed as regards the provisions as to surcharging, the Regulations have opted for ABTAs 30 day period prior to the date of departure as the minimum period whereas the Directive states only 20. In this case the DTI has used the provision of Art.8.

Codes in general impose no legal obligations *per se* but they are used in an evidential way by the Courts in deciding, inter alia, what are the *reasonable* standards to be expected of professional activity. Domestically, members of ABTA who are in alleged breach of the Codes may be reported to their respective councils which operate under the ABTA umbrella. Those against whom complaints are upheld may be reprimanded, fined or expelled from membership. An appeal procedure exists for those found wanting but who object to a council's finding.

At the time of writing the future constitution and role of ABTA is undergoing review as a consequence of the introduction of the Regulations. It may be that the Association will become a purely regulatory body or still retain its trade role. It appears that there is likely to be a general acceptance that there would be a clear separation of the Association's regulatory role from its trade association activities if the two elements continue to co-exist. If a split between operators and agents groups does come about the new travel agent and tour operator trade bodies would be established to look after the interests of their members. If 75% of the ABTA membership agree, a new regime could be in place for October 1993.

Until such time as the issue is resolved the existing ABTA regimes for members will prevail. Even when changes do occur then no doubt those practices which have stood the test of time within the organisation will be adapted to meet the new circumstances.

Arbitration

The first recourse of a dissatisfied tourist is to complain to the agent or operator involved. Should this fail, he may pursue the matter through the courts or elect to use the arbitration scheme set up by ABTA in 1975. It can only be used where there is no dispute between agent and operator as to whose responsibility is in issue. ABTA will, in the first instance, seek to effect conciliation between the parties. If this does not succeed, the customer is invited to apply for an independent assessor to be appointed by the Chartered Institute of Arbitrators. The scheme is informal and governed by several considerations:

1. Claims must not amount to more than £5,000 per booking form, or £10,000 per person.

2. They must not be solely based on personal injury or illness claims.

3. Claims must be brought within 9 months of the holiday concerned.

4. The complainant must agree to be bound by the decision of the arbitrator.

5. The complainant must pay a deposit against the arbitrator's fee and, if unsuccessful, may be called upon to pay the whole fee.

6. Hearings are not in person. The arbitrator bases his decision on the documents submitted to him.

The customer is not obliged to use the scheme and even where booking conditions state that arbitration shall be used to settle any dispute, this cannot oust the jurisdiction of the courts. The provisions of the Arbitration Agreements Act 1988 will apply to this as to any other arbitration scheme.

NOTES:

1. Housing, Town Planning Act 1909.
2. *Guardian* 1 May 1987.
3. Official Journal (O.J.) of the EC No.1159/59 23 June 1990.
4. O.J. No.C115 30 April 1984.
5. 1988 CMLR 695 EC.
6. Travel Trade Gazette 13 February 1992.
7. (1992) IRLR 84 re cases C 6/90 and C 9/90.
8. (1992) CLY 422 20 August.
9. (1987) FTLR 234 CA.
10. (1988) CLY 1058 13 May.
11. (1987) CLY 168 23 November.
12. (1987) CLY 1060 10 November.
13. (1988) CLY 1061 16 February
14. (1988) CLY 1059 15 April.
15. DTI Press Notice No.P/92/756 23 November 1992.
16. (1891) 1 QB 370.
17. (1893) 1 QB 346.
18. (1910) 2 QB 389.
19. (1889) 41 Ch D 295.
20. (1910) 1 QB 215.
21. (1964) 3 All ER 810.
22. (1974) 80 Mx 2d 750.
23. (1973) 75 Mx 2d 750.
24. (1920) 3 KB 497.
25. (1848) 12 KB 310.
26. (1970) 1 QB 311.
27. (1928) 1 KB 498.
28. (1963) AC 465.
29. (1951) 2 KB 854.
30. Para 2.1 (iii)
31. See note 28.
32. Para 2.5.
33. (1936) Ch 575.
34. *Times* 25 Feb 1984

CHAPTER XII

Consumer Protection

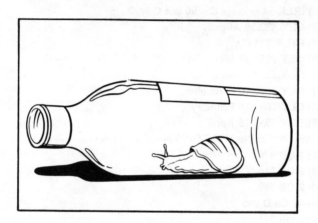

1. THE CONSUMER

A consumer is someone who makes a contract, not in the course of business, with another who sells or supplies goods or services commercially.[1] Such a contract may be in writing on the standard booking form of a tour operator; an oral agreement between a diner and a restaurateur; or the action of putting a coin into an automatic ticket vending machine.

Goods may be bought, such that they become the property of the purchaser, or be supplied to one who merely has the use of them in return for a hire charge. It is usual to speak of services as being supplied rather than bought since they are intangible, e.g. professional advice, or a mixture of goods, services and the use of facilities in the case of hotel accommodation.

Tourists are *consumers* of a wide variety of goods and services which they buy, or hire, in pursuit of their chosen recreational occupations. As such, they come directly into contact with those areas of law which are designed to regulate, inter alia, goods and services which are qualitatively defective, trading practices which are fraudulent, incomplete or misleading information, or restrictive practices which limit freedom of choice. The idea of consumer protection is not a new one in English law. Its effects were experienced very early in the development of the common law by travellers who, of necessity, had to lodge at wayside inns. Controls on the pricing of fares imposed by 19th century statutes on railway companies are more recent examples. The Unfair Contract Terms Act 1977 demonstrates a desire to exercise wider control over numerous business practices which seek to deprive many of protection for the benefit of the few.

Protection of the consumer is linked to administration by units of local government. Justices of the Peace have long dealt with offences in connection with weights and measures and food standards. County courts were created in 1846 to try, on a local basis, cases involving small sums of money. Since 1973, there has been an *arbitration* service within their structure. Currently, where a claim does not exceed £1000, the Registrar can refer the proceedings to arbitration, even if the parties object. If they agree, it can be ordered where larger sums are at issue. Legal representation is permitted but since no lawyers' fees can be recovered by way of costs, litigants tend to appear on their own behalf. Proposals have been made to bring the remedies available within the reach of more people.

The largest category of plaintiff before the *small claims* court is the private citizen. The majority of claimants are successful and a significant number of cases are settled out of court. A large number of claims made by tourists against tour operators and others in the industry have been settled at this level.

Much consumer protection law emanates from parliament. There is remarkable cross-party consensus that consumers should be protected. To some critics this smacks of paternalism. There are a number of reasons why the consumer should be protected, not the least of which is the growth in the inequality of bargaining power. Just as a worker can no longer bargain for wages at a hiring fair, a shopper for goods and services cannot haggle in the market place. Monopolist activities, of which those enjoyed by the major carriers by air, rail and sea are but a sample, have increased with *market forces* becoming a phrase synonymous with decisions of the few affecting the many.

Because litigation has proved expensive, consumer law has aimed at encouraging producers of goods and services to produce Codes of Practice so that complaints can be processed speedily and actual disputes dealt with by arbitration. The alternative is for policing by the criminal law with the threat of sanctions.

2. CRIMINAL LAW

Over the centuries, the criminal law has consistently been used as an instrument for consumer protection. The earliest examples of this branch of the law in action are to be seen in the prosecution of offenders who sold food below accepted quality, and underweight, at excessive prices. The reasons are not hard to discover. The Crown feared that failure to act on the part of the state would lead to people taking the law into their own hands with public disorder being the inevitable consequence.

Prosecutions in connection with the sale of goods were more common than for offences in connection with services. Nevertheless, those who followed the *common callings* of innkeeper and carrier are to be found in the records of court proceedings. Still today, an innkeeper is liable to be prosecuted for refusal to accommodate or supply food and drink to a traveller without lawful excuse.[2] He is also liable at common law for charging excessive prices: *Luton v Bigg (1691).*[3]

Legislation, at first complementing the common law, made an early appearance in consumer protection. There is a reference in Magna Carta in 1215 to a common standard for wine and for other commodities. A series of enactments trace the history of weights and measures down to the Act of 1985. Measures were taken against adulteration of staple foods but not until the Bread Act 1836 was there a general prohibition of such practices. Today standards are protected under the provisions of the Food Safety Act and the many Regulations made in respect of individual items and practices.

Tourists rely heavily on public officials at local level to protect them against fraudulent and dangerous practices. Through inspection, improvement notices and ultimately prosecution, it is hoped that standards can be maintained at the prescribed levels. There is an ever-present danger that because tourists are here today and gone tomorrow they will be the targets for sharp practice and illegal activities.

Trading Standards, or Consumer Protection, Officers are called upon to *police* statutory offences together with Environmental Health Officers. They are asked, by the public, to investigate a wide variety of practices with a view to prosecution. In one case in the Bournemouth area in 1985, the local officers were asked to prosecute the proprietor of a club when a party of lady excursionists were far from satisfied with the performance of a male stripper hired to entertain them!

Prosecuting officers have the right to ask the court to award compensation to injured consumers under the provisions of the Powers of the Criminal Courts Act 1973. Orders are most commonly made by magistrates in connection with trade description offences. The sums are usually small. The largest amounts in compensation would appear to be for offences against section 14 of the Trades Description Act 1968. This makes it an offence for any person, in the course of any trade or business, knowingly, or recklessly, to make a false statement with regard to the provision of any services, accommodation, or facilities. It has caught several unwary or unscrupulous hoteliers and tour operators. The Package Travel etc. Regulations 1992 Schedule 3 require local Trading Standards Officers to enforce the criminal provisions of the Regulations and where an *organiser* contravenes Regulations 5,7,8,16 and 22 then, subject to the *due diligence* defence of Regulation 24, upon conviction he will be liable to a fine.

A complainant seeking compensation would be better advised to pursue his cause in the civil courts. The methods of assessing damages and the levels of awards are higher than those granted in the criminal courts. There is no bar to a civil action on the grounds that the defendant has already faced prosecution and suffered penalty elsewhere. Rather to the contrary, evidence of a criminal conviction can be used as evidence in a civil action based upon the same incident. However, this will not give rise to double awards. If a sum of money by way of compensation has been awarded by the magistrates, this amount will be taken into account when damages are assessed in the County Court. The Package Travel etc. Regulations introduce statutory terms into any contract governed by their provisions and these become part of such contract whether or not the supplier wishes them to be there and any breach of these terms entitles the consumer to remedy for loss occasioned by the breach.

3. TRADE DESCRIPTIONS

The Maloney Committee examined protective legislation. Its criticisms of existing provisions led to the Trade Descriptions Act 1968 which protects consumers and traders alike. For the first time, it included protection against false descriptions applied to the provision of services. It did not include protection against false prices in relation to services, as it did for goods. This omission has now been remedied by the Consumer Protection Act 1987 (q.v.).

Section 1 of the 1968 Act makes it an offence to falsely describe goods, and sections 2-6 develop its provisions. The description applied to goods must be 'false to a material degree' for an offence to have been committed. This qualification is not defined. It depends on the circumstances of each case brought in connection with misdescriptions of size, quantity, composition or fitness for purpose. So, for example, a tourist who buys a watch described as waterproof which turns out not to be so when used in the manner to be expected, will have been the victim of a trade description offence: *Sherratt v The American Jewellers Ltd (1970)*.[4] Similarly, he who buys champagne should get the real article not a Spanish substitute: *J. Bollinger v Costa Brava Wine Co Ltd (1960)*.[5]

The Act does not require that, in the case of goods, there should have been an intention to deceive, nor that any person has indeed been deceived. The use of the word *supply* as opposed to *sale* in relation to goods allows a much wider application of the provisions since it will, for example, encompass hire, e.g. of a car.

False pricing

The 1968 Act created a new offence of false pricing. The purpose was to protect purchasers from being deceived into the belief that they were buying goods at a price different to that advertised. It has not proved very effective in stopping the proliferation of *bargain* offers, despite several Price Marking (Bargain Offers) Orders. It was decided to amend the law in this respect. This has been effected by Part III of the Consumer Protection Act 1987 which replaces section II of the 1968 Act.

Another innovation, introduced by the 1987 Act, is to make new provisions not only in respect of the pricing of goods but also of services, accommodation or facilities.[6] A *consumer* is also redefined in the Act as one who 'in relation to services or facilities ... might wish to be provided (with them) otherwise than for the purposes of any business of his; and in relation to any accommodation means any person otherwise than for the purpose of any business of his'.[7]

The Act is concerned with *misleading* pricing such as would lead a consumer to believe, or reasonably infer, that:

1. The price is less than in fact is the case.

2. That the price is not dependent on other facts or circumstances, but such is not the case.

3. That there are *hidden* additional charges.

4. That the supplier expects prices to be increased/reduced/maintained when this is not so.

5. When the consumer is invited to compare the description against others, on offer as alternatives, but the comparison invited is misleading.

The same rules will be applied where no actual *price* is announced but a *method* of computing it is described and is *misleading*. The new provisions of sections 20 and 21 relate specifically to accommodation and services which were not previously covered: *Newell v Hicks (1983)*.[8]

Other matters which are dealt with by the 1987 Act are the terms upon which the provision of credit, banking or insurance services are offered, or facilities which are incidental to them, together with the sale or purchase of foreign currency.[9] If a business supplier discovers that a statement he made was correct at the time but it has now become untrue such as to mislead consumers, he must take reasonable steps to draw the error to the attention of people who might reasonably rely upon it. If he does not do so then he commits an offence against sections 21, 22 and 23.[10]

The Act provides grounds upon which a supplier may answer charges in relation to false pricing. They are contained specifically in section 24 and generally in section 39. The latter section provides that a defendant is entitled to offer proof that he took all reasonable steps and exercised all due diligence to avoid committing the offence with which he is charged, or that the commission of such offence was due 'to the act or default of another; or to reliance on information given by another'. Such defence is particularly valuable to a travel agent who seeks to rely upon information supplied to him by a tour operator. It is repeated in Regulations 24 and 25 of the Package Travel etc. Regulations 1992.

It is also provided, in section 25, that the Secretary of State shall, after consultation with the Director General of Fair Trading, approve a Code of Practice for Traders on Price Indications. It is not provided that such a Code will itself give rise to criminal charges or civil liability, but that it may be used to rebut defences available to an accused person or facilitate their use. Such a Code is a statutory creation such as those agreed and published in connection with holiday caravans in January 1987.

Provision of services

For an offence to be committed against section 14 of the 1968 Act, a description must have been made knowingly or recklessly by the accused. 'Recklessly' does not imply dishonestly: *MFI Warehouses v Nattrass (1973).*[11] It requires only that the statement should have been made 'regardless of whether it is true or false'. It is not necessary to show that the trader 'has reasons for believing it might be false'.[12] Nor can a statement which was true at the time be rendered reckless by a subsequent intervening event: *Sunair Holidays v Dodd (1970).*[13] Nevertheless, an advertiser must make enquiries about the truth of a statement if he has any doubt concerning its veracity, failure to do so may render his action reckless: *Best Travel Co Ltd v Patterson (1986).*[14] Whether an allegedly false or misleading statement is false to a material degree is a question of fact in each case: *Thomson Travel v Roberts (1984).*[15]

The statement must be false at the time it is made. If it is made in connection with some future event, then it will be difficult to show that it offends against the wording of the statute. A statement made in a travel brochure in 1969, with respect to a holiday in 1970, was not shown to be false: *R v Sunair Holidays Ltd (1973).*[16]

However, an artist's impression supporting statements about a hotel still to be built were held to be representations of existing, not future, facts: *R v Clarksons Holidays Ltd (1972).*[17] Also, a statement may be made false by subsequent events. It may have been innocent when made, but if the trader subsequently discovers that supervening facts make it false, he commits an offence if he does not correct the misrepresentation made to readers of his brochures: *Wings Ltd v Ellis (1985)*.[18]

If a statement promising a future service is known to be incapable of being fulfilled because of a policy of overbooking aircraft seats, then it is an offence: *BAB v Taylor (1975)*[19]

Overbooking

Where a policy of overbooking shows that it is not possible to confirm availability at the time the assurance was given, the statement is false. The person who makes it does not know that a seat will not be available at the time for which it is booked but he cannot confirm it either. If it is made by someone speaking with authority, then it may be possible to show that it was made intentionally or recklessly.

Difficulties arise with regard to bookings by tour operators. They block-book seats on airplanes and hotel space. They allocate to their customers on the basis of the confirmations which have been made to them. If the carrier or hotelier has a policy of overbooking which is responsible for the statements of the operator becoming false, then he is not liable unless he knew that he was making confirmations which he could not guarantee. Knowledge of habitual overbooking by particular hoteliers or carriers might require the operator to check availability before each individual booking which he makes and confirms to his clients.

In order to protect themselves against this problem, operators make contracts with terms based on 'best efforts'. Such terms might say 'The Company does not control the day to day management of the hotels and it is possible that shortly before departure or on arrival at the overseas airport or resort the Company may be advised that the accommodation is not available. In such circumstances the Company will use its best endeavours to provide alternative accommodation. The policy in such cases is to provide a hotel of similar or higher classification at no extra cost or, if this is unavailable, a lower category of hotel and the company will refund the difference in the brochure price plus 5% of the original holiday price.'

Multiple offences

Each brochure containing a false statement is a separate offence. The fact that the same wording is used does not serve to reduce the misrepresentation to a single offence. In 1970, an operator issued 2 million brochures containing an identical false statement; each one constituted an offence: *R v Thomson Holidays (1974).*[20]

Defences

The 1968 Act allows the possibility that the defendant has an answer to the charge, e.g. within section 14 itself, that he did not make the statement knowing that it was false or that he did not do so recklessly. Under section 24, he may avail himself of one of the general defences. He may allege that the false statement was due to the 'act or default of another'. This has even been used in exceptional circumstances to allow an employer to pass the blame on to one of his employees: *Tesco v Nattrass (1972).*[21] The defendant would need to substantiate his claim by proving that he had used all due diligence, but that this did not prevent the commission of the offence as charged. Where the defendant names another as responsible for the offence, that other must be named to the court in advance of the trial and, if the facts confirm him as the person responsible, he may be convicted of the offence.

This seems a particularly harsh rule when the person named is an employee of the person who is primarily liable for publishing the statement. It seems at odds with the principle of vicarious liability which is not unknown in criminal law and is well-tested in civil matters.

The Package Travel etc. Regulations 1992 in many ways mirror the provisions of the Trade Descriptions Act 1968 and it remains to be seen whether or not better protection will be afforded to the consumer by the Regulations rather than by the 1968 Act. The latter has not proved to be effective to far as false statements or false descriptions as to package holidays are concerned. The great weakness of the Act is in the necessary evidence to prove mens rea in order to gain a conviction by the prosecutor. Nor does the threat of prosecution seem to have been an effective deterrent in the past. Low levels of compensation delivered by the Act have caused victims to turn instead to civil actions. As with the Act, so too it would appear with the Regulations which give greater support to a victim in a case for breach of contract than he is likely to recover in criminal compensation awards. Whether this situation meets the requirements of the EC Directive is yet to be tested.

Sugging

The practice of selling under the guise of something other than first appears, SUGGING, is the acronym coined by the Office of Fair Trading. It has lead to a reform of the law in relation to an area where abuse has become common, the selling of timeshares. Such selling has been done most commonly by telesales (cold calling) or by personal contact by off-site personnel contractors (OPCs). These latter may not be so common in the UK but are a familiar feature of many a continental holiday resort where tourists are to be found in plenty. The OPCs induce prospective clients to attend meetings under the guise of 'market research' or in return for promises of luxury prizes or gifts. Timeshare sales are rarely mentioned as the purpose behind the soliciting by OPCs.

It is the job of the OPCs to introduce their clients to the hard sell team. It may not be such a hard sale though since most tourists are in the market already of buying dreams. The timeshare concept induces a client to enter into an agreement for a luxury facility which is guaranteed and at a price which reflects the availability of the facility in its location at a specified time within the year for exclusive use by the owner of that time/space slot. It also offers the chance of profit since the owner can let out his time slot to others if he wishes. The element of luxury is always stressed by the sellers. A luxury which is affordable because the facility is shared with others none of whom could hope to buy the property outright. Often the need to act quickly is stressed since the timeshare is so much in demand it is said. Act now or lose the chance. Sign the paper saying that the agreement has been fully explained to you, whether it has or not and whether or not a copy of the agreement is supplied to the eager buyer.

Variations upon the theme abound including visits, possibly with free flights to the location of the timeshare, a glitzy party for the new owners of the luxury apartments. Nothing illegal has taken place in inducing the customer to sign the agreement forming a binding contract and many reputable sellers of timeshare will allow the customer to take away additional information and allow for a cooling off period during which the customer can change his mind.

Nevertheless, the OFT was not satisfied with self regulation within the timeshare industry and in 1990 proposed a package of reforms to meet what it saw as abuses in the process. They in turn led to the Time Shares Act 1992 which embodies some if not all of the OFT proposals and applies them to situations where the consumer acquires timeshare rights for a period of not less than 3 years. The Act covers both timeshare agreements and timeshare credit agreements where these are not subject to the Consumer Credit Act 1974.

The 1992 Act provides protection where at least one of the parties is located in the UK at the time of the agreement but if both are abroad at the time - the tourist is in Spain or elsewhere when he meets the OPC and signs up - the Act does not apply to the agreement.

Where the Act is operative then the core provision in that the customer is allowed a mandatory 14 days cooling off period from the date the contract is agreed and signed. The sale must be 'in the course of business' i.e. by a professional timeshare seller. Failure to provide notice of the provisions of the Act in this respect renders the seller liable to prosecution. The seller must supply a form which the buyer may fill in if he is desirous of cancelling the agreement within the 14 day period allowed for cooling off. There is no prescribed format which this document must take so long as it shows the buyer's right to cancel and allows him to signify this on the form. The Act also makes provision for the refund of monies paid under the agreement which is cancelled by the buyer.

The Act is somewhat unusual in that it came about as a result of a Private Member's Bill for which the party managers in Parliament found time. Many believe this was to avoid more time having to be spent on a government Bill which could have been rather more rigorous in its terms than the one which has emerged. Many believe the Act does not go far enough while others are concerned as to whether the already hard pressed Trading Standards Officers will have the time or resources to adequately police its rules. It is perhaps best regarded as a stop gap and that sooner or later tougher requirements will be required by an EC Directive. Until such time as this is produced the OFT offers advice not to sign until customers have read the agreement fully and have taken time to consider the terms carefully and possibly have taken legal advice!

4. CIVIL ACTIONS

Where there is a sale or supply of goods or services, a breach of the terms allows the non-offending party to claim under the contract. Where harm is caused to a non-contracting party, the victim must seek redress under another head in tort.

Contract

The freedom to contract is largely illusory today. The use of Standard Form Contracts has allowed the stronger party to dictate terms to the weaker, while the intervention of statute has sought to redress the balance. Statutory terms are implied into contracts and unfair exclusion clauses are negated by operation of law.

Purchasers of goods have been protected since the passing of the first Sale of Goods Act in 1893 signalled the demise of the rule of 'caveat emptor', let the buyer beware. The Supply of Goods and Services Act 1982 has extended the protection to areas of services and hire previously regulated largely by the common law.

Hire

Where goods are bought, the law recognises that the buyer and the seller should be able to seek remedies where the terms of the contract are not fulfilled. The seller will want the buyer to pay him in the manner agreed, and the buyer wants the goods which he has purchased to be delivered to him free from defects not notified to him. He also has a right to expect that the items he has purchased will not only come up to the standard normally expected of such goods, but that they will also be fit for any particular purpose which he has made known to the seller.

There was no good reason why this should not be so in the case of goods which were hired, or services which were contracted for. Under the terms of the 1982 Act, these areas of *supply* are now given statutory protection.

A contract for the hire of goods is described as one 'under which one person bails or agrees to bail goods to another by way of hire'.[22] In such circumstances, terms similar to those found in the Sale of Goods Act 1979 are implied into the contract. They must, therefore, correspond to the description applied to them by the bailor.[23] They must be of *merchantable* quality and *fit for the purpose* for which they are hired.[24] The liability is strict and recalls the rules of the common law which decreed that: 'If there was a defect in fact, even though that

239

defect was one which no reasonable skill or care could discover, the person supplying the article should nevertheless be responsible, the policy of the law being that in a case in which neither were to blame, he, and not the person to whom they were supplied, should be liable for the defect': *Randall v Newsom (1876)*.[25]

In the case of hire, say of a car, the bailor will usually require pre-payment of the charges. If a customer is dissatisfied, he may reclaim his payment and, in addition, seek appropriate compensation for any financial loss sustained in consequence of the defect which might have been reasonably anticipated by the bailor. Alternatively, if the contract is not capable of being rescinded, the bailee may seek repayment of a sum equivalent to the difference in value between the price he paid and the value which he received from a defective vehicle.

The consequential losses which he may claim may be in respect of *disappointment* which he has suffered, or for the cost of hiring an alternative vehicle. He may have elected to take an alternative vehicle from the bailor but this will not prevent him seeking compensation for any loss he has sustained, attributable to the defects in the original vehicle. Where the hire has not commenced, he may reject a vehicle which is not of the type or quality for which he has contracted. If he contracts for a Rolls Royce he cannot be expected to accept a Mini substituted by the bailor!

Services

The terms under which services are provided will be a mixture of express and implied obligations as between the parties. Since 1982, the supplier has been required, under section 13 of the Supply of Goods and Services Act, to exercise 'reasonable care and skill' in fulfilling his part of the bargain. The standard of service required is that of a reasonable man who offers such services, or that higher standard which such a person may claim for himself.

Where the terms of the contract are breached, damages may be claimed not only in respect of a contracting party but for those closely associated with him, e.g. his family: *Jackson v Horizon Holidays Ltd (1975)*.[26]

Damages

The object of damages is to compensate the injured party in monetary terms with such sum as would restore him to the position he would have been in had the contract been performed in accordance with the agreed terms. Where disappointment or nervous shock is concerned this may be no simple matter.

In order to recover compensation, the plaintiff must show that the loss flowed from the breach. It must also not be a consequence which is too remote from the original causation. It will be sufficient to show that the loss was such that it could have been anticipated by the person breaking the contract, or one of which he had notification: *Victoria Laundry v Newman (1949).*[27]

It will be necessary to show that, where the circumstances allow, the victim of the breach attempted to *mitigate* his loss. If he does so, he may be awarded *special damages* for loss which may be assessed directly in financial terms. So, a stranded tourist may recover, from the carrier or tour operator responsible for his misfortune, the cost of getting home by a reasonable alternative method.

General damages are less easy to quantify. They are arrived at by reference to the value which can be attributed to the breach as in *Jarvis v Swan Tours Ltd (1973);*[28] to physical inconvenience and discomfort: *Stedman v Swan Tours (1951);*[29] distress and/or disappointment: *Jarvis* and *Jackson.*

In *Jackson*, damages were awarded to compensate the family of the plaintiff. This has also been extended to friends included in the party of the claimant: *Adcock v Blue Sky Holidays (1980).*[30]

Failure to book the holiday ordered by a honeymoon couple led to the award of compensation against the travel agent concerned: *Cook v Spanish Holiday Tours Ltd (1960).*[31] Where the holiday was booked, but the operator was held not to have exercised reasonable care and skill in selecting a hotel for family holidays, having sent his clients to one which was made unusable not by the hotelier but by hooligan elements at the hotel, the client was awarded damages: *Freemantle v Thomas Cook (1984).*[32]

A claimant who has an action based on contract may also be able to bring an action in tort. Where there is no contractual relationship between the parties, the plaintiff will have recourse only under the appropriate tort head.

Torts

The tort of *Deceit* occurs when one person makes a false statement of *fact* to another, intending that other to act upon it which he does to his detriment. Such a statement must be made 'knowingly or without belief in its truth, or recklessly, careless whether it be true or false': *Derry v Peek (1889)*.[33]

The essence of this tort is the fraudulent intent on the part of the person making the statement. Where it is made innocently, or even negligently, then a claim in *Deceit* will fail. The burden is upon he who alleges the fraud. The difficulty of proof makes this tort little used today. Since most statements are pre-contractual, other avenues are open to a complainant.

In order to induce people to enter contracts, a business enterprise may make boasts or engage in traders' *puffs*. Today, this tends to be classified as creative advertising. Such representations may be mere statements of opinion or they may be held out as fact. Where they induce a party to enter a contract, and the representations are subsequently discovered to have been false, then an action lies for loss attributable to these misrepresentations.

Where the misrepresentation was deliberate, a remedy lay for the fraud similar to that for *Deceit*. But as with that tort it was no easy matter to prove fraud. Courts evolved a way around this by making the representation become a term of the contract, wherever possible, so that an action lay for breach of contract. Alternatively, it was used as a way to allow an innocent party to *rescind* the contract on the grounds that the misrepresentation negatived a genuine agreement: *London Assurance v Mansell (1879)*.[34] No remedy was available at common law for innocent or negligent misrepresentation.

This was remedied in part by extending the tort of Negligence to circumstances where statements were made in circumstances of a special relationship. This would be the case where someone professing special skills and competence makes representations to another who is influenced by them. If the latter suffers financial loss, he may recover damages for negligent mis-statement (q.v.).

The difficulties were finally resolved under the provisions of the Misrepresentation Act 1967. The Act creates a statutory tort in respect of *operative mis-statements*. A negligent mis-statement which induces the addressee to act to his detriment will now be actionable so as to allow the plaintiff to recover damages. In the case of innocent misrepresentation, the old remedy of recission is still available but a court now has a discretion to award damages if it is 'of the opinion that it would be equitable to do so, having regard to the nature of the misrepresentation'.[35]

5. UNFAIR DEALINGS

The common law has always shown a dislike for exemption clauses where one party, by the strength of his bargaining power, seeks to gain an advantage for himself at the expense of the other. The courts have displayed a willingness to set exclusions aside where the circumstances allow. To this end, rules were for mulated to test the validity of such terms within a contract.

The essence of contract is agreement between the parties. Where a term is introduced unilaterally without such consensus, after the contract has been formed, the exemption will not bind the party to whom it is addressed: *Olley v Marlborough Court Hotel Ltd (1949)*.[36] If the term goes to the root of the contract, such that it attempts to render a fundamentally different service than that which was agreed, or which appears to have been in the minds of the parties, then only in exceptional circumstances will it be allowed to stand: *Photo Production Ltd v Securicor Transport Ltd (1980)*.[37] If the clause is repugnant to the main object of the contract it will be struck out: *Sze Hai Tong Bank Ltd v Rambler Cycle Co Ltd (1959)*.[38]

Where there is any ambiguity, such a clause will be construed *contra preferentem* against the party seeking to gain the advantage. The wording will be interpreted literally, and, if it does not refer specifically to that for which the exemption is claimed, the term will not have the desired effect: *White v John Warrick & Co Ltd (1953)*.[39]

Where notice of terms is given by way of reference to them in some document not presented to a contracting party, he will not be bound by them unless it can be shown that he was put on notice. This situation arises in connection with tickets in particular. Whether or not the ticket is sufficient notice of terms contained in another form, e.g. British Rail Conditions of Carriage, is a matter of fact. In some cases the courts have been willing to accept that certain types of ticket are part of the contract such as to incorporate terms not on the document itself: *Thompson v LMS Railway Co (1930)*.[40] In others, they have been unwilling to stretch a point to include all types of ticket: *Chapleton v Barry UDC (1940)*.[41]

In modern business practice *standard form contracts* are commonly used. There is no bargaining between the parties, such agreements are simple *contracts of adhesion*. The economically stronger party is, in effect, saying to the weaker: 'here are my terms, take them or leave them'.

In such circumstances, it has been necessary for Parliament to introduce protection in statutory form. The provisions of the Unfair Contract Terms Act 1977 apply to consumers and businesses alike. It is now less necessary for judges to perform mental gymnastics in order to strike down exemption clauses. Where a person deals as a consumer, the implied terms of sections 13-15 of the Sale of Goods Act 1979, and sections 8-10 of the Supply of Goods and Services Act 1982, can not be excluded. In other cases, the Act looks to the type of loss to which the exclusion refers.

Section 2(1) states that 'a person cannot by reference to any contract term or notice given to persons generally or to particular persons, exclude or restrict his liability for death or personal injury resulting from negligence'. The illiterate passenger in *Thompson* would be able to recover damages for her injuries were the case heard today.

Other loss liability may be successfully excluded if the term in the contract is constructed properly and satisfies the statutory test of *reasonableness*. Section 2(2) of the 1977 Act requires that: 'In the case of other loss or damage, a person cannot restrict his liability for negligence except in so far as the contract term or notice satisfies the requirement of reasonableness'. Section 11(1) explains what is meant by *reasonableness* and section 1 defines *negligence* for the purposes of the Act.

The court is required to have regard to 'the circumstances which were, or which ought to have been known to, or in the contemplation of, the parties when the contract was made'. Schedule 2 of the Act places particular emphasis on the 'strength of the bargaining position of the parties' and requires that account be given to the dominant market position which may exist when considering *reasonableness*.

Notices

Where there is no contractual relationship between the parties, any person wishing to deny liability to another by the display of a notice must show that it is fair and reasonable for him to do so in circumstances where, but for the notice, he would have been liable. Thus, a notice in a car park disclaiming lability for cars parked there which are damaged, by any means, will not protect the proprietor where it can be shown that, but for the notice, he would have been held to account, say for the actions of his employee who damaged a parked vehicle.

Where, by reference to a contractual term, or to a notice displayed, a person seeks to restrict liability to a specified sum of money, and the question of reasonableness arises, the Act requires particular attention to be paid to the personal resources of such person and how far he could have covered the risk by insurance. It is for those who claim that a contract term or notice satisfies the requirement of reasonableness to show that it does.[42] In this connection, it is important to note that section 29(1) allows provisions authorised by statute, or in international agreement to which the UK is a party, to be relied upon notwithstanding the provisions of the 1977 Act. Thus the limits of compensation allowed under the Hotel Proprietors Act 1956 and the Athens Convention are enforceable.

The question of reasonableness has been examined in several cases before the courts since the 1977 Act came into force. British Rail were unable to satisfy the court that the disappearance of a passenger's luggage was not their fault. As a result of their liability, they sought to hide behind a term restricting compensation based on weight contained in a standard form contract. This was held to be unreasonable: *Waldron-Kelly v BRB (1981)*.[43]

However, in another instance, the liability by weight term was upheld since it was said that the bailor could have taken out extra insurance for the items and the British Rail terms were no less favourable than those afforded by other carriers: *Wight v BRB (1983)*.[44] This seems an erroneous assumption. Carried to its extreme, it would mean that because all carriers limited their liability to, say, 1p this would be fair and reasonable because they all conformed to the same derisory level. It is submitted that, unless British Rail or other carriers make insurance at a fair price available at the time they seek to limit their liability, then the restrictions placed upon levels of compensation are unfair within the terms of section 3(1) and (2).

Section 8 of the 1977 Act replaces section 3 of the Misrepresentation Act 1967. Where a person seeks to exclude liability for a misrepresentation, he will be required to show that the exclusion is reasonable.

Standard form contracts

Section 3 of the 1977 Act provides that where one of the parties deals as a consumer under the terms of the other party's SFC, that party is prevented from imposing unreasonable terms on the consumer. He may not, when in breach of contract, exclude or restrict his liability or render a contractual performance substantially different from that which could reasonably be expected from him, or indeed no performance at all.

Even before the Act was in force, the courts had shown a disinclination to allow a substantially different performance to be rendered under the terms contained in a contract where to do so rendered the performance completely different to that which had been envisaged when the contract was made: *Anglo Continental Holidays v Typalos (London) Ltd (1967)*.[45]

Such terms are to be commonly found in SFCs of tour operators, forming an integral part of the booking forms contained in their brochures. Various complaints have arisen from such terms.[46]

The Unfair Contract Terms Act is much concerned with exclusion clauses, to the exclusion of much else. It seeks to protect consumers and others against unfair trading practices in this respect. It could have covered other matters and in fact may be overtaken by events sooner or later.

A draft Directive on Unfair Contract Terms is progressing its way through the EC machinery, although reduced from what was originally envisaged that it should cover. It proposes to regulate contract terms which have not been individually negotiated which is always the case where there is a *Standard Form Contract* prepared by the seller which the buyer must accept as it stands or not at all. The EC refers to such STCs as 'pre formulated' contracts. The fact that a contract has not bee individually negotiated will not make it automatically unfair. The Directive states that it will only be regarded as such if 'contrary to the requirements of good faith, it causes a significant imbalance in the parties' rights and obligations .... to the detriment of the consumer'. As to how this might arise, the Annex to the Directive contains a list of indicative terms which might be unfair - the list is stated not to be exhaustive. The Annex includes any clause in the contract which binds a consumer to those matters with which 'he had no real opportunity of becoming acquainted before the conclusion of the contract'. This issue generally of unfairness will fall to be decided by taking account of the nature of goods or services involved, the circumstances under which the agreement was made or of any other contract upon which it is dependant to some degree.

Further requirements refer to the need for contracts to be in 'plain, intelligible language' and free from ambiguity or doubtful meaning. Where a term is deemed unfair it will be void although the contract as a whole may subsist if it is capable of doing so in the absence of the deleted term. Significantly, the intention appears to be to require regulation of such SFCs and the terms to be a matter for governments and their agencies e.g. in the case of the UK the OFT will probably get the job. The Directive does not appear to intend that individuals shall acquire rights of enforcement although they do appear to have the right to resist enforcement of the term by the beneficiary of the pre-formulated contract. Another significant aspect is that whereas the UCTA 1977 excluded certain types of contract from its regulation, notably contracts of insurance, no such exemptions will exist under the proposals in the draft Directive. All contracts will be covered irrespective of their subject matter.

6. ADVERTISING

There are no general provisions in English law which control advertising. Instead, there are in the order of sixty statutes which, in one way or another, relate to the subject. In addition, there are a number of voluntary Codes of Practice drawn up by interested parties, e.g. ABTA.

The Tour Operators' Code of Conduct does little to enhance consumer protection. Para 4.1 only requires that brochures 'shall contain clear, comprehensive and accurate information to enable the client to exercise an informed judgement in making his choice'. This does not prevent them from stringing together collections of exclusion clauses of a blanket nature. Para 4.12 recites a list of some of the statutes which affect advertising, and para 2.2 lists some of the bodies who set standards.

The Travel Agents' Code of Conduct goes a little further. It compiles the same lists as the TOCC and enjoins members to vet materials for misleading information. Whether agents who fail to do so are more likely to be found liable in negligence, or for misrepresentation, is a moot point. A counter to such claims could be made in the same way that is allowed by section 25 of the Trade Descriptions Act 1968. This permits the defence of *innocent publication* which does not absolve the publisher of false information. It is simply a counter to a charge which requires intent on the part of the accused to be demonstrated. All these provisions need now to be read in the light of the Regulations derived from the Package Travel Directive and legislated for in the UK in 1992.

Advertising standards

The wider control of advertising is left to the industry. The British Code of Advertising Practice was first drawn up in 1962 and has been revised several times since. It is administered by a committee drawn from industry. The intention of the Code is stated to be the desire to reflect the industry's 'sense of responsibility to the consumer'. Advertisements are required to be *legal, decent, honest and truthful*. Complaints of breaches of the Code are to be addressed to the Advertising Standards Authority. The great weakness of the Code is that it is voluntary and has only a persuasive influence on legal decisions. The ASA can impose few sanctions and has been shown to be of very limited support for consumers.

EEC intervention

After a long period of gestation, the EEC adopted a Council Directive in September 1984. The UK government has argued that most of its provisions are already contained in a body of legislation combined with voluntary Codes. The original Draft Directive contained provisions to outlaw claims which, while true, create false impressions, arouse unfulfilled expectations, or omit material infor mation. This was shelved until a later date, to be the subject of a further Directive which has yet to materialise.

At present, a draft Regulation is being considered by the UK Government which would give the Director General of Fair Trading the authority to institute proceedings in the High Court for an injunction to prohibit examples of misleading information. This would require the Court to have regard in particular to matters of *public interest*.

The travel trade

In the six months January to June 1987, the ASA investigated some 33 complaints in respect of holiday advertising. This placed the travel industry fourth in the pecking order of most reported businesses. The number appears small, but the ASA believes that for all industries it is seeing only the tip of the iceberg.

The main complaints concern inaccurate descriptions of facilities, misleading illustrations in brochures, and hidden extras in the price. The position is well illustrated by the tourist who complained that the description of holiday accommodation as being in a 'superb beachside position', omitted to mention that it was necessary to cross a main road to get to the beach and that the hotel was near the airport runway.[47]

In legal terms, the use of the word 'superb' is perhaps no more than a trader's *puff* and does not constitute a misrepresentation nor yet become a term in the contract so as to allow a claim in respect of a breach. Nor would it seem to be caught by the Trade Descriptions Act. The response of the tour operator in this example was novel. He stated that the brochure indicated that the transfer time from the airport to the hotel in question was only 15 minutes, therefore the client should have realised when he booked the holiday that the hotel was near a runway! Such reactions do little to advance the cause of honesty in printed publicity.

It is to be hoped that previously existing loopholes in legislation and often ineffectual self regulatory voluntary provisions of trade organisations will now be overtaken by the implementation of the Package Travel etc. Regulations 1992.

NOTES:

1. Unfair Contract Terms Act 1977 s 12(1).
2. R. v Higgins (1948) 1 KB 165.
3. (1691) Skin 291.
4. (1970) 114 SJ 147.
5. (1960) Ch 262.
6. Consumer Protection Act 1987 s 20.
7. Ibid s 20(6),(b)&(c).
8. (1983) 148 JP 208.
9. Consumer Protection Act 1987 s 22.
10. Ibid s 20(2).
11. (1973) 1 A11 ER 762.
12. Trade Descriptions Act 1968 s 14(2) (b).
13. (1970) 2A11 ER 410
14. (1986) BTLC 119
15. (1984)CLY 3102
16. (1973) 2 A11 ER 1233.
17. (1972) 116 SJ 728. See also Yugotours Ltd v Wadsley (1988) BTLC 300

18. (1985) AC 272.
19. (1975) 3 A11 ER 307.
20. (1974) 1 A11 ER 823.
21. (1972) Ac 153, See also Beckett v Kingston Bros Ltd (1970) 1 QB 606 and Lewin v Rothersthorpe Road Garage Ltd (1984) 148 JP 87.
22. Supply of Goods and Services Act s 6.
23. Ibid s 8.
24. Ibid s 9(1) and (4)(5)(6).
25. (1876) 45 LQBD 364. See also Ashington Piggeries Ltd v Christopher Hill Ltd (1972) AC 441.
26. (1975) 3 A11 ER 92. See also Askew v Intasun North Ltd (1980) CLY 637 and Levine v Metropolitan Travel (1980) CLY 638.
27. (1949) 2 KB 528.
28. (1973) 1 QB 233.
29. (1951) 95 SJ 727. See also Feldman v Travel Service (1957) CLY 934.
30. Unreported CA 13 May 1980.
31. (1960) *Times* 6 February 1960.
32. (1984) *Times* 25 February 1984.
33. (1889) 14 AC 337.
34. (1879) 11 Ch D 363.
35. Misrepresentation Act 1967 s 2(2).
36. (1949) 1 KB 532.
37. (1980) AC 287.
38. (1959) AC 576.
39. (1953) 2 A11 ER 101.
40. (1930) 1 KB 41.
41. (1940) 1 KB 532.
42. Unfair Contract Terms Act 1977 s 11(4)(5).
43. (1981) CLY 303.
44. (1983) CLY 424.
45. (1967) 2L1 61.
46. Holiday *Which* March 1988 pp 112_2113.
47. *Guardian* 12 December 1987 p 23.

CHAPTER XIII

Caterbility

1. PLACES OF REFRESHMENT

All those who travel any distance away from home, and especially those who stop overnight, will require to be provided with food and drink. The availability of refreshment will, to a large extent, depend upon the location of the traveller and the type of fare required.

Under the provisions of the Shops Act 1950, section 74, premises used for the purposes of carrying out any retail trade or business are regarded as shop premises. The Act applies not only to shops in the accepted sense but to any premises in which a retail trade or business is carried on. Such activities which in volve the sale of refreshments or intoxicating liquors come within the definition. Restaurants, cafés, snack bars, public houses, take-aways, wine bars and the public dining rooms and bars of residential hotels are all premises which are governed by the statutory regulation of shops.

The Act specifies general closing hours for shops but enables the administering authorities by order to substitute earlier hours either generally or in relation to shops of a particular class or in a particular area. The time fixed may not be earlier than 7p.m. and cannot apply to the sale of meals or newly-cooked provisions. However, late opening of premises kept open for public refreshment are subject to other statutory restrictions. In most London boroughs (with the exception of the boroughs of Camden, Greenwich, Westminster and the City) it is an offence to use, or permit premises to be used, as a *night café* unless they are registered under Part VIII of the Greater London Council (General Powers) Act 1968. A *night café* means premises kept open for public refreshment at any time between 11p.m. and 5a.m. Under the Late Night Refreshment Houses Act 1969, similar provisions are applied, and licences are required for, premises open between 10p.m. and 5a.m. Premises registered as a *night café* are deemed to be duly licensed. It is always open to local authorities to restrict these hours on public interest grounds if they so choose i.e. to order closing at, say, 3a.m. Such an order was made in respect of premises in Southampton and police officers entering the premises after this time discovered customers still consuming food in the restaurant. The proprietor was prosecuted under the terms of the 1969 Act and convicted. On appeal it was held inappropriate that at the appointed closing time the customers should down knives and forks and leave the premises. They should, it was said, be allowed reasonable 'eating up' time in the way that was permitted in licensed premises for the drinking up of beer etc. As to what the duration of such eating up should be the court was silent.[1] Certain premises are exempted from these regulations. The list includes all those which have a licence to sell liquor for consumption on or off the premises; those with a theatre or cinema licence; bona fide hotels, guest houses or lodging houses; bona fide clubs; comprise undertakings of British Railway Boards or the London Transport Board.

Street traders do not operate 'premises' such as to qualify as shops nor, it would seem, do premises where food is sold for consumption off the premises and no facilities are provided for sitting down to eat come under the provisions regulating either *night cafés* or late night refreshment houses. Street trading will be governed by local byelaws and highways legislation and 'take-away' food services may be regulated by local Acts of Parliament or byelaws which allow local authorities to order closing hours so as to prevent nuisance to local residents. *Kahn v Newberry (1959).*[2]

The hours during which premises licensed for the sale of alcoholic beverages may be open are governed by the Licensing Acts (q.v.). The regulations do not apply to ships, aircraft, railways, trains or coaches.

All premises are governed by controls instituted by the legislation governing town and country planning, public health and those under the Food Safety Act 1990. With the limited exception of members' clubs, discrimination on the grounds of sex or race is unlawful.

Choosing customers

In English law, only the innkeeper is obliged to provide food and drink to travellers. He is required to do so at common law and under the Hotel Proprietors Act 1956. The rules of the common law are upheld save where they are qualified by the statute. This allows the innkeeper to refuse service to someone who is not in a fit state to be received, or who does not appear able and willing to pay a reasonable sum for the services and facilities. It is interesting to note that the Act places the duty to provide food and drink to the traveller before that relating to accommodation.[3]

The Act does not state times during which service to travellers is to operate. This seems to indicate a 24 hours opening time. Section 1(1) preserves the common law duty not to turn away a traveller because of his late arrival or that he arrived on a Sunday: *R v Ivens (1835).*[4] A guest has no right to demand alcoholic beverages to be provided outside permitted hours (q.v.), unless, that is, he has booked accommodation.

The innkeeper is not obliged to provide the traveller with any food other than that which he has available: *R v Higgins 1948.*[5] The fact that the innkeeper does not have any food available, other than that which is already reserved for residents or diners who have booked in advance, is a defence to refusal to serve. However, it is submitted that this is a flimsy excuse today in an age of modern food storage technology. Nevertheless, the fact remains that an innkeeper without the resources to provide for casual visitors is not obliged to send out for food to meet their wants.

What amounts to a sufficient reason for refusing service to a traveller on the grounds that he or she is not in a fit state to be received will be a question of fact: *Rothfield v North British Hotels (1920).*[6] It may be that the innkeeper objects to the manner in which the customer is dressed. In an Irish case, the objection was to the refusal of a customer, who had a cold, to take off his overcoat before sitting down at table.[7]

A request that a traveller go to another hotel in the group because of his colour is unlawful under the common law as well as the Race Relations Act 1976: *Constantine v Imperial London Hotels Ltd (1944).*[8] A request to a lady customer to accept service in another part of the premises may also be lawful if the reason is associated with her clothing: *R v Sprague (1899).*[9] It is likely that such a request would now fall foul of the Sex Discrimination Act 1975.

It is unlawful for any person concerned with the provision of goods, facilities or services, to the public to discriminate on the grounds of sex by either deliberately omitting to provide them or treating the person less favourably than someone of the opposite sex.[10] The legislation applies to both women: *Gill and Another v El Vino Co Ltd (1983);*[11] and men: *Twambley v Jamal's Wine Bar (1982).*[12]

It should be noted, however, that, provided the reason for refusal is not based on sex/race, a licensee may refuse whoever he pleases, if he is not an innkeeper. When the two ladies in *Gill* returned to the bar to celebrate their triumph the licensee declined to serve them on the grounds that he did not like them personally. The point having been made, he later allowed them back in!

It is similarly unlawful to discriminate against a person on the grounds of his or her race alone. It is against the provisions of section 20(1) to refuse service, or to provide facilities of a different or inferior quality. Such discrimination will be attributed also to those who order staff to act in such a manner: *Zarczynska v Levy (1978).*[13]

Subject to the legal duties of an innkeeper and the rules against unlawful discrimination, English law does not compel one man to make a contract with another. Where food is sold or supplied, under contract or otherwise, the law imposes standards both as regards quality and quantity.

2. FOOD AND DRINK

For may centuries the quality of food has been the subject of various statutory controls. The most recent example of this is the Food Safety

Act 1990. It falls within the same generic body of legislation as the Trade Description and Weights and Measures Acts. It imposes sanctions by way of fines and/or imprisonment and other minor penalties on offenders against its provisions. It is not designed primarily as a vehicle by means of which a consumer may pursue a civil claim for compensation although it is possible to cite its breach in claims founded as appropriate for breach of statutory duty. It is possible, although unusual, for a private prosecution to be brought: *Snodgrass v Topping 1952)*[14].

The Food Safety Act 1990 (FSA) replaces most of the Food Act 1984. It is a major piece of legislation with far reaching consequences for the catering industry. Its provisions extend wider than this into all areas of food production and distribution but these mattes are not considered here. The impetus for change came from the increasing number and frequency of food scares and reported incidents of food poisoning. This gave rise to an apprehension that existing legislation was insufficiently effective. The FSA provisions did not take effect immediately but have been introduced in four phases with different commencement orders for named sections. In fact only two sections were implemented immediately in 1990. As with its predecessors the FSA provides that the Secretary of State may introduce such regulations as he may from time to time see fit, the most important of these are the Food Hygiene Regulations which themselves give rise to numerous possible offences. Provision is also made in s.40 for the Minister to introduce Codes of Practice for the food industry.

The FSA covers much more than simply safety. It also governs the composition of food, its quality, labelling and advertising. A small but significant change from previous legislation is that it presumes that all food and food ingredients found on the premises of food businesses is intended for human consumption. It will be for a defendant to a prosecution to prove otherwise to escape conviction for a food offence.

The main provisions of the FSA hinge upon the central offence of supplying food which fails to comply with 'food safety requirements' of which the Act provides no definition. Instead, it sets out what is the position when food fails to meet the standard required as judged by specific offence provisions. The aim of the FSA is, it would appear, to restrict the number and types of defined offences to as to make it easier for the prosecution to secure convictions and less possible for the defendant to escape by claiming he has been charged under the wrong section of the Act.

The principal offences are to be found in Part II of the FSA. The two specified here are:

Rendering food injurious to health   - s.7
Selling food not complying with food safety requirements   - s.8

The former replaces the old section 1 of the Food Act 1984 and the latter consolidates and extends the provisions previously found in ss2 and 8 of the 1984 Act.

Section 7 gives rise to a number of interesting issues. Its intention seems to be to prohibit the doing of anything to food so as to make it injurious to health where the intention is that such food shall be sold for human consumption. The majority of offences created in the FSA are strict liability in nature. This one requires proof of intent to sell for human consumption. Oddly at variance with other provisions as to presumption in the Act.

Under its predecessor, s.1 of the 1984 Act, it was necessary to show that three elements were present for an offence to be committed - adulteration, selling for human consumption (with intent) and the potential for injury to human health. It was the only section of the 1984 Act which required the potential of injury to human health to be a constituent part of the offence. The new section appears not to differ in this respect for it requires there to be a clear demonstration that there has been some addition of subtraction of matter to the food. What is new is the concept of subjecting food to a specific process or treatment which may render it injurious to health. This raises the possibility that processes such as irradiation and as yet undiscovered ways of preserving food may be caught by this section.

Section 7(2) states that when considering injury to health regard shall be had 'not only to the probable effect of the food on the health of the person consuming it but also on the probable cumulative effect .... on the health of the person consuming it in ordinary quantities'. On the one hand this seems to require that regard shall be had to the person - child or adult etc; on the other to look to injury which may not manifest itself for years in a person who has eaten a particular type of processed food. It must be designed to catch the manufacturer of products rather than the retailer since the ability to prove that a particular food product had been consumed in a particular restaurant over a period of years thus leading to a cumulative effect is verging on the fantastic. What is meant by 'ordinary quantities' is unclear. Perhaps the courts are meant to use the common law test of reasonableness to ascertain this. If parallels are drawn from drug related illnesses the ability to prove the injurious nature of a food product in the short as well as the long term may prove extremely difficult.

'Injury' is defined in s.7(3) as being 'in relation to health, including any impairment, whether permanent or temporary'. It is not clear whether this is meant to include food which is decomposed due to bacteriological action such as would have been caught under the 1984 Act it its s.8 as in: *Greig v Goldfinch (1961)*[15]. It appears on the face of it that such an example would fall under s.8(2) of the FSA but to which s.7(2) is also stated to apply.

Section 8 of the FSA appears to be the catch all offence rather in the way that the old s.2 was. The offence which it creates rolls up together the old ss2 and 8 of the 1984 Act. That is to say the old definitions of a sale 'to the prejudice of the purchaser of any food which is not of the nature, or not of the substance, or not of the quality of food demanded by the purchaser' and 'food unfit for human consumption' (otherwise than being injurious to health). Thus this section of the FSA seems to deal with the essential criminality of the sale or supply leaving the later ss 14 and 15 to deal with consumer protection rather more specifically. But as to where the line is now to be drawn between criminality and protection of the consumer is not clear. It may be necessary to have regard to the pre 1990 cases in search of the solution.

FSA s.8 offences would seem to encompass the situations where extraneous matter is to be found in food but which by its nature is not inherently injurious to health. Thus: *J. Miller Ltd v Battersea Borough Council (1956)*[16] - metal in a cake; *Turner & Son Ltd v Owen 1955)*[17] - string in a loaf. The example of the used bandaid found in food as in *Chibnall's Bakeries v E.J. Cope Brown (1956)*[18] may be easier to prove under this section than under s.7 - or perhaps not! Section 8 offences would also catch contaminated food as in the chemical injury case of *Meah v Roberts (1978)*[19].

Section 8(2) associates fitness for consumption with may factors - mould infestation, staleness, contamination with varying levels of unfitness as between each or in respect of individual conditions. It may therefore be that it is left for s.14 to deal with issues of sales not of the substance or quality demanded as was rehearsed in cases such as *Goodfellow v Johnson (1966)*[20] and *Preston v Grant (1925)*[21]. Both cases dealing with the watering down of spirits.

But what of *Smedley's Ltd v Breed (1974)*[22] the case which so excited the House of Lords who referred it back to the magistrates where a fine of £20 was levied? The small green caterpillar which was the culprit in the case was not injurious to health nor did it, it seems, render the food unfit for human consumption. The HL decided that it was a s.2 offence under the 1984 Act. But under the FSA it is a s.8 or s.14 offence.

The difficulty is compounded since the FSA is designed to avoid accused persons escaping liability by virtue of being charged under the wrong section. This matter was resolved under the previous legislation by allowing that is was not a bar to obtaining a conviction if the accused was charged under one section rather than another where some apparent overlapping occurred: *Preston v Greenclose Ltd (1975)*[23]. What the position is now to be under the FSA remains to be seen. It is probable that a charge under s.8 is so all encompassing that all and sundry will be covered by it.

Section 15 is concerned with false descriptions or false presentation of food and seems designed to catch *passing-off* offences and to test the effectiveness or otherwise of disclosure notices supplied in connection with food. In which case *Preston* (q.v.) may fall under this head. Because of its wording the section may give rise to difficulty in relation to the pleading of the offence as charged being 'false description' or 'misleading description' which the courts in the past have treated as separate and non-interchangeable offences, although the line drawn between the two at times seems curiously opaque.

Food

Part I of the FSA revises and extends several pre-existing definition. Food now includes water whether this is sold as bottled water as a product or simply supplied to the customer. It would include water supplied *free* since the definition of sale is extended to the supply of food in the course of business. Thus iced water which is commonly supplied in some restaurants as a way of causing the diner's stomach to contract and to persuade him that the meal is more filling than perhaps is the case, is caught by this provision of the Act. It also applies to water used in the manufacture of food or in any other way specified in an order made by the Minister. From which it would appear that all food supplied in all circumstances to the customer is covered by the Act. Even food given by way of a prize, free sample or gift is caught by the Act. Only those substances which are classified as controlled drugs or licensed medicines are exempted.

Defences

Section 14 creates an offence without providing any defence other than that of *due diligence* as set out in s.21. This defence which applies throughout the FSA requires that an accused person prove that he took all reasonable precautions and exercised *due diligence* to avoid the commission of the offence charged both in relation to himself or to a third party e.g. an employee. The third party defence will only be allowed subject to this requirement. The level of diligence required will vary as provided for in specific sections of the Act. Thus the level may vary in respect of goods provided under a brand name or in the absence of such identification. Where the defendant seeks to pass responsibility to a third party in claiming due diligence he will need to identify that party e.g. the manufacturer, in accordance with the procedures set out in the FSA.

Under the 1984 Act s.102 of that statute allowed what was called the *warranty* defence. This was held to apply where food was received by the defendant under a written description of the food warranting that the goods were as described. If the defendant could show that he had relied on this warranty having no reason to believe that the food was other than was claimed for it and that he had not done anything in relation to the item other than pass it on to the customer he could escape liability: *Tesco Stores v Roberts (1974)*[24]. This usually applied to retail business, it could rarely apply to the catering trade where food is prepared before service i.e. washed and or cooked or at the very least taken out of some form of container. This provision has been repealed by the FSA and has not been replaced. This indicates that the due diligence defence will be a stricter test than its predecessors and that it will be much more difficult for an accused to transfer blame to a third party.

The offences created by the FSA, with the exception of s.7(1) as already noted, are strict liability in nature. Added to this is the intention, raised in s.3, that there is a presumption that any food or article or substance capable of being used in the composition or preparation of food is intended for human consumption when found on the premises of a food business. Taken all round it will be much more difficult under the new regime for a defendant to escape liability.

Labelling and pricing

Section 15 of the FSA deals with food which is either wrongly labelled or likely to mislead the purchaser. Thus a bottle of sparkling wine labelled 'champagne', but originating in Spain, constitutes an offence. Some debate exists over the use of the word 'fresh' as applied to food. It cannot refer to tinned or dried products but with modern frozen or 'sous vide' products does it simply refer to the fact that the food was fresh when prepared or frozen? The matter is unresolved at present.

Section 15 appears at first sight to be little more than old wine in new bottles. It is the old offence of false labelling caught previously by the Labelling of Food Regulations 1984. It does, however, add a twist. It catches a vendor or supplier whether or not he intended to mislead the customer. Further, it is not necessary to have a misleading label on the food, false presentation is sufficient. If the food is got up to give the impression of being that which it is not, then this too will be an offence. Such presentation may be in relation to the shape, appearance or packaging of food. The s.15 offences are therefore much wider in scope than what has gone before.

Pricing is governed by the Price Marking (Food and Drink on Premises) Order 1979. The Order was made under the Prices Act 1974 and applies to all catering establishments where food is sold to the general public. It does not apply where food and drink is prepared by special request or for a price agreed in advance. The Order details prices in relation to the number of items available on a menu. It also requires all prices shown to be inclusive of VAT. Any other additions for service, cover or corkage must also be shown. The display must be at the entrance to the premises which serve table meals or at the point of sale in self-service or take-away operations. Mispricing is now covered also by the Consumer Protection Act 1987, section 20.

Food Hygiene Regulations

Such regulations made by the Minister under enabling provisions in several statutes in the past - notably the Food Hygiene (General) Regulations 1970 - have been a significant source of food law for some time. Indeed they contain much more by way of legal regulation than is contained in the parent legislation. Such regulations lay down rules for the conduct of food business, which title indicates any trade or business for the purpose of which any person engages in the handling of food intended for sale or which is sold for human consumption.

Such regulations are the vehicle by which the makers of legislation can respond to the emerging needs in a given area. Such needs may be social, economic or the result of scientific knowledge or technological change. A statute is too restrictive way of bringing in change when speed may be of the essence or detailed provisions are required. Such regulations are created by designated government ministers who must abide by the limitations set in the parent statute. Failure to do so could result in their being declared ultra vires - outside the powers - of the Minister concerned and therefore ineffective.

In this way it has been possible to react effectively to fears over the advisability of engaging in certain methods of food preservation. Whether or not the fears raised are necessarily calmed by the resulting regulations is a matter for conjecture. The irradiation of food is just such an area which has caused concern and which has given rise to regulation.

Other examples may be seen in relation to the pollution hazards with reference to open food and to food handlers. Regulations are in being to minimise the risk to such food. Amongst these the prohibition on smoking or drinking is pre-eminent. Both employers and employees who disregard the ban imposed by the regulations face fines. Nevertheless, it is still common to find staff serving drinks in bars smoking. The law to prevent this is in place it is enforcement which appears to be lacking.[25].

The FSA contains the facility for the making of may more regulations with regard to food businesses. Tucked away in paragraph 5(3) of Schedule 1 is the authority for regulations to be made requiring persons involved in or intending to be involved in a food business to undergo training in food hygiene. Section 23 of the Act itself empowers food authorities to run or to subsidise the running of courses in food hygiene for employers and employees. The Department of Health was given responsibility for examining how such training might by effected. The result is that there should be no requirement to attend formally recognised courses which provide certification by a recognised provider but that it should be left to businesses to train their own staff. Past experience shows that such de-regulation of training will lead in the main to no training or inadequate provision. Many small businesses will pay lip service to the need if they do anything at all. The notion that the threat of sanctions by way of fine etc. for food offences - will operate to ensure that training is given to an acceptable standard is not borne out by empirical evidence from other areas - health and safety for one.

Many colleges and professional training bodies have always included food hygiene in their courses and always will. But training is not a once and for all activity. All training needs periodic reinforcement and up dating. Will employers generally do this? There are also thousands of catering workers who have never had any formal training of any kind nor achieved any standards capable of formal recognition. Such a situation creates inherent dangers for the consumer.

Registration of food premises

Section 19 of the FSA provides for the making of regulations requiring the control of food premises. Originally it was intended that there should be a system for licensing and registration. The Food Premises (Registration) Regulations 1991 have been introduced but they are a watered down edition of the original. Existing food businesses are required to register and new businesses must do so within 28 days prior to the commencement of trading. The intention being to make the enforcement agency - Environmental Health Officers - aware of the operation in their areas and to inspect the premises which appear on their register as required by the FSA.

It was intended that such premises should in the main be licensed for operation. Not dissimilar in some respects to the licensing of premises selling alcohol where licences could be refused or taken away for specified offences and making it illegal to operate without a licence. In the case of food premises this is not to be the case.

Applicants for a Justices Licence for the sale of alcohol by whatever method have to satisfy criteria as individuals, They need to be fit and proper persons in the eyes of the Justices who will also take notice of training and experience of applicants before granting a licence. The premises where liquor sale are to take place also require a licence. Why this regime should not be required for food premises is a matter of some dispute. Economic factors seem to be behind the failure to adopt such a parallel scheme. Financial considerations for businesses and the administrative base for such a system have won the day over health and safety as they appear to have done in the case of training for food handlers.

The system which has been introduced is purely one of registration. All such a system requires is that notification of a business be made to the local food authority which records details on a register which it is required to maintain. There is a penalty for a business failing to register by way of fine. Registration does not involve the payment of a fee, merely the filling in of a one page form to be returned to the local food authority offices. Once registered there is no requirement for renewal. Some businesses are exempted from registration - retail sales by vending machine are one such together with businesses which operate for a total of less than 5 days in any period of five consecutive weeks. Yet how many customers can a machine infect or how may businesses are there selling fast food at public events, even if operating for less than 5 days etc? Further, the Regulations only apply to permanent and not mobile operations. It is true that the provisions of the FSA apply to all food businesses but except for reasons of administrative expediency and cost it is difficult to see why Regulations of such little real practical effect in the prevention of offences should not extend to all business activities where the sale or supply of food is concerned. Again, if licences were required by all, then even occasional sellers should have to be licensed and much more effective controls could be introduced.

The FSA provides in s.40 for Codes of Practice to be issued giving guidance on the enforcement of Registration Regulations. The response to the Regulations and to such Codes by the EHOs tasked with enforcing FSA provisions is that they are given too little power and that it will be almost impossible to effect any meaningful form of control under the provisions as presently stated.

One problem springs immediately to mind in this context. Where food premises change hands, as they frequently to in the catering trade, or change their operational base - from fast food takaways to table meals for example - notification has to be made to the food authority for the location but de-regulation only occurs when the local authority discovers, almost by accident, that a business has altered or changed hands or indeed may no longer be a food business. The whole system is so full of holes that the scepticism of the EHOs seems well justified.

Enforcement

The FSA makes provision by definition of 'food authorities' and 'authorised officer' in s.5. These largely resemble the position as it existed pre 1990. The main burden of enforcement lies on the EHOs and in some cases Trading Standards Officers (TSOs) with the same degree of difficulty as existed previously as to where in certain cases the line of demarcation between their several duties runs. The line between consumer safety and protection. Where trading is carried out in the context of a market the local authorities also have duties as to the regulation of these activities under Regulations drawn up in 1966. Local authorities also have powers to employ external agencies for policing the system where routine inspection work is to be carried out. The government's rush for privatisation in many fields could also be reflected in areas of food safety. Who then will police the enforcers?

The general provisions as to enforcement are contained in s.6 of the FSA. An 'enforcement authority' is a 'food authority' specifically designated for this activity. The two need not be the same body although in practice they mostly are. Section 6(2) states that 'every food authority shall enforce and execute within their area the provisions of this Act with respect to which the duty is not imposed expressly or by necessary implication on some other authority'. Thus food authorities covered by s.5 are under a duty to enforce the provision of the FSA.

The procedures are very similar to those under the Health and Safety at Work Act 1974 and is clear that this is where they derived their present form. Over the past 20 years the HASAWA provisions have attracted a marked degree of criticism as regards their rigour in terms of powers of enforcement. Although in 1992 the level of fines and other sanctions was increased for HASAWA offences heard before the magistrates this does not mean that the power to enforce has markedly increased - only the level of sanction to those successfully prosecuted to conviction. The same inherent weakness is to be seen in the FSA regime.

Authorised officers under the FSA have a wide range of powers including inspection and seizure; improvement notices; prohibition order; emergency prohibitions; prosecution. These do not of themselves ensure safety as the HASAWA regime has shown. There is no reason to believe that they will be more successful translated to the FSA. It is the political will needed to make them succeed together with adequate resourcing which is the key to success. Great play has been made of self regulation as the most effective form of safety policing in HASAWA situations. The same echoes are to be heard in the FSA system - self training, registration etc. Experience shows that it is not the best of practices without adequate supervision and enforcement agencies.

In the case of prosecution, s.36 of the FSA provides that if an offence is committed by a company both the company and those controlling directors and officers of the company may be prosecuted and if found guilty convicted. Third party offences are dealt with by s.20.

A prosecution must be brought within 3 years of the offence having been committed - obvious difficulties will arise here in connection with s.8(2) issues (Q.v.) - or one year after the matter comes to the notice of the prosecuting authority, whichever is the earlier. Upon summary conviction, penalties for the main food offences are a fine of up to £20,000 and up to 6 months imprisonment. For conviction at Crown Court the level of fine is unlimited and imprisonment up to 2 years may be awarded. Experience of the HASAWA and previous food legislation shows that the upper limits of these sanctions will rarely, if ever, be achieved.

It is difficult to see that the new legislation will live up to the expectations raised for it by the government ministries responsible for the drafting and implementation of the statutes and regulations. If it is seen that they are failing to address the problem adequately through lack of enforcement or whatever then the law will be brought into disrepute and failure to observe all but the basic essentials will become commonplace. The provisions of the Food Premises (Registration) Regulations 1991 have already been seen as at best unenforceable and at worst risible.

Weights and measures

The Weights and Measures Act 1985 consolidates some the previous legislation in the area. Much of its detail has to do with complicated technical matters and with labelling and packaging but some are directly applicable to consumer purchases. Section 28 deals with the giving of short weight, measure or number. 'Any person who, in selling or purporting to sell any goods by weight or other measurement or by numbers, delivers or causes to be delivered to the buyer a lesser quantity than that purported to be sold or than corresponds with the price charged is guilty of an offence.'

This section, allied to sections 29 to 30, creates a number of offences which may be committed by food retailers. He who advertises a '6oz steak' or an '8oz burger', allowing for some shrinkage on cooking and cooling, must sell to that weight. If a dish says, for example, that it contains 'at least three jumbo prawns' then three is the minimum required for the price charged.

Offences against the FSA and the Weights and Measures Acts may also amount to activities caught by the Trade Descriptions Acts. It will be for the officers concerned to decide under which legislation they will bring a prosecution, if any. Compensation may be available upon application to the court by the officer in charge, on behalf of a victim of an offence, but the sums are likely to be less than where a civil action is brought by the latter.

Legislation has for some time strictly regulated the quantities in which beer and spirits may be sold. Except in relation to wine sold by the carafe no such regulation applies to wine sold by the glass. A 'voluntary' code of conduct was introduced for the trade in 1984 but no statutory provision has yet come to the aid of the consumer wondering just how much he should have in the glass supplied to him. Provided the price displayed for a glass of wine is adhered to then no condition applies as to quantity unless this is referred to on the price list. An example where once again self regulation rules the day to the general detriment of the customer.

3. CIVIL CLAIMS

Restaurateurs speak in terms of the *meal experience* when they describe all the components of the package presented to the diner. It includes the quality of food and drink, their preparation and service, the atmosphere of the restaurant and other factors. Depending on the expectations of the customer it may be a good or a bad experience. If it proves unsatisfactory then the customer may seek legal remedy. He may base a claim on contract or in tort.

The contract will be comprised of express terms such as the description of the menu items (allowing for a little poetic licence), the price and additional charge items made known to the customer. In addition, the contract will be affected by terms which are implied by statute in respect of the food and the manner of service.

Sale of Goods Act 1979

The terms *food* and *goods* are synonymous. The Act, therefore, requires, by the operation of section 13, that where goods are sold by description they shall correspond to that description. Food sold as *wholefood* or *vegetarian* must correspond to that definition. If a customer asks for a *vintage* port then he must expect to be served with the item which he himself has described.

The Act requires, in section 14(2), that goods shall be of 'merchantable quality'. As regards goods generally, the phrase has been the subject of much judicial examination. In relation to food, and calling in aid other legislation as a guide only, that which is inedible because it is unfit for human consumption or injurious to health will not satisfy the requirement as to quality. Section 14(6) makes reference to quality being expressed in relation to generally accepted standards for goods of the type in question and the description, if any, applied to them together with the price charged. Thus, if venison is served which has been insufficiently hung to render it digestible, or if the price charged for flank steak is that usually associated with a filet mignon, or if 'succulent' pork is used in relation to leathery chops, the quality may not satisfy the requirement as to merchantability. This does not mean that a customer can return goods which are not to his taste. A diner who complains of the texture of the squid in his 'fruits de mer' is entitled to be told politely that this is its normal attribute. The 'ripeness' of a Camembert cheese is often a matter of individual taste.

If the seller makes known a defect in the product which the buyer is prepared to accept then he has little cause for complaint, especially if the price reflects the quality. A diner who is told that it is the end of the season, that the avocados are not prime quality, and that the price is lower than usual must make his decision based upon the information given to him. Provided the vegetable is not inedible, he has no substance for his complaint as to quality.

Section 14(3) requires that where a buyer makes known a particular purpose for which he requires the goods there is an implied condition that the items supplied are reasonably fit for that purpose. A customer who asks for an Indian dish which is suitable for someone with a delicate stomach is entitled to complain if he is incapacitated after being served with a vindaloo!

Where the buyer does not receive that to which he is entitled under the contract, he will be able to claim against the seller even where the latter cannot be shown to be to blame for the defect in the goods. If the buyer suffers as a result of receiving food not of the standard implied in the contract he may succeed in an action for damages: *Frost v Aylesbury Dairies (1905).*[26]

Where the quality of the food can be shown to be of merchantable quality when the contract was made then, should it be spoiled thereafter, the action will be based not upon sale of goods but for breach of a service. Thus, a steak which was in good condition when it was sold (ordered) by the diner is rendered inedible because of the poor cooking by the chef, or a bottle of port is spoilt when decanted by the waiter. In such circumstances, there is a breach of implied term that the seller, or his servants, will use reasonable care and skill in preparing the dish. This common law obligation is now contained in section 13 of the Supply of Goods and Services Act 1982. The buyer is entitled to reject the goods. Technically, since the steak was his property, he could claim damages, in reality he would be offered another choice. Alternatively, he might choose to accept the original dish at a reduced price.

Where the meal is consumed and the diner later becomes unwell he may claim damages based upon his discomfort and any medical bills incurred: *Priest v Last (1903)*.[27] Where the injury is sustained by a diner who did not purchase the meal, he or she, not being privy to the contract, may not be able to recover compensation: *Buckley v La Reserve (1959)*.[28] In order to overcome the difficulties which this may cause, the courts have shown themselves willing to imply that the person paying the bill for a meal is acting as the *agent* for others in his party: *Charproniere v Mason (1905)*.[29] Where the injured party is the spouse of the party who contracted for the meal, the courts have held the relationship to be the basis for an action on the contract: *Lockett v A.M. Charles (1938)*.[30]

Where the injured party is unable to base a claim in contract he will have to seek redress in tort. He will have to rely on being able to prove a breach of the duty of care necessary to sustain an action in Negligence. This was the essence of the claim in the historic case of *Donoghue v Stevenson*. The action could not be brought against the cafe proprietor who was not at fault, it lay against the manufacturer. The consumer may be defeated in a claim for negligence where he is unable to prove fault: *Daniels v R. White & Sons Ltd and Tabard (1938)*.[31]

The consumer who loses a claim in such circumstances is now protected by the Consumer Protection Act 1987. As a result of an EEC directive[32] on product liability, the 1987 Act imposes strict liability on the manufacturer where goods have undergone an *industrial process*. The Directive allowed member states to include those goods which had not undergone such a process. Nowhere is the term *industrial process* defined. The UK government chose not to include fresh produce in the protection afforded by the Act. Thus a manufacturer will be liable for defects in tinned goods, probably for frozen foods, but not, say, for fresh meat and poultry. The consumer who cannot claim in contract against the caterer will need to resort to an action for negligence and need to prove the fault of the defendant.

The Act defines damage for which compensation may be claimed in terms of personal injury. This may include nervous shock. Pure economic loss will not be the basis for a claim. It will still be necessary to base such a claim on either breach of contract or in tort. None of this should worry a diner who, in the main, is served with many manufactured products and for whom personal injury rather than economic loss is the usual foundation of a claim. All products of brewers, distillers and viniculture are the result of an *industrial process* so the consumer of these manufacturers' goods will benefit from the 1987 Act's provisions, whilst the health food devotee may not be so fortunate!

4. THE LICENSED TRADE

A tourist coming to England or Wales could be forgiven for being confused by the law relating to the sale of alcohol. The deterrent effect upon tourism of the system of *permitted hours* for licensed premises has been the reason given for the change introduced by the Licensing (Restaurant Meals) Act 1987 and the provisions of the Licensing Act 1988, as they affect *permitted hours*.

The licensing system

The common law imposed no restrictions on the sale of alcohol. Licensing is the creature of statute. The Alehouses Act 1828 consolidated the previous statutes whereby the local justices had granted licences to fit and proper persons for the keeping of inns, alehouses and victualling houses. The Act remained the basis of the jurisdiction of the licensing justices until 1911. The licence required, inter alia, that the holder did not adulterate his liquor, use illegal measures, permit his premises to be used by drunken or disorderly persons and that, with the excepted need to receive travellers, he should keep his premises closed during Divine Service on Sundays, Christmas Day and Good Friday. The Licensing (Consolidation) Act 1910 simplified the various statutes relating to the retail sale of liquor and instituted a universal system of licences granted by the justices, with a few exceptions.

Today, all premises selling alcohol by retail need to be licensed, with the exception of boats and aircraft. A theatre which is licensed under the Theatres Act 1968 is also exempt, but may not sell alcohol outside normal permitted hours. Railway trains are exempted provided food is also made available to passengers. Registered clubs also form an excepted class.

The forms of licence which are issued are dependent upon the type of alcoholic beverage to be sold or supplied, the type of premises and the class of customer to be served. The main form of licence which is granted is for the sale of intoxicating liquor of all descriptions. This may be subject to a restriction that service may only be to bona fide members of clubs and their guests.

Another form of licence more in evidence today is the wine-only license. This allows the licensee to sell wines of all descriptions including fortified wines, vermouths and made wines. This type of licence is the one popularly associated with winebars, although many of these are misnamed in that they sell liquor of all descriptions. There are three other forms of licence for beer, cider and wine only, beer and cider only and cider only. These are rarely found today.

The licences associated with public houses and some hotels permit the sale of alcohol for consumption, both on and off the premises, by the public generally. A restaurant licence permits the holder to sell alcohol as an ancillary to substantial meals in premises which are structurally adapted and used bona fide by diners. A restaurant licensed for this purpose must provide a non-alcoholic alternative drink for diners. A residential licence allows the licensee to serve liquor only to guests in residence and their guests, but the latter may not buy their drinks, these must be paid for by residents. It is quite usual to find restaurant and residential licences combined for operation in the same premises. These two forms of license are known as *Part IV* licences from the regulations governing them which derive from that Part of the Licensing Act 1964. The Act is the basis of modern licensing law for England and Wales. Scotland and Northern Ireland have their own systems.

Permitted hours

Until 1914, limits on the hours when liquor could be served were regulated by a method which stipulated when premises had to be closed. A series of measures dealing with the consumption of liquor were enacted during the war and, in 1921, the hours were determined by the Licensing Act which replaced the war-time regulations. This Act established the system of *permitted hours* which has been the subject of many attempts at reform ever since.

The present system allows restaurants to serve alcoholic beverages with meals but only at such times of the day when meals are being provided. The hours of service are from 11a.m. to 11p.m. but if meals are only served at lunch time, or only in the evenings, the hours will be restricted accordingly by the licensing justices.

A hotel or guest house with a residential licence may serve its residents on a 24-hour basis. The 1964 Act stipulates that such premises must have a 'dry room' in which alcohol is not served or consumed. The justices have the power to waive this requirement where they feel that it is appropriate to do so.

The 1988 Licensing Act affected a substantial change in the regime for permitted hours in England and Wales. The Act does not replace its predecessor but significantly amends the Licensing Act 1964. The old regime whereby there was a mandatory break of at least 2 hours in the afternoons Monday - Saturday has been changed. The hours no applied under the provisions of s.60 as amended are:

Monday - Saturday	11a.m. to 11p.m.
Sundays, Christmas Day & Good Friday	12 noon to 3p.m. & 7p.m. to 10.30p.m.

A remnant of the old regime is to be found in the ability of local licensing justices to impose restrictions under s.67A whereby they may order the closure of licensed premises between 2.30p.m. and 5.30p.m. A restriction order may be applied for by the police or persons living or having businesses or schools within the neighbourhood to prevent what is a potential cause of a Public Nuisance it would appear. Such orders are discretionary and subject to appeal against them to the Crown Court. It should also be noted that the justices have a power to allow upon application an extension of 1 hour allowing premises to open at 10a.m. but no earlier 'if satisfied that the requirements of the district make it desirable'.

The same hours generally apply to sales from off licences i.e. those premises where alcohol may be bought but not consumed on the premises. These always had an earlier morning opening time of 8.30a.m. and as a result of lobbying by the big supermarket chains this has been brought forward to an 8a.m. start Mondays to Saturdays.

The concern about drinking in public places, usually with the drink having been purchased from an off licence, has prompted the Secretary of State for the Environment to empower local authorities to make appropriate bye-laws for their local areas banning drinking in public places wherever they see fit.

Premises which are the subject of a restaurant licence or a restaurant and residential licence are also able to serve through what was formerly the afternoon break. This now also includes Sundays unlike other premises where the restriction on afternoon sales continues together with Christmas Day and Good Friday. This concession as with all such licences at all times is subject to the requirement that the consumption of alcohol is ancillary to the main purpose - the consumption of a substantial meal.

Where there is a supper hours certificate under s.68 in force attached to a Part IV licence the premises may stay open for an additional hour in the evenings. Where the certificate is attached to a restaurant facility in a public house or wine bar the same rule applies to evening sales but in respect of the afternoon period it will not cover the period between 4p.m. and 7p.m. when alcohol may not be sold.

The changes in the law do not seem to have produced the mad drinking spree forecast by some opponents of the measures. Nor does it seem to have altered the ways of many licensees. Tourist authorities and others urged changes which they claimed the public wanted. Whatever the public may or may not have wanted some licensees close as they did before in the afternoons. It should always be remembered that a public house is not open at the will of the public. It is a private property governed by public laws. A landlord cannot be compelled to open if he does not wish to do so. Aggrieved parties may object to the renewal of his licence when this is due, but no more.

Many licensed premises chose to shut for economic reasons. If sales to customers do not warrant the expense of staying open then the landlord will close shop. This practice has been prevalent for may years in country areas where opening has been delayed or, in the case of the City of London, few premises open on Sundays because their usual clients, workers in the commercial centres, are not there.

The latest proposal for changes in the law concern the introduction of what is being called the Café-bar. This is said to be modelled on the continental model of café. What it implies is that children below the age of 14 should be allowed in premises where the sale of alcohol is not necessarily linked to the consumption of meals. This is possible now if the children are in a space which is not by definition a bar. What is wanted it seems is to allow children into a new type of general purpose operation to get the best of both worlds in terms of food/drink sales.

The impetus is coming as usual from the big brewers - that element which is often referred to as the 'beerage'. Costs of alcoholic drinks are rising and sales falling. For some time the brewers who control the majority of pub outlets have realised the virtue of food sales to boost their income. Sales of food also offer increased profit margins.

It might be thought that the way would open up for the small proprietor to increase his trade. It might, but the food and alcohol market is dominated by the big brewers and caterers. Such changes as are made will reflect their interests not those of the public. The big brewers have skilfully avoided the intention of the EC as regards the monopolistic structure of the tied trade to date and are past masters at the art of lobbying Parliament to get what they want. If tourists derive any benefit from changes in this direction it will be by accident not design.

Extensions

Permitted hours may be extended by application to the local licensing panel. These extensions are in addition to the 20-minute drinking-up-time at present allowed in premises with *pub* licences and the 30 minutes allowed for licensed restaurants.

A restaurant or *pub* with a bona fide restaurant facility or a club may apply for a supper-hour certificate. This allows alcohol to be served as an ancillary to a meal for an extra hour after the end of the normal permitted hours applicable to the premises.

Two other forms of extension, the Extended Hours Order and the Special Hours Certificate are also available for restaurant and club operations. They are usually associated with the type of activity which is commonly called a *night club*. For this reason they are described under *Clubs* (q.v.).

Measures

The Weights and Measures Act 1963 (as amended by the Act of 1976) prescribes the quantities (or units of measure) in which some classes of alcoholic beverages must be sold.

Unless sold in a sealed container, e.g. a bottle, or used as a constituent of a mixture of three or more liquids (cocktails) gin, rum, vodka and whisky may only be dispensed for consumption in licensed premises in measures of one quarter, one fifth and one sixth of a gill or multiples thereof. A gill is the equivalent of 5 fluid ounces by volume. A notice must be displayed in a prominent position advertising the measure adopted. The adopted measure must be applied to all four named spirits. Other spirits and wine by the glass may be served in whatever quantity the licensee wishes. He is, however, governed by the Price Marking (Food and Drink on Premises) Order 1979 which requires him to display a tariff of prices per item.

The Weights and Measures (Sale of Wine) Order 1976 prescribes the measures by which wine offered by the open carafe must be sold, (25cl., 50cl., 75cl., or one litre). There is a *voluntary* code for the sale of wine by the glass suggested by the industry. Experience shows that this is more honoured in the breach than the observance.

Draught beers and cider may only be sold in quantities of one third, one half and one pint in a capacity measure of the quantity in question. These glasses will be stamped with the official seal as to capacity. Unmarked glasses may be used for bottled or canned beers or where delivery is by a metered pump, officially authorised and the tap of which is clearly visible to the customer. The *head* on beer is not part of the measure but no offence is committed unless the glass is not topped up at the request of the customer: *Bennett v Markham & another (1982).*[33]

Amidst much trumpeting by the DTI it was announced by the Consumer Affairs Minister in the Autumn of 1992 that as from 1994 s.43 of the Weights & Measures Act 1985 would be commenced. This would mean that in determining the quantity of beer or cider to be sold by measure the gas comprised as the *head* should be disregarded. Brim measure glasses will have to be replaced with oversized if not lined glasses as a consequence. Surveys by Trading Standards Officers nationally in 1992 revealed that the average deficiency of liquid beer in any glass was around 5% of capacity; that individual deficiencies of up to 17.5% has been recorded; that in some areas 97% of all 'pints' sold contained less than a pint of liquid beer.

However, a commencement order will be necessary and furious lobbying has been taking place in order to persuade the Minister to change his mind. The beerage is claiming the enormous expense of having to change all glasses used in their tied premises and that any cost incurred will have to be passed on to the customers. When was it ever otherwise?

The change to oversized and lined glasses was mooted several years ago to the same protests from the beerage. If in the intervening years the old brim measures had been replaced on a voluntary basis to replace natural wastage through breakages the problem could have been alleviated. The big brewers have not chosen to do so in the main on economic grounds, the profits they make on under sized measures. It remains to be seen whether or not the Minister will yield to the political pressure being exerted upon him by interested parties.

Beer or cider need not be dispensed in such measures if it forms part of a drink made of two or more liquids, e.g. a shandy. Beer may not be diluted with any liquid unless it is to the customer's order. Spirits may be diluted provided that sufficient notice is given to the customer by means of a prominent display, or to his order.

Age qualification

No one below the age of 14 years is allowed to be in a bar during permitted hours and extensions thereto. A bar, by definition, is any place exclusively or mainly used for the sale and consumption of intoxicating liquor. This does not apply to gardens or 'children's rooms' where liquor is consumed but not sold. Nor does it apply to bona fide restaurants, i.e. where the consumption of alcohol is only ancillary to the taking of table meals.

No person below the age of 18 may buy or consume alcohol in a bar. It is illegal for a person to buy or attempt to buy alcohol for a person below the age of 18 to consume in a bar. A person below the age of 18 may consume non-alcoholic drink but this does not include a 'shandy' made up by the bar staff, only to non-alcoholic shandy in bottles or cans.

No child below the age of five years may be given alcohol to drink in a restaurant. A person under 18, but over 16 years of age, may purchase beer, cider, porter or perry for consumption with a meal in a restaurant.

It should be noted that these ages are stipulated in the legislation as minimum ages. If a licensee wishes to impose a rule of his own that no one below the age of 18 should be allowed in a bar or a restaurant, or under 25 years in a night club, that is his privilege. The public have no right of admission to such premises. In addition, a licensee is required by law to deny admission to his premises to anyone who has been banned by the courts under the terms of the Licensed Premises (Exclusion of Certain Persons) Act 1980.

Special occasions

Where a licensee wishes to extend his permitted hours to cater for a special function or to celebrate a particular event, e.g. New Year's Eve, he may apply to the Magistrates Court for a Special Order of Exemption which, if granted, will describe the limitations of such extension. It should not be confused with a General Order of Exemption which is granted for the benefit of those working in or attending specified markets, e.g. Smithfield. Nor is it the same as an Occasional Licence or Permission, both of which are granted under special rules allowing alcohol to be sold and consumed at places where no licence is in force, e.g. a garden party or fête.

In certain parts of the country, a provision may be inserted in a licence for specified premises that, during certain times of the year, there shall be no permitted hours in the premises. These 'seasonal licences' are to be found in holiday areas and in such places as holiday camps.

The ability of businesses to cater to the wants of the public in places of refreshment depends on many factors. The suitability of the premises and the proprietor are major criteria. Licensing has been a major method for control combined with criminal sanctions against offenders. 'Caterbility' is, therefore, a sum of components which determine what services and facilities may be provided to the public.

NOTES

1.   *The Guardian* 6 April 1993
2.   (1959) 2 QB 1.
3.   s 1(3).
4.   (1835) 7 C & P 213.
5.   (1948) 1 KB 165 (CA).

6.   (1920) SC 805. See also R v Rymer (1877) 2 QBD 136.
7.   See 104 SJ 38.
8.   (1944) 2 A11 ER 171.
9.   (1899) 63 JP 233.
10.   Sex Discrimination Act 1975 s 29(1).
11.   (1983) 2 WLR 155 (CA).
12.   (1982) *Times* 2 October 1982.
13.   (1978) IRLR 532.
14.   (1952) 116 JP 332.
15.   (1961) 59 LGR 304 (QBD).
16.   (1956) 1 QB 43.
17.   (1955) 3 A11 ER 565.
18.   (1956) Crim LR 263.
19.   (1978) 1 A11 ER 97 (QBD).
20.   (1966) 1 QB.
21.   (1925) 1 KB 177. See also Rodbourne v Hudson (1925) 1 KB 225.
22.   (1974) AC 839. See also Newton v West Vale Creamery (1956) 120 JP 318. Greater Manchester Council v Lockwood Foods (1979) Crim LR 593 DC. McDonalds Hamburger Ltd v Windle (1986) unreported.
23.   (1975) 139 JP 245. See also Shearer v Rowe (1985) 149 JP 698.
24.   (1974) 3 A11 ER 74. See also Walker v Baxters Butchers Ltd (1977) Crim LR 479.
25.   Regulation 10(1).
26.   (1905) 1 KB 608.
27.   (1903) 2 KB 148.
28.   (1959) CLY 1330.
29.   (1905) 25 TLR 633.
30.   (1938) 4 A11 ER 170.
31.   (1938) 4 A11 ER 258.
32.   85/374/EEC.
33.   (1982) 1 WLR 1231 (QBD).

Chapter XIV

Paying The Bill

1. TIME FOR PAYMENT

A contract for goods or services is a two-sided affair. Each party promises to provide something of value in exchange for what the other is to provide. The value of a particular item or service is for the parties to determine. Only where there is evidence of fraud or malpractice will the law intervene. It is unusual for the courts to make a bargain for the parties. A rare instance is where an innkeeper has overcharged a traveller. He may be prosecuted for a common law offence and there appears to be no reason why, under the provisions of the Powers of the Criminal Courts Act 1973, the customer should not seek an order for compensation. A remedy in tort may also exist.

The Sale of Goods Act 1979 defines the contract for the sale of goods in section 2(1) as one where 'the seller transfers or agrees to transfer the property in the goods to the buyer for a money consideration called the price'. It is the buyers' duty to pay the seller at the time he agreed to pay in the contract of sale (see section 27). Unless otherwise agreed, delivery of the goods and payment of the price are concurrent conditions (see section 28). It is for the parties to agree time for payment of the bill for goods sold.

In the case of many fastfood operations involving take-away, the seller demands payment before delivery, presumably as a way of ensuring payment. In a restaurant, it is the practice to present the bill at the end of the meal. In self-service cafeterias, the customer pays when he has made his selection from the items on display. In the case of the sale or supply of intoxicating liquor, it is illegal for a person to sell on credit terms. The liquor must be paid for before or at the time when it is sold or supplied. A promise to pay is not enough. Payment must be made in cash or notes or some symbol of cash or notes, e.g. a cheque: *Whitham and Butterworth v Lindley (1920)*.[1] It is presumably not illegal to pay by credit charge card (q.v.) since the monies advanced, or the service provided, are not specifically for the purchase of alcohol and it is not the card company which is in fact selling the items. There appears, however, to be no rush by pub landlords to become involved in such transactions, they have been wary of cheques in the past and shown no marked inclination to change the habits of a lifetime.

The provisions of section 166 of the Licensing Act 1964 are modified in subsection (2) by allowing liquor which is sold or supplied for consumption at a meal, supplied at the same time and which is consumed with the meal, to be paid for together with the meal. This also allows persons who regularly take meals at a restaurant to include the cost of liquor in any arrangements they make with the management for paying bills by account, presented at agreed intervals.

This postponement of payment for liquor is allowed where the items are supplied for consumption by a person residing in premises as a guest. He may pay the price at the time when he is to make payment for the accommodation.

A hotelier may ask for payment in advance from a *chance arrival*. Some hotels receive the bulk of their custom in this way. A receptionist has little evidence about the credit-worthiness of such a customer. If the traveller has little or no luggage, it is usual to take a cash deposit or, alternatively, to make an imprint of any credit card the caller may have. The Hotel Proprietors Act 1956 allows an innkeeper to refuse a guest who does not appear able and willing to pay a reasonable sum for the services and facilities provided. Asking for advance payment is a way of testing this.

Where holidays are booked with tour operators, it is usual for the client to be called upon to pay an agreed deposit and the balance within a stipulated date before the time of departure. These terms are contained in booking forms which accompany brochures and also list the charges due in the event of cancellation by the client.

Tickets for various forms of transportation are almost invariably paid for at the time of booking. Where no ticket is issued, as with a taxi, the fare is paid for on arrival at the chosen destination indicated to the driver by the passenger. The Supply of Goods and Services Act, section 15, implies a term into such a contract that where no charge has been agreed for a service the customer will pay a *reasonable* price. Section 15(2) declares it to be a question of fact as to what is a reasonable charge. Where the taximeter, controlled by the local licensing authority, is the method of determining the fare, it is unlikely that this would be regarded as unreasonable. In other cases, where a taxi or hire car driver is not governed by the meter (q.v.), then the implied terms of the 1982 Act will come into play.

Avoidance of payment

Where one person persuades another that he will pay for services provided by that other, but he has no intention of so doing, then he may be charged with obtaining services by deception under section 1(1) of the Theft Act 1978. *Services* are widely defined in the Act. They can include both the delivery of a restaurant meal (goods) and the hire of a car, entry to recreational facilities, or the provision of board and lodging at a hotel (services). The basis of the agreement is that the services will be paid for in the form of money, e.g. cash, cheque or credit card. Both parties know that a price has to be paid for the service. The offence consists of the dishonesty of the recipient in deceiving the donor of the service.

No deception is required where the offence commonly known as *bilking* occurs, e.g. where a person who has eaten a restaurant meal, or having reached his destination by taxi, runs off without paying. There is no requirement under section 3 of the 1978 Act that the conduct should amount to theft or involve any deception practised by the accused. The offence is committed by a person who 'knowing that payment on the spot for any goods supplied, or service done, is required or expected from him, dishonestly makes off without having paid as required or expected and with intent to avoid payment of the amount due'. Various elements are necessary for the person involved to be convicted.

The person must *make off* either openly or stealthily. It can occur where, at the end of the meal, the diner explains that he has no money but offers his name and address which is accepted. He has not made off but left with consent. If the address is false then consent to his leaving is not real and an offence has been committed. A service must have been provided but where a meal has been eaten or a bedroom occupied, this presents no problem of proof.

The customer must have left without paying. This presents little problem in most cases but the method of payment which is other than cash may raise difficulties. Where the guest pays by cheque supported by a cheque card, or uses a credit card, but exceeds his authorised limit, he is not avoiding payment because the bank or card company will be called upon to pay.

On the other hand, where the departing guest pays with a worthless cheque, one that he knows will not be met, it may be held that the hotelier has not given a real consent to the departure. It has been said that where a cheque is accepted without a supporting card the person who accepts it in such circumstances is taking a risk and allows the rogue to depart. This being so, the accused cannot be said to have *made off*: *R v Hammond (1982)*.[2]

The accused must have acted dishonestly but it does not matter at what stage he decides to act in this manner. It is enough that he is dishonest when he makes off. The offence can only occur in cases where payment on the spot is concerned. If the accused did not appreciate that it was this form of transaction, but believed that it was on credit terms, then he cannot be convicted of this offence. This may occur where the guest believes that someone else is paying the bill. Where this other person is a fellow diner a simple mistake may have been made.

Where all the necessary elements are present such that an offence is committed, any person may arrest someone who is, or whom he, with reasonable cause, suspects to be committing or attempting to commit an offence. If convicted, the accused may be fined and/or imprisoned.

Inability to pay

Where a guest is unable to pay his hotel bill he may have committed the offence of obtaining services by deception but, unless he makes off, he cannot be charged with *bilking*. Where the inability to pay is encountered at an inn, the proprietor may exercise the innkeeper's right of *lien*. This existed at common law but has been restricted by statute.[3]

The lien extends to property brought by the guest within the *hospitium* of the inn. It does not extend to any vehicles or property left in them, nor to any live animals or to property on the person of the guest: *Sunbolf v Alford (1838)*.[4] It does not matter that the property in question is not owned by the guest but by another: *Berman and Nathans v Weibye (1981)*.[5] It may be the property of the wife of a defaulting guest: *Mulliner v Florence (1878)*;[6] or even property brought onto the premises later by the guest which turns out to have been stolen: *Marsh v Commissioner for Police (1944)*.[7]

The *lien* extends to unpaid bills for board and lodging due from residents but it also applies to the property of travellers who have only taken food and drink at the inn. It does not, it seems, apply in respect of damage caused by a guest: *Ferguson v Peterkin (1953)*.[8]

Where property is sent in to an inn by the owner for the use of a guest after the latter has booked in, and the innkeeper is aware of the fact, he may not exercise a *lien* upon the item: *Broadwood v Cranara (1854)*.[9] Where the *lien* is established, it extends to all the guest's property, the innkeeper is not required to pick and choose amongst it to discover value.[10] If a guest manages to fraudulently remove the property from the inn in an effort to defeat the *lien*, the innkeeper may repossess it: *Wallace v Woodgate (1824)*.[11]

The innkeeper is under a duty to look after the goods with the same care he would show towards his own property. The goods may be reclaimed by the guest upon payment of the monies due, these do not include a charge for storage which, if it is levied, may be recovered by the guest: *British Empire Shipping Co v Soames (1860)*.[12]

Powers of sale

An innkeeper is not bound to wait forever to receive payment and his *right of lien* would have little worth if this was all he could do. Under the Innkeepers Act 1878 he has a right of sale at public auction. There was no right of sale at common law and the Act sought to alleviate this burden. It requires that the goods remain unclaimed for six weeks and that notices be placed in the press with a description of the goods and the name of the owner, if this is known. Such notices must be given at least one month in advance of the proposed sale by public auction. Where such goods are despatched to a sale room in advance, the lien is not lost: *Chesham Automobile Supply Ltd v Beresford Hotel (Birchington) (1913).*[13]

Out of the proceeds of the sale, the innkeeper may recoup the monies owed to him plus the costs and expenses of the sale. If there is a surplus he must pay this on demand to the person who left the property at the inn.

Hoteliers, guest house keepers and restaurateurs do not possess this *right of lien*. In respect of their unpaid bills their only redress is to sue the guest in the courts. Where, however, goods have been bailed to any person as security or for safe keeping, that person may rely on his right as a bailee to exercise a *lien* over them for the sum due in respect of the bailment.

An innkeeper may have a right to such *lien* independently of his right *qua* innkeeper. British Rail exercise the authority derived from a term in the Conditions of Carriage of Passengers and their luggage in respect of *left luggage*:

'The Board shall have a particular lien upon any articles deposited for their charges and in the event of such charges or money not being paid within a reasonable time after application for payment thereof, the Board may sell the articles and apply the proceeds of sale towards the satisfaction of any such charges and money and its expenses of the sale.'[14]

The contractual authority would also seem to extend to articles removed to the left luggage office from lockers where the time of hire has expired.

At common law, the master of a ship has a *lien* on the passenger's luggage for unpaid passage money but not on his person or the clothes he is wearing: *Wolf v Summers (1811).*[15] Whether this *lien* arises from *bailment* is not clear. It may arise, like that of the innkeeper, from a *common calling*. The *right of lien* is also available to a pawnbroker. Such a business requires a licence from the Director General of Fair Trading under the terms of the Consumer Credit Act 1974. If the debt is not repaid on the date fixed, the items pledged may be sold. Raising money to pay bills by borrowing may be one method by which debts are settled but it is not the only one.

2. METHODS OF PAYMENT

Cash has long been the traditional way of paying bills, but as prices have risen it is used much less where large sums are concerned. A seller of accommodation, meals, or tickets for entertainment may insist on cash but he is more likely to accept alternatives, depending on the amount involved. In theory, there are upper limits for payment in coins but these are rarely called into use. Notes, even those in foreign currency, are readily accepted.

Tourists from outside the UK often wish to settle their bill in their own currency. Difficulties arise from the problems in determining the exchange rate with a *floating* pound. The rate of exchange offered by businesses generally is less favourable than that which is obtainable at a bank. Channel Islands currency and that of the Irish Republic can be accepted but, like other foreign currency, will need to be exchanged by the business at a bank. This should also be the case with Scottish notes, but in practice they are readily transferable. Some national currencies, like those of eastern Europe, are subject to severe fluctuations and, as a result, will not usually be accepted for the payment of bills.

Cheques

The increase in the use of cheques reflects the decline in the use of cash as a method of payment. The acceptance of these *negotiable instruments* has been greatly assisted by the introduction of the cheque guarantee card.[16]

The Bills of Exchange Act 1882 defines a cheque as 'a bill of exchange drawn on a banker payable on demand'. As such it must also satisfy section 3(1) of the statute as 'an unconditional order in writing, addressed by one person to another, signed by the person giving it, requiring the person to whom it is addressed to pay on demand or at a fixed or determinable future time a sum certain in money to or to the order of a specified person, or to bearer'.

A conditional order to pay is not a cheque. Thus an order to pay on condition that the receipt on the face or reverse of the instrument is signed is not a cheque: *Bavins v London and South Western Bank (1900).*[17] The distinction is of importance to a banker seeking to protect himself against claims for having paid on forged or unauthorised endorsements but need cause little concern to the tourist.

284

It is not necessary to use a cheque printed by a bank. Provided the formalities are observed, the bill may be drawn on any article, e.g. the back of an envelope.

For technical reasons, *travellers cheques* are not usually classified as cheques in law. This is because they are usually drawn subject to a condition that they are countersigned by the holder in the presence of the paying agent. The *traveller's cheque* probably owes its origins more to the old *letter of credit* than to a bill of exchange. The former was used by the private traveller in preference to bills of exchange which were the usual currency of merchants dealing in international markets.

Travellers cheques are issued in fixed denominations by major banks and travel agents of the world. They may be bought in the currency of the traveller's country or that of the places he is visiting. When purchased, they have to be signed and the serial numbers noted by the issuer. A service charge is levied which usually covers the insurance against loss or theft. The cheque is signed again in the presence of the person who is providing the currency required by the customer. Proof of identity may be required in the form of a passport or similar document.

Travellers' cheques are subject to the contractual terms under which they are purchased. It is common to find a term in such contracts that the issuer will replace or refund the value of cheques which are lost or stolen: *El Awadi v Bank of Credit and Commerce International (1988)*.[18] However, this valuable provision protecting the purchaser is subject to terms in the contract which, inter alia, provide that the purchaser properly safeguards each cheque against loss or theft. The onus is upon the purchaser to show that he had properly safeguarded the cheques. If there is a clear link between the failure to take care on the part of the traveller and the loss of cheques then he will not be entitled to claim protection: *Braithwaite v Thomas Cook Travellers Cheques (1988)*.[19]

Cheque cards guarantee payment of the cheque proffered up to the amount agreed by the issuing bank, usually £50. Wherever a card is used the cheque must be signed in the presence of the payee who must himself write the number of the card on the back of the cheque. The use of the card to support the cheque involves the bank concerned in a contract with the payee to honour the payment of the sum indicated. The bank's liability is based upon this contract not on the cheque itself.

The bank has no authority to pay a bill in part. If there are insufficient funds or overdraft facilities in their customer's account the bank cannot pay part of a bill and not the rest. Thus if a bill is for £800, the bank cannot pay £600 which stands to the customer's credit. It must pay all or nothing. Similarly, with a cheque card the bank will only pay the card limit. Only one cheque will be accepted per transaction under the terms of the contract of guarantee. The request of a creditor to be paid by two cheques for a bill which in total exceeds the limit of the card will not be honoured by the bank in the event that there are insufficient funds in its customer's account to satisfy the whole debt.

Some guarantee cards carry the *Eurocheque* symbol, this allows the holder to cash cheques in foreign countries up to the limit specified on the card. The cheque is written in the normal way and converted into foreign currency at the prevailing rate. Some banks, particularly those in France, have adopted a practice of charging extra commission for the service which is contrary to the agreement reached under the scheme. If this occurs, travellers should report the matter to their own bank on return home.

It has become the practice for those writing cheques other than travellers' cheques to add words to the crossing on the face of the cheque in order to provide protection against mis-payments or fraudulent conversions. Such works as *account payee* or *a/c payee* with or without the work *only* are commonly found. On occasion the cheque is drawn to order or bearer which makes the document a bill of exchange in the general sense rather than a cheque.

Until recently the use of words seeking to limit the persons to whom cheques are authorised to be paid by the banker on behalf of the drawer had no statutory authority for rendering them either as cheques or bills of exchange *not transferable*. Nevertheless, crossing a cheque whether in print or manuscript does put the collecting banker on his guard and if he disregards such crossing in circumstances amounting to negligence he is accountable to the drawer: *House Property Co of London v London County & Westminster Bank (1915).*[20]

The Cheques Act 1992 now provides that crossing a cheque together with appropriate words, as indicated above, and with or without the word *only* shall have the effect of making such cheque *non-transferrable* and valid only as between the parties named on the face of the cheque. Protection given to the paying banks by s.80 of the 1882 and 1992 Act is not lost by reason only of the bank failing to pay regard to the crossing. The protection offered to collecting banks by the 1992 Act is extended to cheques which have been made non-transferrable.

Vouchers

These may be issued by travel agents to their clients to enable them to settle hotel bills. One copy is sent to the hotel in respect of specified services and the other is presented by the guest on arrival. Problems may arise where exchange rates change or where agents are using out of date tariffs. Where this happens, a guest may be asked to pay a supplement by the hotel.

Charge cards

These are sometimes called *travel and entertainment cards*. They are not strictly speaking *credit cards* because the issuing organisation is not providing credit to the customer. The holder pays an annual fee for the card and is sent a regular bill which he is expected to pay in full. The issuer derives his revenue from the membership fee and the charge to the businesses which accept the cards in settlement of debts. The two most well known cards in this category are American Express and Diners Club. The basis of the arrangement is the contract between the holder and the issuing organisation and that which exists between the last named and the acceptor who has a *franchise* agreement with the card company. This agreement protects the card holder because, under its terms, the franchisee is not authorised to pass on commission it must pay to the franchiser in the customer's bill. This, allied to the fact that the bills take longer to settle and franchise fees on each transaction are higher than bank credit cards, has made the latter more popular with businesses.

Credit cards, and other forms of consumer credit, are now more commonly used to finance travel and to pay for accommodation and recreational activities. The industry which has grown to meet consumer wants is regulated by statute.

3. CONSUMER CREDIT

A consumer may want credit for a variety of reasons. He may borrow funds in a number of ways. He may obtain a loan from a bank, a finance company, a building society, a pawnbroker or other source.

The credit may or may not be tied to the thing he wants, e.g. a car, a holiday. Alternatively, it may be an advance of money to be put to whatever purpose the individual borrower wishes.

Following criticism of the existing law, the Crowther Committee was appointed to carry out a wide ranging review of consumer credit. The Committee's Report was published in 1971 and followed by a White Paper in 1973. The Consumer Credit Act 1974 provided the framework of the law with details being left to regulations. The supply to individuals, not exceeding £15,000, is brought within its provisions.

An EC Directive on Consumer Credit was agreed in 1986. It seeks to ensure that adequate information is provided on true interest charges, the form and content of credit agreements, terms for early settlement and a system for licensing the sup pliers of credit. The Directive is largely based on the 1974 Act which came fully in to force in May 1985. It does not cover all aspects of credit, nor does it usurp the ordinary common law rules in respect of contracts.

The central plank of the statute is the *regulated agreement* which it defines in terms of personal credit and cash loans, or any other form of financial *accommodation*. The Act applies to any agreement under which credit is advanced including, inter alia, budget and option accounts, credit cards, loans and overdrafts.

Credit cards, by definition of section 14(1) of the Act, come within the area of transactions involving the use of *credit tokens*. Under the provisions of section 51(1) it is an offence to supply unsolicited credit tokens: *Elliot v Director General of Fair Trading (1980)*.[21] The total charge for credit must be stated in such a way that the consumer can see clearly the rate at which he is being offered the advance. This requires a complex system of computation. Basically, it involves calculating the whole charge for credit in a transaction, taking into account all relevant matters, and expressing the total as an annual percentage rate of charge (APR).

All businesses concerned with *regulated agreements* must be licensed, under section 21, by the Director General of Fair Trading. In addition, all who provide ancillary services, e.g. credit brokers, must be licensed. It is an offence to carry on an unlicensed business. Those who *effect introductions* of people desiring credit to persons carrying on a consumer credit business, or other credit brokers, also face criminal charges if they are not licensed: *Hicks v Walker (1984)*.[22] In civil law, the consequence of not holding a licence is that, in respect of a regulated agreement, the debt is unenforceable.

The Act also seeks to protect the consumer from uncontrolled advertising and canvassing for custom away from trade premises for certain regulated agreements. To qualify as an advertisement caught by the Act, it must state the advertiser's willingness to provide credit. The form and content of advertisements, which include radio, TV and films are governed by the Consumer Credit (Advertisement) Regulations 1980. An advertisement is required to be fair and to give a reasonably comprehensive account of the facilities offered, and their true cost, to those at whom the information is directed.

Joint and several liability

Section 75 is an exception to the principle of privity of contract. Where there is a debtor/creditor/supplier agreement, the creditor (not being the supplier) is jointly and severally liable with the seller to the debtor for damages in respect of breach of contract or misrepresentation. Thus where a debtor buys goods or services, using a credit card, he has rights against both the supplier and/or the company advancing credit: *United Dominion Trust v Taylor (1980).*[23] Such provision is useful to consumers who find that the supplier is insolvent, e.g. Laker Airways in 1982.

Consumer credit agreements, together with consumer hire, became regulated agreements only if made after 1 April 1977. This has resulted in those banks which issue credit cards claiming that section 75 applies only to instances where the card was issued to a contracting party after that date. This is an erroneous perception of the law. The agreement with the card company is for *rolling credit*. Each time the card holder uses the card a new and separate contract is entered into. The Consumers' Association hit on the novel idea, used by a reader, of sending back the card and asking for a new one to be issued.[24] When the banks realised the extent of the administration involved, together with the potential loss of custom, they signalled that they would not be trying to evade liability on a technicality. Some have tried to use delaying tactics.

What is clear is that the company which issues the card is liable to meet obligations for goods or services priced at between £100 and £30,000. The companies are unwilling to accept that they are liable for consequential loss as where, say, a tourist wishes to claim not only for failure to provide the holiday services described but for *disappointment* and loss of amenities. It appears that the card companies are willing to make *ex gratia* payments even if still not admitting liability. The companies insist that they are only liable up to the amount advanced for the particular transaction. This was after they had grudgingly agreed, under pressure from the Office of Fair Trading, to accept liability for cards issued before 1977. The better view is that they are jointly and severally liable where only part of the transaction, e.g. the deposit, has been paid for with a card.

Where a debtor wishes to settle his account earlier than expected, he may do so. Under section 95, the Consumer Credit (Rebate on Early Settlement) Regulations 1983 have been introduced for the calculation of rebate charges for credit which are allowed to the debtor. The credit supplier must supply such information within 12 days of receipt of a written request for details.

Where it appears that a credit agreement is extortionate, the court has power to reopen the arrangement. Section 138 provides guidance on factors which are to be taken into account when assessing the merits of the case. The burden of disproving the extortionate nature of any agreement is upon the credit supplier. The court has wide powers to set aside agreements or to rewrite them. It does appear that the terms will have to be *grossly* extortionate for a claim by a debtor to succeed in attracting the support of the courts.

Another area of concern has been the use of *credit reference agencies* to determine the credit worthiness of an applicant. Section 157 requires that, upon his request, the credit supplier must disclose to a debtor the details of any such agency to which reference of the latter's financial standing has been made. Upon receipt of a request in writing from the debtor, such an agency must provide him with a copy of any information relating to him which is held on their files. If necessary, this must be reduced to *plain English*. The debtor must pay a small fee for the service. He must also be provided with details as to how he may seek to have any mistakes rectified. Failure to comply with these requirements of the 1974 Act renders the agency liable to a fine upon summary conviction.

Where a person uses a credit card dishonestly to make purchases exceeding a credit limit, an offence is committed against the Theft Act 1978: *R v Lambie (1981)*.[25] The same is true where a cheque guarantee card is used dishonestly: *R v Charles (1977)*.[26]

Where a credit card is lost or stolen, section 84 operates to protect the debtor. If misuse occurs after the debtor has informed the card supplier of the facts, he incurs no liability for transactions using the card. In any event, liability for accidental loss is limited to a total of £50. The same rules apply to cash cards issued by banks for use in cash dispensers, but not to cheque guarantee cards which are not classed in law as *credit tokens*.

The use of credit cards for placing orders for goods and services, e.g. theatre seats, over the telephone has become widely accepted. Much more use is likely to be made of cards as a means of instructing computer terminals in shops, hotels, travel agents and airports, reducing paperwork. International settlement of card transactions is now widely concluded by electronic data transmission. The cashless and chequeless society is on the move, 'Customers, helped by external cash dispensers and by credit cards, get along surprisingly well without often visiting their bank'.[27]

All manner of services can be paid for by plastic cards. If a traveller wishes to insure himself and his property against risk, he may pay the insurance company in this manner.

4. THE INSURANCE OF RISK

The only thing certain in life is death. We can never be sure that a home will not be destroyed by fire, that a car will not be involved in an accident, that valuable property will not accidentally be lost, or that a traveller will not be taken seriously ill in some remote part of the world. To guard against the financial loss or expenditure which may be incurred, or to provide for the needs of a bereaved family, a person may choose to enter into a contract of insurance to provide for a sum of money to be paid upon the occurrence of a particular event.

There are two categories of insurance: indemnity, which provides an agreed payment against quantifiable loss, e.g. the value of a ship which sinks or a car which catches fire; or contingency, where the sum to be paid is not measured by the loss but is that which is stated in the policy document, e.g. the loss of life or limb.

The law of insurance is essentially that which governs contracts of insurance. Modern insurance law has developed from mercantile practice and the common law. Parliament has intervened little in the field outside marine insurance and compulsory insurance for dangers at work and on the roads. However, two important areas of statutory provision are the powers derived from the Insurance Companies Act 1982 and the Policy-holders Protection Act 1975. Under the former, which consolidates earlier legislation, the Secretary of State controls entry into the industry by a system of *licensing* allied to powers of regulation and investigation. Under the latter, provisions are made for levies to be imposed on the industry as a whole when an authorised insurance company is unable to meet its liabilities.

The essentials of insurance are that an *insurer* assumes the *risks* of the contingency specified, in consideration of a *premium* paid, so that the *insured* who suffers loss will be compensated from a *common fund*. The premiums may be paid periodically or as a lump sum. The contingency must be uncertain as to its occurrence, or if it is bound to happen, as with death, the time of its happening must be uncertain. Because such a contract could be construed as a *wager*, the law requires that, at the time of making the agreement, there shall be an *insurable interest* in the assured. The insured's claim will be based on proof of loss which he has sustained directly or because he must pay for the loss for which he is liable to a third party.

The contract of insurance is based upon *proposal* forms and *policies* which are drafted in a fairly uniform pattern by the insurers. Many of the rules of such contracts are common to all legally binding agreements but, in addition, they are characterised by special rules. It is not necessary for such contracts to be in writing provided that the material terms can, if necessary, be proved: *Murfitt v Royal Insurance Co (1922)*.[28] In practice, they invariably are.

The offer necessary to the construction of the contract is made when the party seeking cover addresses a *proposal* form to the insurer. Once the latter has accepted this, even though a policy document may not have been issued, a binding contract will usually be held to exist.

The particular rules which distinguish contracts of insurance from other legal agreements are those connected with the duty of disclosure placed upon the pro poser, and *warranties* which are widely used to *guarantee* that the facts, as stated in the proposal, are true, which relieves the insurer of the necessity of proving misrepresentation so as to avoid payment of a claim made by the insured. It is these areas which have come in for most criticism.

Disclosure

The insured is required to disclose material facts which he knew, or ought to have known, and which would affect the formation or renewal of a policy of insurance.

The contract of insurance is one which is concluded in terms of *uberrimae fidei*, of utmost good faith. In most contracts there is no duty to disclose facts which are not asked for. With insurance, the proposer must not remain silent where such silence will mislead. 'The insured should help *the insurer* by every means in his power to estimate the risk at its proper value': *Joel v Law Union & Crown Insurance Co (1908)*.[29] He must not wait to be asked but must disclose *material facts*! This phrase can cover a multitude of sins. Failure to disclose anything to an insurer which he deems to be relevant can allow him to refuse to pay out on a claim. This may be so even where the fact not disclosed may have no bearing on the claim whatsoever. It is the feeling of the Insurance Ombudsman at least that, 'an ordinary member of the public should not be expected to interpret the raw material of statutory definition without specific guidance in the form of questions or, at the very least, declarations'.[30]

In 1980, the Law Commission produced a report on Non Disclosure and Breach of Warranty.[31] This recommended that policyholders should only have to give information that a *reasonable man* ought to know would be relevant. The government promised to introduce legislation following talks with the industry. To date nothing has been resolved as to whether legislation will be forthcoming or the industry be left to make voluntary changes. The industry has modified its Statements of Insurance Practice to require disclosure of facts which an insured could reasonably be expected to disclose. In view of this the Trade and Industry Secretary does not seem disposed to change the law.

It is a moot question as to whether a voluntary code will help to alleviate the problems of those refused payment whose cases have been well publicised.[32] Such a one was the holiday cancelled because of a bereavement, the claim being denied because the person who died was ill at the time the policy was taken out. His doctor had said the family could go away without anxiety, but had unfortunately been wrong.

Warranties

These are statements actually made by the assured who fills out a proposal form upon which the contract of insurance is based. If an answer to a question is untrue, the insurers may refuse to pay on the grounds of *breach of warranty*. The Law Commission recommended that a term in a policy should only be deemed a *warranty* if it was material to the risk. Whether a term is a *warranty* will depend on the construction of the policy, no particular form of words is necessary but often the issue is resolved by the inclusion of standard terms. The use of such terms provides a considerable advantage and protection to insurers. Breach of *warranty* need not be based on fault, nor is it possible to allege that the fault, if it exists, is that of someone other than the insured. Liability is strict and the insurer can avoid the policy totally.

Insurers have an advantage over the insured because it is they who draft the policies, usually as standard form contracts expressed in terms very generous to the insurer. Where appropriate, the courts may use the *contra preferentem* rule in the case of ambiguities. It should be remembered, however, that the insurers are able to make wide use of exclusion clauses and exemptions from liability. Under section 1(2) and Schedule 1 of the Unfair Contract Terms Act 1977, the terms of the Act relating to liability for negligence, breach of contract and indemnity clauses, do not apply to contracts of insurance. It remains to be seen whether the draft EC Directive on insurance contracts will ultimately lead to positive reforms in this area.

Travel insurance

About half of all those who take out travel insurance make claims. Many varieties of policy are offered, of variable quality. Every traveller needs to be sure that the policy covers the risks he is likely to encounter, to varying degrees, on the journey he is taking. He may rely on the policy offered by the tour operator in his brochure or upon advice from a travel agent or an independent broker.

The main ingredients of a good policy are:

1. **Medical expenses**. Cover will vary depending on destination, less for travel in the EEC than, say, the US where medical bills are higher.

2. **Baggage and personal effects**. This should cover loss or damage to all luggage and articles worn or carried. Limits are usual for single items and valuable pieces should be insured separately.

3. **Cancellation or delay**. These should cover all non-recoverable costs to the insured and payments on a progressive scale for delays.

4. **Personal liability**. Cover for any loss which the traveller may be called upon to pay to others for harm caused to people or property.

294

5. **Personal accident**. In view of the limits placed upon claims against carriers by international conventions this would seem an essential.

The insurers are well aware of the claims they may be called upon to meet and adjust the premiums accordingly. There has been a tendency to weight these against the older traveller who is more likely to fall sick or die abroad. General exclusions are those which state that people should not travel against a doctor's advice. Nearly every insurer will indicate that 'lack of proper care towards luggage may well prejudice any claim'. Some policies will provide cover where a charter flight has been missed and a more expensive scheduled route has to be taken. This must be for a reason acceptable to the insurer; oversleeping will not suffice!

SUMMARY OF BENEFITS AND EXCESSES PER INSURED PERSON		
	Sum Insured	Excess
CANCELLATION	Not exceeding final invoice cost	£25 (£10 on claims for loss of deposit)
PERSONAL ACCIDENT	(a) Accidental death, loss of one or more eyes or limbs or permanent total disablement £15,000. (b) Accidental death of Insured Persons under 16 years £1,000	
MEDICAL AND OTHER EXPENSES INCLUDING CURTAILMENT	Unlimited (for up to one year's treatment).	£25
HOSPITAL BENEFIT	£10 per day up to max. of £200	
PERSONAL BAGGAGE AND MONEY	Up to £1,000 to include £200 money. Max. per item £200. Jewellery and photographic equipment limited to £200 in all.	£25
PERSONAL PUBLIC LIABILITY	Indemnity limit - £500,000	
COSTS INCURRED THROUGH INTERRUPTION OF PUBLIC TRANSPORT SERVICES	Up to £150	
LOSS OF PASSPORT	Up to £100	
You may ask for a specimen cover note before booking should you wish to examine this in advance.		

Tour operators receive commission for insurance policies which are effected by clients whom they introduce to insurers. Some insist that their insurance *offered* in the brochure is compulsory. There is nothing exceptional in the requirement that a tourist on a package holiday must be insured as a condition of the contract of booking. It is less acceptable that the traveller should be forced to take that which is held out. Often insufficient detail is given of the cover provided such that the individual is unable to assess its worth to him. Some policies are approved by ABTA, which gives some measure of reassurance to the tourist. The table above gives an indication of the type of cover which is usually offered. It is suggested that the maxim *caveat viator* should be applied to all who take out travel insurance.

Some tour operators appear reluctant to provide full details of the policies which they market with packages. When the small print has been deciphered it is often revealed that the contract of insurance contains exclusion clauses which are very much to the advantage of the insurer. Often customers who ask to see the complete policy before they sign are told by the seller that these are only provided after the agreement for the package has been signed! Buyers should beware, such attitudes are against the practice statement of the Association of British Insurers.

Most tourists buy the insurance cover with the holiday package; sometimes there is no choice, the organiser will not provide the package without the specified insurance policy. In which case it might be thought that the matter is subject to the Package Travel Regulations 1992. However, neither the EC Directive 90/314 nor the Regulations made in pursuance of the Directive for operation in the UK make specific reference to the issue of travel insurance. Article 3 of the Directive and Regulation 4 do make reference to 'any descriptive matter concerning a package and supplied by the organiser or the retailer to the consumer ... and any other conditions applying to the contract which contains misleading information' making the organiser or retailer liable to compensate the consumer for any loss which the latter suffers as a consequence. Insurance is not listed in Schedule 1 of the Regulations and it seems unlikely that a claim could be brought if the *information* does not qualify as *misleading*.

What constitutes *misleading information* is less than clear. Case law built up on the Trade Descriptions Act 1968 and the Consumer Protection Act 1987 relates to supplying such information *knowingly* or *recklessly* which words have generated much conflict. The 1992 Regulations are designed to supplement the two criminal statutes in this respect so as to catch in a civil litigation net those who would otherwise escape the criminal trawl of the two earlier legislative provisions.

However, it will take litigation upon the Regulations to determine more precisely their effect in the regard. It would appear that provided that the information in the insurance policy sold is not *misleading* that exclusion clauses, skilfully drafted, will still operate to the benefit of the vendor rather than the consumer.

There is one ray of hope on the horizon for the tourist - the EC Draft Directive on Unfair Contract Terms (OJ 1992 C73/7). Although must modified from its original intended form it does provide an avenue for progress - particularly since such a Directive is subject to the qualified majority voting system of EC legislation which means that individual member states cannot black progress by use of a veto.

On the face of the Draft Directive it does seem as though it offers little more in the areas of the provision of services than that which is contained in the Supply of Goods and Services Act 1982. But in the field of exclusion clauses, which is the sole preoccupation of the Unfair Contract Terms Act 1977, the Directive is much broader in its approach. It deals with 'preformulated' terms in contracts - what in the UK are customarily called standard terms - that is those terms over which the consumer has no effective power to bargain, he must take or leave them. The Directive states that such terms are likely to attract censure by the law if they are 'contrary to the requirements of good faith, (and) cause a significant imbalance in the parties' rights and obligations ... to the detriment of the consumer' which in reality is doing little more than applying the existing UK legal test of *reasonableness*.

In the Annex to the Directive there is a provision that clauses in contracts which bind the consumer to terms 'with which he has not real opportunity of becoming acquainted before the conclusion of the contract.' But if regard is had to the way in which passengers are carried by bus or rail in the UK, they have little opportunity of examining in detail the *Standard Terms* contained in written statements before they travel. They can ask for copies, but seldom do, and in any case they are aware in general terms of the main terms of carriage it has often been stated in the courts.

The Directive does provide some help in that it says that in having regard to the *fairness* or otherwise of *preformulated* terms one of the considerations to be taken into account shall be as to whether or not these are expressed in 'plain intelligible language'. Such that a contract of insurance which falls foul of this provision could be deemed unfair. It goes on to relate that where there is any doubt as to the meaning of a term it shall be interpreted in favour of the consumer. This has long been favoured in UK courts as the *contra preferentum* rule in contract law. It must be added that the Directive creates no presumption of unfairness on the grounds only that the term is not in 'plain intelligible language'.

What is mot significant for the UK is that unlike the provision in the Unfair Contract Terms Act 1977, the Directive does not allow for contracts of insurance, inter alia, to escape its control.

The Directive indicates that the enforcement of its provisions is for member states and it appears unlikely that individuals will be able to use the EC requirements when they are introduced into UK law. It appears likely that the challenge as to *fairness* etc. will fall to be made by a governmental body e.g. the Office of Fair Trading. Originally the Directive was due for implementation by 1 January 1993. This has now been postponed until 1 January 1995.

It should be noted that at the present time all policies of insurance are couched in legalistic language to a greater or lesser extent and prove a daunting task for the layman who seeks to decipher their mysteries. Plain, intelligible language is not the rule:

'The Company shall not be liable in respect of loss, damage or injury or illness or liability which is not or would be but for the existence of this Policy insured by any other policy except to the extent of any excess beyond the amount that is or would be but for the existence of the Policy payable under such other policy.'

What does this mean to the layman? Translated it means that if there is a pre-existing policy giving the claimant cover against the misfortune which has befallen him then he must claim first on that policy and only of the present Policy in so far as there is any sum left uncovered. Thus, if I have a policy which covers me for £75 then if I suffer loss or, say, £100 I can only recover £25 on the second Policy - if the Policy affords cover up to or in excess of this amount.

In making any claim tourists are well advised to collect as much information in support as possible - receipts, reports to local police within 24 hours (a common term), 'property irregularity reports' from carriers, etc. If a claim is rejected by the insurer the issue may be capable of resolution by reference to the Insurance Ombudsman or to such arbitration service as the insurer is party to. Bringing a case before the courts is usually a last resort.

Where a package does not require compulsory vendor supplied cover the tourist is free to shop around; but the same *caveats* expressed as to insurance let outs still apply. Figures for 1992 show that of some 12 million people took out holiday insurance in the year just ended more than three-quarters of a million made some form of claim against insurance - cancellation or curtailment; medical bills; loss o theft of baggage.

When reading brochures consumers should always be wary of the *negative option* inserted by organisers of packages. This states that the customer will be charged for insurance when booking unless he makes it clear that he does not want such cover - always providing there is an option at all. This type of selling insurance, upon which the vendor gains commission for the insurer, must surely be against the principle of fairness in trading. It would be much fairer if the customer had to specifically ask for such cover - *positive option*. To date there are no regulations which make this a legal requirement.

NOTES:

1. (1920) 37 TLR 75.
2. (1982) Crim LR 611.
3. Hotel Proprietors Act 1956 s 2(2).
4. (1838) 3 M & W 248.
5. (1981) 6 CL 658.
6. (1878) 3 QB 484.
7. (1944) 2 A11 ER 392(CA).
8. (1953) SLT 91.
9. (1854) 10 Exch 417.
10. *Daily Mail* 18 May 1984 p3.
11. (1824) 1 C & P 375.
12. (1860) 8 HL Cas 338.
13. (1913) 29 TLR 584.
    N.B. Lien no longer applies to vehicles.
14. BR 25833/22 para 57.
15. (1811) 2 Camp 631.
16. Consumer Credit Act 1974 s 121.
17. (1900) 1 QB 270.
18. (1988) *The Times* Oct 4
19. (1988) *The Independent* Jul 22
20. (1915) 84 LJKB 1846

21. (1980) 1 WLR.
22. (1984) 148 JP 636 (QBD).
23. (1980) SLT 28.
24. *Which.* April 1986 p 143.
25. (1981) 3 WLR 88.
26. (1977) AC 177.
27. D. Vander Weyer. *The Banker*, October 1970.
28. (1922) 38 TLR 334.
29. (1909) 2 KB 683.
30. *Guardian* 28 December 1985 p 23.
31. Law Com no 104 October 1980.
32. *Which.* July 1985.

Chapter XV

Entertainment

1. USE OF PREMISES

The two major preoccupations of English law are the maintenance of public order and the protection of property rights. In a crowded island it is increasingly necessary to reconcile the need for public control over the use of land and the rights of private landowners to have quiet enjoyment of their property.

Protection of these interests is afforded by both the civil and criminal law. The manager and another member of the staff of a hotel in Bayswater were prosecuted for keeping a brothel and convicted. The landlord of the premises gained a court order for the eviction of the tenants. He relied on a covenant in the lease which required that the leasee should not annoy neighbours or himself: *Egerton v Esplanade Hotels Ltd (1947).*[1] Had it been necessary, the tenants might also have been convicted of the offence of public nuisance while neighbours could have sought an injunction on the grounds of private nuisance.

In the event, both public and private interests were met by the due processes of law. At one time anyone could open a hotel. Businesses were almost free from bureaucratic control until the end of the 19th century. A *laisser faire* attitude allowed businesses to operate with little regulation. If a man wanted to build premises he could do so without fear that the design of his building would have been considered out of keeping with the amenity of the area, or that means of access, fire precautions or waste disposal facilities be deemed inadequate.

Planning permission

In 1909, the first Act of Parliament in a series of town and country planning statutes received the Royal Assent[2]. This brief enactment sought to establish proper sanitary conditions and a sense of amenity in the development of land.

The basic principle of planning law is that prevention is better than cure. Permission is necessary from a planning authority in a local area before any substantial building, alteration or development of land can be undertaken. The Town and Country Planning Act 1971, and the Regulations made thereunder, comprise the main body of law in the field. Significantly, the law controls the use to which premises may be put by their occupiers. Only *permitted use* is allowed. Where it is proposed to make a 'material' change in the use of premises, consent must be obtained.

Use classes

Planning Regulations define broad classes of premises by use[3]. Change from one type of business to another, provided it falls within the same class, is permitted without the need for express planning consent. Class II is concerned with *offices* such that an estate agent's office could become a travel agent's without the need for permission. Neither of these businesses could be carried on in premises which had previously been used for dry cleaning since this would fall either under Class I or III. Similarly, permission would be necessary to change a warehouse (Class X) into a nightclub (Class XVIII). Restaurants and cafes, together with other operations which serve liquor under licence, are not within any stated class. As a result, change of use to this form of enterprise will always need permission.

It appears that where a change is envisaged which will only increase additional custom then no permission is needed. Where a hotelier wishes to open his residents' bar to passing trade, no material change of use occurs: *Emma Hotels v Secretary of State for the Environment (1980)*[4]. The proprietor will, however, need to apply for a change in his liquor licence and, wherever structural alterations to premises are carried out, the approval of the justices will be required. Failure to seek their acquiescence could result in the loss of the licence. Under Class XVII, a theatre can become a cinema. If a local authority wishes to prevent this, it can insert a condition in the permission even where the change does not constitute 'development': *Corporation of City of London v Secretary of State for the Environment and Another (1971)*[5].

Other controls

These are derived from various statutory controls affecting premises and activities carried on within them. The construction of buildings is regulated by the provisions of the Public Health Act 1961.[6]

There are some forty Acts of Parliament dealing with the subject of fire prevention in some way or another. Chief amongst these is the Fire Precautions Act 1971. The major change which it introduced was that relating to the content of fire certificates. Previously, the certificates only dealt with means of escape in case of fire. Since 1971 they are much more comprehensive. The Health and Safety at Work Act 1974 amended the 1971 Act to extend its cover to all work places. The Secretary of State may, under the terms of the Act, designate various classes of premises as requiring certificates.[7]

The Local Government Act 1972, sections 144 and 145, together with the London Government Act 1963, give the local authorities wide powers to provide attractions for tourists. Nevertheless, many such amenities require licences to operate in addition to planning permissions.

In law every Public Nuisance is a crime. It is a creation of the Common Law and may best be described as that which materially affects the reasonable comfort and convenience of life of a class of Her Majesty's subjects. Acts which are capable of being such a Nuisance are not easy to state with any degree of precision. They include things so diverse as abuses of the highway; carrying on businesses causing discomfort to others, such as producing noise or smells; keeping a brothel; holding a badly organised pop festival: *Attorney General for*

Ontario v Orange Productions (1971)[8]. In addition to being a crime Public Nuisance may also give rise to a civil claim made by a person who has suffered special damage over and above that endured by a class of persons of which class he is a member.

The crime/private wrong carries with it penalties ranging from life imprisonment to unlimited fine. With so broad a canvas it is fair to ask why then should we need any other criminal offences or actionable definition or wrong at all? In practice the operation of the law of Public Nuisance has been much overtaken by statutory provisions and where the two come into conjunction, statute - the will of Parliament - prevails. Nevertheless, whilst its operation has also been much eroded by the decided cases it is still used as an all purpose filler by the courts where it is felt that a remedy is desirable as a matter of policy but there is no specific head of law to be used. Judges run the risk of being accused of engaging in judicial legislation but it has to be said that in the law of torts at least a remedy has never been refused on the grounds only that the like had never been seen before. Novelty is no bar to a right of action at common law.

Significantly, the recent decision in *Gillingham Borough Council v Medway (Chatham) Docks Co Ltd (1991)*[9] indicates that where a planning permission changes the character of a neighbourhood what once may have been deemed a Public Nuisance before such permission was granted is no longer the case. Or it may be that the correct interpretation is that the statutory authority is a defence to such an action. Whichever is the case, if planning authority is given for the construction of a sports complex or other amenity which benefits many but which is a Nuisance to an identifiable class of HM subjects on the immediate vicinity then such permission changes the nature of the neighbourhood such that the interference with a right of use or enjoyment of land by individuals may no longer be actionable.

2. THEATRES AND CINEMAS

Theatrical performances have been the subject of various controls for many years. The theatre, and the history of those associated with it, has become a major part of the tourist industry. Stratford-on-Avon has become second only to London as the major tourist destination in the UK. In Shakespeare's day there was little control exercised over performances, save where the content might amount to sedition or where a threat to the King's Peace was perceived.

The earliest control of theatrical activities was by the King's Master of the Revels. In 1572, his functions were placed under the authority of the Lord Chamberlain. He equated players with 'vagabonds' and the statutory controls which were imposed upon them were affected by the licensing of theatres and companies of players in and around London.

During the Commonwealth the theatres were closed, to be opened again with much rejoicing with the Restoration of Charles II to the throne in 1660. From this time on, a large number of plays were produced which contained political comment. The nature and extent of such works so infuriated Prime Minister Walpole that, in 1737, the Lord Chamberlain was encouraged to restrict the licensing of plays. The legislation which he introduced acted as a stranglehold on performances which was not removed, and then only partially, until 1843. The much-criticised powers of censorship by the Lord Chamberlain were finally removed by the Theatres Act 1968. Censorship was replaced with recommended standards for theatrical productions.

Theatres require to be licensed by district councils or the councils of London boroughs as appropriate. The licence, where granted, will contain conditions relating to safety precautions and the way in which the premises are to be managed. If performances are given in unlicensed premises, or conditions in the licence are contravened, enforcement may be sought by the licensing authority: *Fisher's Restaurant v G.L.C. (1980)*[10]. Where a licence is refused, appeal lies to the Magistrates' Court.

Obscenity

A theatrical performance is deemed to be obscene if, taken as a whole, it tends to deprave or corrupt persons likely to attend the theatre. Those who oppose certain types of performance have long called for stricter controls. Shortly after the Act came into force, the first productions featuring nudity were staged. A number of *crusades* against the genre were mounted with little success, except for the amount of publicity they attracted.

The provisions of the Act in respect of obscenity are very similar to those contained in the Obscene Publications Act 1959. In considering whether people are likely to be depraved or corrupted, due merit must be given to literary, sociological and ethical content. A prosecution of a producer was brought in London and, after a submission by the defence that there was no case to answer, the judge ruled in favour and stopped the case: *R v Bogdanov (1982)*[11]. The main preoccupation of the anti-liberation lobby is with matters related to the portrayal of sexually explicit material. The Act, however, is also concerned with performances which stir up racial hatred. It must be shown that the result was in fact what the person producing or directing the performance intended. Anything which concerns itself with matters which may make, or keep, someone morally bad, or make him worse, can be the subject of a prosecution: *R v Sumner (1977)*.[12]

Sunday performances

Historically, theatrical performances have long been the target for Sabbatarians. Theatres were caught by the rather confused state of the law dating back to the Sunday Observance Act 1780. This statute is still in force and makes it an offence to provide public entertainment or amusements for reward on Sundays: *Houghton le Touzel v Mecca (1950)*.[13]

Apart from time restrictions, theatres are exempted by the Sunday Theatres Act 1972. Cinemas were also freed from archaic legislation under the Sunday Cinemas Act 1972.

Cinemas

The earliest regulation of cinemas was effected by the Cinematographic Act 1909. A number of statutes followed still adhering to the use of 'cinematographic' to describe their contents. The Cinemas Act 1985 consolidated the various enactments from 1909 to 1982, and certain other legislation relating to premises licensed under those Acts. The law remains substantially unchanged by the 1985 Act, apart from reconciling the definition of 'cinematographic entertainment' in the 1909 Act with that of the Sunday Entertainments Act 1932 which had never been identical. The Law Commission's recommendation on harmonisation has been affected by using the term 'film exhibition' as defined in section 21(1) of the Cinemas Act 1985.

The control of film exhibitions is dealt with in sections 1 to 4 of the Act. All premises must be licensed by the appropriate local authority in whose area the premises are situated. In granting a licence the licensing authority may impose such conditions as they think fit, and are under a duty to impose restrictions, or conditions, to prevent children below the age of 16 years from viewing works unsuitable for them.

Each application will be judged on its merits, but a local authority has a wide discretion in granting licences and in imposing conditions upon the license holder: *Associated Provincial Picture Houses Ltd v Wednesbury Corporation (1947)*.[14]

'Film exhibition' means any exhibition of moving pictures which is produced otherwise than by the simultaneous reception and exhibition of television programmes broadcast by the BBC and IBA, or programmes included in a cable programme service governed by the Cable and Broadcasting Act 1984.

Sex cinemas are subject to additional rules, where a local authority has passed a resolution under section 2 of the Local Government (Miscellaneous Provisions) Act 1982 applying Schedule 3 to that Act in their area.

British Board of Film Censors

The Board classifies films available for public exhibition according to revised categories introduced in 1982. These relate to suitability by age bandings and reference to parental supervision for those below the age of 18 years. These classifications are not legally enforceable but, if a cinema were to disregard the provisions, penalties would follow under the provisions of the 1985 Act which could lead to the forfeiture of a licence.

As a result of the difficulties experienced in the British film industry, the Films Act 1960 introduced a quota system. This is designed to protect domestic films by restricting the number of foreign imports, particularly from the US, which may be shown commercially in the UK.

3. MUSIC AND DANCING

The control of music, singing and dancing was haphazard in its form and application until the introduction of the Local Government (Miscellaneous Provisions) Act 1982. This forms the basis for the grant of licences needed for 'public dancing or music or any other public entertainment of the like kind'.

The application of the statutory provisions is unclear with reference to music played as a background to other activities. It does not apply to Theatres or Cinemas, nor to musical entertainment licences under the Sunday Entertainment Act 1932. It does not apply to open air events, except where these are specifically catered for in the Act. Where the music is only incidental to the main activity, and would not have needed a licence under previous legislation, it is likely that none will be needed now: *Quaglieni v Matthews (1865)*.[15] Where the music is an integral part, or the activity is of 'like kind' to dancing, as with ice skating and roller discos, it is submitted that a licence will be required.

A licence may be annual or of shorter duration. It may be for one or more specified occasions. The concern of the licensing authorities is to see that the premises are safe and managed by suitable persons. Police and fire authorities must be notified of applications and their views considered. Objections may also be heard from members of the public. Applicants are entitled to be informed of the nature of any objections: *R v Huntingdon District Council (1984)*.[16]

In places for which a liquor licence allowing consumption on the premises is in operation, no entertainment licence is required where the entertainment is in the form of radio or television broadcasts, or live music provided by no more than two performers.[17] No reference is made to dancing, and, where this does take place, it is presumed that an entertainment licence will be required. A club is not a place of public entertainment since, by definition, admission is restricted to a class of persons: *Severn View Social Club v Chepstow Licensing Justices (1968)*.[18] The same application of the law will be made in the case of hotels which provide amenities only for their residents and their bona fide guests.

Special entertainment licences

This variety of licence was introduced by the 1982 Act and, though not specifically so designated, it is intended to regulate *pop* and *rock* concerts performed in the open air, on private land, for public musical entertainment. Special procedures are to be followed before the grant of such a licence, but, in allowing it, no special conditions may be attached save those relating to safety, access for emergency vehicles, sanitation and nuisance by noise affecting local inhabitants.

4. CLUBS

There is no legal definition of a *club*. The almost limitless variety of such associations of people makes a precise definition impossible. The one characteristic which they all have is the common interest shared by their members. No legal formalities are required for their formation, although some will be required by those seeking various forms of licence in order to cater to the wants of their members.

Registered clubs

Often referred to as *Members' Clubs*, the assets of the association are owned by its members. They are controlled by elected committees and run on commercial lines according to the rules of their constitutions.

Where such a club applies to the local magistrates for registration within the terms of section 40 of the Licensing Act 1964, no liquor licence is required if such registration is approved. The registration allows members and their bona fide guests to be supplied with alcoholic beverages during such times as are the general licensing hours for the particular licensing area in which the club is situated. Such establishments may apply for a restaurant certificate, extended hours order, or a special hours certificate (q.v.), where appropriate. These forms of extensions to permitted hours are, however, more usually associated with business operations.

At first sight such *private* clubs may have little to offer the tourist. Many of them are *federated* through bodies such as the CIU and the British Legion and others. This allows participants to be in membership of many clubs when they are away from home. The facilities of all such clubs are available for recreational pursuits to the extended membership. Children under 14 are allowed in bars of the Clubs.

Proprietory clubs

These are run as business enterprises with a view to profit for the owners, who may be companies or individuals. They restrict the membership by reserving the right to refuse admission save to those who have been accepted for membership and have paid the appropriate fee.

A liquor licence granted to such a club will have been applied for in the same way as other licences to the local licensing justices. The licence, when granted, will have a condition attached to it stipulating that liquor may only be sold to members and their bona fide guests.[19]

The permitted hours will be those for the locality in which the club is situated. Provided that the premises are structurally adapted, and *bona fide* used for the provision of substantial table meals, a restaurant certificate may be granted upon application. This allows a one hour extension to permitted hours during which alcohol may be served with meals, and a thirty minute 'drinking up' time for diners.

The service of alcohol is ancillary to the service of food, which must be in a part of the premises 'habitually' used for that purpose. The certificate is only available to those who serve meals in the ordinary course of events, and at times when it is customary to serve meals: *Norris v Manning (1971).*[20] What qualifies as a 'substantial meal' is far from clear. The service of sandwiches at a table to diners already present at the beginning of the extra hour was held to be sufficient: *Soloman v Green (1955).*[21]

Where a restaurant certificate is in force, the licensee may apply for an *extended hours* certificate. To qualify, he must habitually provide musical, or other entertainment, in addition to substantial meals. The entertainment must be *live* and must be provided regularly, or on a certain day or days, every week for at least 50 weeks of the year.

Where the entertainment is musical, no entertainment licence is needed by a club; but the club will need a certificate from the local authority to the effect that the premises are suitable for the grant of such a licence, were one needed, before the licensing justices will grant the extension required.

Before a certificate is granted, the justices will want to be certain that both food and entertainment are provided to customers for a substantial period before and after the end of the usual permitted hours. The certificate has the effect of extending permitted hours to 1a.m. but liquor may not be supplied after either the service of meals has ceased or the entertainment has ended. The certificate is usually restricted to certain days of the week and may require that the permitted hours end before 1a.m. Even where all the conditions are fulfilled, the licensing authority has a complete discretion as to whether or not a certificate is granted. The thirty minute *drinking up* time applies to this certificate.[22]

Nightclubs

In order to continue serving alcohol to a late hour beyond 1a.m., a licensee would need to provide both food and facilities for dancing to *live* music. Where the premises are structurally adapted, and bona fide used for both activities, the holder of a justices' licence for the consumption of alcohol on the premises may apply for a *special hours certificate*. This will allow him to serve alcohol as an ancillary to the service of food and the provision of facilities for dancing. He may serve liquor until 2a.m. in the provinces, or 3a.m. in London, with a 30 minute *drinking up* time. If the dancing ceases, or food is no longer available, then the service of alcohol must stop at the same time. The conditions under which the certificate is issued, outside the Inner London area, may set earlier closing hours where there is reason to believe that the *bona fide* use of the premises for which it is granted is likely to end before 2a.m., or that a restriction is necessary to prevent nuisance to neighbours, or to reduce the danger of disorderly conduct on the premises.

An entertainment licence is not needed for a club but, as with an extended hours certificate, the justices need to be satisfied that the premises are such as would qualify for the grant of one were it necessary. The *special hours* certificate will only be granted if all three facilities: food, alcoholic beverages, and dancing are being offered at the same time. The operative word is *offered*. Provided that the facilities are made available, there is no obligation placed on the licence holder to ensure that the customers utilise the amenities provided for them: *Richards v Bloxham (1968)*.[23]

The hours for premises holding a s.70 special hours certificate were varied by the Licensing Act 1988. Subject to the provisions in regard to music and dancing above, permitted hours are now between 11a.m. to the following 2a.m.

Discrimination

Refusal to admit a person to a club solely on the grounds of race or sex is unlawful in the case of proprietory clubs. An anomaly exists in that section 26 of the Race Relations Act 1976 allows people of the same racial or national origins to set up clubs for themselves as long as the criteria for membership is not based solely on colour.

Section 34 of the Sex Discrimination Act 1975 allows all-male or all-female registered clubs. A hotel has been established solely for women on this basis. Recently the CIU has decided on a voluntary basis to recommend to all clubs within its membership that all club facilities should in future be made available to women as well as men.

5. GAMBLING

The control of gambling in its various forms has long been regulated by legislation. The current law is contained mainly in the Betting, Gaming and Lotteries Act 1963 and the Gaming Act 1968. Under the latter, clubs are licensed by the local justices while the Home Secretary makes regulations for the operation of premises in which gaming takes place. Control is exercised by the police and gaming inspectors. Advertising facilities is unlawful save in prescribed ways at the premises themselves.

Betting

Until 1963, *off course* betting was illegal. Under the provisions of the Act a bookmaker may apply for a licence to the local justices for permission to operate a Betting Office. The statute has replaced widespread illegal activities by those which are strictly controlled. The control of advertising and the provisions as to the amenities provided are to be relaxed as a consequence of new regulations to be introduced by the Minister in 1993. The discouragement of punters highlighed in *Wilson v Danny Questel (Rotherhithe) Ltd (1965)* [24] may not be totally abrogated however. It is still the case that a betting shop may not operate as part of another business. It would appear that the exchequer is seeking to maximise revenue by way of taxation from operations which were once deemed illegal.

Betting is prohibited in streets and public places other than licensed racecourses and tracks which are regulated by the 1963 Act. At such venues, betting may only take place on days when racing is taking place there. *Betting* is not defined in any statute but is usually interpreted as meaning an arrangement where money, or money's worth, is risked on the outcome of a future event, e.g. which horse will win a certain race or the outcome of a sporting match. On a strict interpretation of the law, betting amongst bona fide members of clubs would appear to be legal. It would be illegal if members were to place bets with bookmakers. Betting may be distinguished from gaming in that the former is a vicarious activity whereas the latter requires participation. Until recently betting on greyhound races during the evening could only take place at the track. This now to be changed to allow punters returning home in the early evening to place bets in betting shops whilst such are still open. Members of the Greyhound Control Board see the consequence of this as being the closure of many tracks which rely on punters spending money on other amenities at the trackside.

Gaming

The 1968 Act imposes a general prohibition on all forms of gaming in any premises to which the public has access, whether or not a charge is made for admission. Gaming is defined as the playing of a game of chance for winnings in money, or money's worth, whether any person playing the game is at risk of losing any money, or money's worth, or not.[25] Games of *chance* include those which have an element of skill, e.g. some card games. Games of pure skill are not games of chance. Risking money on the outcome of such a game would not be gaming but it could still be caught by the rules against betting.

Gaming has become a recognised and significant element in the field of leisure activities. It has been allowed to operate commercially under the terms of the 1968 Act. Such activities are controlled by the Gaming Board. The Act reverses the policy of the 1963 Act which made all such operations illegal.

Minor exceptions to the general rules are made in the case of games played in public houses for small stakes and games played for *amusements with prizes*. Where a club which is established for a purpose other than gaming wishes to make an admission charge for acts of gaming, it may apply for a registration certificate to permit this. It must not seek to make a profit from gaming in other ways since this is only allowed under the terms of a gaming licence.

Casinos

In order to operate an establishment whose primary object is commercial gaming, a licence is required. An applicant must make representations to the Gaming Board and seek a Certificate of Consent. Strict controls are set to limit the number of such operations in particular localities. They are only permitted in districts with a population of over 125,000. The applicant must identify the location of the proposed premises to the Board which is also concerned with the character of the applicant. It has an absolute discretion in granting a certificate. Its consideration of the proposal must be *fair* but there is no appeal against a refusal to issue a certificate.

Once in possession of a certificate, application must be made to a local authority for a Gaming Licence. The magistrates who sit for this purpose will need to be satisfied that there is an unmet demand for such an operation and that the premises are suitable. They will also consider the fitness of the applicant, notwithstanding that he holds a certificate from the Gaming Board.

Where a licence is granted, it is usual for conditions to be imposed relating to the location of gaming within premises and the games allowed to be played there. These are likely to be the games which provide most profit for the proprietor. They are the *hard core* gambling activities which may only take place on such licensed premises and each of these is governed by rules which are designed to prevent the *house* holding an unfair advantage over the players.

The 1968 Act seeks to prevent excess profits being made from players. In all games where the *house* is participating in the game, no entry charge may be made, nor a levy upon the stakes or winnings of participants. The only exception to this is in the case of a *bona fide* membership subscription to the club. Staff gratuities may not be accepted from members, or their guests, whether voluntary or not.

A number of other provisions regulate the operation of the business. These involve provisions as to membership; the holding of croupiers' certificates issued by the Board; the exclusion of persons under 18 years from the premises; the prohibition on gambling on credit terms, which first appeared in the Gaming Act 1710; prohibitions against dancing and live entertainment; a general ban on advertising. Enforcement of the law is by Inspectors of the Gaming Board. Subject to very minor exceptions, where *gaming for prizes* is allowed, no *Bingo* may be played on the premises.

Bingo

Many clubs regularly operate Bingo sessions for the enjoyment of their members. The origin of the name is alleged to have been the excited cry of a competitor with a full house in a game previously called variously housey-housey, tombola and Crown & Anchor, at the seaside resort of Morecambe in Lancashire! Where such games are played for profit by the organiser, a Gaming Licence issued in respect of Bingo only is required. The same applications to the Board and the local magistrates which apply to *hard core* gaming must be made but only the manager needs to be certified, not his staff as well. The rules for operating Bingo are similar to those for casinos, with minor relaxations.

An admission charge per *session* is allowed, to a prescribed maximum. There can be no more than one session in every two hour period. The waiting time between application for membership and use of the premises is reduced from the 48 hours in the case of casinos to 24 hours. Persons below the age of 18 years may not play but may be present when games are played.

As a general rule, all stakes hazarded are paid out in the form of winnings which may vary from session to session. There is, therefore, no legal limit on the size of stakes or the prizes paid out. A restriction is imposed where a *linked system* operates connecting games played on one premises pooled with those played at others. The most recent regulations of such gaming are contained in the Bingo Act 1985 and 1992. The last named amends the 1968 Gaming Act so as to allow Bingo to be advertised whereas other forms of gaming continue to be strictly regulated by the 1968 Act. The DTI seems keen to arrest the decline of the pastime in recent years saying 'The government has accepted that bingo clubs offer their membership the opportunity to participate in an innocent and congenial social occasion which is unlikely to encourage excessive gambling. They do not therefore require the same close control as does casino gaming'. A laudable sentiment or a realisation of potential revenue to the Exchequer?

The Bingo Act 1985 remains the principal statute regulating the conduct of premises and the activities therein..

Gaming machines

The 1968 Act defines these as 'constructed or adapted for playing a game of chance by means of the machine'. Such machines have 'a slot or aperture for the insertion of money or money's worth in the form of cash or tokens'.

A licensed or registered club is automatically permitted to use such machines. In other places, a registration certificate is required where *jackpot* prizes are paid out. Such a machine is defined in Part III of the 1968 Act as one where a prize is accumulated and remains variable until paid out when prescribed combinations of reels appear.

Certificates for such machines are obtained from the local Magistrates' Court. All prizes must be paid out from the machine itself, not at some other place. A limit is placed on the level of charge for each '*game* which may be varied by the Home Secretary. There are also restrictions on *hold* and *credit* facilities offered by some machines.

Non-jackpot machines are those which are intended for the amusement of the players. They require to be operated by permit. Such games were intended for non-club sites to which the general public has access, e.g. bars and cafés. Application for use is made to the appropriate local body which, in the case of premises with a liquor licence, is the local licensing panel.

Local authorities may place a restriction on the number of such machines in use in a locality or certain types of premises. The number of machines on any one site may also be limited. The local authority has complete discretion in the matter. Complex rules exist for the use of such machines with limitations on the charge levied per 'game' and the small sums which may be offered as 'prizes' in the form of money, or tokens which can be exchanged for money.

Gaming machines may only be sold or supplied by persons who hold certificates for the purpose. Certification extends to those who repair or service machines for reward.

Under the Betting and Gaming Duties Act 1972, and subsequent amending legislation, a gaming licence duty must be paid on most games played in casinos and Bingo premises. The tax is collected by the Commissioners of Customs and Excise. In the case of gaming machines similar *duties* are levied.

6. THE OLDEST PROFESSION

Prostitution is not illegal in England, or in EEC countries. Soliciting for prostitution in public is an offence under the Street Offences Act 1959. Other statutes refer to *common prostitutes*, which term is taken as indicating those willing to provide sexual gratification for clients of their choosing: *R v Webb (1964).*[26] Loitering for the purposes of prostitution is an offence even where no solicitation occurs. It may be performed on foot, or from a vehicle controlled by a prostitute.

The law discourages prostitution in various ways. The most usual are by making it an offence to procure a woman to become a prostitute (rare); keeping a brothel; for men to live off the earnings of female prostitutes; for women to exercise control over prostitutes. All of these constitute offences under the Sexual Offences Act 1956.

The Act does not define a *brothel*, but the premises are well known to the common law. It is an offence to keep a common, ill-governed, disorderly house of which a *brothel* is one variety. The Sexual

Offences Act 1976 extends the offence of brothel keeping, as defined by the common law, to homosexual activities. Provided persons resort to premises for sexual acts outside marriage, the occupier may be convicted of an offence, whether money is paid for services or not: *Winter v Woolfe (1931)*.[27] The presence of one prostitute does not make premises a brothel, there must be at least two working. Hotels letting rooms on an hourly basis need to be on their guard or the proprietors will face prosecution. Even where individual rooms are let separately to tenants the whole may be classified as a brothel: *Donovan v Gavin (1965)*.[28]

Lewd displays

The common law offence of keeping a disorderly house also extends to the performance of indecent acts or exhibitions. Even where visitors attend merely as spectators, an offence is committed: *R v Quinn (1962)*.[29] The conduct complained of must amount to an outrage to public decency, or tend to deprave or be otherwise calculated to injure the public interest, so as to call for condemnation or punishment.

Clients

As late as the case of: *Crook v Edmonson (1966)*,[30] it was held that a man does not solicit for immoral purposes when he does so on his own behalf. In the face of mounting public objection, the practice of motorists' 'kerb crawling' was first attacked in: *R v Dodd (1977)*[31] where under-age girls were accosted by men and *Crook* was distinguished.

The Sexual Offences Act 1985 makes all such activities illegal. A man who persistently solicits one woman, or several, in a street or public place, from a vehicle or on foot, commits an offence. It must be shown that the circumstances are likely to cause annoyance to women or to persons in the neighbourhood. This is to be decided as a matter of fact, no annoyance need actually have taken place.

Soliciting of men by women, except in a public place, is not an offence, nor is the solicitation of one man by another. In this latter case, the law seems to be governed by: *R v Grey (1982)*.[32] Although not specifically stated, the history of the law in this respect shows that Parliament did not intend to exclude such activities from the statute.

Sex shops

The Local Government (Miscellaneous Provisions) Act 1982 empowers local authorities to adopt measures to control sex shops as well as cinemas. These may make the issue of annual licences obligatory for such establishments. They will also be used to bar persons below the age of 18 years from the premises. The Act contains comprehensive definitions of terms which are used in connection with both the premises and the materials within them.

NOTES:

1. (1947) 1 KB 45.
2. The Housing, Town Planning ets Act 1909.
3. Town and Country Planning (Use Classes) Order 1987 SI 764.
4. (1980) 258 EG 64 (QBD).
5. (1971) 23 P & CR 169.
6. Building Regulations 1976 SI 1676 as amended.
7. See Fire Precautions (Hotels and Boarding Houses) 1972 SI 238.
8. (1971) 21 DLR (3d) 257
9. (1991) *The Independent* 20 September
10. (1980) 18 LGR 672.
11. (1982) unreported.
12. (1977) Crim LR 362.
13. (1950) 2 KB 612.
14. (1947) 2 A11 ER 680.
15. (1865) 6 B & B 474: see also Hall v Green (1853) 9 Exch 247.
16. (1984) 1 A11 ER 58.
17. Licensing Act 1964 s 182.
18. (1968) 3 A11 ER 289.
19. Licensing Act 1964 s 55.
20. (1971) 115 SJ 407.
21. (1955) 119 JP 289.
22. Licensing (Amendment) Act 1980 (but not earlier than midnight).
23. (1968) 112 SJ 543.
24. (1965) 2 A11 ER 252.
25. Gaming Act 1968 s 52 (1).
26. (1964) 1 QB 357.
27. (1931) 1 KB 549.
28. (1965) 2 QB 648.

29. (1962) 2 QB 245.
30. (1966) 2 QB 81.
31. (1977) 66 Crim App Rep 87.
32. (1982) Crim LR 176 (CA).

CHAPTER XVI

Spectator Events

1. PUBLIC SHOWS

Spectacles of one sort or another have been organised for the attraction of the public for many years. Modern sporting occasions are the descendants of much older gladiatorial competitions. The range of activities produced for the entertainment of spectators is limited only by the availability of venues and the imagination of promoters.

At one time, crowds would assemble to watch battles. More timorous souls were entertained by displays of the military practising the arts of war on training grounds. These, in their turn, have been replaced by navy days, air displays and military tattoos.

Where the military possessed grounds to display their skills, others relied on public spaces and the streets. The Durham Miners' Gala and the Whit Walks of the industrial north preceded more recent importations in the form of Carnivals with an ethnic theme.

Open air festivals are not a new phenomenon, they have existed, in one form or another with a central theme, for a number of years. They may have a literary theme, as with the annual Dickens Week at Rochester; political overtones such as those associated with the gatherings of trade unionists at Tolpuddle; or associated with gardens, exhibitions, or rallies of many descriptions.

Some public events have disappeared after centuries of popularity. Public executions are a thing of the past. They have gone the way of bear baiting, cockfighting and other violent contests such as prize fighting. Tourists who wish to see such murderous pastimes must now journey to Spain or Mexico to witness bull fights staged for public amusement.

For many years, Association Football has been the major spectator sport in Britain. A crowd of over 84,000 watched a game at the Manchester City ground in 1934, which is still a record for any game outside London or Glasgow. Crowd attendance records in recent years have shown a decline in numbers due, in part, to the growth in numbers of *armchair spectators* with the rise in television audiences. This in no way detracts from the significance of sport as a spectacle. Its value has been acknowledged by government at least for tax purposes, if not in the appointment of a part-time Minister of Sport in the shape of a junior at the Department of the Environment.

The main preoccupation of the Government is, as always in so many areas, with maintaining public order. It has a difficult choice to make between the public good and the public purse. Restrictions on spectator events automatically reduce the revenue from direct taxation and that raised in VAT on many of the activities associated with these occasions.

2. PUBLIC ORDER

There will always be threats to public order where any large crowd gathers. Many examples of violence associated with spectator events can be traced back for centuries. The wide publicity given by television and the press has served to highlight such incidents as those which took place at the Heysel Stadium in Brussels causing the deaths of Italian supporters in 1985, and for which British spectators were extradited to face trial.

These football tourists have gained a reputation for violence which is international as well as domestic. The ban of English clubs from

European competition was the culmination of a series of events. The Football Association has tried, without success so far, to have the ban lifted and the Sports Minister has gone on record as saying that he was 'keen to see English clubs back in Europe but not until we get our house in order'.[1]

In the belief that violence on the pitch provokes reaction amongst spectators, the police are being encouraged to take action against players who assault opponents on the field of play. Such prosecutions are not new. At the end of the last century, a footballer was convicted of manslaughter: *R v Moore (1898)*.[2] Violence amongst spectators at grounds has raised other issues. For many years it has been necessary to prove a breach of the peace has occurred in a public place. It has been argued that a sports ground is not a public place but private property. This has been discounted by the Court of Appeal decision that a place to which the public has access, even where an entry fee is charged, is within the definition: *Cawley v Frost (1976)*.[3]

Following a recommendation of the Law Commission in 1983,[4] the Public Order Act passed into the statute book in 1986. The Act creates a series of offences, graded in accordance with a scale of gravity. The new offences which it establishes replace many older statutory crimes and several at common law, ranging from, at the top end, the offence of 'riot' to 'disorderly conduct' at the lower end.

Part IV is designed to deal with rowdy behaviour at football matches. While these are specifically mentioned, section 37 gives the Secretary of State wide powers to extend the provisions. He may, by statutory instrument, apply the *football* rules to 'a sporting event of a kind specified in the order'.

The statute seeks to both prevent violent disorder and provide a means of punishing offenders. Under section 31, where a person has been convicted of an 'offence connected with football' he may be excluded from any prescribed match. This may last for a period of between three and twelve months. There is no right of appeal against such a ban and if the offender defies the prohibition, he faces fine and/or imprisonment. Where such an exclusion order is made, the court may order that a photograph of the convicted person be taken for use by the police.

The *football offences* to which the exclusion order refers are those committed against section 1 of the Sporting Events (Control of Alcohol etc.) Act 1985. They are concerned with the abuse of alcohol on journeys connected with certain sporting events. The accused must have been on such a journey and have used or threatened violence towards other persons or property. The incident must have occurred during the 'relevant period', defined as 2 hours before the advertised, or actual, start of the match, ending 1 hour after it has finished. The qualifying journey is defined as one which includes breaks and overnight stops.

The principal public order offences are contained in sections 1 to 5 of the 1986 Act. The major crimes of riot, violent disorder and affray require the use, or threat, of unlawful violence to other persons such as would cause: 'a person of reasonable firmness present at the scene to fear for his personal safety'. Section 4 creates an offence of using 'threatening, abusive or insulting words or behaviour' towards another person. This may be in the form of writing, signs or other representations in either a public or private place.

For such an offence to have been committed, it is necessary to show that the accused intended any person so addressed to believe that immediate unlawful violence would be used against him, or that it was intended to provoke a response which itself involved the use of unlawful violence. Where the acts described do not involve either of these two factors, a lesser offence may be committed. Under section 5, where the actions of the accused are likely to cause harassment, alarm or distress to any person within hearing or sight of them, the perpetrator may be prosecuted and convicted.

This latter provision was intended to cover general anti-social behaviour, e.g. chanting, blowing whistles, banging dustbins etc. It was intended to curb hooliganism but not to penalise high spirits. The list of undesirable activities under section 4 includes 'disorderly behaviour'. This is an entirely new offence which does not replace the old offence of 'conduct likely to cause a breach of the peace', specifically retained in section 40(1).

Abuse of alcohol

The availability of alcohol both inside and outside grounds has been blamed for the deterioration of behaviour at public occasions. Following the apparent success of an Act imposing bans on misuse of alcohol, or even possession of the same, at matches in Scotland in 1980, the Scots example was followed by the passing of the Sporting Events (Control of Alcohol) Act 1985. This extends similar provisions to those affecting Scotland to England and Wales.

The measures designed to improve the control of spectators inside grounds have reduced violence inside stadiums. This has resulted in an increase in the number of incidents outside grounds, in the streets where they are less easy to control. The burden on sports clubs has been lightened, it would seem, at the expense of the public in the neighbourhood surrounding sporting venues.

Nor is the problem confined to football. Incidents have occurred at boxing matches and at rugby and cricket grounds. There is the wider international dimension which introduces the prospects of terrorist activities taking place. It is perhaps remarkable that none have so far occurred in the UK, but the lessons drawn from the Munich Olympics of 1972 must be borne in mind by all who are responsible for the safety of the public, wherever they gather in large numbers.

In seeking to control football hooliganism and to fulfil election promises made by the 'party of law and order' The Football Spectators Act 1989 was passed into the statute book. The aim was to control the admission of spectators at designated football matches in England and Wales primarily by means of a national membership scheme with fans being required to register and carry identity cards plus a scheme of granting licences to grounds to admit spectators. In this way the government expected to provide for safety by way of licensing and the revocation or forfeiture of the same; to permit courts to make orders and to enforce them against persons convicted of certain offences; prevent violent disorder at matches both inside and outside the UK - such as were to be designated from time to time in the case of the latter category by the Secretary of State.

The Football Association and many other organisations protested at the unworkability of such a scheme but the government pressed ahead regardless convinced it was right. To date very few of the provisions have commenced and all the signs are that the majority never will be.

Conditions of licences provided for specified seating requirements and admissions procedures. Although many grounds have provided seating this has not prevented pitch invasions which the FA deals with by finding the clubs - a more direct and possibly effective panacea. The restrictions on fans going abroad seem to have had little effect, much less so than the banning of English clubs from European competitions which was a draconian measure adopted by the international football organisations and only relatively recently lifted.

In 1991 the Football Offences Act was passed. It provides for greater control over persons attending football matches in relation to disorderly conduct - specifically creating offences of throwing missiles and the chanting of indecent racial slogans. Entering the playing area without lawful excuse is also made an offence and it for the defendant to prove that he has such lawful excuse - such as would have been the case with those escaping from the fire at Bradford (q.v.) or eventually being allowed onto the pitch at Hillsborough. It is tempting to ask how many of the dead and injured at Hillsborough might have been alive and well today had not the barriers in the ground led to the penning of spectators in what turned out to be killing zones.

3. GROUND SAFETY

In January 1971, crowd barriers at Ibrox Park, Glasgow collapsed and 66 people were killed. Many years before, following injuries at the first Wembley FA Cup Final, a government inquiry recommended a system for licensing stadiums, and for fire precautions, but nothing came of it. Another report, following 33 deaths at Bolton in 1946, recommended similar precautions to those of 1924, with a similar result.

The Safety of Sports Grounds Act 1975 was the first statute targeted specifically at sporting events, coming in the wake of the Ibrox disaster. The Secretary of State has the power to designate any sports stadium with a capacity for more than 10,000 spectators as requiring the possession of a Safety Certificate. The ground in question must be covered by a certificate to be issued by the local authority, specifying the maximum numbers permitted, together with detailed provisions for crowd barriers, exits etc. Such a certificate may be of indefinite duration, or for a specified number of occasions.

Where there is perceived to be a risk of such magnitude that immediate action is called for, a special emergency procedure is available. The Act creates a number of offences which may be committed in connection with the operation of stadiums, but it cannot be used as the basis of civil actions for breach of statutory duty. The controllers of such grounds may claim a defence that they took all reasonable precautions, and exercised all due diligence, to comply with the terms under which the certificate was issued. Where an action for compensation is brought, it will need to be founded in either occupier's liability or negligence.

Fire

In May 1985, a fire broke out after rubbish which had accumulated under a wooden stand, built in 1909, ignited at the Bradford City Football Club. 56 people died and 200 were injured. Under the provisions of the 1975 Act, the Secretary of State had designated all first and second division Football League club grounds as requiring Safety Certificates. He had declined to extend the designation to smaller clubs unwilling, on a voluntary basis, to incur the high cost of ground safety improvements.

The Wheatley Report of the Inquiry into Crowd Safety at Sports Grounds in 1972 had stated that it was unreasonable to expect all minor grounds to be licensed. To this, however, it made a notable exception. In paragraph 54 it stated, 'there is one qualification to this. If in such a ground there is a stand, it seems desirable that it should be made the subject of inspection in view of the possible risk of danger to spectators accommodated in it. Such a ground, in my view, should be licensed even if only to protect the public from that one risk.' The Report also recommended that all licences should be subject to annual renewal.

Shortly after the Wheatley Report, an Inquiry into Safety and Health at Work began its deliberations. The result was the Robens Report which emphasised that the responsibility for instituting safety measures lay with the occupiers of the premises in question whose practices were unsafe. This philosophy of attaching responsibility to people rather than places was embodied in the Health and Safety at Work Act 1974.

An Inquiry into Crowd Safety and Control of Sports Grounds was instituted following the Bradford disaster, resulting in the Popplewell Report of 1986. The recommendations were incorporated in the Fire Safety and Safety of Sports Grounds Act 1987. In addition, under the provisions of the 1975 Act, all Football League club grounds have been designated such that a Safety Certificate is mandatory for them, together with the top two divisions of the Rugby League and major Rugby Union and cricket grounds. The expense has had to be borne by the clubs, no government money has been made available.

The introduction of these statutory measures came too late for the victims of the Bradford fire. Instead they had to seek the aid of the civil courts in gaining compensation.

At Hillsborough Stadium, Sheffield in 1989, 95 people died in the crush and 400 were injured. One of the injured was artificially kept alive until 1993 when support was withdrawn at the request of his parents and with the authority of the Court of Appeal setting a legal precedent in itself.

At Hillsborough, South Yorkshire Police were responsible for crowd control and the chief constable admitted liability in respect of deaths and physical injuries. This incident resulted in many claims for compensation being settled out of court whilst some relatives unsuccessfully brought actions for nervous shock occasioned to them by the incident. Whilst the legal niceties of the cases are outside this text the report of the issues raised before the House of Lords in the case of *Alcock & Others v Chief Constable of South Yorkshire Police (1991)*[5] are commended to the reader.

4. CIVIL LIABILITY

A test case for those affected by the disaster was brought by Mrs Fletcher, who lost three generations of her family, and a police officer badly burned when rescuing victims: *Fletcher and Others v Bradford City Football Club and Others (1986)*.[6] The West Yorkshire County Council and the Health and Safety Executive were joined with the Club as defendants. The case was heard before Sir Joseph Cantley who had gained much experience of such matters as chairman of the inquiry into the fire at the Summerlands Leisure Centre in the Isle of Man. In finding for Mrs Fletcher and PC Britton he said:

'In my view, the continuing negligence of the Club and the continued inaction or in difference of the County Council through its various departments and in both of its capacities, after it had been alerted to the existence of the danger, were concurrent causes of this disaster, and I hold both of them to be liable in damages to the plaintiff .... the primary duty was on the Club and the functions of the County Council were supervisory and its liability is for negligent breach of a common law duty arising out of the way in which they dealt with or ignored their statutory powers. That duty was not to the Club but a duty to the spectators and other persons in the stand. However, the responsibility of the Club is, in my view, greater and I apportion responsibility between the two defendants as to two thirds on the first defendant (the Club) and one third on the third (the County Council).'

The second defendant, the Health and Safety Executive, was dismissed from the case. It was estimated that, as a result of the action, a further

250 claimants sought compensation.

The case emphasises the role of local authorities. Powers are given to county councils but it is the district councils who exercise the planning controls which affect the work necessary to be done on the grounds. The local authority has wide powers in connection with the granting of safety certificates and the conditions attached to them. It may require a club or the occupier of a stadium to take any measures which it considers to be necessary to secure 'reasonable safety'. The cost of the work is not a factor which falls to be considered when granting a certificate. Under the Finance Act (No 2) 1975, the government introduced provisions to assist clubs, and others concerned in the maintenance of grounds, to defray costs by means of tax reliefs.

To assist in achieving the desired standards, the Home Office has issued a 'Guide to Safety at Sports Grounds'. Many of the criticisms highlighted in the Bradford case are included in the voluntary code set out in the publication.

Contract

Every spectator who pays an entrance fee to witness an event enters into a contract with the provider of the entertainment. The precise terms of the agreement are not easy to determine because there are few express terms on which to rely. Those which are spelt out will usually be drawn to the attention of the spectators in posters and other forms of promotional advertising. They may be indicated by reference to a ticket which is issued in connection with the event, either some time in advance, or at the time of admission. In the case of the latter, the purchaser may be entitled to look upon the ticket simply as a receipt. In all cases, it will be a question of fact as to whether the document in question incorporates terms of the contract.

In most instances, the terms of the contract will be such as might reasonably be implied having reference to all the circumstances of the occasion known to the parties. Other than allowing a spectator to occupy the seat or space allocated to him on the ticket, to watch the event as advertised, the obligations of the promoter are somewhat obscure. Section 13 of the Supply of Goods and Services Act will apply to this as any other contract. The use of reasonable care and skill in providing the entertainment is implied into the contract. The promoter may seek to vary this in some way by a notice displayed and brought to the attention of the spectator.

Such a notice cannot deny responsibility for death or personal injury which results from the *negligence* of the promoter. Nor may he exclude, or restrict, his liability for loss caused by his negligence in so far as any other injury is concerned, except it be reasonable for him to do so.[7]

In this respect *negligence* means a breach of express or implied terms to take reasonable care, or exercise reasonable skill, in the performance of the contract. This will include an implied term to have regard to the safety and well-being of spectators. If a spectator is injured by the collapse of a grandstand, from which he is viewing an event which he has paid to see, he is entitled to consider that there has been a breach of contract such as to allow a claim for damages: *Francis v Cockerell (1870)*.[8] The promoter will be liable, notwithstanding that the injury was the result of the bad workmanship of a contractor: *Brown v Lewis (1896)*.[9]

A spectator at a fireworks display is entitled to consider, on the grounds of 'res ipsa loquitur', if for no other reason, that there has been a lack of reasonable care and skill on the part of the organiser when he is injured by a firework: *Whitby v J. Brock (1886)*.[10]

If the defendant can show that he has discharged the duty, there will be no breach of contract on his part so as to deny remedy to the plaintiff: *Piddington v Hastings (1932)*.[11] It may be, however, that a person who pays for admission is expected to accept the possibility that he may be injured by an event which occurs directly from the spectacle he has come to watch.

Volenti non fit injuria

The essence of 'volenti' is that the plaintiff knew of the risk he was running and agreed to accept it. It is sometimes said that he *consented* to the harm being done to him. This may be the case where physical contact is expected within the rules of the game, e.g. boxing, otherwise the consent can only be as to the risk not the certainty. The leading case in this respect, involving spectators, is: *Hall v Brooklands Auto Racing Club (1933)*.[12] In his explanation for the decision to deny compensation to a spectator injured when a car broke through a crowd barrier, Scrutton L. J. said:

'A spectator at Lord's or the Oval runs the risk of being hit by a cricket ball ..... (those) at football or hockey or polo matches run similar risks .....

those who pay for admission or seats in stands at a flying meeting run a risk of the performing aeroplanes falling on their heads..... What is reasonable care would depend on the perils which might reasonably be expected to occur, and the extent to which the ordinary spectator might be expected to take the risk of such perils..... No-one expects the persons receiving payment to erect such structures or nets that no spectator can be hit by a ball kicked or hit violently from the field of play towards the spectators. The field is safe to stand on and the spectators take the risk of the game'.

This interpretation was applied to a small boy hit by an ice hockey puck at a game so as to deny compensation to him: *Murray v Haringey Arena (1951)*.[13] Similarly, it seems that an error of judgement by a participant, which injures a spectator, is not actionable in the absence of evidence that the injury was caused by wilful or reckless disregard for the safety of bystanders: *Woolridge v Summer (1963)*.[14] It will be otherwise where the participants break the rules of the game and in so doing injure spectators: *Payne and Payne v Maple Leaf (1949)*.[15]

A spectator has no claim where a promoter or organiser conducts his business safely, or where participants in the event which the spectator has come to watch abide by the rules or keep within the boundaries of what is reasonably allowable in the circumstances.

Where the plaintiff does not have a full appreciation of the risk, because of the existence of a hazard of which he is not aware, then the organiser cannot escape liability: *Latchford v Spedeworth International Ltd (1984)*.[16] If the accident is in explicable, and no lack of care is apparent, then the organiser cannot be held responsible: *Wilks v Cheltenham Car Club (1971)*.[17] A plaintiff may have no action for breach of contract and may be able to claim under another head.

Negligence

Mrs Fletcher had no contract with the Bradford City Football Club and her action for compensation was based on negligence. The basis of such a claim is the failure to discharge the duty of care owed by the defendant to those he sought to have in mind as likely to be affected, in the way they were, by his acts or omissions. This was the basis of a claim by the widow of a spectator killed in the Ibrox disaster: *Dougan v Glasgow Rangers Football Club (1974)*.[18]

Where a spectator has no claim against the organiser or promoter of the event, he may have an action against one of the participants in the event he is viewing. This will not succeed if the participant can show that the injury was caused by an error of judgement acceptable in the circumstances: *Wilks* and *Wooldridge*.

A spectator who has no contract with the organiser may succeed in a claim for negligence where it can be shown that 'volenti' is inoperative because the injured party was not aware of the particular risk which was responsible for his accident: *White v Blackmore (1972)*.[19]

Notices

The Unfair Contract Terms Act 1977 includes, within the definition of *negligence* under section 1, the common law duty of care and common duty of care under the Occupiers Liability Act 1957. Exclusion of liability, in cases which fall within the provisions of the 1977 Act, are subject to its qualifications. No notice which warns spectators that motor racing is *a dangerous sport* will, of itself, give rise to a defence based on *volenti*.

Section 3(2)(b) does not allow a contract term entitling the beneficiary to render a performance substantially different from that which was reasonably expected of him, or no performance at all, unless this satisfied the test of reasonableness. Thus, a promoter who substitutes an inferior boxer for an advertised contestant on his bill may be protected from an action for breach of contract if there was a term in the contract allowing this for, say, injury to the advertised contestant which was not known, or reasonably could not have been foreseen, at the time the contest was arranged and promoted.

Horse and dog racing

The principle of *volenti* which formed the basis of *Hall* applies to spectators at race meetings. In *Hall*, Greer L.J. remarked:

> 'a man taking a ticket to see the Derby would know quite well that there would be no provision to prevent a horse which got out of hand from getting amongst the spectators, and would quite understand that he was himself bearing the risk of any such possible but improbable accident happening to himself.'

At the same time statutory provisions, such as those contained in the Fire Precautions Act 1971 and the Health and Safety at Work Act 1974, will apply to race tracks. Although breach of statutory regulations may not themselves give rise to an action based upon the breach, failure to observe the required standards can be used as the basis for an action on negligence or occupiers' liability.

The ownership of race-tracks is not uniform. It is a mixture of privately owned or leased tracks and those owned by local authorities. The majority are privately owned and in the hands of a small number of proprietors.

The main preoccupation of the law in relation to racing and the protection of the public is more in the nature of concern for the financial, rather than the physical, well-being of *punters*. It is concerned with ensuring that measures are taken to prevent drug or doping offences. The regulation of horse racing has, since 1750, been largely concentrated in the hands of the Jockey Club. A racecourse needs an annual licence from the club before it can operate. It is also responsible for the licensing of owners, trainers, flat race jockeys, steeple chase and hurdle riders, apprentices, and for the registration of stable employees. The threat of the loss of a licence is regarded as a more powerful weapon than mere fines for *fixing* horses or races. Sometimes its restrictions are considered too restrictive: *Nagle v Fielden (1966)*.[20]

The Jockey Club administers the racing rules, and shares the administration of betting, with the Horse Race Betting Levy Board, the Horserace Totalisator Board, and the Bookmakers' Committee, all three of which owe their existence to the provisions contained in the Betting, Gaming and Lotteries Act 1963.

The Levy Board has a significant part to play in seeing to it that the *punter* has a fair choice of bookmakers with whom to place his bets. This is achieved by the Board issuing certificates for betting areas at race courses. If a greyhound racing precedent which reached the House of Lords holds good for the *sport of kings*, the remedy for failure to allocate facilities to bookmakers lies not with the latter but with the public: *Cutler v Wandsworth Stadium Ltd (1949)*.[21]

As if to demonstrate the difference between the racing of dogs and horses, greyhounds race anti-clockwise whereas the horse proceeds in a clockwise direction! Dog tracks are licensed by district councils and racing is regulated by statutory rules decreeing not more than 130 racing days in a year, and no more than 14 in any one month, on which betting may take place. Betting is controlled, as with horses, by the 1963 Act.

The recent fiasco at Aintree when the Grand National 1993 was abandoned after two false starts has lead some of the national bookmaking firms to declare that they will be seeking compensation from the organisers for monies lost in the promotion and advertising of the event. They cannot claim for loss of expected winnings! An inquiry has been instituted by the Jockey Club headed by a judge, himself a former gentleman rider who has won several races.

Dogs and horses are regarded in law as *mansuetae naturae*. The keeper of such an animal was strictly liable for damage done by it, only if he knew that a particular beast had a propensity for causing harm. Animals *ferae naturae* on the other hand, were regarded as dangerous in themselves to mankind.

5. STRICT LIABILITY

Strict liability is that which arises without fault on the part of a defendant, i.e. he need have acted neither intentionally nor negligently. It arises primarily in association with the carrying on of some particularly hazardous activity, as envisaged under the rule in *Rylands v Fletcher* or in statutory form, e.g. the Control of Pollution Act 1974.

One aspect of such statutory form of strict liability which affects the general public and spectators alike, is that which was created under the Civil Aviation Act 1949, section 40. This makes the owner of an aircraft strictly liable for all material damage or loss caused by it, or by any person in it, or by an article or person falling from it, while in flight, taking off or landing, whether the damage is to people or property.

One aspect of strict liability more likely to be encountered by spectators present at entertainments, is that arising from encounters with animals. These are far more likely to occur than pieces of aircraft falling on the public at air displays.

Circuses

Until the advent of more sophisticated forms of entertainment, circuses were a very popular amusement. Today they are the subject of animal protection campaigns and may be in the last stages of decline, for this and other reasons.

Control of circuses is in the hands of local authorities. They come under the generic heading of *pleasure fairs*. The Public Health Act

1961 empowers local authorities to make byelaws concerning safety, prevention of nuisance, cleanliness and sanitary conditions, and all associated matters, relating to a wide range of outdoor entertainments. Control was extended to fire precautions by the Local Government (Miscellaneous Provisions) Act 1976.

Since local authorities own many of the open spaces in and near centres of population, they also effectively control the sites needed by such entertainments. It may also be that, because of the nature of travelling circuses, they are caught by the provisions of the Public Order Act 1986 which was designed primarily to deal with *hippy* convoys. Where circuses come onto land, and are allowed to remain there, it may be that the landowner will be liable for any *dangerous escapes*: *Attorney General v Corke (1933)*.[22]

Under the common law, the keeper of an animal which was considered dangerous per se was strictly liable for harm which it caused. In the case of *domesticated* animals native to the UK, it had to be shown not only that an animal had a propensity to do harm but also that it had escaped from its keeper: *Rands v McNeill (1955)*.[23]

The whole issue of animals was reviewed by the Law Commission, and reported on in 1967 in Civil Liability for Animals.[24] The Animals Act 1971, which incorporates the findings of the Commission, abolished the common law rules and strengthened the strict liability for dangerous animals by abolishing the requirement for an *escape* to have occurred preceding the harm complained of. The common law concept that some animals are to be regarded per se as dangerous was retained.

Dangerous species

These are defined in section 6 of the 1971 Act and include animals which, while domesticated in their native habitat, are not to be regarded as such when they are found in the UK, e.g. camels: *McQuaker v Goddard (1940)*.[25]

Elephants are commonly employed in circus acts and, although not usually associated with dangerous traits, they may cause harm especially when alarmed or provoked: *Behrens v Bertram Mills Circus (1957)*.[26]

The Act imposes strict liability for harm caused by the keeper of dangerous animals, as defined in section 6(2). In the case of other animals, it must be shown that the damage was of the nature and the severity to be expected if the animal were unrestrained. It also requires

334

that the nature and severity were due to the particular characteristics of the animal concerned and that these were known to the keeper, or anyone in his employ.

The maxim that every dog is allowed one bite is not accurate and certainly does not apply to guard dogs. Under the Guard Dogs Act 1975, such animals must be kept under control and must not be allowed to roam free unsupervised by a handler. The statute was designed to prevent a recurrence of cases in which child trespassers had been savaged by such animals. Section 5 of the Act specifically states that a breach of the statutory duty which it imposes upon those who keep such dogs is not actionable.

The 1971 Act does not remove liability for harm caused by animals which attract claims under other heads of tort. The owner of an animal remains liable in negligence or nuisance: *Gomberg v Smith (1962)*.[27]

Another difficulty which faces circuses is that there are restrictions on the importation of animals designated as needing protection and conservation. The Animals (Restriction of Importation) Act 1964 enables such regulations as may, from time to time, be necessary to be made in connection with such animals. Additional powers exist under the Endangered Species (Import and Export) Act 1976.

Further controls are exercised under the Animal Health Act 1981. Animals, both wild and domesticated, are affected by its provisions. Diseases dangerous to humans, as well as other creatures, may be transmitted by infected beasts. Dangers from the keeping of wild animals were appreciated as arising from the keeping of private menageries. The Dangerous Wild Animals Act 1976 was brought in to control *private* keepers of such animals. Its terms of reference do not apply to circuses or zoos.

Zoological gardens

Zoos have been popular tourist attractions for many years and recognised by both statute and common law: *Filburn v The People's Palace and Aquarium Co Ltd (1890)*.[28]

Escapes have occurred and damage to people and property has been recorded. Many escapes were from the smaller, private collections. As a consequence, the Zoo Licensing Act 1981 requires all zoos to be licensed by local authorities.

The Act contains definitions so as to make clear its terms of reference. A zoo is 'an establishment where wild animals are kept for exhibition to the public'.   Wild animals are those 'not normally domesticated in Great Britain'.   *Zoos* do not include pet shops or circuses, the latter being described as 'a place where animals are kept or introduced wholly or mainly for the purpose of performing tricks or manoeuvres at that place'.   Although district councils and the councils of London boroughs are licensing authorities, there is no prohibition on them which prevents them from operating zoos.

A licence is granted, initially, for a period of four years and for six years upon successful application for renewal.   Licences may be transferred, with permission of the licensing authority, or surrendered.

The grant of a licence may be subject to 'such conditions as the local authority think necessary or desirable for ensuring the proper conduct of the zoo'.   Such conditions include, inter alia, precautions against escapes; records of numbers and types together with health records; births, deaths, disposals and escapes records; the provision of adequate insurance against public liability.

The Secretary of State is required to keep a list of veterinary practitioners as advised to him by the British Veterinary Association who are experienced in dealing with *zoo* animals.   Such specialists, in conjunction with local authority inspectors, carry out periodic inspections of all zoos.   Where zoos are very small, or only small stocks of animals and/or birds are kept, the licensing authority may advise the Minister that the Act should not apply to it, or that its conditions be varied to take account of the nature of the establishment.

Offences against the terms of the Act are punishable by fine.   In serious cases, the authority could refuse renewal or revoke an existing licence.   The Act does not prescribe penalties for escapes or unauthorised releases. This would fall to be covered by other statutory provisions, e.g. the Animals Act 1971.   The type of harm which is envisaged by the 1971 Act is sufficiently wide to take account of injuries caused by attack or the spread of infections.   The omission of the defences of act of God, and of a third party, from the defences available under section 5 of the 1971 Act, mean that these defences are not available to actions under section 2 which cover *dangerous species* and known dangerous animals.   The defence that the plaintiff was wholly at fault, or voluntarily accepted the risk would appear to be available.   Visitors to zoos should beware of poking tigers with sticks or releasing monkeys from cages.

A trespasser to a zoo or a circus cannot seek to call in aid strict liability of the keeper if the former is injured: *Cummings v Grainer*

(1975).[29] The position as regards trespassers will fall to be considered in the light of the Occupiers' Liability Act 1984.   This requires adequate warnings of dangers to be given, and adequate measures to be taken, having regard to what is reasonable in the circumstances.   It is certain that no animal, wild or domesticated, can be kept in any place and left to roam at liberty to deter trespassers: *Lowery v Walker (1911)*.[30]

NOTES:

1. *Guardian* 19 Jan 88 p 28.
2. (1898) 14 TLR 229.
3. (1976) 64 Crim App Rep 20.
4. Law Commission 123.
5. (1991) *The Independent* 29 November
6. (1987) *Times* 24 Feb 87 p 16.
7. Unfair Contract Terms Act 1977 s 2(1) (2).
8. (1870) LR 5 QB 501.
9. (1896) 12 TLR 455.
10. (1886) 4 TLR 241.
11. *Times* 12 Mar 32 p 4.
12. (1933) 1 KB 205.
13. (1951) 2 QB 529.
14. (1963) 2 QB 43.
15. (1949) 1 DLR 369 (Canada).
16. (1984) 134 NLJ 36.
17. (1971) 1 WLR 608.
18. (1974) *Telegraph* 24 Oct 74 p 19.
19. (1972) 2 QB 651.
20. (1966) 1 A11 ER.
21. (1949) AC 398.
22. (1933) Ch 89.
23. (1955) 1 QB 253.
24. Law Commission 13.
25. (1940) 1 KB 687.
26. (1957) 2 QB 1.
27. (1962) 1 QB 25.
28. (1890) 25 QBD 258.
29. (1975) 1 WLR 1330.
30. (1911) AC 10 (HL).

CHAPTER XVII

Leisure Activities

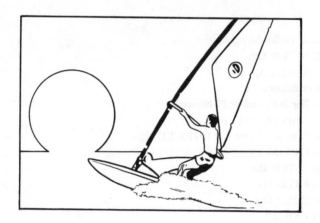

1. LEISURE PARKS

Of all the attractions designed to bring in the paying customer, fairs are probably the oldest form of amusement. Showmen have travelled the roads for centuries, bringing entertainments to towns and villages. The Showmen's Guild has ancient origins, it forms a close society binding its members with rules and expelling those who break its codes of practice: *Lee v Showmen's Guild of Great Britain (1952)*.[1]

Despite many counter-attractions, fairs and showmen still continue to travel, often providing an ancillary service to circuses. Audiences waiting to enter the *Big Top* can pass the time with amusements old and new. The close alliance between fairs and circuses has resulted in their being considered together in the same list of outdoor pursuits in the Public Health Act 1961. Powers are given to local authorities to make byelaws for 'pleasure fairs and roller skating rinks'.[2] The Act is concerned that the places where such activities as are listed in the legislation and provided for the paying public are safe, sanitary, and ordered in such a way that potential nuisances are avoided. Additional powers were conferred on local authorities under the Local Government (Miscellaneous Provisions) Act 1976 for the prevention of fires at fairgrounds. All byelaws must be confirmed by the Secretary of State.

Fairs provide a link between the *watching* and the *doing* elements of recreational pursuits. Fairgoers participate in the activities provided and they also supply entertainment for those who watch the reactions of passengers on roller-coasters, giant octopuses, and other mechanical thrill machines. The amusements have come a long way from the 19th century steam powered Carousel.

As machines became bigger and more powerful they started to be located on permanent sites. Some became leisure parks, basing themselves on the archetype at Coney Island in the US. In the UK, these static attractions became associated with locations which were already a draw to tourists, e.g. Blackpool and Brighton. When combined with accommodation, they were a magnet for families. For an all-in price, food, accommodation, and amusement were packaged and sold to ever-increasing numbers after the successful experiment at Butlin's *camp* at Skegness in the 1930s.

Theme parks

An extension of the Coney Island development has been the theme park. Again, with Disneyland, the US led the way for others to follow. Skilful marketing of popular cartoon characters, allied to fairground events and sophisticated entertainments, has produced a multi-million dollar industry. Other specialised site attractions have been developed, some with themes or combinations of modern amusements featuring water, rides and games. Leading attractions in the UK are those to be found at Thorpe Park, Alton Towers and Beaulieu.

At the end of the list of fairground activities in the 1961 Act is the enigmatic phrase 'Anything similar to the foregoing'.[3] This catch-all category was designed to cover future activities which might be developed at pleasure fairs and which would require regulation. As if to emphasise the possibilities, the Act states that 'Different byelaws may be made ..... for different kinds of pleasure fairs'.[4]

The control of fairs has long been the subject of legislation. The Public Health Acts Amendment Act 1890 enabled byelaws to be made for the prevention of danger from roundabouts, swings and shooting galleries. The long link with *public* Acts of one sort or another reaches from the 19th century to the present day.

Health and Safety

Prior to the passing of the Health and Safety at Work Act 1974, there was no legislation of general application to health and safety. The addition of *work* in the title signals the intention of Parliament to address the problems encountered in the work place, with the emphasis on the prevention of accidents. The title of the statute can give a misleading impression to the casual reader. The Act is not simply concerned with workforces and those who manage them. It is concerned with the obligation of all who control premises and the activities which take place therein.

Every person who has control of premises (other than domestic premises) must ensure, as far as is reasonably practicable, that the premises are safe for all who attend them. Section 3 states that, 'It shall be the duty of every employer to conduct his undertaking in such a way as to ensure, so far as is reasonably practicable, that persons not in his employment who may be affected thereby are not exposed to risks to their health and safety'. Combined with section 4, the wider objective becomes clearer: Those who 'have control of any place where the public may use any plant or substance' must take all reasonably practicable steps to see that the public are kept safe and 'without risk to their health'.

The statute addresses its rules to people rather than places. Personal liability rests on everyone from the chairman of a company to foremen and individual workers. It applies to the self-employed and to those who visit premises. The Act imposes general duties to cover all activities. Where specific activities and types of work are concerned, the Act enables regulations to be made as necessary. The provisions, taken as a whole, are essentially concerned with criminal sanctions as opposed to the recovery of damages following an accident. The provisions apply even where no mishap has occurred. The issue is whether any statutory obligation has been broken. In respect of the *general duties* set out in sections 2 to 8 of the Act, the provisions of section 47 make clear that a breach shall not give rise to civil liability claims based only on the failure to meet the obligations described.

Despite the sanctions of fine and imprisonment allowed for under section 32, few managers seem to appreciate that they are dealing with what are essentially *crimes*. This question of the perception of the offence has not been satisfactorily resolved. One difficulty is that there is a lack of consistency in both enforcement of the legislation and penalties invoked by the courts. In one reported incident, staff at a leisure centre were charging chlorine cylinders for a swimming pool purification system. Chlorine escaped after a valve had been left open. When the gas got into the changing room area, 34 people had to be taken to hospital. Grass over a 100 yard radius was burnt brown. Plants in gardens 200 yards away were damaged. No action was taken.[5]

The enforcement of the law is the responsibility of the Health and Safety Executive (HSE) and is effected by means of the inspection of premises, the issuing of improvement and prohibition notices and prosecution. In carrying out its duties, the HSE is guided by Health and Safety Regulations made by the Secretary of State, usually as the result of proposals made by the Health and Safety Commission (HSC). Following their laying before Parliament, regulations are the subject of an Order made by the Secretary of State which has the force of law.

The HSC is empowered to issue Codes of Practice. These do not of themselves constitute law but they are admissible in evidence before courts and tribunals and are to be taken account of in determining cases.

In addition to the officers of the HSE, under regulations made by the Secretary of State, local authorities have been empowered to appoint inspectors for the prevention and enforcement of the relevant statutory provisions. The title *Factory Inspectors* is applied to these officers but the designation does not correctly describe the wide range of activities, locations or types of undertakings which they are required to supervise.

Fairgrounds, amusement parks and theme parks, in common with all commercial enterprises, are governed in relation to health and safety by the Act. The *industry* has a responsibility to ensure that the public enjoy the amusements provided on properly constructed and maintained equipment and amenities. A Code of Practice was agreed between the *industry* and the HSE in 1986 and its terms have generally been adhered to. The operation of amusements is subject to examination by Factory Inspectors who have reported that, on the whole, standards are good on both fixed and casual sites. The Code requires that *rides* be inspected at least once every 14 months by independent engineers, appointed by the inspectors, and daily by the operators.

An analysis of accidents in 1986 revealed that where accidents occurred, members of the public were 40% to blame; that structural failure accounted for 20%; operator error caused 15% of casualties; the remainder were unattributable to any identifiable cause. In the same year, the HSE gained 5 convictions against leisure operators and issued 17 notices requiring *rides* to be improved or closed.

Despite these measures, there have been a number of accidents resulting in fatalities and serious injuries (2 deaths and 14 injuries in the first six months of 1987). A significant number of accidents have occurred in connection with the latest variety of amusement activities associated with *water complexes*[6]. These have led to calls, notably from the British Safety Council, for greater safety regulations and the appointment of a *Safety Ombudsman*.

Reporting accidents

In 1980, Regulations were introduced requiring the notification of accidents and dangerous occurrences resulting from, or in connection with, a work activity. These have now been entirely replaced by the Reporting of Injuries, Diseases and Dangerous Occurrences Regulations 1985[7] which came into force on April 1, 1986. Every *responsible person*, i.e. the employer or the person controlling the premises at which the incident occurred, has a duty in law to notify and report accidents which result in death of, or serious injury to, any person, whether employee or member of the public. The report must be sent to the local authority as *enforcing authority*. The injuries which must be notified are listed in the Regulations. A record of all such *notifiable accidents* must be kept by the 'responsible person' and kept available for inspection for a minimum of three years. Anyone who contravenes the Regulations is liable, on summary conviction, to a fine not exceeding £2,000 or, on conviction by the Crown Court, to an unlimited fine.

2. LIGHT RAILWAYS

Many theme and leisure parks have *railways* of one variety or another. In addition, there are a growing number of attractions for enthusiasts and the general public provided by light railways. All these operate under provisions established by the Light Railways Act 1896. Several of these railways operate in a dual capacity of providing both a leisure amenity and a means of local transport for the communities they serve, e.g. the Romney, Hythe and Dymchurch Railway.

Such railways may operate under one of two regimes. The Secretary of State may license a project under powers which relate to railways generally,[8] or use a special procedure for light railways and *authorise* such an undertaking.

Neither the 1896 Act, nor the Light Railways Act 1912, define the term *light railway*. Where a *licence* is issued, there is a weight restriction imposed. The locomotive, carriages and vehicles to be used must not exert a weight greater than 8 tons upon the rails by any one pair of wheels. In addition, the train may not exceed 25 miles per hour.[9] Any Order under which a railway is *authorised* will contain similar provisions.

Certain provisions contained in general railway enactments, including those relating to safety, do not apply to light railways unless incorporated in, or applied by, an Order granting *authorisation*.[10] In other respects, the general provisions for railways will be applied. In some cases, additional statutory provisions will apply to light railways, e.g. Public Health Acts: *Wakefield Corporation v Wakefield and District Light Railway Company (1908)*.[11]

Safety is a prime consideration when an application for an Order is being considered. If there appears to be a hazard which constitutes a danger, which is revealed either in the application or in objections made by interested parties, the Minister must investigate. If the danger is substantiated, an application must be denied: *Rother Valley Railway Co Ltd v Minister of Transport (1971)*.[12]

3. PHYSICAL RECREATION

There is a great range of activities from which to select based upon personal preference, affordability and availability. A choice may be made between team events or individual pursuits, competitive games, or personal recreation. Whatever the nature of the activity, it will, to a greater or lesser degree, be regulated by law. It may involve contact with others, the rental of equipment or facilities, entry onto the property of others, or payment for instruction. All of these bring participants into contact with legal rights and duties, not the least of which are those connected with the prevention of accidents, or the award of compensation to casualties, or those suffering other forms of injury.

Bathing

It is debatable whether there is a *right* to bathe in the sea: *Brinckman v Matley (1904)*;[13] but there is no right to use the foreshore for such activities. In most cases, this will be under the control of local authorities who regulate the use of the amenity with byelaws. The Public Health Act 1936[14] provides the statutory authority for control over activities on beaches. The main concerns of the local authorities are related to safety, such that they may, in certain areas, determine where bathing shall be permitted and at what times of the day. Another preoccupation is the preservation of modesty and decency, the standards of which seem to vary with locality and the morality of the moment.

Modern byelaws have had to take into account a *demand* for the right to bathe nude and some authorities have set aside designated areas of their beaches for this activity. In the 19th century, laws were designed to segregate the sexes since men were in the habit of bathing nude. Later, with the freer mingling of the sexes, the emphasis was on the *decency* of the costumes worn by bathers. Today, most authorities are prepared to turn a blind eye to public exposure of the near-naked body unless stirred into action by an outcry against such exposure. In rare instances, it may be that a prosecution at common law might lie for indecency, which includes anything which an ordinary decent man or woman would find shocking, disgusting or revolting: *Knuller Ltd v DPP (1972)*.[15] In the case of the male nude, he might be prosecuted under the Vagrancy Act 1824 for the intention to insult a female!

The rules relating to the beaches will also apply to any estuaries, rivers or lakes, which come under local authority control. Canals and waterways which are regulated by the British Waterways Authority will be governed by its byelaws.

In many of the larger towns and cities the local authorities have, for many years, constructed and operated swimming baths. The basis of law in respect of such amenities is to be found in Part VIII of the Public Health Act 1936, as now incorporated in the Local Government (Miscellaneous Provisions) Act 1976, which considers them as just one aspect of public leisure and recreational activities. The operation of the undertaking will be regulated through byelaws modelled on the 1936 Act. These relate to the general management of the premises and controls to be exercised over persons admitted to them.

Local authorities, like any other *occupiers* public or private, are required to extend the *common duty of care* to all lawful visitors as required by the Occupiers' Liability Act 1957. The Act extends to the premises themselves. Activities which are engaged in by staff and visitors are more likely to be the subject of the wider law of negligence. The standards of care imposed on the authority will relate to the selection and training of suitable staff, for whom they will assume vicarious liability should they be guilty of negligent acts.

Bathers are usually admitted by ticket which will refer them to the terms under which the facilities may be used, thereby making byelaws and other forms of regulation part of the contract. Should the management wish to exclude liability they might incur, e.g. for property left in changing rooms, then they may do so provided notices, or other communications to visitors, do not fall foul of the Unfair Contract Terms Act 1977.

Swimming pools do present particular problems for the management. These arise out of the hazards inherent in water, together with the state of the pool and facilities, such as diving boards which are provided for the use of bathers. The activities of bathers may cause hazards both to themselves and to other users of the amenities. The physical hazards which might be expected to occur, e.g. sharp tiles, slippery surfaces caused by wear, need to be guarded against by regular inspection. Hidden dangers from infection will also demand high standards of hygiene and preventative methods to be employed by the operators.

The standard of care to be displayed in controlling the actions of bathers will be necessarily high. Liability will be determined, inter alia, by whether staff could reasonably have anticipated the event which occurred: *Clark v Bethnal Green Corporation (1939)*.[16] If the management allows the pool to become congested then the likelihood of mishaps occurring becomes greater.

Spectators at the pool side are also entitled to have a duty of care shown for them. This may extend to a parent who suffers nervous shock at seeing a child in danger. The type of *injury* sustained by a parent is reasonably foreseeable by one who does not discharge the duty of care which may be expected of him: *McLoughlin v O'Brien (1982)*.[17]

Sports centres

The modern concept of sports centres can, in most cases, trace its origin to the swimming baths provided by the local authority as a civic amenity. Many are operated by the same bodies today. Centres and swimming baths have a common basis for their existence in the Local Government (Miscellaneous Provisions) Act 1972. The Act lists those activities which it anticipates will be provided in such establishments.[18] As with pools, obligations towards lawful visitors exist in both contract and tort.

Participants who engage in physical activities may reasonably be expected to accept injuries which occur in the ordinary course of events: *Simms v Leigh RFC (1969).*[19] Depending on the physical condition of the premises, a plaintiff may have grounds for a claim where there is a defect which contributes to the injury which he sustains: *Gillmore v LCC (1938).*[20]

Where reliance is placed on the skill or expertise of members of staff at centres, the proprietors will be required to demonstrate that such staff displayed a standard of care commensurate with that which might usually be expected or a higher level where this is claimed for them: *Jones v LCC (1932).*[21]

Inattention towards the safety of those using particular apparatus may result in liability for negligence being attributed to the management: *Gibbs v Barking Corporation (1936).*[22] Where there is a high risk because of the type of apparatus being used, e.g. a trampoline, then the standard of care attributed to supervisors will be higher: *Moore v Redditch and Bromsgrove Gymnastic Club (1981).*[23] Where the supervisor cannot exercise proper control over events, because he is trying to do two jobs at the same time, he will not be able to show an acceptable standard of care towards his charges; nor where activities are taking place in premises unsuitable by reason of inadequate size: *Ralph v LCC (1947).*[24]

Where participants engage in organised games it is expected that the rules will be obeyed. There can be no *volenti* defence where one player breaks the rules and injures another: *Lewis v Brookshaw (1968).*[25] Liability may be incurred because of wilful intent or reckless disregard for the safety of others. Actions may be brought both against a *player* who is alleged to have caused the injury complained of and the organisers: *Harrison v Vincent (1982);*[26] but he who alleges negligence must prove it: *O'Dowd v Fraser Nash (1951).*[27]

A golfer who negligently swings a club may be liable for the injury he causes to a bystander: *Cleghorn v Oldham (1927).*[28] Where balls are hit out of a grounds, and passers by are struck and injured, each case will be judged on its merits such that the remoteness of risk in being hit

346

by an exceptional cricket shot may disallow one claim: *Bolton v Stone (1951)*;[29] but the risk may be judged more likely in the case of a golf shot: *Lamond v Glasgow Corporation (1968)*.[30]

Where it may not be possible to show sufficient lack of care associated with *foreseeability* in order to sustain a claim in negligence, it may be possible to claim under the different rules of Nuisance: *Castle v St Augustine's Links Ltd (1922)*.[31]

4. PERSONAL TRANSPORTATION

The use of the means of transport as a vehicle for enjoyment, and not simply as a matter of necessity, has become part of recreational activity. The earliest form of popular transport for its own sake was the bicycle. Tourist activity involving its use began early in the history of leisure pursuits, both on an individual basis and through organisation by the Cyclists' Touring Club. Other activities combining sport with mobility have extended the range and opportunity for a wider audience.

Riding

Once the privilege of the few, horse riding for pleasure has come within the reach of many. While some may own their own horses, the cost of feed and stabling, together with fees for the service of veterinarians and farriers, has caused more people to hire their mounts from riding establishments. This may be on a fairly regular basis, or the once a year pony trekking holiday.

Anyone who wishes to establish a riding stables must hold the appropriate licence. This requirement was instituted by the Riding Establishment Act of 1964, followed by that of 1970. The issuing authorities are the district councils, the councils of London boroughs, and the Common Council of the City of London.

The licensing authority require to be satisfied as to the experience of the applicant as a horse manager, the adequacy of stabling, and measures proposed in relation to safety and fire precautions. Licences, if granted, are renewable annually. Since there is an inherent risk of accident to riders, a condition for the grant of a licence is that the applicant has sufficient insurance to cover the perils associated with riding.

Considerable attention is also paid to the welfare of the horses. It is an offence to let out or use a horse, for instruction or hire, when it is such a condition that riding would be likely to cause suffering to the animal. A further offence may be committed if a horse is used with defective equipment, so as to be the cause of suffering to the mount, or which may endanger the rider by making him susceptible to accident.

Horses may be ridden on most public highways but in practice, save for access, most rides are on bridleways or on open land. A bridleway is defined in the National Parks and Access to the Countryside Act 1949 as 'a highway over which the public has the following, but no other rights of way, that is to say a right of way on foot and a right of way on horseback or leading a horse'. Bicycles may be used but they must concede right of way to walkers and those on horseback.

The local authority may make an agreement with a landowner for the dedication by the latter of a bridleway over his land. Alternatively, it may make an order for such a right of way where it considers that this would add to the convenience or enjoyment of a substantial section of the public. The rights of all those who have an interest in such land must be considered before such an order is made. It must receive the consent of the Secretary of State before it can become effective and all landowners who are affected by it are entitled to apply for compensation.

Under the terms of the 1949 Act, local authorities are required to produce definitive maps on which bridle paths are marked. Such maps, showing other rights of way as well, must be reviewed and kept up to date at five-yearly intervals. The Countryside Act 1968 requires that every right of way must be signposted at its access points. Anyone removing or defacing such signs is liable to prosecution. Once bridleways are so defined on maps on or after January 1 1960, highway authorities have a duty to maintain them and to see to it that they do not become overgrown.

Aerial Sports

The Air Navigation Order 1972 defines a glider as being in the nature of a 'heavier than air aircraft'.[32] Provided that such an aircraft stays within British air space, and is not used for public transport, no certificate of airworthiness is required.

Public transport is defined in the regulations as 'flying or intended by the operator to fly..... for hire or reward given or promised for the carriage of passengers or goods on such flight'.[33] It also covers situations where passengers or goods are carried gratuitously.

A glider pilot not engaged in public transport does not need a pilot's licence nor does his glider need to be registered. However, no person below the age of seventeen years may have sole control of any glider in motion. Because of the possible danger from collisions occurring at landing grounds, the Air Traffic Control Regulations impose landing controls on aerodromes from which gliders are flown.

These regulations are adequate for airfields but they were introduced before the advent of the *hang glider*. These machines, which more resemble kites than accepted designs for gliders, have caused problems which were not immediately apparent when they started to appear in the skyways. They require no mechanical power to propel them into the air, relying instead on air currents generated on hillside take-offs. This meant that they were not subject to controls which existed in respect of traditional aircraft.

Another spin-off from the original glider concept, allied with the hang glider, has been the development of the powered machine nicknamed the *microlite*. This version comes within the category of light aircraft which were covered by the original regulations. The Air Navigation Order 1985 now covers a much wider listing of all machines, powered or not, and establishes rules for their operation.

The law with regard to the flying of aircraft was examined earlier (Chapter IX) as was the issue of passenger safety. However, it is worthy of note at this point that a passenger engaging in a joy ride when he knows that the pilot is very drunk cannot afterwards claim damages for personal injuries caused by the pilot's negligence. This rule applies even if the passenger himself was drunk at the time when he agreed to the flight so long as he was capable of knowing what he was doing and of appreciating the risks involved: *Morris v Murray (1990).*[34]

The same rule would apply to such a passenger in a balloon, which present peculiar hazards of its own. Hot air ballooning has become a very popular, if somewhat expensive, pastime. The balloonist cannot always predict precisely where his machine will come to earth, or on occasion how! Recently a balloon landed in a farmer's field whereupon it was seized by the farmer who refused to hand it over to its owner until he had been paid £600. He was sued in trespass by the balloonist and was ordered by the court to pay £3,500 by way of damages for trespass to goods - the balloon. In return the farmer was awarded £150 for the trespass to his land but refused compensation for sheep which he alleged has been stampeded by the intrepid balloonist's descent: *Pine v Ingleton (1993).*[35]

Boats

Local authorities have long held powers to control the use of boats on lakes within public parks and on lakes and waterways under their supervision. Those powers are today contained in the Local Government Planning and Land Act 1980[36] which replaces the provisions contained in section 172 of the Public Health Act 1875 in this regard.

Where boats are chartered for leisure services on inland or coastal waters, the Local Government (Miscellaneous Provisions) Act 1976 provides a framework for control. In addition, where privately owned boats operate within coastal waters their activities are regulated by the Merchant Shipping Acts. Such boats, or more correctly *ships*, trading in coastal waters require a licence issued by the Department of Trade. Pleasure boats on inland waterways, other than those under the control of the British Waterways Board (BWD), are licensed by local authorities. The term *pleasure boat*, which refers to craft let for hire to the public or used for the carriage of passengers for reward, is defined in the Public Health Acts Amendment Act 1907, section 94.

Such craft may still fall within the definition even though at other times, when not carrying passengers, they are used for other activities such as commercial fishing. The legislation requires boatmen to be licensed and for byelaws to be made to regulate the operation of boats. These will provide measures to control the use of various craft for activities associated with water skiing and *parascending*. The use of byelaws enables local authorities to carry through measures for the safety and enjoyment of the public generally. New forms of leisure pursuits are constantly being developed which, whilst enjoyed by those who participate, may infringe the pleasure of other water users. The advent of the sailboard has added to the hazards posed to swimmers and created more demands on the rescue services.

The greatest hazards occur in harbour waters. No licence is needed for driving speed-boats. They can be bought and used by complete novices, something not permitted of drivers on the public highway. No safety checks are required and the combination of unseaworthy craft, with powerful engines, in the hands of inexperienced and reckless users, presents a threat to all on the water. In cases where local byelaws are introduced under the provisions of section 76 of the Public Health Act 1961, activities which occur up to 1,000 yards offshore can be the subject of police prosecutions. These measures do not adequately control increasingly-used amenity water and further legislation is overdue.

The hazards from power boats may extend from the water itself to present annoyance to neighbouring landowners. Where organised competitions are concerned, the courts have been prepared to take action. The tort of nuisance has been invoked to tackle the problem: *Kennaway v Thompson (1981)*.[37] This case is notable for the fact that, at first instance, the plaintiff failed to get an injunction but was awarded damages. The Court of Appeal took the view that it was inequitable to allow a defendant to *buy* his way out of responsibility to those affected by his activities. It considered that the noise from boat racing and water skiing events merited the imposition of a limited injunction in addition to the award of damages. Such action is possible where an organiser of noisy activities can be pursued in the courts, but these remedies are not possible in the case of casual individual users. Legislative controls, such as those imposed to silence noise from road vehicles, would seem to be called for.

Canals

A greater degree of control is possible in regard to the recreational use of the canal system. These inland waterways, which were constructed for commercial traffic, have become increasingly popular as a leisure amenity. Many were bought up by the railway companies and allowed to fall into decay and dereliction in order to stifle competition. When the railways were *nationalised* (q.v.) the canals, previously in the hands of the private railway companies, came under the British Transport Commission together with others which had stayed out of the clutches of rail operators. When the BTC was wound up, its duties in respect of canals passed to the British Waterways Board (BWB) under the terms of section 31(5) of the Transport Act 1962.

The duties of the BWB are many and varied. The principal duty of the Board is to maintain the canals for both commercial and leisure use. Part VIII of the Transport Act 1968 classifies the waterways into, 'commercial, cruising and remainder'. The latter category has caused the most difficulty since the Board is not required to keep them in water, or repaired, other than to see that they are not completely destroyed. They have become the target for action by groups of enthusiasts, the jewel in whose crown will be the re-opening of the Kennet and Avon canal linking London with Bristol.

The focus of recreational attention is upon the *cruising* canals. Section 1 to 4 of the 1968 Act describes them as being, 'principally for cruising, fishing or other recreational purposes'. The duty of the BWB is to maintain them in a state which permits their use for cruising in powered passenger boats. One irony of this is that the Board seeks to control, and even prohibits, the use of towpaths by the original form of motive power, the barge horse, because this would require it to keep the paths in a better condition than that which is suitable for ramblers.

The Board has extensive powers to regulate the use of its property under byelaws. Speed limits are strictly controlled because of the potential damage to the banks by the wash from boats and collision hazards at locks and in pounds. The licensing fees charged to commercial and leisure craft, on a sliding scale for footage and use, provide some revenue for the upkeep of the waterways by the Board. The 1968 Act allows local authorities to assist private organisations seeking to maintain or improve canals, or to make them accessible to the public for recreational purposes. The authorities and the water boards have a vested interest in canals since they are valuable sources of local water supply, especially from the splendid reservoirs built by the old canal companies to keep the *cuts* in water. Many important sites of industrial archaeology associated with the canals prove an added tourist attraction.

The canals have become an important part of leisure activity. They provide miniature country walks in urban areas and have long been associated with wildlife and countryside pursuits, not the least of which are fishing and bird watching. The canals bring the countryside within the reach of city dwellers and their use as public routeways along the towpaths has long been recognised: *Grand Junction Canal Co v Petty (1888).*[38]

NOTES:

1. (1952) 2 QB 329.
2. s 75 (3).
3. s 75 (3) (g).
4. s 75 (5).
5. *Management Today* February 1984 p 83.
6. *Independent* 30 Jul 87.
7. SI 1985 No 2023.
8. Regulation of Railways Act 1868 s 27. See also the Cowes and Newport Light Railway Order 1980 SI 1660.

9. Ibid s 28 provisions (1) and (2).
10. Ibid s 12 (2).
11. (1908) AC 293 HL.
12. (1971) Ch 515 CA.
13. (1904) 2 Ch 313.
14. s 231.
15. (1972) 2 A11 ER 898.
16. (1939) 55 TLR 519.
17. (1982) 2 A11 ER 111.
18. s 19 (1).
19. (1969) 2 A11 ER 923.
20. (1938) 4 A11 ER 331.
21. (1932) 96 JP 371.
22. (1936) A11 ER 115.
23. (1981) unreported.
24. (1947) 63 TLR 546 CA.
25. (1968) 120 NLJ 413.
26. (1982) RTR 8.
27. (1951) WLR 173.
28. (1927) 43 TLR 465.
29. (1951) AC 850.
30. (1968) SLT 291.
31. (1922) TLR 615.
32. SI 1972/129 Sch 1 Part A.
33. Ibid Art 89(6)(a)(i).
34. (1990) *Guardian* 14 November
35. (1993) *Guardian* 3 April
36. Sch 34 Part XVI.
37. (1981) QB 88.
38. (1888) 21 QB 273.

CHAPTER XVIII

Countryside Pursuits

1. URBANISATION

Two hundred years ago the great majority of people in Britain lived and worked on the land. With the growth of industrial centres and rapid urbanisation the landscape began to change dramatically. The focus of the new industrial society was the towns and the rural areas, which had once dominated the economy, went into a decline from which it took many years to recover.

The growing industrial and commercial centres made demands on the land for space to expand. Linear expansion along the roads was followed with in-filling in a haphazard manner. The earliest attempts at planning were concentrated on the need to improve health and sanitary conditions. The Public Health Acts of the 19th century coincided with the growth in local government which was being reorganised. The result was that both planning and regulation of public works were concentrated at local level.

Building works in Victorian England reflect both civic pride and growing prosperity. Parks were among the many memorials which industrialists chose to immortalise their achievements. Some were established by municipal corporations comprised of successful local businessmen, others were endowed by individuals. In one sense, the town parks represented attempts to reproduce the private parks of the great landowners. In another, there was a philanthropic desire to provide some breathing spaces within industrial areas where all were admitted without charge. Little green islands, imitating idealised country scenes, began to bloom in the great new industrial centres like Birmingham.

Town parks

In 1875, the *green* movement was given official approval by section 164 of the Public Health Act which authorised urban centres to create parks and to make byelaws for their regulation. Before 1875, it had been necessary to enact private Acts of Parliament to endow and maintain land for the public use.

The 1875 Act remains the basis of the law under which parks are created and maintained. Other statutory provisions have followed the founding enactment but the development has been fragmentary and piecemeal. The Open Spaces Act 1906 enabled land to be taken into public ownership by local authorities to be maintained, at their expense, for the benefit of the communities they served. This, again, represents a reversion to a much older idea, that of public *commons* held to the use of rural populations. The object was not to protect grazing rights but to allow people to enjoy recreational pursuits.

Land has been acquired by various means. Some has been donated by trustees of charitable bodies; old commons, engulfed by towns, have been surrendered by local inhabitants; some has been bought; some, not infrequently, includes disused burial grounds surrendered by various churches. Once acquired, the local authority is obliged to keep the land as an *open space* and to allow controlled public use. The area may be enclosed, or not, and may have some buildings on it, or it may have been waste and unoccupied.

Open land which has not been taken into public protection has been a source of public concern for a number of years. Too often, such land becomes a rubbish tip. Where this happens, local authorities possess powers to compel owners or occupiers to tidy up their property. Where it is felt that the amenity value of any area is 'seriously injured' by the condition in which land is being kept, the authority may serve a notice on the occupier to abate the nuisance within a given time. The Court of Appeal had decided in such a case that whether or not land is properly described as 'open land' is a matter of fact to be judged in each case: *Stephens v Cuckfield RDC (1960).*[1]

Where rubbish accumulates on any land so as to be detrimental to a neighbourhood, notices may be served on owners to remove it. Notices apply to private property and open land alike: *Britt v Buckinghamshire CC (1963).*[2] The deliberate dumping of large objects 'on any land in the open air or on any other land forming part of a highway' is an offence.[3]

The dropping of litter is also an offence under the terms of the Litter Act 1983 which consolidates previous legislation dealing with the problem. An offence is only committed where litter is deposited in any place in the open air to which the public has access without payment. The depositing of material must constitute a 'defacement by litter' at the particular location.[4] Surprisingly, the legislation does not make reference to leaving litter in places to which the public is admitted on payment of an entrance fee.

The 1875 Act authorised local authorities to engage in the 'laying out, planting, improving and maintaining of public walks and pleasure grounds', a policy which was extended by its successors down to provisions for parks in the Local Government (Miscellaneous Provisions) Act 1976. The power to *improve* has been widely interpreted. All manner of recreational pursuits have been provided for in public parks. Bowling greens, tennis courts, boating lakes, bandstands and other amenities are widely encountered.

Horticultural shows, gymkhanas and animal *shows* are often held which require closure of all or some part of a park. Since this is a denial of public use, such closure was allowed for in Public Health legislation.[5] This allows for a closure of no more than 12 days in any one year, with no more than 6 such days to run consecutively, and never including Sundays. The local authority is given a discretion as to whether or not admission charges are to be levied. Parks still host travelling fairs, especially at public holiday times. Circuses too were once frequent visitors, now less so.

The 1972 Act allows parks authorities to close their premises for the performance of open air theatre, concerts, dances and other public entertainments.[6] Where such events are held, there will be attendant car parking problems. Space in parks can be set aside for vehicles,[7] but this is only permitted where it is ancillary to the main purpose of the original activity envisaged by the 1875 Act, i.e. permitting the public enjoyment of an open air space. Parts of parks are not allowed to be used for this purpose where the primary intention of those car-users is to visit a nearby attraction not within the park in question: *Att Gen. v Southampton Corporation (1978).*[8]

Town parks were established for the benefit of local people but they have also grown to be an amenity which attracts visitors. Their popularity with tourists to traditional holiday centres is beyond doubt, as is the world reputation of the London parks.

2. COUNTRY PARKS

It is but a small step from creating stylised images of rural England in town parks to turning the countryside itself into an idealised sylvan pattern. That is how some who live in rural areas view moves to either conserve or develop their localities for uses other than traditional, but declining, agricultural industries. Farm land should be kept for the people who live and work in the countryside, any basic change in land use will only accelerate the further erosion of rural life. So runs one line of argument. 'Applications by farmers to convert their farms into golf courses or leisure parks have already alarmed local citizens .... we have enough golf courses to satisfy demand and leisure parks are surely better as an integrated public effort as rural lungs'.[9]

Be that as it may, the Countryside Act 1968 allows local authorities to establish country parks. The logic seems to be that if town parks have proved their worth, why not do the same in rural areas, at least in locations close to urban centres, since dwellers in rural areas seem to have no need of amenities which exist other than naturally. To add fuel to the flame, power has been given to local authorities to compulsorily purchase land for the creation of country parks.[10]

Such a place is described in the 1968 Act as 'any site on the countryside appearing ... suitable or adaptable ... to provide a country park, that is to say a park or pleasure ground to be used for that purpose'.[11] Such amenities are clearly designed to be run for profit, since the Act specifically excludes section 164 of the Public Health Act 1875 which gave the public free unrestricted use of town parks. The point is also made in section 8 of the Act, which permits the local

357

authority to provide facilities and services for the enjoyment and convenience of the public, including meals and refreshments, parking places for vehicles and lavatory accommodation .... facilities and services for open air recreation'. Foreseeing that such provision might endanger existing facilities and services in such places, the Act decrees that only if these are inadequate to satisfy demand shall additional amenities be provided. This is specious, since existing facilities are bound to be inadequate if demand is to be increased by encouraging a greater volume of visitors.

With this in mind it is worth noting that country parks are not subject to the same rules against closure as those in towns, such sites would seem ripe for commercial exploitation.

In order to maximise the potential for growth, the 1968 Act makes provision for water recreation where a park 'comprises any waterway the kinds of open air recreation for which the local authority may provide facilities and services ..... (which) shall include sailing, boating, bathing and fishing'. The terms of reference are also to include sites which are 'bounded by the sea, or by any waterway which is not part of the sea'.[12]

Such waterways might include those controlled by a Water Authority. Each authority has a duty to 'take steps to secure the use of water and land associated with it for the purpose of recreation'.[13] Reservoirs are frequently used for water recreation, demonstrating authorities' compliance with their instructions to 'use the water and any land associated with it to the best use'.

Development plans

Under the Town and Country Planning Act 1971, Part II, each county council must produce development plans for its area. *Structure plans* are the responsibility of the county authority while *local plans* are generally devolved to district councils. Each must take account of the plans of neighbouring authorities and of the economic planning and development of the region as a whole. Structure plans must be approved by the Secretary of State for the Environment before they become operative.

Generally speaking, such a plan will consist of a map supported by a written statement together with other maps and documents amplifying any proposals. These may relate to the proposed future development of the land to which they refer. In particular, development plans may define sites for 'proposed roads, buildings, airfields, parks, pleasure grounds, nature reserves and other open spaces'.[14]

A development plan must be reviewed with a new survey by the planning authority at least once every five years after the date of approval by the Secretary of State. It may, however, be reviewed at any time for plans are under constant appraisal.

Subject to planning approval, country parks may be developed by private interests. Such developments usually take the form of a multi-use site proposal, usually associated with a *Theme*. A good example of the genre is the Sherwood Country Park built by a Dutch company on former Ministry of Defence land. Its theme is trees and water and the development has led to pressure on ancient broad leaf woodland in a site of *special scientific interest*. The company has similar sites in Holland and Belgium with plans for others in France and Germany and five more in Britain.

Such developments are not without their critics, notably the Council for the Preservation of Rural England. The Council oppose the proliferation of such parks, principally on the basis that commercial development denies public access to woodlands, creating something which is 'wholly irrelevant to the experience of the countryside'.[15]

The Forestry Commission

Development of woodlands by commercial activity is not new. Forest Parks run by the Forestry Commission have been in existence since 1935. The Commission itself was founded by the Forestry Act 1919 with the task of replenishing the stocks of timber consumed in the Great War. By the mid 1950s, it owned over 2 million acres of land. The further potential of Commission property was recognised by the 1968 Act.

The Act specifically empowered the Commission to 'provide or arrange for or assist in the provision of tourist recreational or sporting facilities and any equipment, facilities or works ancillary thereto'.[16] Authorisation was given for accommodation to be provided for visitors, camping and caravan sites, refreshment facilities and general amenities appropriate to the enjoyment of the countryside. The Commission was empowered to make byelaws for the proper management of such activities and for control of visitors to the forests. This was in addition to the wide powers it had already been given in the Forestry Act 1967. These enabled the Commission to prohibit and regulate hazards to its land and amenities while, at the same time, allowing the public to have reasonable access for exercise and recreation.[17]

Offences committed against the byelaws are punishable by fines. Offenders may also be removed from the Commission's land after due warnings have been given. A voluntary Code of Practice is produced for visitors, to prevent breaches of the regulations.

The 1968 Act gave new powers to the Commission to plant woodlands as an amenity, particularly near towns, the purpose being stated as recreational rather than commercial.

3. NATIONAL PARKS

In recent times, there has been a recognition that there is a need to preserve natural resources in the public interest. The Countryside Act 1968, section 11, requires every government department and public body to exercise their functions with conservation in mind. At the same time, due regard is to be had for the needs of agriculture and forestry together with those of the rural communities. Reconciling all these conflicting interests has not been easy or, some would argue, possible.

In some countries, National Parks are recognised as national assets and have been taken into public ownership. After centuries of adherence to the protection of private property rights, the British Government, on behalf of the public, could not bring itself to break with tradition. As a consequence, the land which is designated as part of a National Park is still largely in private hands. The Secretary of State for the Environment and the Secretary of State for Wales do have powers to buy land on behalf of the public or to take leases.

The definition of a National Park is contained in section 5 of the National Parks and Access to the Countryside Act 1949. There are, at present, ten such Parks, the first designated being that of the Peak District in 1955. Another for Mid Wales has been proposed while a Bill presently before Parliament will, if passed, create similar rules for the Norfolk Broads.

The lands comprising the Parks have been taken under public control because of their natural beauty and their amenity value for open air recreation. They have become so popular with the public that many sites are suffering from wear and tear. In 1987, a programme of work on footpaths costing £770,000 had to be launched in the Yorkshire Dales Park. Much of the money has had to be spent repairing the damage caused to the Pennine Way which crosses the Park.

Because the land is still private property, for the most part, control in the public interest is exercised by maintaining access arrangements and by planning controls. The Parks cover about 10% of the land area of England and Wales. Some are entirely within the area of one planning authority, e.g. the Lake District, administered by Cumbria. Others span more than one county. Where this occurs, the Secretary of State can create *Joint Planning Boards* (JPB), as in the case of the Peak District. Where the Park falls mainly within one county, but overlaps others, control may be placed in the hands of the dominant authority. The administrative framework for control of the Parks is set out in Schedule 17 of the Local Government Act 1972.

Where a JPB has been established, the Board will exercise the functions of a planning authority in respect of a Park. In other cases, a committee must be set up to work in conjunction with the local planning authority. Unlike a JPB, a Committee does not enjoy a separate existence but works in conjunction with its Authority. The Authority must discharge certain statutory functions through the Committee but in other matters, e.g. tree preservation and the control of waste land, it exercises powers concurrently with it.

JPBs and Committees are required to produce 5-year plans setting out management policies for the Parks under their control. These are submitted to the Secretary of State for the Environment who, because of lobbying by interest groups and considerations of *policy*, has *modified* many structure plans.

Planning controls

The system of development control for England and Wales was originally established by the Town and Country Planning Act 1947 (now the 1971 Act). Control is effected by the expedient of granting, or refusing, planning permission for 'development'.

Under section 24 of the 1971 Act (as amended), the Secretary of State for the Environment has made the Town and Country Planning General Development Order 1977 (GDO) which has been amended several times since. The time would seem to be ripe for a consolidating enactment.

Schedule 1 to the GDO sets out in detail the 30 classes of development for which planning permission is granted by the Order. These classes do not require planning permission. In the main, they are concerned with what might be regarded as matters which do not substantially affect an area. However, any alteration which affects land within a conservation area, an area of outstanding natural beauty or a National Park, is governed by the Special Development Order of 1985, as amended in 1986 and 1987.[18] These provisions effectively prevent the scope of *permitted development*, allowed by the GDO, from extending to these protected areas. The granting of planning permission in the Parks is, therefore, subject to special scrutiny to ensure that the design and appearance, as well as the location, of any new development fits properly into its surroundings. Attention has to be paid not only to the natural scenery but also to the traditional character of buildings in the area and the use of local materials.

The Government has been contemplating even stricter controls. It is considering whether National Park Authorities should be given power to make Landscape Conservation Orders under section 29 of the Wildlife and Countryside Act 1981.

A major concern has been that tree planting, by the Forestry Commission and private developers, has not been subject to planning control within Parks. The latter may now find that planting trees is no longer as rewarding as they thought. The tax advantages which this gave have been removed by the Chancellor of the Exchequer in his Budget proposals for 1988. Meanwhile, the Forestry Commission's regiments of conifers march on.

The Countryside Commission

The National Parks and Access to the Countryside Act 1949 established the National Parks Commission. The title was changed in 1968 to the Countryside Commission under which name it now appears in the Wildlife and Countryside Act 1981.[19]

The Commission was established as a corporate body which is not an agent of the Crown nor does it hold property on behalf of the State. Its principal duties are to:

1. Preserve and enhance the natural beauty of England and Wales;

2. Encourage the provision of facilities in the National Parks;

3. Promote enjoyment of open air recreation in Parks.

It may charge for its services and may accept gifts and contributions. It is charged with keeping a watching brief over all countryside matters, by liaison with local planning authorities, and advising those who submit proposals for developments. It may engage in experimental schemes, alone or in conjunction with interested public bodies and, with the permission of the Secretary of State, it may manage projects.

Its prime function, under the 1949 and 1981 legislation, is the designation of land for inclusion in a National Park. Once designated, the Commission acts as an advisory, information and education agency and as a *watchdog* for structure plans and proposed developments within Parks.

It is also involved in giving advice and assistance for the creation of 'long distance routes'. Part IV of the 1949 Act makes special provision for the Commission to assist with the creation of these recreational walks for travellers on foot, horseback or bicycle. Plans are made based on reports submitted to the Commission for the maintenance of routes and the provision of ancillary services along the way. Once formulated, the Commission makes proposals to the responsible Ministers, e.g. Transport, Environment, Defence, who may then respond by approving, modifying, or rejecting such proposals and notifying the appropriate local authorities accordingly.

When drawing up their development plans, the local authorities are obliged to confer with the Commission where any Parks are affected. The authorities at County level must also publish maps showing moorland and heath which it is especially important to conserve. Landowners have a right to lodge objections to any Orders which may seek to stop agricultural activities or which forbid forestry work.

The role of the Secretary of State for the Environment is to give directions to the Commission. In the past, this exercise of power has been used sparingly but it is becoming increasingly apparent that the Secretary would like to relax planning constraints on the development of farmland which may affect the Parks.

At a time when the Council for the Preservation of Rural England is arguing strongly for the protection of rural areas, the Secretary of State for the Environment appears to consider that sites in North Yorkshire, within the North Yorkshire Moors National Parks, might be suitable for the dumping of nuclear waste. Meanwhile, the Nature Conservancy Council is carrying out an audit of state-owned nature reserves with a view to selling them off to commercial enterprises.[20]

The value of the Parks as tourist attractions is not lost on

Government. The number of individual visits, daily, during one month in the summer of 1987, was put at 200 millions. In any one year, there are about 90 million visitors. The greatest danger to the Parks is from the gradual breakdown of the European Common Agricultural policy. Upland farmers may be worst hit and will seek alternative 'cash crops' in the form of tree plantations. The alternative might be to pay farmers to carry out conservation policies, but farmers in Snowdonia have already voiced their objections to becoming *Museum Pieces* as they see it.

4. CONSERVATION

In addition to its specific duties in respect of National Parks, the Countryside Commission has a general responsibility to advise the Secretary of State for the Environment on matters affecting the natural beauty of the countryside generally.[21]

In exercising this function, the Commission may issue Orders designating *Areas of Outstanding Natural Beauty*. Local interests must be consulted, before the Order is made, and it will require confirmation by the Secretary of State. Where designation is confirmed, powers similar to those which exist in respect of Parks will be provided. Whereas byelaws may be made in respect of Parks, the same does not appear to be the case for *Areas*. In Parks, wardens may be appointed to enforce the local authority byelaws; in *Areas* wardens, if appointed, may only *advise* visitors. These differences seem to illustrate the lack of an overall policy for the countryside.

Often there is opposition to the designation of *Areas*[22] and some authorities seem unwilling to incur expense in preserving or enhancing natural beauty although, as with the Parks, they have powers to give grants or make loans for this purpose.[23] Local authorities are required to review maps of their areas every five years and to update the information contained therein as it relates to areas of mountain, moorland, foreshore, and cliffs. These maps, showing places with important conservation needs to be protected, must be put on sale to the public.

Areas of Special Scientific Interest

The Wildlife and Countryside Act 1981 places upon the Nature Conservancy Council a duty to identify *sites of special scientific interest*, such need having been first identified in the 1949 Act. The special interest may be by reason of flora, fauna, or geological importance. Where an interest is identified, the Council is required to notify the local planning authority, the Secretary of State, and the owner or occupier of the land.[24]

The notification will list activities which are likely to harm the site. Should any of these activities be carried out without giving a minimum three months' notice to the Council, an offence will have been committed. In an emergency, the requirement as to notice may be waived. The procedure seems to have little deterrent effect for some landowners.[25]

More extensive powers exist under which the Secretary of State may make Orders forbidding specified operations on such sites in order to protect the survival of plants or animals, where it is in the national or international interest to do so. Where the Secretary fails to live up to expectations, he may find himself in conflict with the European Commission, a fate which has befallen his colleague at the Scottish Office.[26] Where a person is convicted of breaking the terms of an Order, the court has the power to order the land to be restored to its original condition at the expense of the individual responsible.

The 1981 Act makes it an offence to kill many types of animals and birds, or to destroy specified plants. Both visitors and landowners may be guilty of offences.[27]

Coastlines

Large stretches of coastline are within National Parks, or Areas of Outstanding Natural Beauty, and may also feature Areas of Special Scientific Interest. The coastline is particularly vulnerable to development and the Department of the Environment has issued guidelines for its conservation in the hope that a flexible approach to controls, allied with good management, may be the best way forward.[28]

The 1981 Act enables the Nature Conservancy Council to seek designation of the foreshore, or sea bed, as marine nature reserves to be managed by the Council or in co-operation with local landowners. If such measures are inadequate, there are provisions for the compulsory purchase of the land in question. With the possibility of *privatisation* of nature reserves, the powers seem unlikely to be called in aid.

In 1985, the Countryside Commission published an *Access Charter* to assist visitors to the countryside.[29] It makes several worthwhile points which are meant to keep the peace between landowners and land-users. It emphasises that whilst trespassers may be required to leave land, they must not be threatened with firearms or deliberately injured. The old ploy of keeping a bull in a field, as a deterrent to those seeking to use a right of way, is highlighted as an offence punishable by fine under the 1981 Act, combined with the provisions of the Health and Safety at Work Act 1974.

The Charter deals with a variety of other matters, included amongst which is information concerning camping and picnicking. Such activities may not be engaged in on private land without the consent of the occupier or owner. Nor may the public use commons or village greens for these purposes.

The use of caravans has long been associated with use of the countryside and may, in any numbers, be a threat to the amenity of National Parks and other areas. To control this potential nuisance, a system of licensing for sites was introduced by the Caravan Sites and Control of Development Act 1960.

A prerequisite for the granting of a licence to a landowner, wishing to provide facilities for caravans, is planning permission. If the permission is limited by time, so too will be the licence granted by the district council for the locality concerned. Each licence is distinctive in that it will relate the statutory guidelines to the particular features of individual sites. Conditions may be imposed on the use of the site. These are not necessarily related to public health requirements but usually reflect the opinion of the council as to the impact which it is believed a site will have on local amenities: *Esdell Caravan Park Ltd v Hemel Hempstead UDC (1965).*[30] Schedule 1 to the 1960 Act lists exceptions to the requirement for licensing, but this does not obviate the need for planning permission: *Klein v Whitstable UDC (1958).*[31]

Local authorities have a discretion, under the Countryside Act 1968, as to whether they will provide picnic sites or car parking facilities. If they decide to do so, they may acquire land compulsorily for these purposes and either run the facility as a commercial venture themselves or let it to an individual at a commercial rent.

5. WILDLIFE

The Charter for Access to the Countryside notes that going out into the countryside is one of Britain's most popular recreational activities. It adds that 'watching birds, observing the natural life of the countryside and studying wildflowers are increasingly popular pastimes'.

It is notable that, until the Wildlife and Countryside Act 1981, there was no general prohibition against killing any wild bird or against taking, damaging, or destroying their nests or eggs. It is now a serious offence to harm some especially endangered species of birds or mammals, reptiles, amphibians and invertebrates. For the rest, they must take their chance against man in general or man the hunter in particular. Times are changing none the less as is shown by the fact that the legislation to protect badgers which already existed in the statutes of 1973 and 1991 has recently been both consolidated and extended in the Badgers Act 1992.

Hunting

For centuries there have been laws to protect animals from being taken by any save those who possessed what was in the nature of a property right over game. Subject to the statutory provisions relating to the protection of wildlife, a landowner may hunt over his own property or bestow the privilege on others. An exception is made in the case of the taking of hares, for which a licence is required.[32]

Sporting rights attach to land and, where such land is leased to another, the lessor may reserve the rights to himself save those in relation to hares and rabbits. If the lessor does not keep down the numbers, the tenant may claim for losses which he has sustained: *Seligman v Docker (1949)*.[33]

Game rights can be a very valuable form of *property* and, for their protection, the law of trespass provides one means of barring intruders: *Merest v Harvey (1814)*.[34] Trespass does not require physical entry onto the land, it may be effected by the firing of a gun or the sending of a dog onto land. Such an act may even be committed by one who is on a public highway and, by his actions there, threatens the property: *Harrison v Duke of Rutland (1893)*.[35]

It should also be noted that a person in charge of a hunt may be liable in trespass if he knows or ought to know that there is a real danger that hounds under his charge are likely to enter prohibited land, provided that he either intended this incursion or was negligent as to its prevention. An intention could be inferred from the fact that it is virtually impossible to stop hounds in pursuit of a terrified stag from entering such premises: *League Against Curel Sports v Scott (1985).*[36]

In recent years there has been much opposition to blood sports and violent incidents have occurred between hunt saboteurs and hunt followers. Deaths have occurred. In other incidents actions have been brought against the police for over zealous restraint and excessive use of force. Such issues are outside the scope of this text but it must be heard not to envisage a time when enough is enough and the activities of the hunting field will be outlawed in the same way as the pursuit of otters, badger baiting and cock fighting have been. Such activities seem out of place when the 21st century approaches.

Poaching

A person unlawfully in pursuit of game, by daytime, can be required to give his name and address to a gamekeeper or constable with a view to his prosecution. If he continues on the land thereafter, or gives a false name or address, he may be arrested.[37] Where the taking, or destroying, of game or rabbits unlawfully takes place at night, an offence is committed.[38] Upon conviction, following trial on indictment for a third offence, a sentence of imprisonment for up to 7 years may be imposed!

A poacher who kills and takes away game is not guilty of theft.[39] If he takes eggs of game birds, or young birds unable to fly, he may be convicted of an act of theft.

A landowner or occupier may not deliberately set traps on his property so as to intentionally harm a trespasser: *Bird v Holbrook (1828).*[40] A poacher, by night, may be arrested with a reasonable degree of force, which may also be used to eject other trespassers by day; but a deliberate intention to cause harm is unreasonable.

During certain times of the year, there is a *close season* for various types of game which may not be taken or killed at such times, e.g. pheasants are *safe* between February 1 and October 1. It is an offence to kill game on Sunday, at any time of the year, or upon Christmas Day.

Subject to certain exceptions, e.g. by members of the Royal Family, it is unlawful to kill game without a licence. The issuing authority is the local authority and licences may usually be bought over the counter at Post Offices. A register of licences issued is kept and failure to produce a licence on request is an offence. In order to deal in game by wholesale or retail, a dealer's licence is necessary. A dealer must possess both a game licence and an excise licence. It is an offence to deal in game without such permissions.

Deer

The Deer Act 1991 contains specific provisions in connection with the killing of deer. Close seasons are defined by type of animal. It is an offence to wilfully kill a deer by night. The operative word is *wilfully*, motorists who accidentally run down a deer at night would otherwise face penalty. Deer are not *game* within the definition of the Game Act 1831, but a game licence is needed to kill them.

Firearms

Various types of *sporting gun* are used for taking game. Such weapons are defined under the Firearms Act 1968. It is an offence to purchase, acquire, or possess a weapon without a firearms certificate issued by the local police. As a result of a number of firearms being used in criminal activities, a Bill is presently before Parliament to amend the Firearms Act 1968. Under the terms of the Bill, a number of types of weapon, including pump-action shotguns, will be prohibited. Before shotgun licences are issued, or renewed, applicants will have to satisfy a senior police officer that they present no danger to the public. They will also have to show good reason for wishing to acquire a certificate. Any transfer of a shotgun ownership will have to be notified to the police. At present, over 840,000 shotgun certificates are on issue in England and Wales.

Fishing

In terms of the numbers of those participating, angling is the single largest recreational sporting activity in Britain. The right to fish inland waters runs mainly with the property rights in land. Some waters are extremely valuable assets for their owners.

Fishing of inland waters is now subject to the consolidating measures contained in the Salmon and Freshwater Fisheries Act 1975. The Act prohibits certain methods of taking fish and certain types and conditions of fish. Part II of the Act sets out *close seasons* for various types of fish and offences are listed in Part IV.

Licences for fishing are issued by Water Authorities under the Water Act 1973. The licences refer to salmon, trout, all other freshwater fish, and eels. The licence describes the location where fish may be taken, the duration of the permission, and the name of the holder.

A person entitled to an exclusive right to fish certain waters may be granted a *general* licence. The holder may authorise other persons to fish the waters to which such licence refers. Such licences are often held by angling clubs and associations. On the authority of an Order confirmed by the Secretary of State, Water Authorities may limit the number of any licences issued in order to conserve fish stocks.

Private rights to fish waters may be bought and sold. In non-tidal waters, the law assumes the right of fishing as accruing to an owner of the river banks out to the middle of the water. Some of the rights can be very valuable and a great tourist attraction. Under the Theft Act, it is an offence to unlawfully take, or destroy, fish in any water which is private property or over which there is a private fishing right.

NOTES:

1. (1960) 2 QB 373.
2. (1963) 2 All ER 175.
3. Civic Amenities Act 1967 Part III.
4. s.1.
5. Public Health Acts 1890 s.44 and 1961 s.53.
6. s.145(2).
7. Local Government (Misc Provisions) Act 1976 s.19(1)(f).
8. (1978) P & CR 281.
9. *Guardian* 4 Jan 87 p4.
10. Countryside Act 1968 s.7.
11. Ibid s.7(1) and (2)(b)(c).
12. Ibid s.8(1) and (2).
13. Ibid s.22 and Water Act 1973 s.20.
14. Sch 5 para 1(3).
15. *Guardian* 24 Aug 87 p2.
16. s.23(2).
17. s.46.
18. SIs 1985/1012: 1986/8 1987/349.

19. s.47 and Sch 13.
20. *Guardian* 11 Jan 88 p5.
21. National Parks and Access to the Countryside Act 1949 s.85.
22. *Sunday Times* 24 Mar 88 p8.
23. Local Government Act 1985 s.44.
24. s.28.
25. *Guardian* 29 Apr 85 p4.
26. *Guardian* 2 Jul 87 p8.
27. *Guardian* 26 June 87 p5.
28. DOE Circular 12/72.
29. Countryside Commission CCP 186/85.
30. (1965) 3 All ER 737. See also Mixnam's Properties Ltd v Chertsey UDC (1965) AC 35.
31. (1958) 10 P & CR 6.
32. Hares Act 1848 and Game Licences Act 1860.
33. (1949) Ch 53.
34. (1814) 5 Taunt 442.
35. (1893) 1 QB 142 CA.
36. (1985) 2 All ER 489
37. Game Act 1831 s.31.
38. Night Poaching Act 1828 s.1.
39. Theft Act 1978 s.4(4).
40. (1828) 4 Bing 628.

CHAPTER XIX

Heritage Management

1. HISTORIC HERITAGE

'Britain is one gigantic genuine historic theme park. We have 450 stately homes open to the public and some lovely decrepit dukes to wheel out for the tourists. Our product is splendid.'[1] Such was the view of the retiring head of the English Tourist Board in 1986.

The *splendid product* described by Michael Montague is one way of looking at a complex pattern of buildings, objects and ideas built up over centuries. 'Theme park' or not, there is no doubt that the historic heritage of Britain, or any other country, can be packaged and sold.

Another way of looking at it is that it is comprised of 'everything that survives from the past (which) is not only historic because it is of the past, but it is also of our heritage because it is handed on to us by our predecessors of past ages'.[2] This definition includes things of historic value, buildings, archaeological remains, works of art and literature together with a heritage of ideas. A tourist may look at the Palace of Westminster both as a building of architectural merit and as a symbol of British parliamentary democracy.

A whole industry has grown up to present, or even reproduce, artefacts and scenes from bygone ages. Museums no longer simply contain cases filled with dusty exhibits. There is a growing policy of relating display items to the age in which people lived and worked. Museums today provide an infinite range of attractions for visitors. Some concentrate on a single theme, as with the National Railway Museum at York. Others maintain a theme but offer an extensive range and variety of exhibits, the Natural History Museum for one. Some seek to combine exhibits with a wider range of tourist attractions, as at Beaulieu Abbey which houses the National Motor Museum.

The concept of heritage extends into the libraries and galleries, many of which are associated with, or are part of, museums. The British Library has its own exhibition galleries where items of historic interest such as Magna Carta and the first folio edition of Shakespeare can be seen.

2. CULTURAL HERITAGE

The first step in public recognition of the value of preserving the national heritage was the Museums Act 1845. Conscious no doubt of its place in history, the city fathers of Canterbury opened a museum under the umbrella of the statute and used this as a device to provide a library at the same time. The Act did not set out to establish museums, merely to encourage their foundation by allowing local authorities to expend public monies on such ventures.

The Act was soon replaced by a more extensive enactment, the Libraries Act 1850, which authorised the collection of library materials and examples of art and science for 'the instruction and recreation of the people'. For the first time, library facilities were being made available to the public. Collections of books and artefacts had long existed in private hands. All great houses had libraries, such as those which exist at *stately homes*, e.g. at Longleat; others had much simpler collections. The private collectors also gathered curios to decorate their houses. These came, at first, from Europe and, later, from the expanding Empire. Many of these found their way into public collections by way of gifts or loans. Most museums today have exhibits which they are forced to store for lack of display facilities.

The great contribution of the 19th century legislation was not that it created collections but that it enabled public resources to be put to use for displaying materials to the public. Not only could municipal revenue be used, but the power to borrow for the purpose of buying exhibits was conferred on the authorities by the Treasury. Many of the museums, libraries and galleries are housed in premises custom-built for the purpose and which themselves are today architectural attractions in their own right.

Libraries

The present law governing libraries is contained in the Public Libraries and Museums Act 1964. The service is provided by library authorities whose duty it is to provide amenities for local residents and those in full time education. The range of materials has greatly expanded. Stocks are no longer confined to books but contain pictures, records and films. In addition to lending, they serve as valuable storehouses for local materials available for reference to interested users drawn from a wider audience than that which exists locally.

Libraries are subject to the law governing the protection of visitors to premises, liabilities which they share with many other undertakings which welcome the public through their doors. They are protected from the more troublesome elements which may visit them. The Libraries Offences Act 1898 contains provisions for dealing with those visitors who act to the *annoyance or disturbance* of other users. The statute prescribes disorderly conduct; the use of violent, abusive or obscene language; gaming; remaining on the premises having been requested to leave at closing time. To these offences, others may be added by local bye-laws designed for the management of the service.

The nature of public libraries as lending institutions has raised issues of copyright protection. Libraries are forced to consider whether the actions of their readers may involve them vicariously in liability. With the increase in the technology of reproducing materials and its availability at comparatively cheap prices the problem has grown. The test of *culpability* is whether the library can be said to have in any way approved or authorised the actions of its clients: *CBS Inc. v Records and Tapes Ltd (1981)*.[3]

The Copyright Act 1956 does not prevent absolutely the copying of materials held by libraries in their stocks. It is allowable to make limited amounts of copied works available to users. Such a facility is of obvious benefit to those who make use of libraries for the purpose of personal or other research. Many libraries contain local archive material of particular interest to those who have come to visit an area to trace their ancestors or to discover facts about the locality generally. Such facilities hold much attraction for tourists from the 'Old' Commonwealth and the US.

Art collections

As with libraries, art galleries are a legacy of 19th century enlightenment. Some charge for admission, others do not. In addition to their own collections, local authorities may provide grants to aid private exhibitions.

Many of the great institutions which attract visitors worldwide owe their existence largely to bequests and donations. Those which have been offered to the nation, as distinct from specific institutions, are administered by the trustees of the National Gallery. This body was established by statute in 1856. Its affairs, together with those of the Tate Gallery, are currently regulated by the National Gallery and Tate Gallery Act 1954.

There is continuing concern that too many antiques and works of art are being exported from Britain. In 1986/87 there was a gap of some £90 million between the value of works exported and those imported to the UK. The Government has powers to control the export of goods of all descriptions by a system of licensing,[4] especially of items 'manufactured or produced more than 50 years before the date of exportation'.[5]

Export licences are required where objects with an individual value of more than £16,000 have been in Britain for more than 50 years. A Reviewing Committee on the Export of Works of Art maintains a watching brief on the trade in such items and has registered disquiet at the scale and range of exports.[6] At the same time, grants by central government to museums and galleries have been restricted, raising fears that items in private hands will be sold abroad. Allied to this has been the practice of buying works of art and antiques as investments by individuals and associations. Between 1974 and 1980, the British Rail Pension Fund invested £40 million in this way. The fear is that they, and other organisations, will sell their property in foreign markets to raise capital. Public galleries and museums will not be able to compete for lack of funds.

Museums

Public museums are required to operate within the guidelines set out in the Public Libraries and Museums Act 1964. Many are run by local authorities but, in addition, there are a number which are foundations organised and run under the enabling provisions of other legislation, e.g. the British Museum Act 1963.

The 1964 Act allows charges to be made for admission but moves to do so have led to public objection. It seems inevitable that, in the face of economic pressures, the larger institutions will have to resort to raising funds in this way to meet their running costs. The need was realised in 1972 with the passing of the Museums and Galleries Admission Charges Act.

The National Heritage Act 1983 established a Memorial Fund. The objects of the statute were to preserve items of importance to the national heritage. The trustees are empowered to make grants or negotiate loans. Monies are advanced in order to protect objects or collections which are of outstanding historic, artistic or scientific interest. In recognition of the value of the Victoria and Albert Museum as the repository of may works of fine and decorative art, a separate Board was established under the Act in respect of the institution. The V & A is not a single entity but is made up of a number of collections, e.g. the Theatre Museum housed at Covent Garden, and has needs peculiar to it.

Loans

For many years, a system has operated whereby individual items, or whole collections, which are privately owned may be lent by their owners for public display. To this has been added the practice of inter-museum loans. Such *travelling* collections are often on semi-permanent loan from major institutions like the V & A.

Loans may be contracted for on a formal legal basis or on an informal basis. Whichever is the case, the host for the time being becomes the bailee of the objects entrusted to him. The duties of such a bailee are to take proper care of the items. If they are lost or damaged it will be for him to disprove negligence, or that no failure on his part caused or contributed to the loss. A prudent bailee does well to insure against such an eventuality.

3. REMOVAL OF ITEMS FROM PUBLIC PLACES

With a few notable exceptions, e.g. motor vehicles, it is not an offence to dishonestly use the property of another unless there is an intention to deprive that other of the property permanently. The Criminal Law Revision Committee considered whether or not to create a general offence of *dishonest use*, but decided against it.[7]

During the passage of the Theft Bill through Parliament a case was made out for making *temporary deprivation* an offence, although not one of theft. This followed a history of the removal of items from places open to the public. The most notorious of these had been the removal of the Goya portrait of the Duke of Wellington from the National Gallery. The picture was returned after an interval of some years. The person responsible had demanded that a large ransom for the picture be paid to a charity before it was returned. He was acquitted of theft of the picture and only convicted of the theft of the frame which had not been recovered.

Section 11 of the Theft Act is a result of Parliament's wish that powers should exist to deal with such actions and those like them. It is now an offence to remove from a building, or its grounds, the whole or part of any article displayed, or kept for display, in any building to which the public has access for the purpose of viewing it or part of it. The section does not apply where the display is for the purpose of *effecting sales or other commercial dealings*. The offence is one of some complexity and several factors must be present for a successful conviction to be obtained.

The public must have access to the building in order to view the building, or part of it, or a collection, or part of a collection housed in it. Access must be available to the public generally, although to exclude children from an exhibition considered unsuitable for them would not constitute a denial of access. It is not necessary that an entrance fee is charged. Exhibitions in parks and streets are not protected. If, say, a statue were removed from an open park this would not be an offence under section 11. By the same token, if such an item were removed from the garden of a house open to the public the section would not apply for it is concerned with property inside buildings.

A way round this difficulty is for an exhibitor who wishes to hold what is essentially an open-air display to ensure that at least one item from the *collection* is housed indoors for viewing. In this way, all of the items forming the *collection* will be protected. If entrance to the house was only for the purpose of taking refreshments or using toilet facilities, this would not suffice.

The items must be displayed or kept for display. Objects such as crosses in churches which are used for acts of worship are not *displayed* within the meaning of the Act. The purpose of setting out the object in question must be for exhibition to the public. An ashtray placed for the convenience of visitors would not be such an object. It is sufficient that the item was 'kept for display', e.g. in the storeroom of a gallery: *R v Durkin (1973).*[8]

It is also necessary for the article to have been *removed* from the premises. Such taking need not be at a time when the public are allowed access. It would be an offence to take an exhibit from a museum or gallery when such premises were closed. If the exhibition is temporary, it seems that the removal of the object must be on a day when the public have access for an offence to have been committed against the terms of section 11.

The Act refers to the removal of the *whole or any part of any article*. The meaning of *article* is not immediately apparent. In some statutory interpretations the term has been held not to apply to animals, whilst in others it has. In deciding the application of the word here, it is necessary to consider the *mischief* which the statute was intended to cure. It is, therefore, submitted that to take a plant from a National Trust property or a valuable snake from the London Zoo could be an offence.[9]

There are some anomalies in the section. If a stately home is open for a Bank Holiday only and a person hides on the premises and waits until midnight before taking the article, no offence against the Act is committed. Again, a single item cannot constitute a *collection*. The position where it is part of a *collection* housed elsewhere is not clear. It would, of course, be protected if its presence was ancillary to the main purpose, that of viewing the building.

The term *collection* was only used, it seems, in the sense of a gathering together of items which could be of interest to the public. It is not essential that they should be so. A collector might have brought them together for his own satisfaction or enjoyment. He would be protected by section 11 as much as any other. If the occupier of the premises simply allowed artists to display their works there so that they might sell them, this would not be a *commercial dealing* so as to deny them protection. The purpose of the artists might be commercial but *dealing* is not the purpose of the proprietor.

378

It should be remembered that section 11 is intended to deal with those activities which do not in law amount to theft. Where the facts show otherwise, offenders may be charged with theft or some other offence prescribed by law.

Treasure trove

Where gold or silver in the form of coins, bullion or plate has been hidden in the ground or other secret place, then it is classified as treasure trove. Under the Royal Prerogative, it is the property of the Crown. Only if the true owner can be discovered does it pass to that person. It is necessary that the items were hidden not merely lost or abandoned: *Att. Gen. v Overton Farms Ltd (1982).*[10]

In order to encourage a finder to surrender his discoveries, which are often of historical importance, it is the practice of the Crown to compensate him with the full market value of his discovery. Should the Crown not wish to keep the objects, even where the Coroner's Court has declared them to be treasure trove, they will be returned to the finder.

Many such finds may be of value but they are not covered by the official designation if the articles are not of gold or silver: *R v Thomas and Willett (1863).*[11] In such cases, the occupier of the premises on which they were found has a prior claim to that of the finder: *Parker v British Airways Board (1982).*[12] Such a person might, of course, sell items which could be a loss to the nation. In such a case, the use of the export protection licensing system could be called in aid.

In a trial for theft of property which it is alleged is treasure trove, the jury must not convict unless they are sure from the evidence that the property in question is treasure trove. The mere *possibility* of its being such is not sufficient to support a conviction: *R V Hancock (1989).*[13]

Treasure trove comprises any coin or other object of gold or silver which was hidden at some time in the past by someone who intended to recover them and who or whose present heirs or successors are unknown. The law which dates back to 1195 in this regard has been referred to, with good cause, as *archaic* and the British Museum for one would like to see a change made. The wrath of the Museum was occasioned by the discovery in a Norfolk field of a hoard of artefacts together with objects of gold and silver.

The original discovery was made on private land by someone given permission by the occupier to be there and to use a metal detector. The Kings Lynn coroner ruled that the gold and silver items were all treasure trove but that the other artefacts belonged to the owner of the field. It is with such objects that the difficulty really arises. The majority are not gold or silver in nature or are only alloys of precious metals. In the case of the latter they may only be classified as treasure trove if they contain a *substantial* proportion of gold or silver. No definition of *substantial* exists with any degree of precision to guide the coroner.

Even where excavations are carried out by museum staff it is necessary to get them to sign waivers in favour of the museum or they could be adjudged entitled to a reward. The expense of paying *ex gratia* rewards can mean that a museum is unable to afford to keep that which it finds. Even allowing that there is no duty to pay a reward to do so to a finder is of great practical importance for it persuades the latter to reveal his find rather than to conceal it and sell it later for profit - even though such sale may be illegal. Such an inducement is obvious from the Norfolk example where the non treasure trove items were valued at £20 million.

The change in the law is desired by the British Museum and others is that wherever artefacts are discovered in the same cache as gold and silver items *all* of the find should be classified treasure trove.

Metal detectors

The use of these devices in the search for *buried treasure* has become a popular pastime. If they are used on property without the permission of the owner of the land, this constitutes an act of trespass. Where the land is publicly owned, the appropriate action must be taken by whichever body controls the land on behalf of the community.

Their most obvious use is in areas which are likely to yield interesting discoveries. Many of these are likely to be *protected places* within the definition of the Ancient Monuments and Archaeological Areas Act 1979. Such places are scheduled under the statute or owned or under the guardianship of the Secretary of State or a local authority. Alternatively they may be designated as 'Areas of Archaeological Importance'.[15]

The Act may designate such places by Order.[16] It then becomes an offence to investigate them without prior notice and consent from the controlling authority. It is thus an offence to use a metal detector in a protected place; to remove objects of archaeological interest found in such a manner; or where entry has been permitted, to break a condition which was imposed on such entry. The Act defines a metal detector as 'any device designed or adapted for detecting or locating any metal or mineral in the ground'. Adaptation may take various forms: *Popperwell v Cockerton (1968).*[17]

Site controls

Under the 1979 Act the Secretary of State may list *scheduled monuments*, such listings not being subject to challenge. The list includes Hadrian's Wall, medieval village sites and ancient burial grounds, as well as the Tower of London. If work is carried out on them without permission, or they are damaged or destroyed, the Act prescribes prosecution of those responsible[18.] It is as much an offence for the owner of the site to cause the harm as for a stranger.[19] An interesting case involving the Marquis of Hertford came before the courts: *English Heritage v Marquis of Hertford (1987).*[20] Lord Hertford was charged at Warwick Crown Court with damaging an ancient monument, the site of a Roman settlement, by ploughing up two meadows on his land. The site had been listed since 1964. He was fined £10,000. In the wake of the plough, the site was vandalised by treasure hunters with metal detectors. English Heritage estimate that 200 such sites are damaged each year.

The Secretary of State also possesses powers to repair monuments as necessary. Alternatively he may purchase sites compulsorily if need be. As an alternative to scheduling, he may also take such properties into 'guardianship'. In this way he, or a local authority, assumes full responsibility for managing the monument. Private rights are thus protected and the guardianship may be ended and occupation by the owner resumed.

Wrecks

The definition of a monument is very wide. It can include the remains of a vehicle, vessel or aircraft which are protected by the provisions of the 1979 Act.[21] It does not extend to those wrecks which are the subject of scheduling under the Protection of Wrecks Act 1973. This statute allows the Secretary of State to designate wrecks by Order. This is designed to protect sites of historic, archaeological or artistic importance. They may not be interfered with or visited without authorisation. The measures are designed both to protect valuable sites and to keep intruders away from what are, in many cases, dangerous places.

In recent years, unauthorised skin divers have become the equivalent of the menace of those with metal detectors on land. Without effective protection artefacts from sites such as that of the *Mary Rose* could have been lost to the nation and the tourist industry.

Occupiers liability

Heritage sites are protected from the unlawful activities of visitors. Such visitors are themselves protected from harm by the provisions of the Occupiers Liability Act 1957 and 1984. All occupiers of premises are required by the provisions of s2(1) of the 1957 Act to afford visitors a 'common duty of care' such duty being described in s2(2) as 'reasonable' and allowing the court to consider all the circumstances of the case. The antiquity of a site may be just such a circumstance: *Hogg v Historic Building & Monuments Commission for England (1988).*[22]

Similarly, where fencing has been erected to deter adventurous persons and even where such persons are children who are specifically provided for in s2(3) of the 1957 Act the test again is whether 'in all the circumstances ... the visitor will be reasonable safe in using the premises for the purposes for which he is invited or permitted by the occupier to be there' notwithstanding that an occupier must be prepared 'for children to be less careful than adults': *Moloney v Lambeth B.C. (1966).*[23]

4. THE NATIONAL TRUST

This unique institution dates its origins from the joint enterprise, in 1895, of a social worker, a parson and a solicitor. Their aim was to preserve both buildings and the countryside which were of *historic interest and natural beauty* for the nation. Its first properties were a minute stretch of Welsh cliffs and a small house in Sussex. Today the Trust is third only to the Forestry Commission (q.v.) and the Ministry of Defence in extent of its land holdings in England and Wales. It owns more than one third of the historic houses which are open to the public.

These were not the original priority of the foundation. In the 1890s, many such properties were still in private hands and occupied as family dwellings. Escalating maintenance and repair costs caused numerous houses to fall into decay, many being demolished as a result. In 1937, the Trust established a Country House Scheme to save threatened properties by accepting them as donations to the Trust by their owners. They, for the main part, continued to live in the houses while access was allowed to the public in return for the support of the foundation. The result was that the image of the Trust changed and it became associated with the stately home industry.

Despite its name, and having been incorporated under the National Trust Act 1907, itself later modified by the 1937 Act, the Trust is not a government institution. An essential provision of the legislation is that the Trust's properties shall be *inalienable*. That is to say, they may never be sold or mortgaged, although, with the permission of the Charity Commissioners, a property may be leased.

The Trust is the largest charitable body in Britain, controlled by its members through general meetings at which the Council is appointed for the purpose of carrying out Trust business. This includes, inter alia, accepting property in trust under the system which allows the State to accept payment of taxes by receiving land in lieu of money. The government is not obliged to accept such land, it has a discretion to accept or require the property to be sold to satisfy the debt owed to the State. In 1984, the government refused to accept Calke Abbey despite acknowledging that the house was of considerable architectural and historic interest. The Trust managed to buy the house for £7.5 million. This price did not include the estate which the government wanted sold. In many cases it is by good management of an estate that the Trust can afford to support the buildings. Nevertheless, it was intended that the Abbey would open to the public in 1989.[24]

The principal objectives of the Trust are:

1. To acquire and protect sites of major archaeological importance, including a growing number of industrial locations.

2. To preserve the landscape by woodland management.

3. The care of a wide variety of buildings of architectural and historic interest, with an increasing emphasis on small properties.

4. The landscaping and management of gardens, many with unique features.

5. To safeguard the coastline. Enterprise Neptune launched in 1965 expects eventually to have some 900 miles under protection.

6. The preservation of wildlife. There are at present 57 nature reserves and 414 Sites of Special Scientific Interest in the portfolio.

The Trust is not the only agency involved in such work. It has been joined by the National Trust for Scotland, the Historic Houses Association and English Heritage. The latter being an offshoot of the Department of the Environment.

Byelaws

For a number of years, the Trust has been empowered to make byelaws for the management and protection of its assets. The powers derive principally from the National Trust Act 1971. They allow the Trust to exclude visitors from parts of the properties and to remove those who offend against accepted standards of behaviour. They are used to prohibit such potentially harmful activities as lighting fires, digging up and removing plants, and depositing rubbish. Offenders may be brought before the courts and fined for offences against the byelaws.

Liability

The Trust must act in accordance with the remit of the enabling legislation, but the wide powers which this gives seem to preclude the likelihood of the foundation being accused of acting *ultra vires*. It may make *reasonable charges* for admission to its properties or for use of its facilities which probably means that an *unreasonable* charge might be construed as *ultra vires*.

As an occupier of premises, the Trust is subject to the provisions of the Occupiers' Liability Acts 1957 and 1984; for dangerous escapes under the rule in Rylands and Fletcher; for the tort of Nuisance; and for offences against the Control of Pollution Act 1971. It will be liable, in a wide variety of situations, under the Health and Safety at Work Act 1974.

The duty of the Trust as a landowner is not only to take care of the property in its possession but also to take such measures as are necessary to prevent harm befalling the land of neighbours by proper management of its affairs. Thus failure to avert a landslip from an ancient burial site, the potential danger being known, rendered the Trust liable in damages: *Leakey v National Trust (1980)*.[25]

5. PROTECTION OF THE BUILT ENVIRONMENT

'We now see an almost obsessive interest on the part of John Citizen in the environment and its preservation. Formerly, the environment did not mean a thing.... (now) John Citizen and a few planning authorities have realised that the environment is not automatically here to stay. It is only here as long as valiant efforts are made to preserve it.'[26] This comment on the advance of the 'concrete jungle' in towns and cities reflects the need for constant vigilance in the interests of preserving that which is best and worthwhile keeping. In hard economic terms it represents the assets of the tourist industry.

In 1990 four Acts were passed to consolidate the existing legislation in respect of town and country planning. The principal amongst these were the Town and Country Planning Act (TCPA) and the Planning (Listed Buildings and Conservation Areas) Act (PLBCA). The latter is closely aligned with the former some of whose provisions it replicates in so far as they can be applied to listed buildings and conservation areas.

The provisions as to scheduled monuments remain separate and are governed by the Ancient Monuments and Archaeological Areas Act 1979. A building may at one and the same time to scheduled and listed in which case the 1979 Act prevails.

The TCPA is compendious, running to 337 sections and 17 Schedules. It details planning authorities, development planning, controls on development, compensation orders, rights of owners, enforcements and special controls amongst its principal provisions. This consolidation of the law was carried out by the Law Commission and its work was deemed necessary in order to represent the existing law in a satisfactory form.

The TCPA plans may be strategic (involving substantial areas if not the whole country); local plans (implementing strategic policy); unitary (dealing with specific locations). Control over development is effected by the need for planning permission.

Any development carried out without permission is unlawful and may be the subject of enforcement actions by the local authority. Controls are applied in respect of operational developments (building, engineering etc.) and use change (making a material change in the use of any building or other land). With regard to the former it is not lawful to build a leisure complex or excavate a swimming pool or build a roadway or rail link without the necessary permission. The provisions of the latter preclude the turning of farmland into golf courses or houses into hotels at the whim of a developer. At certain points the two heads of control may overlap while at others there are marked differences particularly with regard to the procedural issues especially enforcement.

The wide provisions of the TCPA are within an area of specialist study but, nevertheless, their operation impacts strongly upon leisure activities and the tourist industry.

Trees

Part VIII of the TCPA deals with 'Special Controls' which includes substantial reference to tree preservation orders. In both the TCPA and the PLBCA provisions are made for trees to be protected against unauthorised topping, lopping or felling where such trees have been specified and subject to requirements for consent. The Batho Report in 1990 which was commissioned by the department for the Environment fully reviewed the position with regard to the existing position as regard trees and recommended the inclusion of additional controls for hedgerows.

Where trees are unlawfully removed, uprooted or otherwise destroyed in contravention of a tree preservation order, the owner of the land can be required to plant another of an appropriate size and species at the same place so soon as he reasonable can.

Further limited protection is given to trees generally where they are within a conservation area by virtue of s.211 of the PLBCA. This requires that prior notice of any felling of a tree or trees be given to the planning authority. It is an offence to do any act in relation to a tree within a conservation area which is capable of being protected by a tree preservation order notwithstanding that no such order has yet been made. Essentially this provision puts the planning authority on notice so that it may make an order protecting a tree or trees.

Conservation areas

The PLBCA deals specifically with conservation areas and listed buildings. Control is effected with regard to the former by means of designation and effect, control of demolition and developments within such areas. Thus established, Part II of the Act comes into play effectively applying many of the provisions as to listed buildings set out in Part I to whole areas.

The purpose of establishing conservation areas it to provide a broader form of protection than just for listed buildings. The concept was first introduced in the Civic Amenities Act 1967 to extend protection to buildings which are only historically or architecturally interesting and not worthy of listed building status and yet are seen as part of a rural or urban area which is itself of special interest in representing a grouping of buildings whose character and appearance is worthy of preservation and/or enhancement. Such areas may even attract designation in rural settings where there is no architectural interest as such but special historic interest only.

In DOE Circular 8/87 para 54 the Secretary of State advised:

"Clearly there can be no standard specification for conservation areas. The statutory definition is 'areas of special architectural or historic interest, the character or appearance of which it is desirable to preserve or enhance'. These areas will naturally be of many different kinds. They may be large or small, from whole town centres to squares, terraces and smaller groups of buildings. They will often be centred on listed buildings, but not always. Pleasant groups of other buildings, open spaces, trees, an historic street pattern, a village green or features of historic or archaeological interest may also contribute to the special character of any area. Areas appropriate for designation as conservation areas will be found in almost every town and many villages. It is the character of areas, rather than the individual buildings, that [section 69 of the Planning (Listed Buildings and Conservation Areas) Act 1990] seeks to preserve or enhance."

No formal designation procedures exist. Designation is effected by the appropriate resolution of the authority concerned. It derives from such a resolution and does not form an integral part of the local plan process set out in the TCPA 1990. There is however an intention to link the two together more closely in the future. At present notice of designation has to be published in the London Gazette and at least one newspaper circulating locally in the geographical location of the designated area. There is no legal requirement that owners of properties affected should be notified individually.

Consequences of designation are that demolitions are controlled, as is the growth of trees, advertisement signs are restricted together with other alterations which could change the nature of the area. As a quid pro quo, grants and loans are made available to owners to assist in maintaining buildings etc. in keeping with the ethos of the location. Permitted developments are also restricted in respect of domestic dwellings, industrial works, statutory undertakings and telecommunications.

Listed Buildings

These are now protected by Part I of PLBCA 1990 which provides for a regime of selectivity. In 1990 some 450,000 buildings were listed. The impetus for change was provided by the destruction of the Firestone factory in 1980 shortly before it could be granted listed status allowing the vandals to escape liability.

Only a 'building' may be listed but the term is widely interpreted by the TCPA 1990 s.336(1) as including 'any structure or erection, and any part of a building, as so defined, but does not include plant or machinery in a building.'

A building does not cease to be such by reason only of demolition without authorisation provided that sufficient of its component parts remain in being enabling it to be identified. Such was the case where the owner of a barn in Leominster demolished it for shipment to the USA. He was ordered to re-erect it and an appeal against this order made by the district council was rejected by the Secretary of State: *Leominster District Council v British Historic Buildings & S.P.S. (1987)*.[27]

The criteria for listing are currently to be found in Appendix 1 to DOE Circular 8/87. The listing of a building confers protection not only on the building itself but also any object or structure fixed to the building. In this context an object is anything which is within the curtilage of the building even though not affixed to it but form any part of the land and has done so since before 1948: *Debenhams v Westminster City Council (1987)*.[28]

'Building' has been applied to some rather strange edifices for the purposes of listing - horse troughs, railway viaducts, towers, follies, pillar boxes, a toilet once frequented by Charles Dickens and the original Butlins Chalet in Skegness.

The 'list' of buildings is maintained by the DOE. The categories set out in the PLBCA 1990 are Grade I structures - those of exceptional interest - which presently comprise some 2% of all buildings listed; Grade II which are those of special architectural or historic interest warranting every effort being made to save them. Within this latter category a building may be designated Grade II* denoting that it is especially interesting.

Structures do not qualify solely on the basis of antiquity. There now exists a rolling 30 year rule by means of which all buildings more than 30 years old dating back from the time of consideration for listing may be designated. In exceptional cases some no more than 10 years old may be listed where appropriate.

When considering listing the Secretary of State must inform the owner but he his not required to consult with any party prior to making his decision. This extend to the Historic Buildings and Monuments Commission which statutory body he is required to inform but not to consult. In making his decision he is entitled to consider not only the building itself but also its surroundings and any other man made features: *Cotswold District Council v SOS Environment (1985)*.[29]

Once a building is listed prior consent must be obtained before any alteration, enlargement or demolition in connection may be effected. Public notices of any proposals must be posted enabling interested parties to object. Where work is done without consent the person responsible may be fined and/or imprisoned. An interesting provision of the PLBCA is that the level of fine may be set so as to reflect the financial benefit which has accrued to the wrongdoer by reason of his unlawful act. In addition the person convicted of damaging or demolishing a listed building could be ordered to restore it to its original form: *Solihull Borough Council v Doyle (1985)*.[30]

There is no appeal against listing but an aggrieved party can write to the Secretary of State requesting delisting. Special dispensations as to listing apply to ecclesiastical works and redundant churches. Grants may be made available to assist with repairs of listed buildings.

Where work is authorised in connection with a listed building conditions may be attached to the consent. If such a condition is not complied with this also constitutes an offence. In considering applications regard is taken of the setting in which the property stands and any features of architectural or historical importance possessed by the building. A listed building which is not regarded as being properly maintained may be made the subject of a compulsory purchase order. The owner may be compensated but where it appears that the owner has deliberately neglected it so as it becomes dilapidated, thus affording him the excuse for demolition, the Secretary of State may order that the building having been compulsorily purchased, the owner be given only minimum compensation.

The law relating to scheduled monument (q.v.) remains separate from the provisions of the PLBCA 1990. A building may be scheduled and listed at the same time. In such circumstances the provisions of the Ancient Monuments and Archaeological Areas Act 1979 shall prevail.

Preservation notices

Where the building under threat is not listed but the local authority considers that it is of special architectural or historic interest it may issue a building preservation notice which has the effect of staying any alteration or demolition work for 6 months giving the structure *de facto* listed protection until such time as a decision is reached as to whether or not full listed status shall be granted. Where the danger is imminent, the notice may be affixed to a prominent position on the building itself: *Maltglade Ltd v St Albans RDC 1972).*[31]

6. DAMAGE TO PROPERTY

The Criminal Damage Act 1971 extends protection to all property against the actions of 'a person who, without lawful excuse, destroys or damages any property belonging to another, intending to destroy or damage any such property or being reckless as to whether such property would be destroyed or damaged'. Such a person is guilty of an offence under section 1(1) of the Act.

Property includes land or building on the land. The offence may only be committed against the property of another. The owner of a *listed* building could not be charged with an offence committed against his own property.

The offence will be committed by those who deliberately or recklessly vandalise property of others. Carving of initials or spraying an ancient monument with graffiti would constitute an offence against the Act and also against section 28 of the Ancient Monuments and Archaeological Areas Act 1979. The difference is that, under the 1971 Act, the actions must be wilful or reckless; the 1979 Act allows negligent behaviour to be the basis of a prosecution. In Lord Hartford's Case (q.v.), the court accepted that the action of ploughing was not done deliberately with the intention of destroying the site. Nor could the noble lord be convicted of criminal damage since it was his own land which was affected.

The 1971 Act may also be the basis of a prosecution against those who damage goods. Where a piece of furniture is damaged, or a painting attacked, property will be regarded as having been *destroyed or damaged* because its value has been diminished. It does not matter where the property is located so long as it can be shown to be owned by another, e.g. a museum, the National Trust, a local authority or an individual.

NOTES:

1. *Guardian* 14 Mar 86 p 12.
2. Royal Society of Arts Journal Jul 78 p 42.
3. (1981) 2 All ER 812.
4. Import Export and Customs Powers (Defence) Act 1939.
5. Export of Goods (Control) Order 1981 SI 1641.
6. 33rd Report of the Committee.
7. 8th Report of the Committee.
8. (1973) 2 All ER 872 CA.
9. *Observer* 7 Feb 87 p 5.
10. (1982) 2 WLR 397. See also Att Gen v Trustees of the British Museum (1903) 2 Ch 598.
11. (1863) 169 ER 1409.
12. (1982) 2 WLR 503.
13. (1989) *Guardian* 28 Jul
14. *Observer* 10 March 1991
15. s.42.
16. s.33.
17. (1968) 1 WLR 438
18. s.57.
19. s.28.
20. (1987) *Guardian* 10 Feb p 6
21. s.1(4)..
22. (1988) CLY 2573.
23. (1966) 110 SV 406.
24. *Times* 8 Dec 83 p 6.
25. (1980) QB 485
26. SW D. Heap - Hamlyn Lectures 1975
27. (1987) JPL 350.
28. (1987) AC 396.
29. (1985) JPL 407.
30. *Chartered Surveyors Weekly* 28 Nove 1985 p.766
31. (1972) 3 All ER 129

CHAPTER XX

The Common Inheritance

1. A GREEN AND PLEASANT LAND?

In 1990 a Government White Paper was produced[1] which sought to examine issues raised by the need to protect the environment.. It highlighted the growing concern generally felt for the well being of the UK from a domestic standpoint but also bearing in mind the wider dimension of the European Community (EC) and the international forums. Much earlier a conference had been held at Stockholm in 1972 which almost for the first time focused the attention of the international community on the need to control abuses of the ecosystem. In the years between these two events there developed a growing awareness that measures needed to be put into effect before irreversible changes in the environment of the world occurred. The main difficulties were appreciated as being what needed to be done, how could effective measures be taken and by whom.

The environment has become a major item on all national and international agendas. It is a big issue in terms of economic, political and social terms which are all interrelated with the physical element. It is not an easy matter to describe the scope of all that is encompassed within the single word *environment*. In general terms it can be taken to signify the external surroundings in which life forms exist and which influence that existence and the way in which life forms develop. These surroundings may be natural or man made. Above all it is the activities of man which have given rise to perceived threats to his existence and which are self generated.

The planet is some 4,600 million years old but its future existence as a home fit for human inhabitation will ultimately depend upon what decisions are taken in the immediate future to safeguard its well being.

'Earth (is) a person of 46 years of age . . . only at the age of 42 did (it) begin to flower . . mammals arrived only 8 months ago; in the middle of last week ape like humans (evolved) . . . Modern humans have been around for four hours. During the last hour we discovered agriculture. The industrial revolution began a minute age. During those sixty seconds of biological time, humans have made a rubbish tip of paradise.'[2]

The Environment

A precise definition of the *environment* is conditioned by the context in which it is used. So it is possible to consider the content of economic, social and political environments to name but three. In the sense that it is being used here it is perhaps best to consider it from the way in which it is viewed by those who are in a position to make an impact upon it for better or worse, namely the law makers and the law givers. A major enactment affecting the topic was the Environmental Protection Act 1990. For the purposes of the statute *environment* is described as:

'all or any, of the following media, namely the air, water and the land; and the medium of air includes the air within buildings and the air within other natural or man-made structures above or below ground.'[3]

The Preamble to the Act describes the purpose for which the statute was enacted as being 'to make provision for the improved control of pollution arising from certain industrial and other processes'. This signifies recognition that it is these latter which have given rise to the need for protection from *harm* which the Act describes as being to:

'the health of living organisms or other interference with the ecological systems of which they form part and, in the case of man, includes offence caused to any of his senses of harm to his property'.[4]

As in many other areas of law it seems that the ownership of property is worthy of at least equal treatment as living organisms including man himself! The statute demonstrates that it is the physical environment in both natural and man made forms which is worthy of protection and it is upon this basis that this text is written. Nonetheless, at every point in an examination of the topic so described economic, political and social factors impact upon the physical environment. Most notably, at a time when economies throughout the world are suffering some degree of recession and all are seeking growth as a solution to their ills, the *cost* of environmental protection is uppermost in the minds of those who are empowered to make political decisions which will have repercussions on the social well being of their constituents.

The *'industrial and other processes'* cited in the UK legislation are the providers of goods and services, together with employment, for millions of people. Political decisions on the environment which seek to regulate the activities of businesses may have the effect of causing businesses to close or to go into decline or to move to locations where governments are less concerned, or able to be concerned, about the impact of such business on the environment.

The developed world of richer nations has developed a throw away environment disposing of artefacts in preference to repairing and reusing them. The third world, as a matter of necessity, repairs and recycles, activities to which their better off neighbours are beginning to turn for a variety of reasons. Not the least among these is the build up of waste which they have increasingly accumulated and which pollutes the environment in one form or another. Some have tried exporting their waste to other, often poorer, nations where the disposal may be scientific but more than likely is not; but in any event its presence causes a hazard for the new host.

That the political decision makers are grasping the problem of environmental harm may stem primarily from pragmatic rather than altruistic roots. Concern amongst people generally, fanned by pressure groups, has awakened public consciousness to the dangers which threaten everyone. The cause of the environment has grown and to be *Green* is seen to be equated with good. the message is not lost upon politicians of all persuasions. Generally their response has been reactive rather than pro-active although it is perhaps fair to say that in the context of sophisticated planning law which has developed in the UK more than in any other nation, pro-activity has played a major part.

The Case of the Whale

In 1986 in response to many years of campaigning by pressure groups, the International Whaling Commission (IWC), a UN recognised body, imposed a ban upon commercial whaling. The signatories to the prohibition upheld it on a voluntary basis. The only sanctions against any who might break ranks was that of loss of esteem within the international community, allied with the possibility of some forms of trade embargo. The strength of international opinion is what kept the ban in place until 1993. In May 1993 the IWC meeting again agreed to a continuation of the ban but dissenting voices were raised more loudly than before. There was general approval to continue as before but immediately after the meeting broke up, Norway announced through its foreign minister that she would resume catching certain whales. Other members, some of whom has agreed only reluctantly to continue the moratorium on the killing, registered their strong disapproval. They were powerless to prevent any member country within the IWC pursuing what it saw as its national i.e. economic interest. In the eyes of commercial interests whales = money. Dead whales that is.

Over the years the whale has become the symbol of what is deemed best in an environmental sense where conservation and environment are regarded as synonymous. It also points up all that is worst with the pursuit of commercial and political interests outweighing environmental issues. It emphasises the lack of enforcement power where decisions are taken in a voluntary, albeit, international forum. No-one is going to go to war over a whale!

Those governments which oppose the ban, notably Norway and Japan, argue that some national governments are supporting activists so as to pretend to their electorates that they are environmentally caring - Green. Whereas in fact, they argue, such governments are cultural imperialists dictating how individual, often smaller nations, should behave. Yet others see the issue as between urbanised and rural cultures. People in cities do not need to throw harpoons, rural economies it is suggested must.

Supporters of commercial whaling argue their case on the basis of resource management backed by scientific study of whale populations. For long whales were killed on the basis that a study was needed to show how many and what species existed! Opponents of whaling are seen as being tools of conservationists who are economic with the truth in order to pursue their own political agendas.[5]

In this area of environmental/conservation debate another phrase has been coined, *sustainable development*. This appears to mean that each generation should be entitled to do much as it pleases with the environment so long as it does not leave the earth a poorer place than when it inherited it. This it is said promotes choice and salves the consciences of governments and businesses alike. The concept is enshrined in the UN Convention on Biodiversity and is seen as the best idea the international community has so far come up with in the field of environmental protection. This it would appear was the verdict of the Summit held in Brazil in 1992. Small comfort to the whale and other life forms, some of which have been hunted to the point of extinction by man.

The whale has thus become the symbol of conflicting environmental ideologies, highlighting paradoxes and inconsistencies of approach by individuals and nations which often defy scientific analysis and are far from rational. No-one believes that the world will come to an end if marine mammals of the order *Cetacea* became extinct. Many do believe that the world would be a poorer place if homosapiens suffered the same fate. Others believe it might be a better place. The final irony in the saga of the whale is that the financial benefits from watching rather than killing whales would appear to be greater. This tourist industry inspired activity earns more today than selling whalemeat to Japanese diners at $140 a pound. Ecology tours are big business, conservation can be seen to pay.

There are of course greater issues on the environmental agenda than the life and death of whales. Foremost amongst these are what to do with toxic waste produced by industry - notably nuclear products; the effects of ozone destroying chemicals - principally chlorofluorcarbons (CFCs), leading to human illness and possibly death; global warming and the 'greenhouse effect'; the destruction of tropical rain forest. Only ten years ago global warming was seen as something fit only for the realms of science fiction. That certainty has now been undermined and governments are seriously concerned about the phenomenon.

The Impact of Tourism

Whale watching is only one of the by products of the tourist industry which has become a major contributor to the GDP of many countries. Another has been environmental pollution by tourists.

'Its that time of year again. Fifty strong units of people in anoraks along the streets of London. Coaches . . . park on the pavement and discharge the refuse of Europe on to the road. Yes, its the tourist season - not as many imagine, a minor irritant but a major phenomenon that goes to the heart of Britain's economic malaise . . . Many of the anoraks . . . head for our free museums like rats for drainpipes . . . they stand in the middle of the busiest pavements . . . not content with making London unbearable for a few months of the year (they) refuse to go home . . . The net result if not as the tourist industry would have you believe a bonanza of earnings from tourism. Our deficit on tourism is expected to reach £4 billion (in 1993).' [6]

A personalised view of tourism no doubt but it finds echoes amongst the Cornish who describe tourists as *emets* (ants) or in the West Country generally where the term *grockle* is used. These reactions, however prejudiced, indicate that the phenomenon of people in numbers, especially concentrated in particular geographical locations and/or at particular times of the year can themselves be seen as polluting the environment for those whose surroundings are invaded.

Added to this, the tourist industry generates increased demand for transport facilities - road, rail and air - which adds to the increased levels of CFCs in the atmosphere. The transport itself requires facilities to meet and move the consumers of its services. Airports, stations and other termini eat into the land stock, require buildings as economically efficient if not aesthetically pleasing as possible, more resources are consumed and energy sources required. Again the environment is affected.

Tourists require accommodation. Hotels and other living space is created at a price to local communities and their environment as even a cursory glance at the shores of the Mediterranean will reveal. The phenomenon of sprawling caravan sites in the post war period in UK caused much the same impact on the British environment. Purpose built leisure attractions for the tourist add to the bill for the impact on the environment.

Increased movement to site locations at seasonal peaks leads to congestion of roads, demands on water and sewage disposal and more than usual levels of noise from many sources. The impact on the tourist may also be evidenced by illness, frequently food generated; polluted beaches and unhygenic accommodation take their toll. The tourist industry is built upon the notion of selling dreams and of such stuff dreams are not made. The expectations of the natural and built environment promoted by the advertising may fall short of the ideal.

The impact on local communities throughout the world by the tourism phenomenon can be viewed as a polluting agent for many environments physical, economic and social. It is the regulation of this and other polluting agents within acceptable bounds which is the problem which faces many governments for it is at this level that the problems of environmental damage must be tackled if remedies are to be effected.

2. THE ROLE OF LAW

Law by itself cannot solve problems it can only contribute to the regulation of human activity in an attempt to achieve a level of behaviour which is generally accepted and which has a better than average chance of being supported by those it is designed to protect. This is particularly true with respect to legal measures designed to protect the environment from mankind's worst excesses. Herein lies another issue, is the law designed to protect people, or the environment *per se*? The issue must turn on the concept that by protecting the environment in which people live they themselves are being protected. In the event, much of what is deemed to be environmental law is the setting out of rules of conduct resolving procedural issues which often outweighs the substantive element. This is most evident in statutory regulation rather than in the common law.

A consideration of what may be deemed to be environmental law shows that almost anything could be included from the financial measures necessary to order national budgets to the individual consumer or person at work. These are areas which are themselves the proper subject for study and it is necessary to narrow the field in order to get at the roots of the tree. Much of the law relating to the protection of the environment in the UK is to be found in the public domain. That is to say it is the well being of citizens as a whole which fall to be considered and provided for rather than the rights of individuals. Which is not to say that individual rights are not provided for. Both the common law and statutory tort actions are essentially designed for this purpose.

The laws which are created will necessarily take into their protection the few as opposed to the many where it is the environment as a whole which is to be protected. The few here are taken as being sub groups of the main population, which category will cover tourists allowing for the fact that the vast majority of the population will be in this category at one time or another and for varying durations. The tourist may, however, be entitled to regard himself as paying twice over for protection. Once as a member of the public and then again as a tourist spending on his chosen recreational activity. He may, therefore, feel doubly aggrieved as the victim of pollution or other environmental hazard.

The classification of the law as it presently exists in Britain does not easily allow what has become termed environmental law to fit into any simple mould. That a body of the law with this title has been forming is without doubt but where the boundaries begin and end is far from clear. What is certain is that much of what can be said to fall under this heading is statutory in origin and relies for its enforcement more on administrative processes than on the courts. Very often no privately enforceable rights are afforded by the statute in question or the Orders and Regulations made under its umbrella. the common law does afford a limited degree of what may be regarded as environmental protection. Indeed the tort of Nuisance was at one time the main vehicle for the maintenance of private rights. Its offshoot, the tort based upon the rule in *Rylands v Fletcher* also figures in this field. The torts of Negligence and Trespass have their parts to play but it is an inescapable fact that it is statutory regulation which dominates what is now the broadly described area of environmental law.

An area of the common law which for a time straddled both camps was and is, Public Nuisance. Essentially it is an area of criminal law and thus firmly in the public domain. As broadly drawn by the courts it concerns those actions which affect the lives of identifiable classes of Her Majesty's subjects and for the transgression of which criminal sanctions have been held to apply. Its province is so potentially all encompassing that one authority was caused to remark:

'with such a broad concept in existence, backed with such broad remedies, what need have we of any other criminal offence or torts?'[7]

In essence public nuisance is essentially part of criminal law.

'Every person is guilty of an offence at common law, known as public nuisance, who does an act not warranted by law, or omits to discharge a legal duty, if the effect of the act or omission is to endanger the life, health, property or morals, or comfort of the public, or to obstruct the public in the exercise of rights common to all Her Majesty's subjects'. [Archbold].

A person who commits a public nuisance incurs a possible penalty of life imprisonment and unlimited fines. It was this very uncertainty as to what were the boundaries of this crime that led to its decline in use. Public nuisances are dealt with by way of indictment or by an action by the Attorney General or a local authority.

They can constitute a tort where an individual who is a member of an identifiable group or class can maintain an action provided he is capable of demonstrating that he has suffered more than other persons of the class. Where an action is brought damages may be recovered.

It might be thought that public nuisance is an ideal vehicle for actions in the area of environmental law and indeed it has been used for such: *Attorney General v PYA Quarries (1957)*[8] concerning the blasting operations at a quarry which caused the Court of Appeal to uphold the decision of the judge at first instance that a public nuisance had been caused and to grant an injunction.

The issue was examined recently in *Gillingham Borough Council v Medway (Chatham) Dock Company Ltd (1991)* where the right of the authority to bring an action was overridden by the fact that planning permission had been given to change the nature of a locality i.e. the environment of the area and therefore the standard of what was acceptable as a level of nuisance was to be decided in the light of its new characteristics not those which existed before the permission was granted. Needless to say this decision has been the subject of some controversy in environmental law circles.[9]

Public Nuisance has not disappeared from view as a crime or a tort but it has rather been overtaken by the creation of a number of statutory provisions.

Statutory intervention has resulted in some offences at common law being made into more precisely defined statutory offences. In other instances statutes have created categories of statutory nuisances which are in effect a bridge between the common law controls of environmental matters and the more usual statutory provisions in the field. A number of statutory nuisances are to be found in the EPA 1990 s.79 and each local authority is under a statutory duty to inspect their localities for such nuisances. To constitute such a statutory nuisance the matter complained of must either be prejudicial to health OR a nuisance. Such things as smoke emission, fumes, dust, steam, smells, noise, animals and any other matter declared by enactment to be a statutory nuisance. The object of the provisions is to have the nuisance abated as quickly and effectively as possible. The local authority can itself issue an abatement notice without the necessity of resorting to a court action. Indeed if the authority is satisfied that such a nuisance exists it is under a mandatory duty to issue a notice. A person who is served with such a notice an appeal against it to a magistrate's court. An unusual provision of the EPA 1990 is that by virtue of S.82 a complaint may be made to a magistrate's court by any person who is aggrieved by the existence of a statutory nuisance once it has occurred but not in anticipation. The court can issue an abatement notice and also levy fines where such a notice is ignored. Where appropriate a local authority can apply to the High Court for an injunction prohibiting or restricting a statutory nuisance. The use of the provision is to tighten up a possibly weak abatement order where the nuisance warrants such a step.

Private Nuisance

This tort is a creation of the common law. At one time it was the mainstay of such environmental protection law as existed. It is essentially a cause of action arising when one person by his actions or omissions interferes with the use or enjoyment of his neighbours land. The prime reason for its existence is to protect use and enjoyment not give grounds for compensation for damage to property, which it can do, or for personal injury which seemingly it cannot although there being no case directly on the point the matter is open to some doubt. Unlike the tort of Negligence with which Nuisance shares a family connection, there is no need to prove fault or malice although the latter will negative the defence that the defendant was not making an unreasonable use of his own land from which the offending activity is claimed to have emanated. Remedies of injunction and damages are available as is the right of the victim to abate the nuisance by his own intervention. This latter is not one which finds much favour with the courts.

The locality where the nuisance occurred can be taken into account but only in so far as ascertaining the degree of unreasonableness of a defendants activities in relation to what was normally to be accepted in a particular locality. It is no defence to claim that a plaintiff came to the nuisance of his own accord and therefore must like it or lump it. The tort is strict in the sense that once nuisance has been established it is no defence to claim that all reasonable steps had been taken to avoid it. Actions have been brought for water pollution; smells; noise; dust and many of the matters which today are regulated by statutes as nuisances. The tort has lost ground as a form of redress mainly as a consequence of the cost involved in bringing an action before the courts.

A cousin of Nuisance which may be mentioned here is the form of tort which again is land based namely that which relies on the rule in *Rylands v Fletcher*. Briefly this states that where a person for his own purposes brings onto his lands and collects and keeps there anything which is likely to cause harm if it escapes does so at his peril for if it does escape and cause harm to another's property the keeper from whose care the thing escaped will be strictly liable for the damage to property, that is without proof of fault. The tort is essentially one of the escape of dangerous things. It too has been much overtaken by specific statutory provisions for the dangers from hazardous substances e.g. the Nuclear Installations Act 1965 and also the wider provisions of the EPA 1990. There is also the added difficulty of proving non natural use of the land where recently the Court of Appeal felt it easier to find for the plaintiff in nuisance preferring to leave the peculiar aspects of *Rylands* to one side where there was an escape of chemicals causing ground pollution and damage to a water supply: *Cambridge Water Company v Eastern Counties Leather plc (1991)*[10] the decision at first instance being reversed by the Court of Appeal.

There remains the possibility that an action in the nature of a claim in tort could be brought with regard to the violation of an interest protected by statute, or breach of statutory duty as it is more commonly, though not so precisely, known. The basis of such a claim is that the statute provides for a civil remedy either expressly or on a construction of the wording used and that it does not expressly deny the right or provides only one remedy for breach thus disallowing claims under another head. It is a difficult area of statutory construction not the least of which involves demonstrating that the alleged victim of the breach was a person whom the statute sought to protect and that the damage suffered was of the type that the statute was designed to protect against.

It must be stressed that with all the heads of tort considered above, including public nuisance seen as a tort, the victim can only complain after the event, that is to say where harm has occurred. They cannot in most cases be the subject of preventive action except in unusual circumstances allowing a *quia timet* injunction to be sought. But certainly no preventive action for damages can be entertained.

This is where statutory provisions which seek to prevent the harm occurring in the first place are more effective in this respect and certainly come into their own in the issues involved in environmental law.

Statutory provisions

It is perhaps not surprising that a nation consisting of a collection of small islands with a growing density of population, which was the birthplace of the Industrial Revolution followed by the factory age of the late 19th century should find activities within its shores the subject of controls aimed at environmental protection. These appeared at a relatively early period in the evolutionary movement from a land based to factory based economy. Major statutory provisions in the shape of the Public Health Act 1895, River Pollution Prevention Act 1876 (although little used and largely ineffective), and the Housing and Town Planning Act 1909 made their appearance and until the 1970s provided the main platform for developments in controls on land use and issues of what we now choose to include in the generic category of environmental protection laws. They also demonstrate the piecemeal nature of the development of environmental protection with different regulations and enforcement agencies.

Britain has a relatively long history of anti pollution measures and some of the earliest systems of inspection to accompany them. These stemmed from the way in which the industrial economy developed; but the measures introduced did not prevent much dumping of industrial waste in unsuitable ways and often on unmarked sites; discharges of raw sewage and industrial products into the water supplies was commonplace. Although much has been done by way of improvement Britain has been referred to as the Dirty Man of Europe in recent years largely as the result of pollution of the atmosphere and the sea emanating from the UK finding its way into the backyards of our EC partners and for failing to come up to standards which have been achieved on the continent.

The first statute which sought to deal with the issue of pollution in a holistic way was the Control of Pollution Act 1974 although this Act called forth much criticism during the time it was in force until 1990 when it was largely repealed and replaced by the Environmental Protection Act. This legislation deals extensively with waste disposal, statutory nuisance and seeks to establish a system of integrated pollution control (IPC). This replaces the ad hoc approach adopted in previous legislation in relation to environmental protection. The effect is that issues in relation to air, land and water are to be considered together when the impact of all industrial processes are scrutinised for the effect which occurs when their products are released into the environment.

IPC regulation is the responsibility of Her Majesty's Inspectorate of Pollution while in the area of atmospheric pollution local authorities are charged with regulation for Air Pollution Control (APC). The statute also deals with the apprehension of stray dogs! ss.149-151. It may be that it is just possible to accept that this is an environmental measure but the real reason is that the Government wished to attend to this issue of dog control and a convenient bill was passing through parliament at the time allowing the dogs their day as it were!

It has to be said that the initiatives for upgrading the law on pollution have come from the EC. Past experience has shown a marked reluctance on the part of the UK Government to respond enthusiastically to EC Directives claiming that excessive bureaucracy prevents enterprise and holds back the economy from growth. There are many instances of the UK seeking to water down EC law and a marked delay in incorporating it into the domestic legislation. On a number of occasions the UK has been forced to comply under threat of litigation before the European Court of Justice (ECJ).

Much play has been made of the development of *subsidiarity* in relation to the introduction of EC law into domestic legislation. The UK Government interprets this as the ability to introduce as much, or often as little, as they choose to suit domestic political policy. This is not what the EC intends. *Subsidiarity* means that it should be for national governments in member states to introduce legislation through the mechanism which is appropriate to each one at the level of operations which is most suitable for the effective introduction of the measures to be brought into effect Regrettably, during the last decade there has been a growth of centralisation of government in the UK with a consequent reduction in local responsibility and by gathering power to the centre local responsibility and accountability to local people has been eroded. This has meant, in the case of the environment, that local government has less control over decisions operating for the benefit of local people. This despite power of regulation and enforcement being placed on the shoulders of local authorities; they are merely the agents of central government not the controllers of their own affairs.

The attitude of the EC to this interpretation has been to view the actions of the UK as anti-competitive practice. That is to say the cost of introducing measures across the Community should be the same for all members, more or less, and depending upon their past record in specific areas. By Britain claiming that compliance with EC law pushes up costs and hampers UK industry this is tantamount to admitting that by not coming up to EC standards Britain is able to sell its products at prices which undercut competition from Europe thus disadvantaging those who have complied with the levels set by the Commission.

There is a view in some quarters that what is being introduced by way of legislation is foreign so far as the UK is concerned. Much flag waving and trumpeting over the sovereignty of Parliament disguises the fact that Britain acceded to the treaties making this country part of the EC and expressly declared in the European Communities Act 1972 that henceforward EC law was part of the domestic law of the UK. This having been said, EC law does not affect all domestic laws and where it does, it has a greater impact on some than on others. Thus planning law in the UK is largely unaffected by EC legislation while in matters of safety and competition the effect is much more pervasive throughout the UK system.

The European Dimension

The Treaty of Rome was signed by the original members of the EC in 1957 and in its original form did not contain specific provisions for the protection of the environment other than Article 235 enabling the Council of Ministers, acting unanimously, to take *appropriate measures to achieve any of the objectives of the Community*. It could be inferred from this that in the 1950s there was a lack of concern for environmental matters. This was remedied thirty years later under Article 25 of the *Single European Act 1987* which set out three principal objectives for EC action on the environment:

405

-   to preserve, protect and improve the quality of the environment;
-   to contribute towards protecting human health;
-   to ensure a prudent and rational utilisation of natural resources.

The main and specific areas of EC activity so far have been in relation to water pollution, atmospheric pollution, noise, chemical products, waste disposal and nature protection. It is no co-incidence that these have been the main bases for recent UK legislation.

Further, in interpreting the objectives via the legislation four clear themes can be identified:

-   preventive action is required to protect the environment;
-   environmental damage should be rectified at its source not at the point if impact alone;
-   the polluter pays the cost of the damage and for its rectification;
-   in every policy promulgated via the EC environmental protection shall be a constituent part.

It is clear from this that the EC is in the driving seat for improvements in environmental protection. Three key Directives point the way to future EC policy:

The Directive on the Assessment of Effects of Certain Public and Private Projects on the Environment - 85/337.

The Directive requires that developers supply and make public information on certain projects together with details as to how they propose to avoid or reduce the environmental effects. The Directive places the developer under a duty to consider preventive measures *before* the project is undertaken.

It is one of the few areas of EC legislation which impacts directly on UK planning law and is best exemplified in its application to major public works - road, airports and long distance rail routes together with commercial ports and inland waterways.

The UK Government has done no more than the minimum required by the Directive. It is possible that in some instances this minimum has not met the required standards. The extension to the M3 motorway at Twyford Down near Winchester went ahead despite vociferous protests from any national and local objectors. The route chosen represented the most economic in the Government's eyes and the most ecologically damaging in the eyes of the protesters. The matter was referred to Europe with a challenge based on alleged UK failure to carry out a proper environmental impact assessment as required by the Directive. This challenge was narrowly defeated by the Government. There are more other projects in the pipeline in other locations and the Government faces further challenges. The main cause for concern is the way in which matters are progressed at ministerial level with piecemeal applications by way of statutory instruments. These actions, or minimalist approach, shown by the UK may convince the Commission that EC regulation of this policy needs to be strengthened in order to make developers more responsive to their obligations.

Directive on Civil Liability for Damage caused by Waste - COM(91) 219 Final.

This is still a draft directive with the Dutch and the UK notably carrying out a rearguard action to delay, if not prevent, its introduction. The intention is that a wide civil liability for damage shall be imposed including damage to the environment.

When introduced it will make a radical change to UK law. The intention is that the producer of waste shall be made liable for damage to people, property and the *unowned environment*. Specific proposals are:

- The liability of the waste produced shall be strict i.e. without the need for the victim to prove fault based liability thus radically altering the common law tort of Negligence in this regard. It will also affect Nuisance and the rule in *Rylands* because although it is not necessary to prove fault, certain infections from Negligence into these torts has moved them nearer to fault bases than when they were originally conceived as causes of action.

- actions can be brought by interest groups rather than individuals and damages, where awarded, could be very large since the Directive proposes that damages should reflect the cost of reinstatement of the damaged environment;

- injury to the *unowned environment* extends the law beyond injury to the person or to property such that damage to wildlife or destruction of habitat will be actionable.

This Directive would also avoid the degree of inconsistency in the way in which claims for environmental damage are dealt with by the courts. It is not without significance that the House of Lords Select Committee on the European Community considered the draft of this Directive and opposed its introduction.

Directive of Freedom of Access to Information on the Environment - 90/313

The objective of this Directive is to ensure freedom of access to, and dissemination of, information on the environment held by public authorities and to set out the terms and conditions on which such information should be made available. At present the public has only limited rights to such access under the EPA 1990 and the Water Act 1989 and via reference to such planning applications/permissions held by local planning authorities (LPAs). The Directive obliges public authorities to give information to any person on request without the need for the applicant to justify such request. It does, however, allow authorities to conceal information behind a cloak of commercial and industrial confidentiality. There is every sign that the UK Government intends to make extensive use of this proviso in order to minimise the impact of the Directive.

The three Directives taken together will have a major impact on activities in the UK particularly in connection with waste disposal. There are signs that the obsessive secrecy which besets politics in the UK will be used to defeat the openness of the EC regime and that in the absence of an official register of waste disposal sites and releases into the atmosphere the public interest will continue to be poorly served.

The changes and proposed changes inherent in the Directives outlined are not as extensive and those regimes currently in operation in the United States. Nor has the UK moved as far in their direction as has, for example, Germany.

There are in addition a number of subject specific Directives which have been introduced and which impact on UK law e.g. Bathing Water-76/160.

Public International law is that which regulates the conduct of affairs between nations and specifically those who are signatories to documents signifying agreement at various levels. The highest level is that of a Treaty, with lesser agreements being signified by Conventions and Protocols. Such agreements do not automatically become part of the domestic law of a nations unless such nation decides to include all or any international agreements into its municipal law by whatever is the usual process used to make law in that jurisdiction. An example may be found in the international conventions on carriage of passengers by land, sea and air which have been incorporated into UK law and that of many other nations whilst the provisions of certain protocols covering the same fields have not. By virtue of s.156 of the EPA 1990 the Secretary of State may make regulations to modify parts of the Act in order to comply with International agreements to which the UK is a signatory.

In terms of environmental law there are relatively few - Ramsar Convention on Wetlands of International Importance 1971 and the Vienna Convention for the Protection of the Ozone Layer 1987 are two examples.

3. TOWN AND COUNTRY PLANNING

This is an area of UK law which is relatively unaffected by extra-territorial influences. It is also a field which has a distinguished and much documented pedigree. Some matters - planning controls and the national heritage - have been addressed earlier in the text and it is not proposed to reopen these issues here.

Town and Country planning first became the task for government at central and local level when issues of public health and housing policy became a matter for concern. The main driving force was the growth in population and the attendant urban expansion which accompanied the phenomenon in the UK during the late 19th century[11]. As it is presently constituted, planning law extends to cover not only land use but the design and structure of buildings. It also has the unusual characteristic in UK law of anticipating developments and seeking to control them before they get underway. The main arbiter of whether or not a particular development should be carried through is the LPA for the area in which the development is to be carried out. Appeal against *permissions* which are granted is to the Secretary of State.

Usually, LPAs have a specific duty to consider *all material factors* impacting upon local development[12] whereas other regulatory bodies which are the creatures of statute are much more narrowly constrained in their terms of reference.

The scope of planning law is very wide given that economic, social and political factors weigh heavily upon it. Environmental factors are an additional element which have to be considered by the LPAs. It is an area of specialist knowledge and application with almost a life of its own. It is not possible to examine more than in outline the complexities of the subject in a book of this size. Nevertheless, there are general principles which do bear examination in outline.

Development plans

These set out the general policies and strategies which a LPA proposes to follow for developments within its jurisdiction. They do not comprise a detailed programme and some aspects which are considered in the plan may never be followed up. *Development* is widely interpreted in this context and applies to both new structures and to change of use for existing premises. *Permissions* for new projects or changes in use are granted in the light of the overall development plan, Government policies and *other material considerations* e.g. an environmental plan.

Where permission is granted for a proposed project it may be granted subject to conditions attached to it. Rights of appeal, against refusals or permissions which are subject to conditions, are exercised to the Secretary of State but there is no appeal against a development which has been granted only the process of judicial review with reference to the manner in which a decision was reached but not on the merits of the development itself.

LPAs are public bodies exercising democratic powers granted to them in enabling legislation. Their decisions may be challenged on the basis that they have either exceeded their powers as granted in legislation, that is they have acted *ultra vires* or that the process which they have used by which to arrive at a decision is flawed; an issue which may be remedied on judicial review or by administrative process.

In consequence of the very wide powers possessed by LPAs they are able to resist many of the restraints placed upon other regulatory bodies e.g. the National Rivers Authority (NRA). A judicial review does not involve the rehearing of the substantial merits of a case it only operates as a check on the administrative abuse of power by a public body. In the light that a review finds in favour of the objector the matter is referred back by the High Court to the LPA where the issue is looked at by a different officer who may come to the same conclusion as his predecessor. Even where an abuse is demonstrated to the court, the objector still has to satisfy the court that he has *suffered prejudice* to his position as a consequence and ought to be granted relief.

The system does ensure that at present the developments are considered at an appropriate level, locally. Decisions are guided by Government from the centre but decisions are still taken locally. It also allows for liaison and consultation with the interested parties in a real way and that where it sees fit to impose conditions on a permission the LPA is ensuring that it maintains control over developments as they take place or changes of use as they are effected with the whole process being monitored along the way.

In planning matters it has become evident that pressure groups can exert considerable pressure provided they can bring themselves within a category of those with a *sufficient interest* in the proceedings where the subject matter is being challenged by way of judicial review[13]. Examples of the process in action can be seen in a series of recent cases, notably *R v Secretary of State for the Environment ex parte Rose Theatre Company Trust (1990)*[14] which involved an application against the refusal by the SoS to schedule the site of the Rose Theatre, Southwark as an ancient monument. The decision revealed that no-one had a right to challenge the SoS's use of his prerogative power and that his verdict was final! In *R v Poole Borough Council ex parte Beebee (1991)*[15] the issue was over the power of a local authority to overrule regulations concerning a Site of Special Scientific Interest (SSSI) in order to build a housing estate. The standing of bodies such as the British Herpetological Society and the National Conservancy Council as having *sufficient interest* in the matter was upheld by the court.

Planning controls cover many proposed activities involving *inter alia* waste disposal and other specifically controlled issues thus affording regulation not only under the terms of the particular and relevant legislation appropriate to the activity under review but also under the general powers of a LPA. Thus environmental issues can have the benefit of double indemnity as it were.

It has been said that planning law is largely a matter of procedure rather than of substantive law and this is generally true in the sense that if the terms of reference are followed to the letter and the administration is carried out in accordance with the guidelines laid down then if the LPA has exercised discretion allowed to it in reaching its decision then this is not open to challenge.

Town and Country provisions appear to encompass any development and extend beyond simple issues of public health and land use. Under the Planning Compensation Act 1991 which amends the previous legislation is appears that a principle is established whereby a *development plan* formulated by a LPA should be followed giving emphasis to the plans of the LPA rather than allowing them as before to be driven by the developers who are seeking permissions. This gives considerable scope to the LPA to steer the environmental plan for a whole locality where it is, as it were advising itself of changes which it wishes to make[16].

At the same time, the emphasis has been shifted from land use and the provision of amenities in an area to socio-economic considerations with political overtones with pressures on LPAs from the minimalist lobby of the pre-market approach to life, the universe and everything, to those who seek strong regulation of developments to avoid the worst excesses of the marketeers. People versus profits as it is sometimes described in the media. As it is, planning control is required for any *development*[17] and a development is defined as:

> 'the carrying out of building, engineering, mining and other operations, in, on or under land, or the making of any material change in the use of any buildings or other land'[18]

The courts have long since decided that whether or not there is a development is a matter of fact and degree to be decided in each situation which comes before them. The LPA or the SoS decide as a matter of law whether such *development* has taken place whereas the courts will confine themselves to consideration of the way in which the decision was taken and whether or not such decision may be seen as perverse.

In relation to *material change of use*, statute gives very little guidance leaving the precise meaning deliberately vague. As part of the so called 'deregulatory' measures of the 1980s designed by the Government to facilitate flexibility any change within one of the designated 16 Classes of use set out in the 1987 Regulations is not to be considered as a development as so is not to be considered the subject of planning controls.[19] Some of the classes are very wide allowing the starting up of businesses unfettered by planning restrictions provided they fall within the deliberately wide banding prescribed by the Regulations.

4. POLLUTION CONTROLS

Clearly the quality of the environment is the legitimate concern of all those who may be affected by a diminution in the levels of quality in air or water, none more so than the tourist on socio-economic grounds alone before considerations of safety are taken into account.

Air

Nothing is more fundamental to the quality of life than the air which we breath:

> 'An average person requires over thirty pounds of air a day or about six pints every minute, and he has to take it as it comes. He would not readily stand in sewage or drink dirty water. Yet daily the individual draws 26,000 breaths, between 18 and 22 each minute, many of which - if not all in some cases - are filthy'.[20]

Atmospheric pollution has been a well known and well documented phenomenon for a considerable time. Some of the earliest 19th century environmental regulations deal with smoke pollution. The range of atmospheric pollutants has increased considerably since those early years. The piece meal regulation has persisted until the present day with some general controls under public health legislation and some industry specific controls being introduced. The manifest failure of the controls was evidenced in the numerous smog effects which resulted in respiratory illnesses and sometimes, death. In response to this problem the Government set up an Inquiry - the Beaver Committee - with the result that its recommendations were adopted and legislation introduced to deal with specific forms of emissions into the atmosphere - the Clean Air Act 1956 and the later statute of the same name in 1968. But with the decline of one form of pollution others have appeared as industrial processes developed, most notably the advent of *acid rain* largely resulting from discharges of sulphur dioxide into the atmosphere from power stations. The Beaver Committee in 1953 had wanted to see the fitting of desulphurisation equipment but this had been rejected in favour of building taller chimneys! The issue has been one of a long running dispute between the UK and the Scandinavian countries. The EC has proposed a desulphurisation programme and although some steps have been taken along this path it remains to be seen whether or not it will succeed.

The EPA 1990 seeks to control all forms of noxious pollutants other than smoke under the APC regime in Part I of the statute. This is supplemented by Regulations made under the enabling statutes targeted at specific processes and substances.

At the present time the emissions from motor vehicles are governed and controlled by setting standards not of acceptable levels of pollution but by tackling the problem at source by requiring the machinery itself to be subject to standards set for it. This has been done mainly by use of the powers allowed to the Minister by the Road Traffic Act 1988 as amended in the light of EC Directives, notably 88/76 which sets new limits on allowable levels of gases emitted from new vehicles which came into use after 1990 and requiring all such vehicles to be capable of running on unleaded petroleum products. It is the EC Directives which have been the prime movers throughout in seeking to set standards for environmental quality by controlling atmospheric pollution.

Water

Regulation is largely effected through the enforcement powers of the National Rivers Authority (NRA) under the Water Act 1989 and subsequent amending legislation. Water pollution can take many forms as a result of contamination by organic waste, chemicals, toxic materials, bacteria and temperature affecting the biology of water. The degrees of pollution also vary widely resulting in various different consequences.

Modern controls may be seen to stem from the Rivers (Prevention of Pollution) Act 1951 and further developments up to and including the Control of Pollution Act 1974 which extended the geographical limits for controls beyond inland water to underground and coastal areas as far out to sea as the three mile territorial limits. The EPA 1990 which has largely replaced the 1974 COPA does not alter the regime created by the latter. The establishment of the NRA in 1989 was the first occasion on which an attempt to establish a national policy for the prevention and control of water pollution was made.

The impact of the EC on water pollution law in the UK cannot be underestimated yet it does not cover all forms of pollution. The water Directives follow two identifiable regimes - one to control emissions and the other to establish quality objectives in relation to the use which is to be made of different forms of water supply. Perhaps the most significant is Directive 76/464 on Dangerous Substances in Water which has effectively changed UK law by requiring domestic legislation to tighten up on the many discharges into water previously allowed by the granting of *consents* and by the introduction of an integrated pollution control regime for all forms or prohibited substances.

Under the quality approach system staged approaches are adopted in determining what standards are acceptable in given circumstances. Of particular note in the interests of tourism and the tourist are those Directives which deal with Bathing Water (76/160); Freshwater Fish (78/659); Shellfish (79/923) and Drinking Water (80/778).

The Bathing Water quality system sets out 19 levels within which all such waters must comply, with set levels of tolerance for each. The standards were created with little enthusiasm in the UK with the cost of improvements being the main cause for opposition. Others in Government viewed them as just another example of over jealous EC bureaucracy. Initially the UK identified only 27 beaches UK wide which were to be regulated - less than regulated places in Luxembourg which has no coastline! After pressure from the EC this was increased such that there are now over 400 listed. This has still not prevented the UK being taken to the ECJ for failure to implement the Directive[21].

At one time it was a boast heard often in Britain that it was safe to drink the tap water anywhere and that it was only in primitive European countries that this was not so. Such a boast now has a hollow ring to it. The Directive on Drinking Water sets out 62 standards relating to all water intended for human consumption. Britain delayed implementation of the provisions until after the date set by the EC for universal implementation mainly because of difficulty in reaching the standards required. The UK Government engaged in protracted arguments seeking to gain exemption from many of the standards by the process of *derogation* which is part of EC procedure. It has not so far succeeded in this and formal infringement proceedings are yet again being taken against the UK for non-compliance.

Despite this the EC regulations have succeeded to a large extent in improving matters as regards both bathing and drinking water. Public opinion once mobilised has had a profound effect on the Government. An attempt by the UK Government to allow the newly privatised water companies in the UK to be self regulating as regards standards has not been accepted by the EC. The NRA has also come under criticism for being too docile in its pursuance of standards.

Sewage

Closely allied with the water issues the disposal of sewage has often caused problems because of the potential for water pollution from this source. Those engaged in sewage undertakings are treated in the same way as other operations which discharge products into the water supply. *Consents* for discharges are required from the NRA. In many cases these *consents* were relaxed prior to the Water Act 1989 and in advance of the EPA 1990 because the Government feared that if it were otherwise there could be a spate of private prosecutions in the run up to water privatisation. A substantial number of sewage undertakings were breaking the law when the position was reviewed in 1989.

In all issues associated with pollution it seems to be an inescapable fact that the UK Government in the 1980/90s has been opposed to all or any EC measures which affect the profitability of British industry. There are signs of a change in this attitude in the 1990s but there should be no reliance on the reported sightings of green shoots until the flowers themselves come into bloom!

People

That the environment is at risk from the pressure of people in increasing numbers and with increased wants cannot be denied. There are increased demands on both essential and amenity resources with levels of expectation on quality issues being heightened in the light of scientific and technological advances. Yet people themselves as consumers of the resources and as an agency for environmental pollution have a case to answer. National Parks are a prime example of the dangers of success. Eleven exist and the New Forest is destined to add to the number yet they provide a microcosm of the harm that can be brought about by sheer weight of numbers. So much so that calls are being made for restriction on access and for *sustainable development* with controls on *Developments* within the Parks which would only be allowed after it had been shown that these were in the national interest and lack of practical alternatives were available outside their boundaries:

'The pressure of tourism - 100 million visits to the Parks - attracts applications for inappropriate developments. These range from holiday complexes to many sports that are more suited to the fringe'.[22]

Even the horse so beloved of the English, it is alleged, has come in for its share of criticism:

'The riding boom is . . . churning up country footpaths and damaging ancient woodlands . . . conservation authorities are cracking down, introducing strict limits on the numbers of horses allowed in some areas and obliging them to wear licence discs . . . The National Trust has taken tougher action. It will allow members of specially formed associations only, limited to 150 riders to use certain of its properties'.[23]

If three of our most cherished institutions, the heritage, the horse and the National Trust are under threat of further necessary controls who can doubt that the impact of tourism on the environment will provide an increasing source for debate? It is even claimed that by the way in which the history of the nation is presented to the general public by museums and the heritage industry we may be corrupting the minds of visitors by giving a false impression of what the past represents and of institutionalising concepts of a false national culture.[24]

5. A JUDICIAL VIEW

In 1985 that noted scourge of the judiciary J.A.G. Griffiths stated that 'Judges tend to favour established political authority'[25]. Lord Bridge delivered himself of the view in *SAVE v No1 Poultry Ltd (1991)*[26] that:

'The public controversy over this case arises from differences of opinion about the traditional and contemporary architectural styles. These arouse strong feelings but are no concern whatever of the courts . . . our concern is solely with the legality of the decision making process, not at all with the merits of the decision'.

Perhaps Sir Harry Woolf, as he was the, should be allowed the final word. He entitled his lecture to the Environmental Law Society - "Are the Judiciary Environmentally Myopic?" He included in his talk the following observations:

'It has become increasingly clear that the public has a great concern about the threat to the environment. A problem which should concern us all is whether our legal system is capable of adapting so as to provide an effective mans of protecting the environment . . . At the present we rely on no

417

single legal procedure or remedy. Instead we rely on the long established common law actions for public and private nuisance; in part on the public law procedure of judicial review; in part on statutory appeals and applications and generally on the criminal law. Combined these procedures provide a formidable array . . . their deployment can result in a succession of proceedings (which) may each frustrate the ability of others to do justice . . . The EC dimension itself creates tensions for our existing institutions and the traditional English approach'.[27]

Nowhere more than in the field of environment protection is there a more dynamic process underway and it will need new approaches and new solutions to the many problems with which we are faced. Not the least we need a new system for resolving legal regulation of essential matters which the present system does not appear capable of producing.

NOTES:

1. This Common Inheritance. Cmod 1200/90
2. Against All Odds. Greenpeace 1993
3. Environmental Protection Act 1990 s.1(2).
4. Ibid. s.1(4)
5. Weeping and Whaling. J. Vidal *Guardian* 7 May 1993
6. The Tourist Trap. D. Atkinson. *Guardian* 14 June 1993
7. Public Nuisance - a critical examination (1989) CLJ 55
8. (1957) 2 QB 169
9 Public Law Rules - O.K.? *Environmental Law Journal* Vol.4, No.2 1992
10. (1991) *Times* 23 October 1991
11. Town and Country Planning in England and Wales. J.B. Cullingworth
12. Town and Country Planing Act 1990 s.70
13. Supreme Court Act 1981 s.31(3)
14. (1990) 1 AllER 754.
15. (1991) JPL 643
16. Town and Country Planning Act 1990 s.54A
17. Ibid s.57(1)
18. Ibid s.55(1)
19. Town and Country Planning (Use Classes) Order 1987 SI 1987 No.764
20. *Man and Environment*. R. Arvill. Penguin Books 1967
21. Filthy British Beaches etc. G. Lean *Observer* 30 May 1993
22. Ponies are Chewing up the Countryside G. Lean. *Observer* 2 May 1993
23. *The Representation of the Past*. K. Walsh. Routledge 1993

24. *The Politics of the Judiciary*. J.A.G. Griffiths. Fontana 1985
25. (1991) 1 WLR 153
26. *Journal of Environmental Law* Vol.3 No.2 1991
27. Ibd.

FURTHER READING

Bonner, G.A. *British Transport Law by Road & Rail,* David & Charles, 1974.

Davies, K. *Local Government Law,* Butterworths, 1983.

Downes, T.A. *Textbook on Contract,* Blackstone, 1993

Drury, A.C. and Fenner, C.W. *Credit Cards,* Butterworths, 1984.

Field, D. *Hotel and Catering Law in Britain,* Sweet & Maxwell, 1988.

Filed, D. *Practical Club Law,* Sweet & Maxwell, 1979.

Field, D. and Pink, M. *Liquor Licensing Law,* Sweet & Maxwell, 1990.

Fox, C. *The Countryside and the Law,* David & Charles, 1971.

Fridman, G.H.L. *Law of Agency,* Butterworths, 1990.

Gaskell, N.J.J., Debattista, C. and Swatton, R.J. *Chorley & Giles: Shipping Law,* Pitman, 1987.

Goodwin-Gill, G.S. *International Law and the Movement of Persons,* Clarendon Press, 1978.

Grayson, E. *Sport and the Law,* Butterworths, 1988.

Green, W. *Guide to Environmental Law,* Sweet & Maxwell, 1992.

Harte, J.D.C. *Landscape, Land Use and the Law,* E. & F. Spon, 1985.

Harvey, B.H. and Parry, D.L. *The Law of Consumer Protection and Fair Trading,* Butterworths, 1992.

Holloway, J.C. *The Business of Tourism,* MacDonald & Evans, 1992.

Howarth, W. *Freshwater Fishery Law,* Financial Training, 1987.

James, L. *The Law of the Railway,* Barry Rose, 1980.

Jones, M.A. *Textbook on Torts,* Blackstone, 1993.

Kahn-Freund, *The Law of Carriage by Inland Transport,* Stevens, 1964.

Martin, J. *Shawcross & Beaumont: Air Law,* Butterworths, 1992.

Martin, J.N. *Paterson's Licensing Acts,* Holt, 1992.

Palmer, N. *Bailment,* Sweet & Maxwell, 1992.

Pannett, A. *Principles of Hotel and Catering Law,* Holt 1991.

Robertson, G. *Freedom, The Individual & the Law,* Pelican 1989.

Roddis, R.J. *The Law of Parks and Recreation Grounds,* Shaw, 1970

Scott, M. *The Law of Public Leisure Services,* Sweet & Maxwell, 1993.

Shoard, M. *This Land is Our Land,* Paladin, 1987.

Smith, J.C. *Law of Theft*, Butterworths, 1989.

Stanton, K.M. *Breach of Statutory Duty in Tort*, Sweet & Maxwell, 1986.

Street, H. *Freedom, the Individual and the Law*, Penguin, 1982.

Suddards, R.W, *Historic Buildings The Law and Practice,* Sweet & Maxwell, 1993.

INDEX

A full list of principal statutes and a table of cases affecting tourism activities is given at the front of this book on pages vi-xi and xii-xxii respectively.

424

425

431

435

O

P

438

443

The Legal Framework - Sir Leonard Jason-Lloyd

The Constitution - pbk, 64pp.	1 85450 059 7
Tutor's Manual - A4 binder	1 85450 091 0
The English Courts - pbk, 80pp.	1 85450 064 3
Tutor's Manual - A4 binder	1 85450 097 X
Criminal Sanctions - pbk, 110pp.	1 85450 054 6
Tutor's Manual - A4 binder	1 85450 099 6
The Modern Company - pbk, 64pp.	1 85450 069 4
Tutor's Manual - A4 binder	1 85450 089 9
The European Community - pbk, 96pp.	1 85450 074 0
Tutor's Manual - A4 binder	1 85450 039 2
Police Powers - pbk, 78pp.	1 85450 079 1
Tutor's Manual - A4 binder	1 85450 145 3

The Criminal Justice Act, '91 as amended by **The Criminal Justice Act, '93:** a guide. pbk, 240pp, A5 binder + updates

Exercises in Business Law - Fiona Golby

Large number of varied user-friendly exercises, crossword and other puzzles & materials for 1st level post-experience students. BTEC National & HND Business Law module. Pack may be *freely copied for student use*. GNVQ & A level.

Tutor's Manual - A4 binder   1 85450 093 7

* * * * * * * * * *

Case Studies in Business Law - Jeffrey Young

20 topical case studies on a range of issues in business law from liability to description, from property to personal problems. Level beginners plus.

pbk 96pp   0 946139 98 9

Tutor's Manual - A4 binder   0 946139 93 8

* * * * * * * * * *

Case Studies in Employment Law - Jeffrey Young

17 topical & typical case studies on employment law issues and problems, from unfair dismissal to wage reduction, from maternity rights to changes of job. Level beginners plus.

pbk 96pp   1 85450 047 3

Tutor's Manual - A4 binder   1 85450 067 8

* * * * * * * * * *

Tourism and Leisure in the Countryside -
Richard Sharpley

Material for a full year's course with 9 stand-alone chapters on countryside recreation, management, planning and the law.
Level HND plus.

pbk, 320pp   1 85450 095 3

Tutor's Manual - 1 year's class materials, exercises1 85450 185 2

* * * * * * * * * *

Travel and Tourism: 2nd edn - Patrick Lavery

Introduction to the main sectors of the tourism industry, defining and outlining the development in UK, Europe and USA, plus transport deregulation. Level HND plus.

pbk, 224pp.   1 85450 120 8

Tutor's Manual - exercises, notes, OHPs   1 85450 024 4

From Tourist Attractions to Tourism Heritage - Pat Yale

From museums to stately homes, castles, palaces and gardens, religious buildings, archaeological sites and ancient monuments, industrial and transport heritage. Level PG Diploma, degree etc.

* * * * * * * * * *

Tourism in the U.K. - Pat Yale

BTEC National/A level text on the business and management of tourism, with commentary on UK tourist attractions. Level BTEC National plus.

pbk, 320pp (maps/charts/diagrams)   1 85450 017 1

Tutor's Manual with maps, OHPs, case studies   1 85450 094 5